DOGMATIC THEOLOGY

Volume II
Christ's Church

by Monsignor G. Van Noort, S.T.D.

Translated and Revised by
JOHN J. CASTELOT, S.S., S.T.D., S.S.L.
WILLIAM R. MURPHY, S.S., S.T.D.

THE NEWMAN PRESS
Westminster, Maryland
1957

The present volume is a translation of the 5th edition of Msgr. Van Noort's *Tractatus de Ecclesia Christi*, edited by J. P. Verhaar. Because of the extensive revision made by the translators, the English translation may be called the 6th edition of Msgr. Van Noort's dogmatic treatise.

Nihil Obstat: PAUL F. GENOVESE, S.S., S.T.D.
Censor Deputatus

Imprimatur: EDWARD CARDINAL MOONEY
Archiepiscopus Detroitensis
die 26 Octobris, 1956

The *nihil obstat* and *imprimatur* are official declarations that a book or pamphlet is free of doctrinal and moral error. No implication is contained therein that those who have granted the *nihil obstat* and *imprimatur* agree with the opinions expressed.

Library of Congress Catalog Card Number: 55–10552

Copyright © 1957 by THE NEWMAN PRESS

Printed in the United States of America

TO OUR PARENTS
THROUGH WHOM WE FIRST
CAME TO KNOW AND LOVE
CHRIST'S CHURCH

Preface

A man might well despair of trying to paint even a miniature picture of America in a single volume. How hopeless, then, must seem the task of attempting a miniature of the Roman Catholic Church within the same space limits? This Church existed for almost 1500 years before America was dreamed of; it continues to flourish with unabated vigor after America has reached maturity, and, if history alone were used as a plausible basis for prophecy, it promises to exist long centuries after the American experiment has become an artifact like countless other civilizations through which this Church has lived.

Still, theologians have always been known for a perverse inclination to attempt the apparently impossible. And theologians do continually try to make a rough sketch of the Church in a single volume. This book exemplifies one such effort.

Given the nature of the task, one can understand why Msgr. Van Noort had to be literally ruthless in pruning the matter to meet his specific aim. That aim was twofold: 1) to present a brief, apologetic demonstration of the fact that the Roman Catholic Church is that very Church which Jesus Christ founded many centuries ago; 2) to give a brief theological description of the structure of that Church: its hierarchical organization, its powers, its mysterious supernatural life.

In nontechnical language, the author's bipartite division of the matter may be described this way: "The Church viewed from the outside" (apologetics), and "The Church viewed from the inside" (dogmatic theology).

The first section gives a glimpse of what any outsider can discover about the Church simply with the aids of history, reason, and patient study. The second section gives a glimpse of the Catholic Church which is appreciable only in the light of revelation and of faith. To adopt the beautiful figure suggested by the late Father Mersch,* the Catholic Church may be compared to an immense

---

* *The Theology of the Mystical Body*, p. 492.

PREFACE

cathedral which can be viewed from either the inside or the outside. A tourist who looks at the cathedral from the outside can immediately grasp its immense size and the solidity and grace of its construction. And, if his aesthetic sensibilities are overrefined, he may even be repelled by the marks left by wind, weather, and migrant birds. But only the tourist who ventures inside can catch the breath-taking beauty of its stained glass windows, the chaste simplicity of its linen-laid altar, and the intense, holy silence that surrounds its tabernacle.

Two approaches to the Church are, then, open to the ecclesiologist: the one apologetic, the other theological. Some authors concentrate exclusively on the one or the other. Van Noort has attempted to squeeze a bit of both into one volume. Needless to say, that takes a lot of squeezing. Of course, such an approach may disappoint readers who wish to approach the Church exclusively from one point of view. And undoubtedly it will simply outrage those who grow fatigued by the demands of scientific presentation and wish simply to read a beautiful, glowing book of devotion on the Church of Christ.

Still, the method employed by Msgr. Van Noort has its advantages for the more general type of reader. For those whose hearts might be too easily swayed, it provides the hard rocks of science in the apologetic section; for those whose heads might be too deeply submerged in such a purely rational approach, it provides a good jolt of authority and at least a hint of the mystery of the Church in the theological section. For the total beginner, it provides at least a starting point for further exploration along either line of investigation.

Revisions

It has been our difficult task to attempt some large-scale revisions of the book in the light of recent ecclesiology. The literature on the Church in the past thirty years has become a veritable deluge. A chorus of voices rises on the one side impatiently shouting: "Why don't textbooks treat the Church *this* way?"; it is always counterpointed by a dozen or so other choruses demanding some other form of treatment. In the midst of this hue and cry, we have modestly clung to the generally accepted ecclesiological approach, leaving to more venturesome—and competent—souls a totally new approach. Our reason is a simple one: it is very easy to talk about

PREFACE

"a whole fresh approach to ecclesiology," but quite another matter to produce one, and, at the same time, remain simultaneously scientific, original, and doctrinally sound. Nonetheless we have tried to incorporate such points as seem solidly established by more recent studies, and to take some notice of present trends. The attempt to incorporate new matter and prune old, in the work of an author outstanding for lucidity and terseness, has cost us many tears. If we have not succeeded very well, it has not been from any lack of effort.

The following are some of the major revisions. The statistics and information on dissident Christian Churches have been thoroughly overhauled. A new, revised, chapter on the Mystical Body has been added. What was merely an appendix on Church and State has been expanded into a complete chapter which includes both the standard principles and an evaluation of Leo XIII's teaching. The chapters on members of the Church and the necessity of the Church for salvation have both been revised in the light of *Mystici Corporis* and recent ecclesiological writing. We have added a new appendix giving a full discussion of the primacy text in the Gospel of Matthew; the basic importance of this text to the whole discussion seemed to demand some special treatment. A new select bibliography for the Church in general has been drawn up, with special attention to recent works in English. Several special bibliographies have been added for questions like Church and State, membership in the Church, etc. Apart from these major revisions, innumerable details that have been either deleted, added, or made more precise in both text and notes will be apparent to anyone who makes more than a casual comparison of this book with the Latin edition on which it is based.

A word about biblical theology and manuals of theology in general. Numerous writers keep calling for a fuller biblical approach to theological material. They are disturbed by the fact that standard manuals usually lump texts together without bothering to give a thorough exegesis of them or a comparative study of the same point as it appears, now dimly, now brightly, in various other scriptural *loci*. The complaint has its merits. It also poses some mighty methodological—and pedagogical—problems. The difficulty of using such an approach, without expanding an ordinary textbook into an encyclopedia, does not always seem to register in the minds of the critics. For example, the appendix on the primacy text runs to about 15 pages. Were this treatment accorded other important texts, the present volume would end up as a thousand, instead of just several hundred, pages. Furthermore, since the proximate norm of the faith is the Church's *magisterium*, not Sacred Scripture, and since manuals of theology are designed for beginners, not specialists, we feel justified in restricting such a biblical approach to a selected number of questions. Not everyone will agree with our particular selections; but we do feel that there is need for some such selection. For the rest, we have indicated sources where further information is available for the reader eager to do a bit of research along scriptural lines.

A few *cautions:*

1. The fact that a book is often cited does not necessarily mean that its contents are embraced *in toto*. On the other hand, express disapproval of this or that section of a book does not mean that the whole book is regarded as useless.

2. Should any non-Catholic read this book, we hope he will bear in mind that uncomplimentary remarks aimed at doctrines are not aimed at persons. This book aims not at exalting *my* Church at the expense of *your* Church. It aims simply at delineating the characteristics of Christ's Church—a Church which Christ founded not simply for *you* or for *me*, but for the whole human race.

3. If the opinions of any theologians have been misrepresented in the discussion of theological controversies, we utter a heartfelt apology in advance.

4. Above all, if we have written anything contrary to what the Catholic Church holds and teaches, we wish it considered as not uttered.

5. Many points alluded to in the theological section (particularly in the chapter on the Mystical Body) may well prove fairly unintelligible to readers unacquainted with other tracts of theology. That chapter presumes much which will be discussed specifically and at length only in later tracts in this series: Christology, the Redemption, grace, etc. If, indeed, the Church is the Mystical Body of Christ, one can appreciate this aspect of the Church's nature only after one has a thorough knowledge of what Christ is, what He has done, and what He continues to do.

We should like to express publicly our thanks to Mr. John J.

PREFACE

McHale, Mr. John L. Maddux, Mr. E. J. Foye, and other members of the Newman editorial staff for their patience and helpful suggestions in the whole work of preparation. Thanks are due also to some heroic typists and researchers: the Revs. Joseph Hrabovsky, David Brock, Charles O'Neil, and Richard Van Mullekom. Finally, a word of thanks to reviewers and critics, whose suggestions are always listened to and appreciated, even when painful.

JOHN J. CASTELOT, S.S.
WILLIAM R. MURPHY, S.S.

St. John's Provincial Seminary
Plymouth, Michigan

October 11, 1956: Feast of Our Lady's Divine Maternity

Acknowledgments

We wish to thank the following publishers for permission to quote from their publications:

AMERICAN ECCLESIASTICAL REVIEW, Washington
  The translation of Pope Pius XII's *Ci Riesci*.

AMERICA PRESS, New York
  The Mystical Body of Christ. Encyclical of Pope Pius XII with Introduction and Notes by Joseph Bluett, S.J., 1955.

GEOFFREY BLES LTD., London
  Russia and the Universal Church by Vladimir Soloviev, 1948.

THE BRUCE PUBLISHING COMPANY, Milwaukee
  The Christian Churches of the East by Donald Attwater. Two volumes, 1948.
  The New Testament Rendered from the Original Greek with Explanatory Notes. Translated by James A. Kleist, S.J. and Joseph L. Lilly, C.M., 1956.
  Dictionary of Dogmatic Theology by Pietro Parente, Antonio Piolanti, and Salvatore Garofalo. Translated from the second Italian edition by Emmanuel Doronzo, 1951.
  Paul the Apostle by Giuseppe Ricciotti. Translated by Alba I. Zizzamia, 1953.

CAMBRIDGE UNIVERSITY PRESS, New York
  Medieval Manichee by Stephen Runciman, 1955.

B. HERDER BOOK COMPANY, St. Louis
  Christian Denominations by Konrad Algermissen. Translated from the German by Rev. Joseph W. Grundner, 1945.
  The Theology of the Mystical Body by Emile Mersch, S.J. Translated by Cyril Vollert, S.J., 1951.
  The Church Teaches. Documents of the Church in English Translation. Translated and prepared by John F. Clarkson, S.J., John H. Edwards, S.J., William J. Kelly, S.J., and John J. Welch, S.J., 1955.

ACKNOWLEDGMENTS

P. J. KENEDY & SONS, New York
Pio Nono by E. E. Y. Hales, 1954.

THE MACMILLAN COMPANY, New York
Popular History of the Catholic Church by Philip Hughes, 1949.

THE NATIONAL CATHOLIC WELFARE CONFERENCE, Washington
Translation of Pope Pius XII's encyclical, *Humani generis*, 1951.

NOTRE DAME UNIVERSITY PRESS, Notre Dame
The Catholic Church in World Affairs

OXFORD UNIVERSITY PRESS, New York
The Oxford English Dictionary, 1933.

THE PAULIST PRESS, New York
Translations of Pope Leo XIII's encyclicals *Libertas* and *Immortale Dei*.

SHEED & WARD, INC., New York
A History of the Church by Philip Hughes. Three volumes, 1949. *The Church of the Word Incarnate.* A Essay in Speculative Theology by Charles Journet. Translated by A. H. C. Downes. Volume One: *The Apostolic Hierarchy*, 1955.

WILLIS KINGSLEY WING, Authors' Representative
"The Onward March of the Christian Faith," by Paul Hutchinson. *Life*, December 26, 1955.

List of Abbreviations

AAS	*Acta Apostolicae Sedis*
ACW	*Ancient Christian Writers*
AER	*American Ecclesiastical Review*
Bibl	*Biblica*
BLE	*Bulletin de littérature ecclésiastique*
CBQ	*Catholic Biblical Quarterly*
CCHS	*A Catholic Commentary on Holy Scripture*
CIC	*Codex Juris Canonici*
Coll. Lac.	*Collectio Lacensis*
CTSA	Catholic Theological Society of America— Proceedings
DAFC	*Dictionnaire apologétique de la foi catholique*
DB	Denzinger-Bannwart, *Enchiridion Symbolorum*
DTC	*Dictionnaire de théologie catholique*
ETL	*Ephemerides theologicae Lovanienses*
Greg	*Gregorianum*
HE	Eusebius, *Historia ecclesiastica*
ID	*Immortale Dei*
Kirch	*Enchiridion fontium historiae ecclesiasticae antiquae*
KL	Kleist-Lilly, *The New Testament*
LZ	Lebreton-Zeiller, *The History of the Primitive Church*
MCC	*Mystici Corporis Christi*
ML	Migne, *Patrologia latina*

LIST OF ABBREVIATIONS

NRTh	*Nouvelle revue théologique*
QP	Quasten, *Patrology*
RJ	Rouët de Journel, *Enchiridion patristicum*
RSPT	*Revue des sciences philosophiques et théologiques*
RSR	*Recherches de science religieuse*
ScG	St. Thomas, *Summa contra gentiles*
S.Th.	St. Thomas, *Summa theologica*
TCT	*The Church Teaches*
ThD	*Theology Digest*
ThGl	*Theologie und Glaube*
ThQ	*Theologische Quartalschrift*
ThR	*Theologische Revue*
TS	*Theological Studies*
VD	*Verbum Domini*
ZkTh	*Zeitschrift für Katholische Theologie*

Contents*

	Page
PREFACE	vii
ACKNOWLEDGMENTS	xiii
LIST OF ABBREVIATIONS	xv
GENERAL BIBLIOGRAPHY	xix
INTRODUCTION: THE TREATISE ON CHRIST'S CHURCH	xxv

SECTION I

The Church Viewed from Outside (Apologetics)

I. THE FOUNDING OF THE CHURCH	5
Article I. The Fact of the Founding of the Church	5
Article II. Why the Church?	20
Article III. The Perpetuity of the Church	25
II. THE CHURCH'S NATURE	31
Article I. The Church as a Hierarchical Society	31
Article II. The Church as a Monarchical Society	59
III. THE PROPERTIES OF THE CHURCH	102
Article I. The Church's Infallibility	102
Article II. The Church's Unity	126
Article III. The Church's Holiness	135
Article IV. The Church's Catholicity	143
Article V. The Church's Apostolicity	151

* A detailed outline is found at the beginning of each article.

CONTENTS

		Page
IV.	THE MARKS OF THE CHURCH	158
	Article I. The Marks of the Church Founded by Christ	158
	Article II. Which Christian Society Verifies the Marks of Christ's Church?	171

SECTION II

The Church Viewed from Inside (Dogma)

I.	THE CHURCH: THE MYSTICAL BODY OF CHRIST . . .	216
II.	THE MEMBERS OF THE CHURCH	236
	Article I. Conditions for Membership in the Church .	236
	Article II. Necessity of Belonging to the Church . .	255
III.	THE ROMAN PONTIFF	273
	Article I. Preliminary points	273
	Article II. The Nature of the Roman Pontiff's Primacy .	279
	Article III. The Infallibility of the Pope	289
	Epilogue: The Pope's Temporal Sovereignty . . .	313
IV.	THE BISHOPS	319
	Article I. The Bishops Considered Singly	319
	Article II. The Bishops Considered Collectively . .	329
V.	CHURCH AND STATE	343
	Article I. Teaching of the Church	349
	Article II. Theological Value of Leo XIII's Teaching .	390

APPENDIX. THE PRIMACY TEXT IN THE GOSPEL OF MATTHEW 395

SCRIPTURAL INDEX 411

INDEX OF PROPER NAMES 415

GENERAL INDEX 421

General Bibliography

Books

ADAM, K. *The Spirit of Catholicism*. Revised edition. Translated by Justin McCann. New York, 1954.

ALGERMISSEN, K. *Christian Denominations*. St. Louis, 1945.

ATTWATER, D. *The Christian Churches of the East*. 2 vols. Milwaukee, 1947.

BAINVEL, J. V. *De ecclesia Christi*. 1925.

BATIFFOL, P. *The Early History of the Church*. London, 1914.

———. *Catholicisme et papauté: Les difficultés anglicanes et russes*. 1925.

———. *L'église naissante et le Catholicisme*, 1922.

BELL, G. *Documents on Christian Unity*. 2 vols. London, 1948–55.

BELLARMINE, ST. ROBERT. *De controversiis Christianae fidei*. vol. I. 1590.

BENSON, R. H. *Christ in the Church*. St. Louis, 1914.

BILLOT, L. *De ecclesia Christi*. Rome, 1927.

BLUETT, J. *The Mystical Body of Christ*. New York, 1943.

BONIFACE VIII. *Unam sanctam*.

CALCAGNO, F. *Theologia fundamentalis*. 1948.

CAVANAUGH, J. *Evidence for Our Faith*. Notre Dame, Ind., 1952.

CERFAUX, L. *La théologie de l'église suivant Saint Paul*. Paris, 1948.

DE BROUWER, F. *Tractatus de ecclesia Christi*. 1882.

DE SAN, L. *Tractatus de ecclesia et Romano pontifice*. 1902.

D'HERBIGNY, M. *Theologia de ecclesia*. 1927.

DIECKMANN, H. *Die Verfassung der Urkirche*. 1923.

———. *De ecclesia*. 1925.

DORSCH, E. *De ecclesia Christi*. 1914.

FRANZELIN, J. *Theses de ecclesia Christi*. 1887.

GOOSSENS, W. *L'église, corps du Christ, d'après St. Paul*. Paris, 1949.

GENERAL BIBLIOGRAPHY

GRABMANN, M. *Die Lehre des heilige Thomas von der Kirche als Gotteswerk.* 1903.

GRUDEN, J. G. *The Mystical Christ.* St. Louis, 1936.

GURIAN, W., AND FITZSIMONS, M. *The Catholic Church in World Affairs.* Notre Dame, Ind., 1954.

HASSEVELDT, R. *The Church: A Divine Mystery.* Translated by William Storey. Chicago, 1955.

HERBERG, W. *Protestant—Catholic—Jew.* New York, 1955.

HUGHES, P. *A History of the Church,* 3 vols. New York, 1949.

——————. *Popular History of the Catholic Church.* New York, 1949.

JOURNET, C. *The Primacy of Peter.* Translated by John S. Chapin. Westminster, Md., 1954.

——————. *The Church of the Word Incarnate.* Vol. I, *The Apostolic Hierarchy.* Translated by A. H. C. Downes. New York, 1955.

KOESTERS, L. *The Church: Its Divine Authority.* Translated by E. J. Kaiser. St. Louis, 1938.

LEBRETON, J., AND ZEILLER, J. *The History of Primitive Christianity.* Translated by E. C. Messenger. 2 vols. New York, 1947.

LECLERCQ, J. *La vie du Christ dans son église.* Paris, 1947.

LERCHER, L. *Institutiones theologiae dogmaticae.* Vol. I. Revised and edited by F. Schlagenhaufen. Barcelona, 1951.

LUBAC, H. DE. *Catholicism.* New York, 1950.

——————. *The Splendour of the Church.* New York, 1955.

MAAS, J. *De Kerk van Christus.* 1927–8.

MERSCH, E. *The Whole Christ.* Milwaukee, 1938.

——————. *The Theology of the Mystical Body.* St. Louis, 1951.

MONTCHEUIL, Y. DE. *Aspects of the Church.* Chicago, 1955.

MURPHY, J. L. *The Living Christ.* Milwaukee, 1952.

OTTIGER, I. *De ecclesia Christi.* 1911.

PALMIERI, D. *Tractatus de Romano pontifice cum prolegomeno de ecclesia.* 1902.

PARIS G. *Tractatus de ecclesia Christi.* 1929.

PIUS IX. *Quanta cura.* December 8, 1864.

PIUS XII. *Mystici Corporis.* June 29, 1943.

——————. *Humani generis.* August 12, 1950.

QUASTEN, J. *Patrology*. 2 vols. Westminster, Md., 1950–3.
RANFT, J. *Die Stellung der Lehre von der Kirche in dogmatischen System*. 1927.
RICCIOTTI, G. *Paul the Apostle*. Translated by Alba I. Zizzamia. Milwaukee, 1953.
ROUSE, R., AND NEILL, C. *A History of the Ecumenical Movement: 1517-1948*. London, 1948.
SALAVERRI, I. *Sacrae theologiae summa*. Vol. I. Madrid, 1952.
SCHULTES, R. *De ecclesia Christi*. 1925.
SERTILLANGES, A. *The Church*. London, 1922.
SIMON, P. *The Human Element in the Church of Christ*. Westminster, Md., 1954.
SOLOVIEV, V. *Russia and the Universal Church*. Translated by Herbert Rees. London, 1948.
SPEDALIERI, F. *De ecclesia infallibilitate in canonizatione sanctorum quaestiones selectae*. Rome, 1949.
STRAUB, A. *De ecclesia Christi*. 1912.
TAVARD, G. A. *The Catholic Approach to Protestantism*. New York, 1955.
TROMP, S. *Corpus Christi quod est ecclesia*. Rome, 1937.
TYSZKIEWICZ, S. *La sainteté de l'église Christoconforme*. Rome, 1945.
WEIGEL, G. *A Survey of Protestant Theology in Our Day*. Westminster, Md., 1954.
WILMERS, G. *De Christi ecclesia libri sex*. 1897.
ZAPALENA, T. *De ecclesia Christi*. 2 vols. Rome, 1950–4.

Articles

CERFAUX, L. "L'église et le règne de Dieu d'après St. Paul," ETL, 181 (1925).
CHOUPIN, L. "Le pouvoir coércitif de l'église," NRTh, 209 (1908).
———. "Heresie," DAFC, II, 442 ff.
CREHAN, J. "Scripture, Tradition and the Papacy," *Scripture*, 7 (1955), 6 ff.
DANIÉLOU, J. "Cross Currents in Modern Protestantism," ThD, 3 (1955), 73 ff.

DE VISSCHER, H. "Soloviev and the Universal Church," ThD, 2 (1954), 125 ff.

DULLES, A. R. "The Protestant Concept of the Church," AER, 132 (1955), 328 ff.

FENTON, J. C. "The Apostolicity of the Roman See," AER, 118 (1948), 444 ff.

———. "The Catholic and the Church," AER, 113 (1945), 377 ff.

———. "The Church and Catholic Dogma," AER, 120 (1949), 123 ff.

———. "The Church and God's Promises," AER, 123 (1950), 295 ff.

———. "The Church and the Non-Catholic," AER, 113 (1945), 44 ff.

———. "The Church and the World," AER, 119 (1948), 202 ff.

———. "The Church in Adequate Perspective," AER, 133 (1955), 258 ff.

———. "The Communion of the Saints and the Mystical Body," AER, 110 (1944), 378 ff.

———. "The Extension of Christ's Mystical Body," AER, 110 (1944), 124 ff.

———. "Father Journet's Concept of the Church," AER, 127 (1952), 370 ff.

———. "The Invocation of the Holy Name and the Basic Concept of the Catholic Church," AER, 129 (1953), 343 ff.

———. "The Local Church of Rome," AER, 122 (1950), 454 ff.

———. "*Magisterium* and Jurisdiction in the Catholic Church," AER, 130 (1954), 194 ff.

———. "The *Mystici Corporis* and the Definitions of the Church," AER, 128 (1953), 448 ff.

———. "The New Testament Designations of the Church and of its Members," CBQ, 9 (1947), 127 ff.; 275 ff.

———. "Our Lord's Presence in the Catholic Church," AER, 115 (1946), 50 ff.

———. "The Proof of the Church's Divine Origin," AER, 113 (1945), 203 ff.

———. "St. Peter and Apostolic Jurisdiction," AER, 120 (1949), 500 ff.

---. "Scholastic Definitions of the Catholic Church," AER, 111 (1944), 59 ff.; 131 ff.; 212 ff.

---. "The Twofold Origin of the Church Militant," AER, 111 (1944), 291 ff.

---. "The Use of the Terms Body and Soul with Reference to the Catholic Church," AER, 110 (1944), 48 ff.

---. "Vicarius Christi," AER, 110 (1944), 459 ff.

FITZMYER, J. A. "The Function of the Papacy," AER, 121 (1949), 34 ff.

GRAHAM, A. "The Church on Earth," *The Teaching of the Catholic Church*, New York, 1947. II, 691 ff.

HUARTE, G. "Quomodo ecclesia Christi, quae visibilis est, possit esse objectum fidei," Greg, 78 (1922).

MYERS, E. "The Mystical Body of Christ," *The Teaching of the Catholic Church*. New York, 1947. II, 659 ff.

STANLEY, D. M. "Kingdom to Church: The Structural Development of Apostolic Christianity in the New Testament," TS, 16 (1955), 1 ff.

ST. JOHN, H. "Authority and the Ecumenical Dilemma," *Blackfriars*, 37 (1956), 196 ff.

WRIGHT, JOHN J. "The Eternal Church," *Voice*, 34 (1957), 5 ff.

Introduction

The Treatise on Christ's Church

The treatise on *The True Religion* demonstrated that the religion which the Catholic Church teaches was divinely revealed in Christ. Now attention must be focused on the Catholic Church itself, that society in which the divine religion of Christ is embodied, and by which it is preserved and practiced.[1]

The term church (*ekklēsía* from *ekkaleín* "to call forth") signifies an assembly of people called together. This assembly may be secular,[2] or, more properly, religious.[3]

Christ's Church, then, indicates in a general way the whole host of people who join themselves to God through Christ. Since this group includes some who are living in triumph in heaven, some who are suffering in purgatory, and still others who are fighting life's battle on earth, the Church in this broad sense consists of three parts: the Church Triumphant, the Church Suffering, and the Church Militant. The former two do not fall within the scope of the present treatise.[4]

The *Church Militant* can in turn be understood in a broad or a strict sense. In the broad sense it includes all men on their way to heaven who have, from the time of Adam's fall, worshiped God through allegiance to the Christ who would one day be born or who has already been born. Consequently, we may distinguish the *Church of the law of nature*, that *of the Mosaic law* (the Synagogue), and that *of the law of the gospel*. In the words of St. Augustine,

> All the just who have ever existed, from the very beginning of time, have had Christ as their Head; for they believed that He would come whom we believe to have already come, and by their faith in Him they were saved as we are by ours.[5]

But in its proper and strict sense, the Church of Christ is limited to the Church of the law of the gospel, and embraces those people

INTRODUCTION

on earth who profess the religion which Christ Himself founded.

Still, even in this limited sense, the term *Church* is used in various ways. At times it denotes the whole body of Catholics throughout the whole world,[6] or again, some particular group.[7] At times it is applied to the whole body without distinction between those in authority and those under authority, while at other times it may indicate only the former,[8] or only the latter.[9] However, the precise meaning is usually clear enough from the context in which the term appears.

The present treatise considers the Church of Christ in the ordinary, strict sense, that is, the Church Militant of the New Testament, universal, whole, and entire.

2   **Definition.** The Church, according to the above acceptation, may be defined as follows: *The society of men who, by their profession of the same faith and by their partaking of the same sacraments, make up, under the rule of apostolic pastors and their head, the kingdom of Christ on earth.*[10] This definition is given here at the very beginning of the treatise in the interests of clarity. That it is a true and legitimate definition will become clear as the exposition proceeds.

3   Among our *adversaries* may be numbered in general all those who glory in the name of Christian but live beyond the pale of the Roman Catholic Church: all heretics and schismatics, many of whom are so steeped in Rationalism that they have held on to hardly any part of Christian revelation aside from the principles of morality.

The sources to be used throughout the treatise are all those documents from which one can gain a knowledge of the beginnings of the Christian religion and of the Christian Church: the books of the New Testament and the writings of the early fathers. The works of the apostles are cited merely as historical documents, and although they are held in reverence as being apostolic, it is their historical authority rather than their apostolic origin which is of prime import in the present discussion. On the other hand, one should not overlook the fact that many of our opponents agree with us in accepting all or nearly all the books of the New Testament as divinely inspired compositions. In discussions with people who share this view, then, these books may be adduced as possessing not only historical worth but the authority of the word of God as well.

INTRODUCTION

Division. The subject matter falls into two sections. The former will treat of *the Church as a whole;* the second, of *each of the Church's hierarchical ranks in particular.* The former study will be largely apologetic in character, the latter more theological.

Notes

1. See J. Ranft, *Die Stellung der Lehre von der Kirche im dogmatischen System* (1927).
2. *E.g.,* Acts 19:32, 39; Ps. 25:5.
3. See Acts 5:11: *Great fear came over the whole congregation (ekklēsia) and on all who heard of this;* see also Gal. 1:8; J. C. Fenton, "New Testament Designations of the Church and of its Members," CBQ, 9 (1947), 127 ff.; *idem,* "The Meaning of the Name 'Church'," AER, 131 (1954), 268 ff. The Greek word *ekklēsia* is the basis of the word for church in the Latin, Romance, and Celtic languages. Thus we find: *ecclesia* (Latin), *église* (French), *iglesia* (Spanish), *chiesa* (Italian), *eglais* (Irish and Gaelic), *iliz* (Breton). As for the word in Teutonic and Slavic languages:

> The ulterior derivation has been keenly disputed. The L. *circus,* and a Gothic word *kelikn* 'tower, upper chamber' (app. originally Gaulish) have both been proposed (the latter suggested by the Alemannic *chelihha*), but are set aside as untenable; and there is now a general agreement among scholars in referring it to the Greek word *kyriakón,* properly adj. 'of the Lord, *dominicum,* dominical' (f. *kýrios* lord), which occurs, from the 3rd century at least, used substantively (sc. dôma, or the like) 'house of the Lord', as a name of the Christian house of worship.—*The Oxford English Dictionary,* II (Oxford, 1933), 403.

Thus we have the words: *church* (English), *kerk* (Dutch), *circe* (Old English), *Kirche* (German), *kyrka* (Swedish), *kirke* (Danish), *kirkko* (Finnish), *cerkov'* (Russian), *cerkiew* (Polish, but only with reference to the "Greek Church").

4. See J. C. Fenton, "The Communion of Saints and the Mystical Body," AER, 110 (1944), 378 ff.
5. *In psalm.* 36, *Sermo* 3, 4. See Leo XIII, *Humanum genus* (April 20, 1884); J. C. Fenton, "The Twofold Origin of the Church Militant," AER, 111 (1944), 291 ff.; *idem,* "New Testament Designations of the Church and of its Members," CBQ, 9 (1947), 127 ff.; *idem,* "The Church and the World," AER, 119 (1948), 202 ff.; *idem,* "The Church and God's Promises," AER, 123 (1950), 295 ff.; *idem,* "The Church in Adequate Perspective," AER, 133 (1955), 258 ff.; J. Leclercq, *La vie du Christ dans son église* (Paris, 1947); R. Hasseveldt, *The Church: A Divine Mystery,* translated by Wm. Storey (Chicago, 1955). A key thought developed in the above works is that the Church is more properly and fruitfully considered as the kingdom of God on earth, that kingdom which has existed throughout all the ages, in constant opposition to the kingdom of the devil, the world. This was the approach of the classical ecclesiologists, and it is, happily, being revived today. As a matter of fact, the custom of defining the Church exclusively in terms of the New

INTRODUCTION

Testament did not become the vogue until about the nineteenth century. Msgr. Journet states the matter as follows:

> Now what are we to say of this act by which God has produced the Church, His abode among men—whether we call the Church a miserable hovel on account of human sin, or a temple on account of the Guest it shelters? Has it known but a single form, unchanged down all the ages? Did God from the beginning produce His Church as it stands to-day, and has time no other part to play than to lend endurance to what was perfect from the start?
>
> The answer is clear. The divine act that produced the Church has been marked by several phases. These might be called the various divine regimes under which the people of God have lived during the course of the ages, the divine regimes of the Church. For God led the Church through various successive states, and the purpose of time is to enable this Church not only to endure, but also to progress until it reaches that state which is to be the last one in this world, the state in which it enters the era of the Incarnation and of Pentecost.—*The Church of the Word Incarnate. I, The Apostolic Hierarchy,* translated by A. H. C. Downes (New York, 1955), 1 f.

6. The *universal Church,* as in Eph. 5:25: *Christ loved the Church, and delivered himself for her.*

7. Particular churches, as in I Cor. 1:1: *Paul . . . to the congregation (ekklēsía) of God at Corinth.*

8. The *teaching Church,* as in Matt. 18:17: *"If he pays no attention to them, then notify the Church."*

9. The *Church taught,* as in Acts 20:28: ". . . *in which the Holy Spirit has placed you as bishops to rule the Church of God."*

10. Thus Pesch, *Praelectiones dogmaticae,* I, no. 309, following Bellarmine, *De ecclesia,* I, III, cap. 2. A shorter and less exact definition might be: *The society which professes the religion of Christ.* See J. C. Fenton, "Scholastic Definitions of the Catholic Church," AER, 111 (1944), 59 ff.; 131 ff.; 212 ff.; idem, "The *Mystici Corporis* and the Definitions of the Church," AER, 128 (1953), 448 ff. These articles constitute, incidentally, a splendid survey of the history of ecclesiology. See also C. Journet, *op. cit.,* 45 ff.

SECTION I

The Church Viewed from Outside (Apologetics)

Chapter I. THE FOUNDING OF THE CHURCH

Article I

THE FACT OF THE FOUNDING OF THE CHURCH

I. *Opinions of Opponents:*

    1. Orthodox Protestants (the Reformers)
    2. Modern Protestants
    3. Modernists
    PROPOSITION 1: Christ personally founded a Church which is a true society.
        Proof: 1. from the promise of Christ
                2. from the deeds of Christ
                3. from the earliest available historical records
        Scholion 1: Christ established only one Church.
        Scholion 2: When did Christ establish the Church?
        Scholion 3: The distinction between the primitive Church and the Synagogue.
    PROPOSITION 2: It is due to the institution of Christ Himself that the Church is visible.
        Proof: 1. from the threefold bond which Christ Himself imposed
                2. from the manner of speaking of Christ, the apostles, and the fathers
    Objections

SECTION I

The Church as a Whole

With reference to Christ's Church considered in its ensemble, four points must be studied: its founding or institution, *its nature or* constitution, *the* properties *which adorn it, and the notes or* marks *by which it is recognized.*

CHAPTER I

The Founding of the Church

This chapter will determine: (1) the *fact of the founding of the Church,* (2) the *purpose for which,* and (3) the *time for which* it was founded.

Article I

THE FACT OF THE FOUNDING OF THE CHURCH

I. Opinions of Opponents

1. **Orthodox Protestants.** It would be quite some task to give an accurate presentation of the various opinions of the Reformers concerning the Church and its institution, especially in view of the fact that they seldom agreed with one another. A summary of Protestant teaching might run about as follows: [1]

a. There does exist a Church founded by Christ Himself. It consists of the just (Lutherans) or of the predestined (Calvinists). This is the "Church of the promises," in which are verified the promises of Christ. It is holy and indefectible, etc. But, although it joins the holy or the elect to Christ, it does not join them together with each other; and indeed it cannot, because God alone knows who belongs to it. It is the *invisible Church,* the kingdom of God on earth.

b. The true members of Christ, desirous of manifesting their faith and of stirring it up by outward gestures, joined together and formed the *visible Church,* or rather, *visible churches.*[2] And so the visible Church is a human institution, and can adopt various social forms as localities or the fashions of the times require. It can even disintegrate and fall apart. But as long as it is based on truly evangelical principles, it is good and legitimate, and in this sense it can be called the true Church. Not even then, however, is it identical with the invisible Church, for it always harbors a certain number of hypocrites. On the other hand, the invisible Church is not separate from the visible, for a great crowd of the holy or elect always[3] lies hidden in the "ecclesiastical mass." But if the visible Church should become so corrupt as to start contradicting evangelical principles, it would thus turn out to be a false Church. This is what happened, under the papacy, to the Roman Catholic Church, which the older Reformers dubbed the Synagogue of Satan and the Church of Antichrist.

2. **Modern Protestants** take the following view of the matter. All Christ preached was an elevated form of morality and the love of God, "the Father, who is in heaven." He neither separated Himself from the Synagogue of the Jews nor enjoined this separation on His disciples. Therefore He founded no Church, any more than He taught a new religion. But His disciples, driven by the hate and persecution of the Jews, soon set up separate communities, from which, particularly under the active influence of the Roman community, the Catholic Church was pieced together about the middle of the third century. Before this time a universal Church existed only in the minds of the Christians, as a sort of ideal Church. But the Catholic Church, by inventing dogmas borrowed in large part from Greek philosophies, and by adopting a social structure based on that of the Roman Empire, wandered far from the spirit of Christ and the pure gospel. It evolved along the lines of a progressive corruption, although it always managed to hold on to a part of the gospel.[4]

3. **Modernists** deny the genuineness of many Gospel passages and advance the following views. The Christ of history, who thought the end of the world was just around the corner, did not even dream of founding a Church worthy of the name: "The founding of a Church as a society which would enjoy a centuries-long existence on earth was altogether foreign to the mind of Christ; as a matter of fact, in the mind of Christ the kingdom of heaven was on the point of being inaugurated together with the end of the world."[5] Therefore in its own good time the Church was born of a twofold need. The more remote was that which individual believers felt for sharing their faith with others; the immediate need was that felt by the multitude, now steeped in the one faith, for gathering into a society which would safeguard, increase, and spread the treasure they held in common. Furthermore, every society needs a governing authority; in the Church

also, necessity gave birth to authority. This latter developed, little by little, with the help of historical circumstances, into that hierarchy at whose head is the Roman pontiff.[6] Still, add the Modernists, the founding of the Church and of the hierarchy is attributed to Christ by the faithful. In the realm of faith, every Christian consciousness is included by some vague force in the consciousness of Christ. If this be granted, then whatever came forth from the Christian consciousness in the course of time can be said to have come forth at least indirectly from the consciousness of "the Christ of faith."[7]

Against all of these opponents, then, the Catholic theologian must set forth and defend the Catholic doctrine of the real and immediate founding of a Church by the Christ of history. Accordingly, the question is no longer whether Christ preached a new, and divine, religion, but only whether the historical Christ Himself gathered His disciples into a society worthy of the name or not.

PROPOSITION 1: *Christ personally founded a Church which is a true society.*[8]   5

This proposition contains a twofold assertion. *a.* Christ Himself *directly* founded a Church. This rules out any indirect founding through the agency of others to whom Christ would have entrusted or left the whole affair. *b.* This Church is, as Christ Himself founded it, *a society in the strict sense,* not merely a religious academy.

A *society* is a *permanent assembly of many people united for the attainment of a common goal.* Not any and every group of people is a society, but only one which pursues a common goal in a permanent manner. Now this stable unification of many people is effected by means of certain bonds which unite the minds and the active efforts of the group. The chief of these bonds is authority. And so the *matter* of a society is the group itself; its *form* is the unifying bonds, authority in particular; its founder or *author* is he who unites the group by applying the bonds.[9]

This proposition is a *dogma of the faith* in both its parts, for it is contained equivalently in the Vatican Council, which asserts that "the eternal Shepherd and Bishop of our souls determined to build a holy Church." The council then proceeds to reproach those who pervert "the form of rule established by Christ the Lord in His Church," and, finally, adds the remark that "St. Peter was established by Christ as the visible head of the whole Church," and that he "directly and immediately received from the same our Lord Jesus Christ the primacy of real and genuine jurisdiction."[10] So also the *Oath against Modernism:* "With unshaken faith I believe that the Church was immediately and directly established by the real and historical Christ Himself while He was living in our midst, and that this same Church was built upon Peter, the head of the apostolic hierarchy, and upon those who will succeed him to the end of time."[11]

6   *Proof:*

1. From *the promise of Christ.* If Christ, the true envoy of God, promised anything, then beyond the shadow of a doubt He fulfilled the promise. *"You are Peter, and upon this rock I will build my Church. . . . I will give you the keys of the kingdom of heaven, and whatever you bind on earth shall be bound in heaven, and whatever you loose on earth shall be loosed in heaven."* (Matt. 16:18–19). Now that Church, compared as it is to a house founded on a rock, and to a kingdom in which Peter will have supreme power, will most certainly be not an amorphous mob of people, but a group gathered together into unity, or a society.

Quite to the point here also is the fact that Christ preached, right from the beginning of His public life, and had others preach, that *"the kingdom of heaven is close at hand,"*[12] and the fact that He said He was to gather His sheep together from among Jews and Gentiles so that there would be *"one flock, one shepherd"* (John 10:16). For just as a house and a kingdom carry with them the ideas of cohesion and unity, so does a sheepfold.

7   2. From *the deeds of Christ.* Our Lord Himself bound all His disciples together with a threefold bond: the profession of the same faith, the same rites, the same rule.

a. He enjoined upon all the profession of the same faith: *"Preach the gospel to all creation. He that believes and is baptized will be saved; but he that does not believe will be condemned."*[13]

b. He commanded all to *share in the same rites,* at least in baptism and the Eucharist. *Baptism:* *"He that believes and is baptized will be saved,"* and *"Unless a man is born of water and the Spirit, he cannot enter the kingdom of God"* (John 3:5). The *Eucharist:* *"The bread which I shall give is my flesh given for the life of the world . . . unless you eat the flesh of the Son of Man, and drink his blood, you have no life in you.*"[14]

c. He subjected all to *the same rule*. To the apostles alone, to whom He had previously promised the power of binding and loosing (Matt. 18:18), did He entrust the power of preaching, baptizing, ruling, and absolving (Matt. 28:19–20; John 20:21–23). Furthermore, to Peter alone did He give the task of feeding all His sheep (John 21:15–17).

3. From the *earliest historical records* available.[15] They bear witness to the facts that (*a*) Christ's disciples were from the very beginning united in a real society, and (*b*) the establishment of this society or Church was even then attributed to Christ Himself.

8

a. The book of Acts and the epistles of the apostles make it abundantly clear that the disciples were linked by the aforementioned threefold bond immediately after Christ's Ascension.

They *professed the same faith* and were obliged to profess it— that faith, namely, which the apostles preached: *Those who accepted his* [Peter's] *word were baptized. . . . They gave steadfast attention to the teaching of the apostles* (Acts 2:41–42; see 8:12, 37; 10:33 ff). *One Lord, one faith* (Eph. 4:5). *Let me tell you that if even we ourselves or an angel from heaven should proclaim to you a gospel other than we have proclaimed, let him be accursed.* (Gal. 1:8; see Rom. 16:17; Tit. 3:10–12; II John 9–11).

They performed *the same rites,* baptism and the Eucharist: *On hearing this . . . they said to Peter and the rest of the apostles, "Brothers, what shall we do?" "Have a change of heart and mind," Peter told them, "and be baptized everyone of you." . . . Those who accepted his word were baptized, and there were added that day (to the Church) about three thousand persons. They gave steadfast attention to the teaching of the apostles and to union, to the breaking of bread and to the prayers* (Acts 2:37–42). *There is one Lord, one faith, one Baptism* (Eph. 4:5). *In fact, by a single Spirit all of us, whether Jews or Greeks, slaves or free men, were introduced into the one body through baptism* (I Cor. 12:13). *Because the bread is one, we, the many who partake of that one bread, form one body* (I Cor. 10:17).

They were subject to *the same pastors,* i.e., the apostles. *Those who sell property deposit the returns at the apostles' feet* (Acts 4:34–35). *The apostles call together the multitude for the selection of the first deacons and impose hands on those chosen* (Acts 6:2–6);

they appoint presbyters throughout the different cities (Acts 14:22); they solve authoritatively the question of the binding force of the prescriptions of the Old Law and issue some relevant commands (Acts 15:5 ff; I Cor. 11:34); they claim for themselves the right to inflict penalties, and actually exercise this right (II Cor. 13:10; I Cor. 5:3 ff).

b. The apostles themselves attribute the founding of this Church to Christ. They teach that the faithful form *a spiritual edifice*, built *on the foundation of the apostles and prophets with Christ Jesus himself as the chief cornerstone* (I Pet. 2:4–5; Eph. 2:20; see Heb. 3:6); that Christ is *universal head of the Church, which is truly his body* (Eph. 1:22–23); that Christ bought the Church *"with his own blood"* (Acts 20:28); that the Church is the bride of Christ, whom He *loved* and for whom He *delivered himself, that he might sanctify her . . . in order to present to himself the Church in all her glory* (Eph. 5:25–27). Add to this the fact that the apostles openly claim to have received their authority over the faithful from Christ (II Cor. 10:8; 13:10).

9   *Scholion 1. Christ established only one Church.*

The arguments alleged above demonstrate the further point that Christ founded not two or more Churches, but one single Church. Indeed if one gives heed to *our Lord's own words*, one notes that He always spoke of His kingdom or Church in the singular, and, in fact, explicitly stated that all His sheep were to be gathered into "one flock."[16] If one considers *Christ's actions*, one sees that He subjected all His worshipers of all nations to the apostolic college, and entrusted His entire flock to the care of Peter alone. As a result, the most ancient witnesses knew of only one Church. According to the apostles, all the faithful and all the individual churches in various places form one body, make up one Church.[17] According to the *Didache*, the Church is to be gathered together from the four corners of the earth: "Remember, O Lord, thy Church. . . . Gather her together, sanctified, into thy kingdom from the four winds" (10. 5). In the words of St. Justin, "those who believe in him (Christ) are one soul, one congregation, one Church" (*Dialogue with Trypho* 63). Finally, St. Cyprian unequivocally declares: "There is one God, one Christ, one Church, and one See, founded on a rock at the Lord's command" (*Epist. 40 ad plebem* 5).

Scholion 2. When did Christ establish the Church?

Our Lord did not do everything affecting the Church at one and the same time. For, having announced—from the beginning of His public life—that the Church would soon be established (Matt. 4:12–17), He made the *immediate preparations* for its establishment before His Passion, so that only the determination of its definitive form yet remained. During that time, while preaching His doctrine, He joined to Himself a group of believers, instituted the more important sacraments (baptism and the Eucharist), taught His pastors-to-be, and promised them a sacred power. Still, it was only after the Resurrection that He *put the final touches* to the construction of the Church, when He definitively conferred upon the apostolic college and upon Peter their sacred ruling power.[18] The Church is clearly a society, and no society has been properly constituted until its authority has been established. Strictly speaking, then, the Church was established by Christ after the Resurrection, and it was *promulgated* or made public on the solemn occasion of Pentecost and hence became obligatory from that day on.

Scholion 3. The distinction between the primitive Church and the Synagogue.

From the fact that Christ, during His earthly sojourn, and the disciples, even after Pentecost, observed the ceremonial prescriptions of the Mosaic Law, some have concluded that the Christians in the early days after Pentecost did not form a society distinct from the Synagogue and that consequently the Church had not been founded by Christ Himself.

The principal objection of these adversaries has already been met above (no. 8). For since the Christians, immediately after Pentecost, professed their own special doctrine, performed rites peculiar to themselves, obeyed their own leaders, it is clear that they did indeed make up a society distinct from the Synagogue.[19] One further point: they also held their own assemblies.[20]

As for the observance of the ceremonial (legal) precepts: the fact that Christ—and the apostles during His lifetime—kept the Law presents no difficulty; for all the observances of the Old Law remained *alive* or obligatory up to the death of Christ, who at that time established the New Covenant in His own blood.[21] With our

Lord's death the Old Testament went out of existence, and from that moment the precepts of the Law became *dead*, i.e., no longer of obligation.

Nevertheless the apostles and the first converts from Judaism kept the legal prescriptions for a while; and this was a prudent arrangement, for it showed more clearly the connection between the two Testaments and gave the defunct Synagogue a decent burial (much like that of a cherished mother, whose lifeless corpse is not tossed hurriedly into a ditch, but is kept for a while and then borne reverently to the grave by a massed crowd of sons and daughters).[22] But later, when the gospel had been sufficiently promulgated, the ceremonial precepts of the Law became positively *lethal*, in the sense that they could no longer be carried out by Catholics without serious sin.[23]

12 PROPOSITION 2. *It is due to the institution of Christ Himself that the Church is visible.*[24]

This proposition is *certain*.

That the Church is visible follows necessarily from the fact that it is a real society, for there can be no genuine society in the world of men unless it be visible. But since Protestants constantly attack with might and main the visible character of the Church which Christ founded, it is necessary to give the question special consideration. The visible form of the Church which is the subject of this present discussion must not be confused with what is strictly its knowability. It is one thing to ask whether the Church which Christ founded is a public society, and quite another to ask whether that society can be recognized *as the true Church of Christ* by certain distinguishing marks. Its being formally recognizable presupposes its being visible, but the two are not identical. Furthermore, the present discussion centers on the visible character of the Church insofar as it is a society. No one denies that the Church's members are visible, for they are flesh-and-blood people; but some do question whether, by the institution of Christ Himself, these members are bound together by external bonds so as to form a society that can be perceived by the senses, a society of such a nature that one can readily discern who belongs to it and who does not. Mark well the words "the institution of Christ Himself," for the question is precisely this: Did Christ personally found a visible Church, one which by its very nature would have to be an external (public) society, so that an invisible Church could not possibly be the true Church of Christ? For once one proves that the one and only Church which Christ founded is visible from its very nature, then it necessarily follows: (a) that an invisible Church such as that to which Protestants appeal is a pure fiction, and (b) that all the promises which Christ made to His Church refer to a visible Church.[25] Note, lastly, that to insist on the Church's being visible is not to claim that all its elements are immediately apparent to the senses. Just as a man is really visible even though one cannot see his soul directly, so too the Church must be adjudged truly visible even if some element which is an essential part of its make-up cannot be seen directly—provided that this element be by its very nature joined to and externally manifested by some visible element.

Proof:

13

1. From the *threefold bond* which Christ Himself imposed. It was indicated above how our Lord founded the Church by enjoining on His disciples the profession of the same faith, participation in the same rites, and obedience to the same authority (no. 7). It is by these bonds that the Church is drawn into unity and held together; without them there is simply no Church of Christ. Now, since these bonds are external things which people can see, they necessarily make the Church an external, visible society. One can discern, using one's external senses, which men profess the same doctrine, frequent the same sacraments, and obey the same rulers. It is, then, clear that the Church is visible by the very institution of Christ, or, in other words, that its visibility flows necessarily from its very nature.

2. This conclusion is corroborated by the *manner of speaking* employed by Christ, the apostles, and the earliest fathers, who clearly had in mind a visible society whenever they spoke of the Church.

Christ compares His Church to a kingdom, to a flock, to a house, to a net let down into the sea, to a field producing wheat and weeds, to a city built on a mountain peak. He teaches, besides, that sinners whose reformation is proving difficult are to be reported to the Church.[26]

The *apostles* call the Church a body in which many members are joined together and are mutually interdependent; the house of

God in which pastors live; the pillar and mainstay of truth; the flock in which the Holy Spirit has placed the bishops as shepherds.[27]

The *earliest fathers* urge the absolute obligation of belonging to the Church of Christ and clearly teach that it is easily discernible;[28] they could have done neither were the Church not visible. A further consideration is the fact that long before this the *prophets* had described the kingdom or Church of the Messias as a very high mountain which attracts people to itself precisely because it can be seen from anywhere.[29]

14 *Objections:*

(1) Christ Himself gave clear enough indication that His Church was invisible. For (a) He compared it to *"a treasure buried in the field"* (Matt. 13:44), and (b) when the Pharisees asked, *"When is the kingdom of God coming?"* He replied, *"The kingdom of God comes unawares. Neither will they say, 'Behold, here it is,' or 'Behold, there it is.' For behold, the kingdom of God is within you"* (Luke 17:21).[30]

Answer to *a.*: The purpose of this parable is to point up the value of the Messianic kingdom, and so the word *"buried"* is not to be stressed. And anyway, how could one find an *invisible* treasure?

Answer to *b.*: These words rule out both a political and an eschatological kingdom of the type to which the Pharisees were looking, but not every type of visible kingdom. The meaning is as follows. The kingdom of God will not come all of a sudden with a great to-do and with all the worldly trappings such as we associate with a triumphant king of whom the crowd shouts, "Here he is!", "There he is!", nor will its inauguration be accompanied by celestial fireworks. The kingdom of God will grow little by little by little, step by step, imperceptibly. In fact *"the kingdom of God is already in your midst"*; it has already begun to take root and to grow in the midst of you. Since the words *entòs hymôn* are addressed to the Pharisees, they do not signify "in your souls," but rather "in your midst," i.e., in the midst of the people of which you form a part. See Knabenbauer and CCHS on this passage.

(2) If the Church were visible, the Creed would not propose it as an object of *faith:* "I believe ... holy Church."

Answer: What one *sees* in the Church is one thing; what one *believes* about that same Church is quite another. One sees the Church's external social structure; one believes that the same Church which has this particular social structure is of divine institution and has the power to lead people to holiness and to supernatural salvation. In the same way, the apostles saw Christ walking about after the fashion of all men, and at the same time they believed in His divinity.[31] Note the phrase "the same Church," for one does not see an amorphous "ecclesiastical mass," in which the invisible Church of Christ would be hiding, but one does see the very Church of Christ.

Notes

1. See G. Weigel, S.J., *A Survey of Protestant Theology in Our Day* (Westminster, Md., 1954); A. R. Dulles, S.J., "The Protestant Concept of the Church," AER, 132 (1955), 328 ff.; J. Daniélou, S.J., "Cross Currents in Modern Protestantism," ThD, 3 (1955), 73 ff. For an interesting study of the views of an outstanding Russian Orthodox theologian on the Church, see H. de Visscher, "Soloviev and the Universal Church," ThD, 2 (1954), 125 ff.

2. At the present time some orthodox Protestants are of the opinion that a *visible* Church was founded by Christ and is therefore of *divine origin*. See, for instance, F. W. Grosheide in *Geref. theol. Tijds.*, 31 (1930), 257.

3. Calvinists apparently do not rule out the case—although they admit it but rarely—in which a person can be saved even though he be *outside* the Church. Thus, for instance, H. Bavinck, *Gereformeerde Dogmatiek* (2nd ed.), IV, 311.

4. This is, for all practical purposes, the view of A. von Harnack, *Lehrbuch der Dogmengeschichte* (3rd ed.), I, 41 ff.; see also *ibid.*, 439 ff.

5. The decree *Lamentabili*, prop. 52 (DB 2052).

6. See the encyclical *Pascendi*, and the decree *Lamentabili*, prop. 54–6 (DB 2054–6).

7. See the encyclical *Pascendi* (DB 2088, 2091).

8. See F. Reisinger, "Christus Stifter der Kirche nach den Briefen des hl. Paulus," *Theol.-prakt. Quarts.* (Linz, 1927), p. 447 and 704.

9. See J. Maritain, *Man and the State* (Chicago, 1953).

10. Constitution *De ecclesia Christi*, preamble and ch. 1.

11. DB 2145.

12. Matt. 4:17, 23; 10:5–7; Mark 1:15. The terms *kingdom of heaven* and *kingdom of God* in the gospels signify, at times, our *heavenly home*, at other times, God's *kingdom on earth*. This latter can be either the *internal kingdom* (Messianic peace) or the *external kingdom*, that society which Christ uses as an instrument for the planting and fostering of His internal reign in the souls of individuals (see Eph. 4:11 ff.; I Cor. 3:22). Therefore, although not all the texts which speak of the kingdom of heaven here on earth refer directly to the Church, still they err badly who claim that none of these texts

is to be understood as referring literally to the Church. See B. Bartmann, *Das Himmelreich und sein König* (1904); M. Cordovani, *Il regno di Dio* (1918); L. Cerfaux, "L'église de le règne de Dieu d'après St. Paul," ETL, 181 (1925); *idem, La théologie de l'église suivant St. Paul* (Paris, 1948); I. Salaverri, *Sacrae theologiae summa* (Madrid, 1952), I, s.v. *Regnum*.

13. Mark 16:15–16; see Matt. 28:19–20. It has been said that the chief bond is not purely and simply the same faith, but the *profession* of the same faith, for *merely* inner faith does not bind men together into a society. And Christ did not demand internal assent alone, but also its external manifestation. Since He ordered that baptism be administered to those who believed, He evidently expected some outward token of this belief. That token is given by external profession.

14. John 6:52–54; see Luke 22:19; I Cor. 11:23–30. When we say, "*at least* baptism and the Eucharist," we prescind from the question as to whether Christ prescribed other rites as well. But the two we have mentioned, about which no one who admits the historicity of the Gospels can raise any question, will suffice for the present discussion.

15. See P. Batiffol, *L'église naissante et le Catholicisme* (1922); H. Dieckmann, *Die Verfassung der Urkirche* (1923).

16. Matt. 4:17; 10:7; 13:31, 34; 16:18; John 10:16; see 11:52.

17. Acts 9:31–32; 15; 16:4; 20:28; I Cor. 10:17; 12:13; Eph. 4:11–16.

18. John 20:21; 21:15–17; Matt. 28:16–20. See J. C. Fenton, "The Proof of the Church's Divine Origin," AER, 113 (1945), 203 ff.; D. M. Stanley, S.J., "Kingdom to Church: The Structural Development of Apostolic Christianity in the New Testament," TS 16 (1955), 1 ff.; T. Zapalena, S.J., *De ecclesia Christi*, I (Rome, 1950), 86–141.

19. Acts 5:11: after relating the incident of Ananias and Saphira, St. Luke tells us that *great fear came on the whole congregation (ekklēsía) and on all who heard of this*. He indicates thereby a real distinction between the *ekklēsía*, the Church, on the one hand, and the Jews on the other. See CCHS, 826 f. Gal. 1:13: . . . *beyond all measure I persecuted the Church of God and ravaged it*. Certainly, in the eyes of the ardent Pharisee, Saul, the Christians formed an easily discernible society, a society distinct from Judaism and from the Synagogue that it could be the clear target of his misguided zeal.

20. *Daily with one accord they attended the temple, and, breaking bread at their homes, took their food with gladness and simplicity of heart* (Acts 2:46). *They gave their steadfast attention to the teaching of the apostles and to union, to the breaking of bread and to the prayers* (2:42). *With one accord they all met in Solomon's portico . . . no one of the rest dared join them* (5:12–13; see 3:11).

21. Heb. 9:11 ff. Christ Himself was of course not held to the observance of the Law, (Matt. 12:6–8), but He wanted to fulfill all that the Law prescribed for righteousness in order to leave us an example of humility and obedience.

22. St. Augustine *Epist.* 82. 16. In somewhat the same strain G. Ricciotti writes:

THE FOUNDING OF THE CHURCH

The child developing in its mother's womb already has a life of its own distinct from that of its mother, even though it is as yet incomplete and dependent on the mother's life. But during this period of formation it is being prepared gradually for its own independent life by a provident nature. And even when the child has been born, there is still a slender cord binding him to his mother. Only when this has been cut does the new life become completely independent.

It is historically accurate to say that the Christian Church—in its externals—was conceived and formed in the womb of the Jewish Synagogue, and that for a certain length of time its life was united with that of the latter, although it was distinct from it and clearly directed toward complete independence. The last tie binding it to the Synagogue was the observance of the rites prescribed by the Law of Moses. Once this was severed, the Church acquired an autonomous life, entirely independent of the Synagogue.

The one who dared to cut this bond, with incalculable consequences for the history of mankind, was Paul. In this sense he may be said to have "delivered" the Church.—*Paul the Apostle*, translated by Alba I. Zizzamia (Milwaukee, 1953), p. 272.

23. Gal. 5:2–4; See DB 712; S.Th. I-II, q. 103, a. 4; Pesch, *Praelectiones dogmaticae*, V, no. 519 ff.

24. See J. Walz, *Die Sichtbarkeit der Kirche* (1924); J. C. Fenton, "The Catholic and the Church," AER, 113 (1945), 377 ff.; *idem*, "Our Lord's Presence in the Catholic Church," AER, 115 (1946), 50 ff.; *idem*, "Father Journet's Concept of the Church," AER, 127 (1952), 370 ff.; *idem*, "The Invocation of the Holy Name and the Basic Concept of the Catholic Church," AER, 129 (1953), 343 ff.

25. See J. C. Fenton, "The Church and God's Promises," AER, 123 (1950), 295 ff.

26. Mark 1:15; John 21:15–17; 10:16; Matt. 16:18; 13:47, 24; 5:14; 18:17. See J. C. Fenton, "New Testament Designations of the Catholic Church and of its Members," CBQ, 9 (1947), 127 ff. 275 ff.

27. I Cor. 12:12 ff.; see Eph. 4:11 ff.; I Tim. 3:15; Acts 20:28; I Pet. 5:2–4.

28. For example, St. Ignatius *Ad Philadelph.* 3. 3: "If a man runs after a schismatic, *he will not inherit the Kingdom of God*" (ACW translation). St. Irenaeus *Adv. haer.* v. 20. 1: "This [Church] is a seven-branched (*heptámochos*) candelabra bearing the light of Christ." Origen *Series comm. in Matt.* 47 (on Matt. 24:27), "The Church is suffused with light from east to west, it is filled with the true light, it is the pillar and solid foundation of truth." St. Cyprian *De unitate eccl.* 5–6: "Our Lord's Church is radiant with light and pours her rays over the whole world. . . . You cannot have God for your Father if you have not the Church for your mother" (ACW translation).

29. Isai. 2:2–3: *And it shall come to pass in the latter days that the mount of Jahweh's house shall be set above the mountains, and exalted above the hills; and all nations shall stream unto it, and many peoples shall go and say: "Come, let us go up to the Mount of Jahweh, . . . "* (trans. E. J. Kissane). It is interesting to note that the prophets foretold the Church even more clearly than they did Christ. See St. Augustine *In psalm.* 30; Hasseveldt, *op. cit.*, 60.

30. The translation used for this passage is that of the *Confraternity New Testament* (Paterson, 1941). Fr. Kleist's translation renders the true meaning, and thus makes the passage useless as the basis for an objection.

31. See G. Huarte, "Quomodo ecclesia Christi, quae visibilis est, possit esse objectum fidei," Greg (1922), 78; Msgr. Journet (*op. cit.*, p. 20–1) writes:

> When the divine virtue passed through the human nature of Christ to bring grace and truth to the sinners among whom he lived, then, although it remained essentially mysterious, it embodied itself in space and time, and became in a measure manifest, on account of the visible means it borrowed. Thus too, the same mysterious virtue of which to-day the Church is formed in the world, having come from its source in the Trinity and passed through the human nature of Our Lord now glorified and ascended into heaven, continues, by passing through the hierarchy, to incarnate itself in space and time and to make itself in a measure visible, by reason of the means whereby it enters into sensible contact with us. It is thus invisible and mysterious in its inner depths, but visible and evident up to a point in virtue of the sensible vesture with which it clothes itself in order to reach us.
>
> We need no faith to perceive the sacramental signs and the jurisdictional organization of the Church. Faith will be needed, however, to recognize that these signs and this organization are the envelope of a hidden, divine, and ever-active virtue, without which the very being and existence of the Church would soon founder into nothingness. That is the mystery we confess when we say, in the words of the Nicaeo-Constantinopolitan Creed: "I believe in the apostolic Church." We believe—it is a truth of faith revealed in Scripture—that a supernatural virtue penetrates the hierarchy, the apostolic body, for the forming of the Body of Christ in the world.
>
> Yet, however mysterious in itself, the divine virtue that forms and maintains the Church is revealed, inadequately no doubt, in one of its effects: the marvellous permanence of the Church. To anyone who is alive to the impermanence and fragility of all known societies, the uninterrupted substantial continuity of the Church, in the midst of the revolutions of the Western world, must surely seem a sociological fact for which no natural explanation will suffice. The permanence of the Church under one same hierarchy is not a mystery to be seen only by the eye of faith; it is a fact verifiable in history; and its miraculous character bears witness to the divine origin of the Church.

Article II

WHY THE CHURCH?

PROPOSITION: The Church was founded in order that through it and in it the Christian religion would be practiced and men would be made holy.

Proof: 1. from Christ's commission to the apostles:
    a. to preach the gospel;
    b. to administer the sacraments;
    c. to instruct people in His precepts.
2. from the mission of the Church as a continuation of Christ's.

Scholion 1: It follows from all the above that the Church is a religious, spiritual, supernatural society.

Scholion 2: It follows, too, that the Church is the religion of Christ in concrete form.

Article II

WHY THE CHURCH?

15 PROPOSITION: *The Church was founded in order that through and in it the Christian religion would be practiced and men would be made holy.*

This proposition is *certain*.

Now that the fact of the Church's institution has been established, its *purpose* must be studied—not its ultimate purpose, about which there can be no question, but its immediate and special purpose. This purpose includes two elements, but they are so intimately conjoined as to be practically inseparable: the practice of the Christian religion and the sanctification of mankind.

Under the heading of the *practice of the Christian religion* are included the preaching (safeguarding, explanation, presentation) and profession of Christ's teaching, the celebration of Christian rites (sacrifice and sacraments), the instruction of people in Christian morality, and the actual living of life according to the norms imposed by this teaching.

The supernatural sanctification of mankind is accomplished in no other way than by the practice of the Christian religion; people become holy by professing the Christian faith, by taking part in Christian rites, and by obeying Christian precepts. However, the holiness to be attained in this life is attained with a view to the bliss of the life to come. It follows, then, that the Church has a further purpose, eternal salvation itself.

The statement of the proposition contains the words *through and in it*, for it is through the efforts of the Church (or more explicitly, of its official personnel) that Christ's religion is preserved and practiced by the members of the Church. Again, it is through the active influence of the Church (of its official personnel) that the members of the Church are made holy.

The Vatican Council indicates the Church's purpose in the following words: "The eternal Shepherd and Bishop of our souls determined to found a holy Church in order that He might extend the salutary work of redemption throughout all ages."[1] Of course the work of redemption as perpetuated by the Church is not the Redemption itself. It is not the offering of the price, which was the personal task of Christ Himself (Heb. 10:14), but rather the application of the Redemption, which application consists in the sanctification of mankind through the practice of the Christian religion.

Proof:

16

1. Christ gave the Church's pastors no other commission than that of preaching the gospel, of administering the sacraments, and of instructing people in His precepts: *"Go, therefore, and initiate all nations in discipleship: baptize them . . . teach them to observe all the commandments I have given you"* (Matt. 28:17-20; see John 20:23). Consequently, all He expected of the peoples to whom He sent the apostles was that they accept His teaching, use His rites, and obey His commands: *"He that believes and is baptized will be saved; but he that does not believe will be condemned"* (Mark 16:16). But it is in precisely that way that the practice of the Christian religion is realized. The purpose of the Church, accordingly, is the practice of this religion. And a simultaneous conclusion is that the Church has as its purpose also the sanctification of mankind. For, granting the obvious fact that the honor of God is the ultimate goal which the Christian religion has always in view, the practice of this religion has no other purpose than to make men holy.

2. The Church's purpose is to continue Christ's mission: *"As the Father has made me his ambassador, so I am making you my ambassadors"* (John 20:21; see Luke 10:19). But the object of Christ's mission was the sanctification of mankind: *"I have come that they may have life, and have it in abundance"* (John 10:10); *"After all, it is the mission of the Son of Man to seek and to save what is lost"* (Luke 19:10; see Matt. 1:21). Therefore the Church's purpose is the sanctification of mankind; and this can be accomplished only through use of the means prescribed and provided by Christ, i.e., by the practice of the Christian religion. The conclusion is evident.

Scholion 1. It follows from all the above that the Church is a religious, spiritual, supernatural society.

17

Societies are classified especially on the basis of the goal at which they aim, and so we distinguish political societies, economic societies, literary societies, etc. But the purpose for which the Church was founded is something religious, spiritual, and supernatural. The conclusion is evident. And so the Church is quite different from a civil society, which seeks to advance the temporal welfare of its citizens. This is what Christ meant when He said, *"My kingdom is not a worldly one"* (John 18:36; see Luke 12:14), i.e., it is not a kingdom like those which earthly kings govern; its purpose is not limited to the sphere of the temporal; it is not a political kingdom: "Give ear, then, Jews and Gentiles; listen, all kingdoms of the earth: I do not stand in the way of your exercising sway over this world."[2] One can see at the same time that the spiritual character of the Church does not at all militate against its being an external, visible society. In the words of Leo XIII, "From the point of view of the Church's ultimate purpose and of the proximate causes by which it produces holiness, it is definitely spiritual. On the other hand, from the point of view of the people who make it a cohesive group and of the actual rites which are productive of spiritual gifts, it is an external and necessarily conspicuous society."[3]

18 *Scholion 2. It follows, too, that the Church is the religion of Christ in concrete form.*

One can gather from what has been said that the Church and the religion of Christ, though logically distinguishable, are as a matter of fact absolutely inseparable. For Christ Himself so joined His religion to the society He founded that the one became inextricably intertwined and, as it were, cemented together with the other. Who in fact got from Christ the power and the duty of preaching His doctrine, of celebrating His rites, and of instructing the nations in His commands? None other than the pastors of the Church. What do people do who want to practice Christ's religion? They profess the doctrine preached by the Church's pastors, they make use of the rites performed by them, they live according to the disciplinary norms handed down by them. In a word, they submit to the teaching authority, to the ritual ministrations, to the rule of the Church. Therefore our Saviour gave expression to His religion so completely in the Church that apart from that Church and without its ministrations, it is absolutely impossible to observe that religion in its integrity and to practice it properly.[4]

Notes

1. Constitution *De ecclesia Christi*, Preamble.
2. St. Augustine *Tract. 115 in Joannem* 2.
3. Encyclical *Satis cognitum* (June 29, 1896).
4. That is why this canon had been prepared for the Vatican Council: If anyone should say that the religion of Christ is not extant and manifest in any special society founded by Christ Himself, but that it can be followed and practiced by each person individually without his paying any particular attention to whether one society may be His true Church, let him be anathema (See *Coll. Lac.*, VII, 576d).

Article III

THE PERPETUITY OF THE CHURCH

PROPOSITION: In founding His Church, Christ made it indestructible.
    Proof: 1. from the promises of Christ
            2. from the Messianic prophecies
            3. from the testimony of earliest times
Corollary.

Article III

THE PERPETUITY OF THE CHURCH [1]

PROPOSITION: *In founding His Church, Christ made it indestructible.*

19

This proposition is *certain*.

The present question has to do with the perpetuity of that Church which alone was founded by Christ, the visible Church. Any society can fail in either of two ways: it can simply cease to be, or it can become unfit for the carrying out of its avowed aim through a substantial corruption. The Church cannot fail in either way. Since its aim, namely, the supernatural sanctification of mankind, cannot be achieved except through the proper administration and practice of the religion of Christ, the Church would corrupt and fall apart if it either abandoned or adulterated Christ's religion in its dogmatic or moral content. Hence indestructibility comprises two elements: (a) that the visible Church will endure until the end of the world, and (b) that, right up to the end of time, it will keep Christ's religion incorrupt. "Right up to the end of time," for as long as there are men wandering about on earth, they will depend for their sanctification on Christ working through His Church. After that, the kingdom of glory will take the place of the Church Militant.

Proof:

20

1. From the *promises of Christ*. *"And I, in turn, say to you: You are Peter, and upon this rock I will build my Church, and the gates of hell shall not prevail against it"* (Matt. 16:18). It follows that the Church of Christ, whose stability is indicated in this promise by the mention of its rock foundation (see Matt. 7:24-25), can never be vanquished by hostile forces. But it would be vanquished not only if it ceased to be, but even if it became corrupt.[2]

"Absolute authority in heaven and on earth has been conferred upon me. Go, therefore, and initiate all nations in discipleship:

CHRIST'S CHURCH

... and teach them to observe all the commandments I have given you. And mark: I am with you at all times as long as the world will last" (Matt. 28:18-20). The phrase *"as long as the world will last"* is a clear reference to the end of the world (see Matt. 13:40; 24:3). And so, until that day comes, Christ will be at the side of the apostles as they teach, sanctify, and rule. He will be at the side not only of the apostles personally—for they were soon to die—but at the side also of those who will take up the work of the apostles throughout the centuries and will thus form with them one moral person. He will be there, He to whom all power has been given. It is, therefore, a truly efficacious assistance which is here promised. And what will be the aim of this assistance? Precisely that they may teach, sanctify, and rule properly. And it is an absolute promise; there are no strings attached, and none are to be presumed, either, for there is no question here of reward or payment on condition of work performed; rather it is a question of safeguarding the means to salvation. Therefore, the visible Church will last forever, and in an incorrupt state. It will go on forever safeguarding the doctrine of Christ, administering His sacraments, and instructing all peoples in His precepts.

The parables of the field (Matt. 13:24-30, 38-40) and of the net (13:47-50) imply the same thing, i.e., that the kingdom of Christ will last until the end of the world.

21 2. The *Messianic prophecies* offer further proof. They clearly assert that the kingdom of the Messias will be everlasting and unfailing.[3] The angel who announced Christ's conception repeated the following prophecy: *"And the Lord God will give him the throne of his father David. He will be king over the house of Jacob forever, and to his kingship there will be no end"* (Luke 1:32-33). The kingdom over which the Messias is to exercise His kingship is none other than the Church in which Christ gave concrete expression to His religion. But if the Church ever became corrupt, it would by that very fact cease to be the kingdom of the Messias.

3. *Testimony from earliest times* corroborates the foregoing proofs. Both the apostles and the earliest fathers considered the Church indestructible, and so they must have been aware of the divine promises on this score. *The apostles* call the Church *"an unshakable kingdom"* (Heb. 12:28); they predict that the Eucharist will be celebrated until Christ comes to judge the world (I Cor. 11:26). To quote just a few of *the fathers*, St. Ignatius says, "The

Lord permitted myrrh to be poured on his head that He might breathe incorruption upon the Church" (Ephesians 17. 1. ACW trans.) St. Athanasius, in explaining the words of the Psalm: *"His throne shall be like the sun before me,"* writes:

> Take the throne of Christ to mean the Church, for it is therein that He dwells. Hence the Church will go on enlightening the world with its brilliance and existing forever, just like the sun and the moon (*In Psalm.* 88:38).

And St. Jerome:

> We understand accordingly that the Church can be stricken with persecutions right up to the end of the world but can never be overthrown; it can be attacked, but never overcome. And this will be, because the Lord God almighty, its [the Church's] God, promised that He would see to it, and His promise is the very law of nature.[4]

Corollary 22

There is no reconciliation possible between the divine promises guaranteeing the indestructibility of the Church and the following heterodox notions. (1) Calvin taught that the Church of Christ under the papacy did not completely cease to be, but that it nonetheless collapsed so wretchedly that there was nothing left but the foundations and a heap of rubble.[5] (2) The Synod of Pistoia asserted that "in these last centuries a general pall of obscurity has been spread over the most important truths, truths which concern religion and which are the very foundation of the faith and of the moral teaching of Jesus Christ." Pius VI declared this statement heretical.[6] (3) Many religious systems have, at different times and under various guises, predicted a new Church, an improved system of salvation, a more lavish effusion of the Holy Spirit. Such were, among others, the Gnostics, Montanists, Cathari, Anabaptists, Quakers, Swedenborgians, Irvingites, Latter Day Saints, etc.[7] (4) The Modernists claim that the Church, like every other natural society, is subject to the laws of continuous evolution, and that the monarchical and autocratic structure of the Church, based as it is on a common error of the ancients about the Church's direct divine institution, can and must give way to a democratic structure in accord with the demands of the modern mentality; and furthermore, that the Church, by stubbornly clinging to unchangeable dogmas, is unequal to the task of effectively safeguarding the gospel ethic.⁸

Notes

1. See *above*, Art. 1, note 31.
2. See C. Journet, *op. cit.*, p. xxvii:
Looked at in this way, the Church is composed of just men and sinners. But that statement needs further precision. The Church contains sinners. But she does not contain sin. It is only in virtue of what remains pure and holy in them, that sinners belong to her—that is to say in virtue of the sacramental character of Baptism and Confirmation, and of the theological habits of faith and hope if they still have them. That is the part of their being by which they still cleave to the Church, and are still within her. But in virtue of the mortal sin which has found its way into them and fills their hearts, they belong chiefly to the world and to the devil. "He who commits sin is of the devil" (I John iii. 8). . . .
Thus the frontier of the Church passes through each one of those who call themselves her members, enclosing within her bounds all that is pure and holy, leaving outside all that is sin and stain, "more piercing than any two-edged sword and reaching unto the division of the soul and the spirit, of the joints also and the marrow, and discerning the thoughts and intents of the heart" (cf. Heb. iv. 12). So that even here below, in the days of her pilgrimage, in the midst of the evil and sin at war in each one of her children, the Church herself remains immaculate; and we can apply to her quite fully and without any restriction the passage of the Epistle to the Ephesians (v. 25-28): "Christ also loved the Church and delivered himself up for it: that he might sanctify it, cleansing it by the laver of water in the word of life: that he might present it to himself a *glorious Church, not having spot or wrinkle or any such thing, but that it should be holy and without blemish.*"
See also *ibid.*, 95 ff.; R. H. Benson, *Christ in the Church* (St. Louis, 1914).
3. II Kings 7:12-16; I Par. 17:11-14; Ps. 71:5-7; Isai. 9:6-7; Dan. 2:44.
4. *In Amos* (conclusion).
5. *Institutes of the Christian Religion*, IV, 2, 11.
6. In the constitution *Auctorem fidei*, (1794); see DB 1501.
7. See *Coll. Lac.*, VII, 594.
8. See the encyclical *Pascendi* and the decree *Lamentabili*, prop. 52, 53, 63.

CHAPTER II

The Church's Nature

Article I

THE CHURCH AS A HIERARCHICAL SOCIETY

I. *Errors:*
   1. Protestants
   2. Modernists
   3. Synod of Pistoia

II. *The Church of Christ is a Hierarchical Society:*

   PROPOSITION 1: Christ established a sacred authority in His Church when He directly bestowed on the college of the apostles the power to teach, to function as priests, and to rule.
   Proof: 1. from Christ's words;
   2. from the apostles' manner of acting.
   Some Objections Answered
   Scholion: Charismatics and co-workers of the apostles.

   PROPOSITION 2: It was Christ's will that the sacred ruling power which had begun in the apostolic college should continue forever.
   Proof: 1. from the indestructibility of the Church;
   2. from Christ's explicit promise;
   3. from the apostles' manner of acting.
   Scholion: The personal prerogatives of the apostles.

   PROPOSITION 3: The sacred rule which began with the college of the apostles continued on in the college of bishops.
   Proof: 1. indirect testimony of the earliest records;
   2. direct, formal testimony of these records.
   Scholion 1. Therefore the individual or monarchical episcopate takes its origin from the apostles.

Scholion 2. This same episcopate comes, not only from the apostles, but, through the apostles, from Christ Himself.

Scholion 3. What of St. Jerome's remarks?

III. *Theological Corollaries on Extent and Nature of Power Conferred on Church's Rulers:*

1. Temporal punishment
2. The powers of orders and of jurisdiction.

CHAPTER II

The Church's Nature

The preceding chapter demonstrated the fact that Christ founded a Church for a specific supernatural purpose and that this Church enjoys a promise of perpetuity. The stage is thus set for a close study of its nature. For this latter depends both on the social structure which the Church received from its Founder and on the purpose for which He founded it. Now because of the way our Lord set it up, the Church is a *hierarchical* society: *Article* I; and a *monarchical* society: *Article* II.

Article I

THE CHURCH AS A HIERARCHICAL SOCIETY [1]

An association in which all the members enjoy basically equal rights of authority, so that no individual may exercise authority without being commissioned thereto by the others (as is the case especially in voluntary associations)—such a society is called equal or democratic. But if the running of the society belongs by special right to one or a few of the members, then the society is called unequal. If it is a sacred society, it can be called a hierarchically constituted society, or simply a hierarchical society, for hierarchy (*hierà arché*) etymologically signifies sacred rule.[2] Consequently if there exists within the Church a group of men distinct from the other members, and if this group wields a sacred power by divine right (i.e., not from any delegation by the Church, but from the institution of Christ Himself), then the Church will be an unequal or hierarchical society.

I. Errors

1. With the exception of the Anglican High Church, all Protestants in general deny that there is any hierarchy which can claim establishment by divine right. According to them, all Chris-

tians are equal in the matter of spiritual power, since aside from the "royal priesthood," in which all share, there is in the New Law no priesthood strictly so called. Among the Protestants, those who act as ministers of the divine word and the sacraments, and likewise those who administer the affairs of the churches, fill offices set up by the Church itself, not by Christ. At the most, some admit that the church has a divine commission to set up such offices.

2. **In like manner, Modernists** deny that there is any hierarchy *of divine right*. When one disentangles all their involved verbiage, one discovers that they attribute the whole setup of the Church to natural evolution: "The elders who performed the task of watching over the meetings of the Christians were appointed by the apostles as priests and bishops to provide for the necessary management of the growing communities, but not precisely to perpetuate the mission and power of the apostles"; and, "Dogmas, sacraments, hierarchy—as far as both the idea and the reality are concerned—are only interpretations and evolutions of the Christian consciousness, which took the tiny seed hidden in the gospel, developed it, and embellished it with external trappings."[3]

3. **The Synod of Pistoia** taught that sacred power was given directly to the whole community of believers, which in turn delegated it to the bishops and the supreme pontiff. If this be admitted, then the Church's rulers are nothing but the tools and servants of the Christian populace. Pius VI condemned this doctrine as heretical. It is still the view of the Jansenists in Holland.

II. The Church of Christ is a Hierarchical Society

Catholic teaching holds that Christ Himself established a sacred authority in His Church, and that this authority, invested first in the apostolic college, was uninterruptedly perpetuated, and in fact perdures today in the college of bishops.

25 PROPOSITION 1: *Christ established a sacred authority in His Church when He directly bestowed on the college of the apostles the power to teach, to function as priests, and to rule.*

The first part of this proposition affirms the general truth that the Church, by the institution of the Lord Himself, is an unequal society, i.e., one in which some govern and others are governed. The second part states precisely who were put in authority over the others and what powers put them in a class apart. A proof of this latter statement will suffice.

The power *to teach* is the right and the duty to set forth Christian truth with an authority to which all are held to give internal and external obedience.

The power *to function as priests* or ministers is the power to offer sacrifice and to sanctify people through the instrumentality of outward rites.

The power *to rule* or govern is the power to regulate the moral conduct of one's subjects. Since this power is exercised chiefly through legislation and then through judicial sentences and penalties, it comprises *legislative, judicial,* and *coercive* powers.[4] The power to pass judgment and to punish is a necessary complement of the power to make laws, for all by themselves, laws usually have little effect. They must be bolstered by courts and by penalties.

The threefold power to teach, to function as priests, and to rule corresponds to the threefold office with which Christ as man was invested, for He was Prophet, Priest, and King.[5] And so, by bestowing on the apostles the aforesaid threefold power, He made them sharers in the same powers which He (in His human nature) received from the Father, although not in the same fulness.

We frequently mention in this connection the *college* of the apostles; the aforementioned powers were given to the apostles, not as to so many individuals having no ties one with the other, but inasmuch as they constituted a unit, a "college." Indeed, why would Christ, who wanted to found one Church, have given the power to rule to eleven men completely independent of one another? This matter will be treated explicitly in *Article II.*

Finally, the sacred power was conferred on the apostolic college *directly.* This rules out the opinion of the Synod of Pistoia mentioned above.

The proposition is a *dogma of faith,* as we know from various definitions of the Church. See the Council of Trent, *Sess.* 23, c. 4; the Vatican Council, constitution *De ecclesia,* Preamble (DB 960, 1821).

Proof:

1. *From Christ's words.* (a) For all three powers at once: "*As the Father has made me his ambassador, so I am making you my*

ambassadors" (John 20:21). Christ had been sent by the Father as a prophet (teacher), as a priest, and as a king. He now transfers to the apostles the offices and the powers which He had received, in sending them forth to make disciples, to baptize and sanctify, and to regulate the moral conduct of the disciples (Matt. 28:18–19). (*b*) For each power separately: *the power to teach: "Go into the whole world and preach the gospel to all creation. He that believes and is baptized will be saved; he that does not believe will be condemned"* (Mark 16:15–16). The *priestly power: "Do this as my memorial"* (Luke 22:19), and: *"Whenever you remit anyone's sins, they are remitted; when you retain anyone's sins, they are retained"* (John 20:23). The *power to rule: "I tell you with assurance, whatever you bind on earth shall be bound in heaven; whatever you loose on earth shall be loosed in heaven"* (Matt. 18:18).

There can be no doubt that it is a question of real power in the texts cited. That this power is bestowed not on all indiscriminately but on the apostles alone is clear from the fact that the words are addressed exclusively to the apostolic college, i.e., to those men of whom Christ had made special choice a long time before, and whom He had trained with a view to the duties He was to entrust to them.[6]

27   2. From *the apostles' manner of acting.*[7] (*a*) They assert in general terms that they have acquired a *ministry* (Acts 1:17), an *apostolic ministry* (Acts 1:25); that they are to be esteemed as *subordinates of Christ and stewards of God's mysteries* (I Cor. 4:1), to whom God *has entrusted . . . this ministry of reconciliation . . . entrusting to us the message of reconciliation* (II Cor. 5:18–20) —men, therefore, who are carrying out a mission for Christ, God as it were exhorting through them.

Furthermore, (*b*) the apostles, either by words or by deeds, claim for themselves each of the three aforementioned offices. That of *teaching: But they went forth and preached everywhere* (Mark 16:20; see Acts 5:42; 10:42); *"But I count my life as nothing . . . if only I accomplish my course and the ministry that I have received from the Lord Jesus, to bear witness to the Good News about God's grace."*[8] That of *the priesthood: Then Peter and John laid their hands on them, and they received the Holy Spirit* (Acts 8:17); *I remind you to stir up God's grace of office which you have through the laying on of my hands* (II Tim. 1:6). That of *ruling: "It is that the Holy Spirit and we have decided to lay no further*

THE CHURCH'S NATURE

burden upon you but this indispensable one, that you abstain from things sacrificed to idols and from blood and from what is strangled and from immorality." [9] And the apostles claim for themselves not only *legislative* power, but *judicial* as well: *As for me, though absent in body, I am present in spirit, and have already, as if present, reached the decision . . . to deliver this man to Satan for the destruction of his corrupt tendencies that his spirit may attain salvation on the day of the Lord Jesus* (I Cor. 5:3–5); and *coercive: What is your choice? Shall I come to you provided with a rod, or with love, with a spirit of gentleness?* [10]

Objections: 28

Christ did not establish any hierarchy, for: (1) He expressly forbade any one of His disciples to consider himself greater than the others or to lord it over the others: *They also had a discussion among them as to which one in their group should be considered the greatest. He said to them: "The kings of the Gentiles lord it over them, and their princes have themselves styled benefactors. That must not be your way! No, the greatest in your group must be like the youngest, and the leader like the servant"* (Luke 22:24–26). And so, (2) both St. Peter and St. John ascribe the title *holy priesthood* to all Christians without distinction (I Pet. 2:5, 9; Apoc. 1:6); and (3) St. Paul teaches accordingly that the sacred ministers exercise their office only as the result of being in some way delegated thereto by the faithful: *All things belong to you, whether it is Paul, or Apollos, or Cephas* (I Cor. 3:22).

Answer to 1: Our Lord wanted to eliminate from His followers not authority, but arrogance in the exercise of authority and pride in general. That is why He set Himself up as a model of humility, even though He enjoyed the fulness of authority: [11] *"I am in your midst like a waiter in attendance"* (Luke 22:27).

Answer to 2: St. Peter and St. John attribute a priesthood to all, but a priesthood in the broad sense, by virtue of which all offer "spiritual," i.e., not strictly official, sacrifices; namely, prayers and good works. How little the alleged texts rule out a priesthood in the strict sense, reserved for certain definite persons, is especially evident from the fact that God had said to all the Israelites indiscriminately: *"You shall be to me a kingdom of priests"* (Exod. 19:6). And yet He had set apart among the chosen people a specific class of men to whom were reserved the official functions of the priesthood. It is not difficult to see that the apostles alluded to these words of the Old Testament to indicate that in the Christian people was perfectly realized what God had once affirmed of the nation of Israel.[12]

Answer to 3: St. Paul states this one fact, that ecclesiastical offices were established *for the benefit* of the faithful. The context from which the text is lifted makes this quite clear.

29 *Scholion. Charismatics and co-workers of the apostles.*

1. In the first years charismatics contributed in no little degree to the building up of the Church. These were men who had been endowed by God with various extraordinary gifts: the gifts of knowledge, of prophecy, of tongues,[13] etc. These charismatics (as such) held no real authority in the Church, did not belong to the hierarchy, but on the contrary were subject to the real rulers of the Church, i.e., the apostles, even in what concerned the use of their charisms in the meetings of the faithful (I Cor. 14:28–30). Those Protestants were therefore quite wrong who taught that the beginnings of the hierarchy were to be sought among the charismatics, as if offices or specific functions in the Church had been instituted only when charisms began to wane.

2. Aside from the charismatics, there were definitely some men in this primitive era who, though not members of the apostolic college, nonetheless performed functions in the Church and were armed with a sacred power. We read, for example, that Philip the deacon preached and baptized (Acts 8:5, 38), and that, together with the apostles, there were also "elders" gathered together for the Council of Jerusalem (Acts 15:2, 6, 23; 16:4). But although these men were at times nominated by the community, they received their actual office and power not from the community of the faithful, but from the apostles, as is clear from Acts 6:1–6 [14] for the deacons; and from Acts 14:22 for the elders. Furthermore, they held a position subordinate to that of the apostles.[15] This very fact backs up our conclusion that the apostles enjoyed real power, a power which they had received from God. For not only did they exercise their power personally, but they also delegated part of that power to various co-workers.

This is not the place to consider whether or not the development of the hierarchy through the institution of the lower orders was effected by the apostles at Christ's command. One remark will suffice. It is clear that after the Resurrection, our Lord instructed the apostles in matters concerning His Church: . . . *appearing to them throughout forty days and discussing matters pertaining to the kingdom of God* (Acts 1:3). What precisely He enjoined upon them is not recorded in Scriptures and so will have to be inferred from the activities of the apostles and the traditions of the ancients. But from the nature of the case it seems quite probable that the general plan for the organization of the churches is to be attributed ultimately not to the apostles but to Christ Himself.

PROPOSITION 2: *It was Christ's will that the sacred ruling power which had begun in the apostolic college should continue forever.*

30

This proposition is concerned with the same threefold power which we have proved to have been given to the apostles. It asserts that this power was granted by Christ with the following stipulation: that it be handed on to an endless line of successors. We are not concerned at the moment with the subordinate co-workers of the apostles. The only point to be proven here is that it was Christ's will that the apostolic college should continue forever, in such a way that there would always be in the Church a body of men invested with that threefold power which the apostles enjoyed. This thesis is a *dogma of faith,* as we know, e.g., from the Council of Trent, *Sess.* 23, c. 4 (DB 960).

Proof:

31

1. From the *indestructibility of the Church.* Christ willed that His Church should last until the end of time, and in an incorrupt state (nos. 19 ff.). Therefore He wanted all those things to last forever without which the perpetuity of the Church would be impossible. But the Church as He founded it is completely dependent on the teaching, priestly, and ruling powers of the apostles. The conclusion is clear.

Proof of the minor.[16] The Church depends essentially on the teaching, priestly, and ruling powers of the apostles. For the following factors determine its very existence: that all profess the doctrine which the apostles taught; that all take part in the same rites which they used to celebrate; and that all obey their rule. If the preaching, priestly ministration, and government of the apostles were to stop, the Church would by that very fact immediately vanish. To put it another way, remove the chains which bind into unity that society which we call the Church, and that unity, that society, would disperse and come to naught.

2. From *Christ's explicit promise*. When our Lord gave the apostles their definitive mission to teach, sanctify, and rule, He went on to say, in the clearest of terms: "*And mark: I am with you at all times as long as the world will last*" (Matt. 28:20). But how could He possibly be forever present to the apostolic college in the work of teaching, sanctifying, and ruling, unless that college itself were to last forever; unless the apostles were to have a never-ending line of successors in their work as teachers, priests, and rulers?

32 3. From *the apostles' manner of acting*. There can be no doubt that the apostles understood the mind of their Master, and so, if they themselves transmitted their threefold power to their successors, we must of course conclude that they were carrying out the Lord's will in this matter. As a matter of fact, the apostles did take care to appoint men to succeed them.

a. In the canonical Scriptures there is, e.g., the case of Timothy, whom Paul, precisely because he senses the nearness of his own death, urges to carry out his ministry carefully: *But as for yourself, you should be self-controlled in all things, bear trials patiently, work as a preacher of the gospel, discharge your ministry. As for me, I am already being poured out in sacrifice, and the time of my departure is at hand* (II Tim. 4:5–6). Now Timothy's *ministry* included the offices of teaching, of the priesthood, and of ruling. (1) The office of *teaching: Preach the word, be urgent in season, out of season. Convince, rebuke, exhort people with perfect patience and teaching, for a time will come when they will not endure sound doctrines.*[17] (2) The office of the *priesthood: Do not hastily impose hands on any one* (I Tim. 5:22). (3) The office of *ruling: Do not listen to an accusation against a presbyter unless it is supported by two or three witnesses. Rebuke habitual sinners in the presence of all, that the rest may stand in fear* (I Tim. 5:19–20).

b. Among the earliest fathers, St. Clement of Rome wrote:

> And so, after receiving their instructions and being fully assured through the Resurrection of our Lord Jesus Christ, as well as confirmed in faith by the word of God, they went forth, equipped with the fullness of the Holy Spirit, to preach the

good news that the Kingdom of God was close at hand. From land to land, accordingly, and from city to city they preached, and from their earliest converts appointed men whom they had tested by the Spirit to act as bishops and deacons for the future believers. . . .

Our Apostles, too, were given to understand by our Lord Jesus Christ that the office of bishop would give rise to intrigues. For this reason, equipped as they were with perfect foreknowledge, they appointed the men mentioned before, and afterwards laid down a rule once for all to this effect: when these men die, other approved men shall succeed to their sacred ministry. Consequently, we deem it an injustice to eject from the sacred ministry the persons who were appointed either by them [the apostles], or later, with the consent of the whole Church, by other men in high repute.[18]

Quotations from other early witnesses will appear in the proof of the next proposition.

Scholion. The personal prerogatives of the apostles. 33

It was stated above, and with deliberate caution, that Christ willed the transmission, from the apostolic college to an endless line of successors, of the threefold power of teaching, sanctifying, and ruling. But not every single thing which God granted the apostles was to be handed down to their successors. The apostles exercised, as it were, a twofold function, that of the *apostolate* and that of the *pastorate* or episcopate. They were first and foremost apostles (taking this word in its strict sense), i.e., legates commissioned by God to promulgate all of His revelation, and to start or set up Christ's Church. Then, secondarily, so to speak, they were the first pastors of the Church to which they had given form. It is readily understandable that the apostolic office demanded certain prerogatives which the pastoral office as such did not require. Therefore, as *apostles*, each of them had (*a*) a direct divine mission to carry out both of the aforementioned tasks all over the world. Furthermore, (*b*) they enjoyed the charisms (1) of revelation, (2) of infallibility (in matters pertaining to their mission), and (3) of miracles.

The apostolate was, to begin with, by its very nature an extraordinary gift, confided to these men alone.[19] The gifts conferred on them by reason of their apostolate did not pass to subsequent

(39)

pastors of the Church, since they were not simply, and in every respect, successors of the apostles, but *only in the pastoral office.* But the essence of the pastoral office consists precisely in the threefold power of teaching, of the priesthood, and of ruling.

34 PROPOSITION 3: *The sacred rule which began with the college of the apostles continued on in the college of bishops.*

This proposition is a step nearer the question of precisely which men in the ancient Church were in fact the apostles' successors in the pastoral office. Note that the title *successor* fits only him who steps into another's place in such a way as to receive in its fulness the office which the latter had administered. And so, for a man to be reckoned a successor of the apostles, it is not enough that some one apostolic power be conferred on him (like the power of the priesthood, in full or in part). No, he must have the whole range of power which constituted the apostles pastors of the Church. The present proposition states furthermore that the apostles' successors, in the sense just set forth, were those officials of the Church whom all of Christian antiquity, at least from the beginning of the second century, called *bishops.*[20] Just as it was a question above of the apostolic college, so is it now a question of the college of bishops; for the present proposition does not assert that each single bishop is the successor of an individual apostle, but rather that the apostolic college was succeeded by the college of bishops or the episcopate.

This proposition is a *dogma of faith.* See the Council of Trent, *Sess.* 23, c. 4 (DB 960).

35 *Proof:*

The question, which men received their pastoral office and powers from the apostles, can be answered in two ways: (1) by tracing back and discovering, in the light of ancient historical records, who ruled the Church after the apostles had died; and (2) by gathering together the formal testimony of the ancients concerning the successors of the apostles.

1. The *earliest historical records* make it clear that soon after the death of the apostles there were bishops in charge of each of the churches. In fact, these records even furnish direct proof, in the case of several episcopal sees, that these latter go back to the apostles themselves.

THE CHURCH'S NATURE

The letters of St. Ignatius Martyr show beyond cavil that, at the beginning of the second century in each of the churches of Asia Minor, there was, besides the subordinate ministers (priests and deacons), one bishop, who functioned as teacher, priest, and ruler. St. Ignatius' manner of expression gives sufficient indication that this episcopate was not a novel institution.[21]

Hegesippus journeyed from the East to Rome about the middle of the second century, and on the way visited "very many bishops," and found the same doctrine being taught in "each of the episcopal lines of succession (*en ekástē diadochē*)."[22] And so in the middle of the second century there could be reckoned in many cities a line of bishops who had succeeded to the posts of their predecessors.

About 180 A.D. St. Irenaeus, "since it would be very tedious to list the lines of succession of all the churches," drew up the list of the Church of Rome alone, tracing it from Sts. Peter and Paul to Eleutherius, who "now holds the episcopate in the twelfth place from the apostles" (*Adversus haereses* iii. 3. 2–3). The same Irenaeus tells us that the holy apostles handed on this Roman episcopate to Linus, and that St. Polycarp had been appointed Bishop of Smyrna by the apostles (i.e., by St. John; *ibid.* 3–4; see Tertullian *De praescriptione* 32).

Tertullian writes that, in the churches instituted by St. John, the line of bishops, when traced to its origin, stops with St. John, who began it (*Adversus Marcionem* 4. 5).

Clement of Alexandria relates how St. John, after his return from Patmos to Ephesus, sometimes traveled to neighboring provinces to appoint bishops (*Quis dives* 42; cited by Eusebius HE 3. 24).

Origen testifies that St. Ignatius Martyr was the "second after St. Peter to be bishop of Antioch" (*In Lucam homilia* vi).

Finally, Eusebius gives us, besides the list of Roman pontiffs, that of the bishops of Antioch back as far as St. Peter; of Alexandria back as far as St. Mark; and of Jerusalem back to St. James, "the brother of the Lord."[23]

2. Furthermore, *formal testimony* establishes the fact that the early fathers unanimously considered the bishops as successors of the apostles.

St. Irenaeus says that if we want to discover the true tradition of the apostles,

36

we can enumerate those who were appointed as bishops in the churches by the apostles and their successors to our own day, who never knew and never taught anything resembling their [that is, the Gnostics'] foolish doctrine. Had the apostles known any such mysteries, which they taught privately and *sub rosa* to the perfect, they would surely have entrusted this teaching to the men in whose charge they had placed the churches. For they wished them to be without blame and reproach to whom they handed over their own position of authority.—*Adversus haereses* iii. 3. 1; see QP, I, 301.

Elsewhere he mentions "episcopal lines of succession, through which they [the apostles] have handed down that Church which exists everywhere (*ibid.* iv. 33. 8). Again, he says of the heretics, "All these [heretics] are of much later date than the bishops to whom the apostles entrusted the churches" (*ibid.* v. 20. 1).

Tertullian hurls this taunt at the heretics:

Let them make public the origins of their churches; let them unroll the scrolls containing their bishops' names, tracing the lines of succession back to the beginning, in such a manner that their first bishop may [be seen to] have as his consecrator and predecessor some one of the apostles or someone from apostolic days, but one who has persevered in loyalty to the apostles. For this is the way apostolic churches hand on their records.— *De praescriptione* 32.

St. Cyprian: "For it is for this, brother, that we work and must work hardest of all: to maintain as far as in us the unity which has been handed down by the Lord through the apostles to us their successors" (*Epistula* 42. 3).

In the Council of Carthage held under St. Cyprian about 256, Clarus of Mascula said:

That commission of our Lord Jesus Christ is quite clear which He gave when He sent forth His apostles and entrusted to them alone the power which He had been given by the Father. We are their successors, and we govern the Church of God in virtue of the same power.—ML, III, 1111.

Firmilian, bishop of Caesarea in Cappadocia:

Therefore, the power of forgiving sins was given to the apostles and to the churches which they founded in virtue of a mandate from Christ, and to the bishops who succeeded them in their office by being ordained thereunto.—*Epistula ad Cyprianum*; see ML, II, 1217.

St. Jerome: "All [bishops] are successors of the apostles" (*Epistula* 146. 1); and, "With us, the bishops take the place of the apostles; with them [the Montanists], the bishop takes third place" (*Epistula* 41. 3).

St. Gregory the Great: "Indeed, the bishops now take their [the apostles'] place in the Church" (*In Evangelia homilia* 26. 5).

Scholion 1. Therefore the individual or monarchical episcopate[24] *takes its origin from the apostles.*

The arguments adduced yield this conclusion also: that the men to whom the pastoral office of the apostles passed were, immediately after the death of the apostles, real bishops; in this sense, that they *alone*, as individuals, governed their individual churches; armed with teaching, priestly, and ordinary ruling power. In fact, not one of the authorities cited gives even so much as the slightest hint of a so-called "plural" or "collegiate" episcopate; many of them clearly rule it out.[25] Moreover, the first traces of a monarchical episcopate are already discernible in the books of the New Testament. Several passages in the Acts of the Apostles favor the view that James, the brother of the Lord, was the bishop of the church at Jerusalem.[26] The pastoral Epistles (those to Timothy and Titus) seem to leave little doubt that Timothy exercised the office of bishop at Ephesus and Titus in Crete. The "angels" of the churches, to whom St. John sends letters (Apoc. 1–3), can hardly be other than the bishops of those churches. Therefore it is certain that the monarchical episcopate takes its origin from the apostles. Furthermore, if it had not been started by the apostles, it would not be possible to understand how it could have been foisted on all the churches before the middle of the second century (i.e., before synods were held, and at a time when the primacy of the Roman pontiff made its authority felt quite sparingly).[27]

Once the apostolic origin of the monarchical episcopate has been established, it makes little difference whether the apostles put a bishop in charge of each of the newly founded churches *right from the beginning;* or whether they sometimes placed these latter in the care—for the time being—of a college of "presbyters" (priests of the first or, according to others, of the second class), who would rule the faithful as a sort of common council, as delegates of and under the watchful eyes of the apostles, until the proper time arrived for bishops to be appointed.[28] And so we can leave to historians and exegetes those questions which concern the precise meaning of the names *epískopos* and *presbýteros* in first century documents; as well as questions concerning the primitive organization of the churches while the apostles were still alive.[29]

38 *Scholion 2. This same episcopate comes not only from the apostles, but, through the apostles, from Christ Himself.*

Christ arranged for the Church to be governed forever by successors of the apostles. The latter, following out this direction of their Master, put individual bishops in charge of each individual church. Now it is altogether reasonable to believe that they were executing a divine order also when they thus set up "monarchical" bishops. Certainly, Christ personally and directly founded the Church; and so He Himself must have determined its essential framework and structure. Above all else, the order, the rank of bishop (setting aside for the moment the question of primacy) belongs to this structure. As a matter of fact, the earliest witnesses assert—at times rather vaguely, at times quite explicitly—that the episcopate such as they know it, i.e., the "monarchical" episcopate, is of divine right.

St. Clement of Rome teaches that the apostles, "after receiving their instructions," and "equipped as they were with perfect foreknowledge," took care to select co-workers and successors for themselves (*Epistula prima ad Corinthios* 42. 3, 44. 2).

St. Ignatius Martyr calls the bishop a "grace" and a "commandment" of God (*Epistula ad Magnesios* 2; *Epistula ad Trallianos* 13. 2); concerning the bishop together with his priests and deacons, he says that they were "appointed in accordance with the wish of Christ" (*Epistula ad Philadelphenses* Inscription); and so he adds elsewhere that "Apart from these, no church deserves the name" (*Epistula ad Trallianos* 3. 1). Now why would it be impossible for a legitimate church to exist without a bishop, etc., except that it

(44)

be the fact that Christ Himself had ordered the appointment of the bishop (and of priests and deacons)?

St. Cyprian, after remarking that the Church is founded on the bishops, and that every act of the Church is governed by these same rulers, adds, "Since this was therefore established by divine law, I wonder that some . . . " (*Epistula* 27, *De lapsis*).

St. Basil, writing to his disciple, Chilo, mentions "bishops of the churches of God, [bishops] appointed by God" (*Epistula* 42. 4).

Now in truth if the Church is founded on bishops by the order of Christ Himself, and if *"the Holy Spirit has placed . . . bishops to rule the Church of God"* (Acts 20:28); then it follows that this arrangement is immutable. It is therefore necessary that the Church of Christ be ruled until the end of time by the college of bishops, each of whom rules over one of the many districts of the Church.

Scholion 3. What of St. Jerome's remarks?

St. Jerome apparently contradicts the doctrine just set forth when he writes:

> The same person is also priest and bishop, and before the time when, under the instigation of the devil, there arose parties in the Church, . . . the churches were governed by the council of priests. But when each one wanted those baptized by him to belong to him and not to Christ, it was decreed in the whole world that one of the priests should by election be set over the others, and that he should have the care of the whole church and suppress the seeds of the schism. Therefore let bishops be apprised that they are superior to priests by custom rather than by a true decree of the Lord.—*Commentarium in Epistula ad Titum* 1. 5; see LZ, I, 352.

He writes in the same strain elsewhere, when defending priests against the encroachments of deacons (*Epistula* 146, *ad Evangelum* 1).

These passages are quite difficult, so difficult indeed that some authors think that St. Jerome should not be listened to on this score, since he departs from the common teaching of the ancients. Still, the following remarks may throw some light on the problem.

If St. Jerome's words be taken literally, he contradicts even himself. For elsewhere he expressly acknowledges that there has been a distinction between bishops and priests from the very beginning of the Church. He writes, for example, that the apostles "ordained bishops and priests throughout each of the provinces" (*Commentarium in Matthæum* 25. 26–28). Therefore, they were even then distinct orders. The bishops were real, individual bishops, for the saint rejects as impossible the supposition of several bishops' ruling in one place.[30] In addition, he himself testifies that at least some of the churches have had monarchical bishops right from the beginning.[31] Therefore, unless one is willing to grant that the holy doctor contradicted himself, one must give his words a more favorable interpretation. In this whole matter, it must be noted, firstly, that St. Jerome's aim in both the objectionable passages was to extol the office of the priest; and, secondly, that quite often he let his pen run away with him. In view of this, his probable meaning would seem to be the following: at first bishops and priests were, for all practical purposes, scarcely distinguishable, since they conducted all their affairs in a spirit of fraternal helpfulness. But later custom gave the bishop considerable preeminence over his priests not only in right, but also in conduct and practice.[32]

III. Theological Corollaries on the Extent and Nature of the Power Conferred on the Church's Rulers

40 1. **Temporal punishment.** It was pointed out above (no. 5) that a part of the power to rule is coercive power, in accord with which penalties are leveled against lawbreakers. One must then maintain that the Church can punish those who violate its laws by inflicting, not only spiritual penalties, but temporal ones as well.[33]

A *penalty* differs from a penance precisely in that it is imposed on one against one's will. A penalty is *spiritual* when it deprives a person of spiritual benefits. Examples are excommunication and suspension. By *temporal* or corporal punishment is meant that which directly deprives one of material goods or bodily comfort. Examples of this type of penalty are fines, imprisonment, and the like. Note the word *"directly"*; for a spiritual penalty too can often bring about a loss of this world's goods; for example, the loss of revenue accruing to a benefice may result from a suspension.

The governing power which our Lord gave His apostles is universal and consequently embraces everything which may contribute to the Church's aim and which is not at odds with its native character. The Church's aim is of course spiritual, but everyone knows that temporal punishment, too, can contribute most effectively to the carrying out of a spiritual purpose. It can do so by inducing the guilty parties to come to their senses and by making others think twice before committing a crime. And if capital punishment strikes many as being too much at variance with the mild and gentle character of the Church, still the same objection is not valid for all temporal punishment. In fact the Catholic Church has explicitly condemned the doctrine of those who insist that "the Church has no right to inflict temporal penalties in disciplining those who violate her laws."[34] Accordingly, the Code of Canon Law states: "It is the native and strict right of the Church, independently of any human authority whatsoever, to discipline her refractory subjects with both spiritual and temporal penalties" (c. 2214).

One may object: "If Christ had given His Church the power to inflict temporal punishment, He would have provided it with an armed force to execute those penalties. But as the matter stands, He gave it no soldiery." The answer is that the Church has the right to invoke the aid of secular power to discipline those who break her laws. "Both," says Boniface VIII, "are in the Church's power, the spiritual sword and the material.[35] But the latter is to be used in the Church's behalf; the former is to be wielded by the Church. The former is in the hands of the priest, the latter in the hands of kings and soldiers, but at the will and with the permission of the priest."[36] But if secular rulers should not come to her aid, then God, who gave His Church the assurance of indestructibility, will aid her yet more. For further details on this matter, consult works by canonists.[37]

A final remark: it is one thing to inquire into the right and power of the Church, and quite another to inquire into the judicious use of that power. For since the Church received its power for constructive rather than for destructive purposes, it must adapt, and has always adapted, the exercise of its rights to varying circumstances of time and place. Consequently, since the character and the needs of our modern times are quite different from conditions in the Middle Ages, the Catholic Church's foes have no right to claim that if it were not for the fact that it now has no military power it would be exercising its coercive power in the same way as it did in centuries past. Does not civil society now proceed in correcting and punishing quite differently from the way it did in ages past? And the Church, as history attests, has always been more gentle than the civil administration.[38] They are guilty of calumny who insist that the Church wants to revive all those things which were in other circumstances quite just and beneficial.

41   **2. The powers of orders and jurisdiction.** The oft-mentioned tripartite division of the Church's power: teaching, priestly, and ruling, is not the only possible one. There is still another division which is at once quite useful and quite common. It divides the whole of sacred power into the powers of orders and of jurisdiction. The power of orders is the same as that of the priesthood. It has as its immediate object the worship (in the strict sense) of God, and also the internal sanctification of souls through the infusion of grace. It takes its name from the sacrament of orders or sacred ordination, by which it is conferred on a person.

The power of jurisdiction is the moral power to place others under obligation, to bind and to loose, and comprises at once the two powers of teaching and ruling.[39] It has as its immediate object the governing of people in the realm of belief (through doctrinal decrees), and conduct (through disciplinary laws, judicial sentences, penalties). Finally, it directs the faithful in acquiring holiness through their own personal efforts. This power is conferred on a person when a superior imposes it, or when the person is given a legitimate mission.

This treatise considers the power of jurisdiction in a general, over-all sense, and so it is only in passing that its division into jurisdiction of the external and internal forum is mentioned here. Jurisdiction of the *external forum* is that whose primary and direct object is the advantage of the Church as a society. Jurisdiction of the *internal forum* has as its primary and direct object the personal advantage of the faithful as individuals.

There are many points of difference between the powers of orders and of jurisdiction.

(1) They differ in their immediate objects and in the manner in which they are conferred, as has already been said.

(2) They differ on the score of *permanence*. The power of jurisdiction can be limited and taken away by a superior.[40] The power of orders, however, being inseparately joined to the ineradicable sacramental character, can be neither restricted nor

taken away; and so, all things being equal, it can always be *validly* exercised. Still, the power of orders can be controlled by that of jurisdiction to some extent, i.e., in what concerns its legitimate use. Accordingly, its exercise can be forbidden by a superior and thereby rendered *illicit* or sinful.

(3) They differ in their *basic nature*. The power of orders is merely instrumental or ministerial. Since God alone can produce grace as its principal, efficient Cause, the official personnel of the Church have no proper or native power to do so. They act merely as God's instruments, or, since they are rational beings, as His ministers. Consequently, they can impart grace only by performing the rites instituted by Christ. The power of jurisdiction, on the other hand, involves not merely instrumental, but real principal causality.[41] For, although the Church's rulers may have to set forth the teaching and the precepts of Christ, they enjoy also their own personal power of teaching and ruling (even though this power be given them by another). As regards teachings, they not only declare what has been revealed, but use their own prudence in deciding the proper time and the precise manner in which they will make such declarations. They decide, furthermore, what is in harmony with revealed truths; what is directly or indirectly opposed to them; and on their own authority they prescribe that revealed truths be accepted as the word of God and that matters related to these truths be accepted as certainly true. As regards ruling, they not only declare what the divine law enjoins, but on their own authority they enforce these (divine) precepts, and decide when and how they are to be observed. And so it is with their own power, and in the capacity of principal agents, that they frame laws and inflict penalties. True it is that even in these cases they are acting as ministers of Christ, but here their power is not merely instrumental. Is there not a great difference between the power of a servant who can only make known and put into effect the king's commands, and that of a royal governor sent to rule a province? They are indeed both ministers, but the former is invested with instrumental power only, the latter with principal power as well. It is in the light of the foregoing considerations that the power of orders or of the priesthood is often called the power of *ministry*.

The powers of orders and of jurisdiction may exist separately in different persons, but the institution of Christ calls for their being ordinarily and, as a rule, joined in the same person. And this is quite fitting: for right order demands that the same ones who sanctify men by imparting grace to them, should also, by exercising jurisdiction, guide them towards the production of results befitting their holiness.

Notes

1. There is an excellent treatment of this whole matter in A. Mertens, *De Hierarchie in de eerste eeuw des Christendoms* (1908); H. Dieckmann, *Die Verfassung der Urkirche* (1923); I. Salaverri, *op. cit.*, p. 509 ff.; T. Zapalena, *op. cit.*, p. 173 ff.

It was only when God, inaugurating the final era of history, chose to pour out at last upon men the supreme favours reserved for them from all eternity, that He established the Church in its definitive temporal status by bringing the regime of visible mediation to its highest point of perfection. This brought with it at once the deepest joy and the most effective help, but also the hardest trial and the most exacting exercise of our faith: the greatest joy and help, because there is nothing so connatural to man as to receive divine things humanly; the hardest trial and effort, because there is no more surprising mystery than this collaboration of the uncreated with the created, of omnipotence with indigence, of eternity with time, of immensity with place. First the Word is sent from heaven into our flesh, and then, having promised the help of the Holy Spirit, He sends His own disciples into the world: "As the Father has sent me, so also I send you" (John xx. 21). Hence the perfect regime of the Church militant involves a double visible mediation: that of the Incarnation and that of the hierarchy.—C. Journet, *op. cit.*, p. 6.

2. Although the word "hierarchy" etymologically signifies nothing other than sacred power, it has by custom come to mean especially that sacred power wielded by several persons *subordinated one to the other*. We shall see later on that the Church was founded as a human organization in the second sense as well.

3. See the decree *Lamentabili*, prop. 50, 54.

4. See C. Journet, *op. cit.*, p. 184-6:

We may easily verify the presence of this distinction in the recent documents of the magisterium. Thus, on the 28th August 1794, Pius VI condemned "as leading to a system already condemned as heretical" the fifth proposition of the Synod of Pistoia stating that the Church "has not received from God this power which, not content with advising and persuading, goes on to make laws, and then to constrain the rebellious by exterior judgments, and by salutary punishments." Here we recognize the division of the Church's power into legislative, judiciary and coercive. The same three-fold division is indicated by Leo XIII in the Encyclical *Immortale Dei* of the 1st Nov. 1885: "Jesus Christ gave to his Apostles unrestrained authority in regard to things sacred, together with the genuine and most true power of making laws, as also the twofold right of judging and punishing, which flows from that power."—p. 185.

THE CHURCH'S NATURE

5. See Van Noort, *The True Religion*, nos. 151-2; and C. Journet, *op. cit.*, p. 9-10, 17-8, 123-4.

6. See Luke 6:14; Matt. 10:1 ff.; Mark 6:7 ff.; Luke 9:1 ff.

7. By the term "apostles" is meant here all the men who were members of the apostolic college, even those who were admitted only after Christ's Ascension. For just as anyone who had been chosen as an apostle by our Lord, during His sojourn on earth, and had later resigned from the college (this is a mere hypothesis and does not imply that such a thing could actually have happened after Pentecost)—just as such a one would have forfeited his mission and would have ceased to be an apostle, so too, those who were later legitimately (i.e., under the action of God Himself) joined to the college of the apostles, are to be considered on the same plane as the others. This happened not only in the case of St. *Matthias* (Acts 1:15-26), but also in that of St. *Paul*, who was chosen by God Himself for the apostolate (Acts 9:1-18; see 22:6-16; 26:12-18), received his mission from Him (Acts 13:2-4), and was recognized by the other apostles (Acts 9:27; 15; Gal. 1:18-9; 2:9; II Pet. 3:15). Some number St. *Barnabas* among the apostles (in the strict sense), while others do not. It is true that he did not see the Lord, but he did get his mission directly from God (Acts 13:2-4), and worked in close cooperation with the other apostles (Acts 4:36; 9:27; 11:22; 15; Gal. 2:9). This may be why he is at times called an apostle in the Scriptures themselves (Acts 14:4, 13). It is to be noted, however, that the term is not always used in its strict sense in the Acts and Epistles.

8. Acts 20:24; see I Cor. 9:16; II Thess. 2:15; I Tim. 1:19-20; II Tim. 2:17-18.

9. Acts 15:28; see 16:4; I Cor. 11:2; II Thess. 3:14.

10. I Cor. 4:21; see II Cor. 10:3-8; 13:2, 10.

11. See John 13:13.

12. See J. C. Fenton, "New Testament Designations of the Church and of its Members," CBQ, 9 (1947), 127 ff.; J. E. Rea, "A Note on the Nature of the Common Priesthood," AER, 118 (1948), 422 ff.; Pius XII, *Mediator Dei* (Nov. 20, 1947); H. F. Davis, "The Priesthood of the Faithful," ThD, 1 (1953), 49 ff.

13. See I Cor. 12:8-11; S.Th., I-II, q. 111, a. 4.

14. The title "deacons" does not occur here, but there is hardly any doubt that the seven men referred to were raised to that order which was later called the diaconate. See St. Irenaeus *Adversus haereses* i. 26. 3; iii. 12. 10; iv. 15. 1; CCHS, 820d, 828a.

15. One can understand without difficulty that the apostles might, quite frequently, have assigned offices in the Church to men with some charism or other. This seems to be the explanation of the fact that the *inspired spokesmen and teachers* who were at Antioch celebrated the sacred liturgy (Acts 13:1-3). However, in the phrase, *As they were celebrating the liturgical worship of the Lord and fasting*, the subject "they" may well be impersonal, and does not necessarily refer to the spokesmen and teachers mentioned in the preceding sentence. On the other hand, the *Didache* (10. 6) mentions "prophets" who celebrated the Eucharist.

16. For those not familiar with formal reasoning processes, it may be well to point out that such a process, called a syllogism, consists of two statements, called respectively a major and a minor premise, from which a conclusion logically follows. Most often, the major is a universally accepted truth needing no proof. The minor, however, may have to be substantiated by additional evidence.

>Major: Every man has a soul.
>Minor: But Christ was a man.
>Conclusion: Therefore, Christ had a soul.

17. II Tim. 4:2–3; see 2:23–5; I Tim. 4:6–7.

18. *Epistula prima ad Corinthios* 42. 3–44. 3; ACW transl. The words, "when these men die" (*eàn koimēthôsin*), are taken by some as referring to the apostles; by others, as referring to the aforementioned bishops; see *De Katholiek*, 119 (1901), 455. However you take these words, St. Clement still says that the apostles provided for hierarchical succession, and, indeed, at the Lord's command.

19. In O. Cullmann's *Peter: Disciple, Apostle, Martyr*, translated by Floyd V. Filson (Philadelphia, 1952), about which work we shall have more to say later, this poses a dilemma. In Cullmann's view, apostolic grace must either perish with the apostles or survive them in its entirety. Catholic teaching resolves this dilemma by distinguishing between a mission of the apostles which is an extraordinary, noncommunicable charism relating to the *founding* of the Church, and an ordinary communicable charism relating to its *preservation*. See C. Journet, *The Primacy of Peter*, translated by John C. Chapin (Westminster, Md., 1954), p. 50, 53. Idem, *Church of the Word, op. cit.*, p. 127–8:

>This distinction between the extraordinary and the permanent jurisdiction is attested by a double fact. On the one hand it seems absolutely certain that the Apostles had privileged powers which were to cease with them: the power, for instance, of communicating new revelations or of writing inspired books. On the other hand it seems absolutely certain that the Apostles were the first depositaries of a power to teach the nations, a power that was to pass to their successors and to be perpetuated till the end of time. Consequently, there are two ways in which the Church is said to be apostolic: first because the Apostles, in virtue of their ordinary powers, founded her and gave her the first impulsion, the first orientation; and next because the Apostles bequeathed her their ordinary powers.

20. We say, "at least from the beginning of the second century," because there is a great deal of discussion about the rank and function of those men who, in first century documents (the New Testament, the *Didache*, St. Clement's *Epistula prima ad Corinthios*) are called "bishops." Some think (*a*) that the words *epískopos* and *presbýteros* are used indiscriminately for priests of the first and second rank; others hold (*b*) that the title *presbýteros* was a common designation for priests of the first and second class, but that the title *epískopos* was restricted to those of the first class; others, finally, think (*c*) that both words refer to priests of the second class only. See *De Katholiek*, 119 (1901), 442 ff.

A word on the above terminology: a presbyter of the first class would be what we now know of as a bishop, possessing the fulness of the priesthood; a presbyter of the second class would be a simple priest. See LZ, I, 352–3; P. Hughes, *A History of the Church*, I (New York, 1947), 61–71; T. Zapalena, *op. cit.*, II, 47; Journet, *Church of the Word, op. cit.*, p. 80, n. 4.

21. *Epistula ad Ephesios:*
However, since affection does not permit me to be silent when you are concerned, I am at once taking this opportunity to exhort you to live in harmony with the mind of God. Surely, Jesus Christ, our inseparable life, for His part is the mind of the Father, just as the bishops, though appointed throughout the vast, wide earth, represent for their part the mind of Jesus Christ.
Hence it is proper for you to act in agreement with the mind of the bishop; and this you do. Certain it is that your presbytery, which is a credit to its name, is a credit to God; for it harmonizes with the bishop as completely as the strings with a harp.—3. 2–4. 1; see 6.
Epistula ad Magnesios:
But for you, too, it is fitting not to take advantage of the bishop's youth, but rather, because he embodies the authority of God the Father, to show him every mark of respect—and your presbyters, so I learn, are doing just that: they do not seek to profit by his youthfulness, which strikes the bodily eye; no they are wise in God and therefore defer to him—or, rather, not to him, but to the Father of Jesus Christ, the bishop of all men.—3. 1.
Epistula ad Philadelphenses:
Regarding this bishop I am informed that he holds the supreme office in the community not by his own efforts, . . . No, he holds it by the love of God the Father and the Lord Jesus Christ.—1. 1.
Surely, all those that belong to God and Jesus Christ are the very ones that side with the bishop; . . . —3. 2.
Take care, then, to partake of one Eucharist; for, one is the Flesh of Our Lord Jesus Christ, and one the cup to unite us with His Blood, and one altar, just as there is one bishop assisted by the presbytery and the deacons, . . . —4.
I cried out, while in your midst, and said in a ringing voice—God's voice: "Give heed to the bishop and to the presbytery and to the deacons."—7. 1.
Epistula ad Smyrnaeos:
You must all follow the lead of the bishop, as Jesus Christ followed that of the Father; follow the presbytery as you would the Apostles; reverence the deacons as you would God's commandment. Let no one do anything touching the Church, apart from the bishop. Let that celebration of the Eucharist be considered valid which is held under the bishop or anyone to whom he has committed it. Where the bishop appears, there let the people be, just as where Jesus Christ is, there is the Catholic Church. It is not permitted without authorization from the bishop either to baptize or to hold an agape; . . .
He who does anything without the knowledge of the bishop worships the devil.—8. 1 – 9. 1.

All the foregoing excerpts are from the ACW translation. See also *Epistula ad Trallianos* 3. 1; 7; *Epistula ad Polycarpum* Inscription; 6. 1; A. Mertens, *op. cit.*, p. 284 ff.; J. C. Fenton, "New Testament Designations of the Church and of its Members," CBQ, 9 (1947), 275 ff.; LZ, I, 421–4; Hughes, *op cit.*, I, 61–71; QP, I, 63–76.

22. Eusebius HE 4. 22; see 11.
23. In the *Chronicon* and HE; the pertinent passages may be found in Franzelin, *Theses de ecclesia*, p. 271.
24. Some modern writers, especially those outside the Church, make a distinction between the *monarchical* or *unitarian* episcopate, in which one *episkopos* governed his church all by himself; and the *plural* or *collegiate* episcopate, in which several men, all called *episkopoi*, ruled a church after the fashion of a board of directors. Monarchical bishops then would be nothing other than bishops in the traditional Catholic sense. But the term "monarchical bishop" is to be used discreetly, so as not to cast aspersions on the primacy of the sovereign pontiff. For it is now the common custom to call him alone the monarch who holds supreme and independent dominion. See Hughes, *loc. cit.*; J. C. Fenton, "The Apostolicity of the Roman See," AER, 118 (1948), 444 ff.
25. See also H. Dieckmann, "Das Zeugnis der Chronik von Arbela für den monarchischen Episkopat," ThGl (1925), 65.
26. Acts 12:17; 15:13; 21:18; Gal. 1:19; 2:12.
27. See De Smedt, "L'organisation des églises chrétiennes," *Congrès scientifique international des catholiques tenu à Paris 1888*, II, 335.
28. See LZ, I, 478; Journet, *Church of the Word, op. cit.*, p. 82, n. 1:
According to Batiffol the name of "presbyters" would, at the outset, have been used alike for laymen and for the ordained. The liturgical and social functions were reserved for deacons and for *episcopoi*. The *episcopoi* or presbyter-bishops had the power of bishops. They formed a college in each Church. At the death of the Apostles the plural episcopate was dismembered, so as to give birth to the sovereign episcopate of the bishop and the subordinate priesthood of the priests. However, the plural episcopate subsisted for a long time at Alexandria; the whole *presbyterium* was composed of bishops; but only one of them, designated by election, exercised the power of ordaining. Cf. *Études d'histoire et de théologie positive*, Paris 1920, p. 226 and 280. But Duschesne observes that if things began in more than one place with the collegiate episcopate, the unitary episcopate was not unknown to the primitive institutions; we find it in the mother-church at Jerusalem, at Antioch, Rome, Lyons, Corinth, Athens, and in Crete (*The Early History of the Church*, London 1914, vol. I, pp. 63–9).

See also *ibid.*, p. 390, n. 2.
29. See A. Michiels, *L'origine de l'épiscopat* (1900); *De Katholiek*, 119 (1901), 433 ff.; J. Rostworowski, *Charakter i znaczenie biskupstwa w pierwszyck dwoch wiekach dziejow Kosciola* (1926); LZ, *loc. cit.*; CCHS, 658a–659f.
30. *Commentarium in Epistulam ad Titum, loc. cit.*: "Of course there could not have been in one city several bishops, as we now understand this office." *Epistula* 146, *loc. cit.*: "Let no one heatedly insist that there were several bishops in one church."
31. *De scriptoribus ecclesiasticis* ii. 15. 17; *Chronicon of Eusebius* 45. 64.
32. See Wilmers, *De ecclesia*, p. 331; Michiels, *op. cit.*, p. 420; CCHS, *loc. cit.*; LZ, *loc. cit.*, P. Hughes, *loc. cit.*
33. See Salaverri, *op. cit.*, I, 940, 952–56, 966–71; C. Journet, *Church of the Word, op. cit.*, p. 298–99:

THE CHURCH'S NATURE

The jurisdictional power founded by Christ has for its first mission the announcing of the good news of the Gospel (declaratory power), and for its secondary mission the effectual organizing of the conduct of those who welcome this good news (canonical power). And the Kingdom of God in its wholeness, that is to say the divine order resulting from the descent of the Holy Trinity into history and from Its habitation among men, cannot, in virtue of a divine intention expressly signified in the Gospel, find its final perfection, its perfect realization, save by the integral functioning of the jurisdictional power, involving first a genuinely legislative power (whose essential and general decisions are ratified in heaven), and in consequence a judicial and coercive power. When therefore those who have given their hearts to the Church begin to revolt against her laws, she is entitled to act against them and inflict penalties.

These penalties, always spiritual if you look to the power that decrees them and the end that justifies them, will be, in their immediate and intrinsic tenor, either directly spiritual—as excommunication, expressly provided for in Scripture—or else temporal, material. To deny this last point—to deny that the Church can decree, subject of course to the demands of prudence according to time, place and circumstance, penalties that touch her subjects in the goods of fortune, in the goods of the body, in the use of liberty—would be to deny her power—always exercised of course, for spiritual ends —over the whole man; it would be to deny her all power to descend into the realities of practical life, thereby limiting not only her coercive power but even her judicial and legislative power; lastly, it would be gravely to misconceive her spiritual nature, for while this certainly forbids her to use temporal things in the manner of, and for the ends of, the State, it does not forbid but rather requires her to make use of them according to her own spiritual laws and for her own spiritual ends.

There are here two errors to be avoided: that which denies the Church's right to dispose of temporal things, contesting her character as a perfect and autonomous society, a kingdom effectively organized to exist *in* this world; and that which grants her the power of disposing of temporal things in the manner of and for the ends of the State; making her a kingdom *of* this world.

However, the means of coercion open to the Church are limited. The following remarks of Msgr. Journet are quite to the point (*ibid.*, 194-195):

Her resemblance to political societies is analogical only, not univocal. Hence the resemblance of her canonical power to the political power is also only analogical; and that of her legislative, judiciary and coercive powers to the legislative, judiciary, and coercive powers of the State, is merely analogical likewise. . . .

It further results that the means of coercion open to the Church to bring her rebellious children back into the ways of obedience and love will not be identical with those used by the temporal society. Since the Church is a society which is not *of* this world, a spiritual society, ecclesiastical penalties will be always spiritual by reason of their end. But since the Church is a society which is *in* this world, a visible society, she can touch delinquents in their visible, temporal and material goods; but, even then, such penalties, remaining spiritual in aim, will be distinct from those inflicted by civil society. They will have another measure; they will be lighter and will not, for example, go so far as the shedding of blood and the death penalty. . . .

Yet Popes have issued decrees for setting holy wars on foot, and for compelling princes to hunt down heresy, and I believe that they did so legitimately. But what I propose to dispute is that they did so in virtue only of their canonical power, and of essential and permanent exigencies of the Kingdom of God.

See CIC 2214, §2:

Let the bishops and other ordinaries remember that they are pastors, not persecutors, that they should rule their subjects, not lord it over them, but love them as sons and brothers, and try to turn them from evil ways by advice and exhortations, for fear of having to be severe when they sin. But when human frailty has led them to fall into sin, let the bishops, conformably with the word of the Apostle, *reprove, entreat, rebuke in all patience and doctrine,* since sinners are often more easily brought back to the right way by benignity than by sternness, by persuasion than by threats, by charity than by authority. But if, on account of the gravity of the sin, chastisement becomes inevitable, then let sternness be tempered with gentleness, justice with mercy, severity with sweetness, that necessary and wholesome discipline may be preserved without harshness, that those corrected may amend, or at least, if they will not come to a better mind, that others may be deterred by the salutary example of their punishment.

See also Journet, *loc. cit.,* p. 193 ff., 253, 268 ff., 280 ff., 298 ff.

34. Encyclical *Quanta cura,* December 8, 1864 (DB 1697); see St. Gregory the Great *Epistulae* ix. 65 *ad Januarium calar.;* Council of Trent, Session 25, chapter 3, *De reform.;* S.Th., II-II, q. 10, a. 8, *corpus;* L. Choupin, "Le pouvoir coércitif de l'église," NRTh (1908), p. 209; *idem,* "Hérésie," DAFC, II, 442 ff.

35. See C. Journet, *Church of the Word, op. cit.,* p. 251 ff., esp. 254.

36. In the bull *Unam sanctam, Extravagantes communes,* bk. I, title 8, chap. 1; see *Syllabus of Errors,* prop. 24 (DB 1724).

37. See, for example, F. Cavagnis, *Institutiones iuris publici ecclesiastici* (Rome, 1906), I, no. 288 ff.; 336 ff.; L. Bender, O.P., *Ius publicum ecclesiasticum* (Bussum, 1948); A. Bonghi, *Stato e Chiesa* (Milan, 1942); F. Cappello, *Summa iuris publici ecclesiastici* (Turin, 1932); M. Coronata, *Ius publicum ecclesiasticum* (Turin-Rome, 1934); A. Ottaviani, *Institutiones iuris publici ecclesiastici* (Rome, 1935); *Compendium iuris publici ecclesiastici* (Rome, 1943); Saviano, *Sovranità della Chiesa e sovranità della Stato* (Milan-Rome, 1934).

38. Read CIC, 2291 and 2298, where are listed the vindictive penalties in ordinary use in the Church.

39. Still, it is to be understood that the word "jurisdiction" is often used in a more restricted sense so as to be coextensive with only the power of rule or dominion. See J. C. Fenton, "*Magisterium* and Jurisdiction in the Catholic Church," AER, 130 (1954), 194 ff.

40. Although the supreme pontiff is elected by men like himself, he receives jurisdiction directly from God; and so, no man can block or restrict it. The pope himself, however, can abdicate.

41. See Journet, *Church of the Word, op. cit.,* p. 124 ff.; also p. 10, 163, and especially p. 160 which contains an excellent outline of the power of jurisdiction; J. C. Fenton, *art. cit.*

Article II

THE CHURCH AS A MONARCHICAL SOCIETY

I. *Errors*

II. *Catholic Doctrine*

> PROPOSITION 1: Christ appointed St. Peter as visible head of His whole Church by bestowing upon him directly the primacy, i.e., a primacy of real and strict jurisdiction.
>
> *Proof:* 1. from the words of Christ's promise;
> 2. from the words of the fulfillment of the promise;
> 3. corroborated by many instances in which Peter is given preference over the other apostles or in which he acts as their head:
>   a. bestowal of a new name on Peter;
>   b. special honor given him;
>   c. first place given him;
>   d. task of strengthening his brothers entrusted to him;
>   e. his active leadership after the Ascension;
> 4. corroborated further by testimony of the ancients.
>
> *Objections*
>
> *Scholion:* The relationship of St. Peter to the other apostles and to St. Paul.
>
> PROPOSITION 2: It was Christ's will that the primacy, begun with St. Peter, should continue forever.
>
> *Proof:* 1. from nature and purpose of primacy;
> 2. from the words of Christ;
> 3. from testimony of ancients.
>
> PROPOSITION 3: Peter's primacy lives on in the Roman pontiff.
>
> *Proof:* 1. argument of exclusion (by process of elimination);
> 2. genealogical argument (by tracking down source of Roman primacy);

3. historical argument (testimony and facts from first centuries).

Objection: Canon 28 of Chalcedon.

Scholion: Why do the Roman pontiffs often profess to be acting "on the authority of the holy apostles Peter and Paul"?

III. *Epilogue: The Roman Catholic Church is the True Church of Christ*

Article II

THE CHURCH AS A MONARCHICAL SOCIETY

42 The preceding article established the fact that Christ's Church is not a democratic society. There remains the further question: is it aristocratic or monarchical?

An *aristocratic* society is one in which the highest authority rests by right with a group of noblemen of equal rank. Accordingly, if Christ had conferred the sacred power on the apostles as a group, and in such a way that no one of them would be superior to the others, then the Church's regime would be aristocratic in form. But if, within the group of apostles, He placed one above the others so that the sacred ruling power in all its fulness would be his and, in time, his successors', then the Church would be a *monarchical* society.

I. Errors

43 1. The *High Church* of England, the *Greek Church* and *eastern sects* in general agree, for the most part, with the doctrines set forth in the preceding article. But at the same time they hold that all bishops are by divine right on an equal footing.[1] They therefore deny that our Lord conferred on St. Peter and his successors any real power over other bishops and over the universal Church. Many will grant that Peter himself was given a certain pre-eminence in the matter of power or prestige; a few acknowledge even some sort of primacy of honor in Peter's successors.[2]

2. Likewise the Old Catholics and the Jansenists of Holland, at least the modern ones, reject all primacy which lays claim to divine right.

3. Again, in the seventeenth century, Edmund Richer and Marco Antonio de Dominis; in the eighteenth century, Nicholas de Hontheim, the Synod of Pistoia, and, in general, all the older Gallicans and Jansenists busied themselves with repressing or restricting the primacy of the Roman pontiff. They claimed that the fulness of sacred power belonged at least originally and basically

to the Church as a whole, or to the bishops as a group, and limited the pope's power to that of an inspector or adviser. But more about these errors later, in the second section.

The Catholic doctrine is that Christ directly conferred upon Peter alone the sacred power of rule in all its fulness; that He willed this primacy, begun in Peter, to continue forever; and finally, that this primacy does as a matter of fact perdure in the Roman pontiff.[3]

II. Catholic Doctrine

44 PROPOSITION 1: *Christ appointed St. Peter as visible head of His whole Church by bestowing upon him directly the primacy, i.e., a primacy of real and strict jurisdiction.*

The *first* part of the proposition affirms the monarchical form of the Church's rule, and the *second* explains what kind of power Christ gave St. Peter.

Primacy, in its etymological meaning, signifies pre-eminence over others. Peter's primacy is called *primacy of real and strict jurisdiction* to show that he was given pre-eminence not of honor only, but of real authority, so that he surpassed all in power, and all others were given the bounden duty to obey him. But since the sacred power of jurisdiction comprises, as seen above, the power to teach and to rule, Peter's primacy may be defined as the *full and supreme power to teach and to rule the universal Church.*[4]

By virtue of this primacy St. Peter became the visible head of the whole Church Militant. Mark well the qualification *"visible,"* for Christ Himself remains the principal, but invisible, head of His universal Church. It is in His name and by His authority that Peter presides over the visible Church. Peter takes His place not in the absolute sense, but insofar as he exercises external control (teaching and ruling) over the Church Militant. Peter is therefore usually, and quite fittingly, called the Vicar of Christ on earth; vicar, not successor, for he alone can be called a successor who steps into the place of one who has laid aside his authority.[5]

The proposition states that the primacy was conferred on Peter himself directly, in order to rule out the opinion of those who have taught that the fulness of sacred power was given directly to the whole assembly of the faithful, or at least to the whole apostolic college, and was thence delegated to Peter as a minister of the Church. They would call Peter a "ministerial head."[6]

THE CHURCH'S NATURE

The proposition is a *dogma of faith,* as the Vatican Council tells us: "If anyone should say that St. Peter the apostle was not appointed by Christ the Lord as prince of all the apostles and as visible head of the whole Church Militant, or that this same St. Peter received directly and immediately from the same our Lord Jesus Christ the primacy of honor only and not of real and strict jurisdiction, let him be anathema."[7]

Proof:

1. From the *words of the promise.* Christ had asked the apostles, *"But you, . . . who do you say that I am?"* and Peter alone had answered, *"You are the Messias, the Son of the Living God." Jesus acquiesced and said to him: "Blessed are you, Simon, son of Jona. It was my Father in heaven that revealed this to you, and not flesh and blood. And I, in turn, say to you: You are Peter, and upon this rock I will build my Church, and the gates of hell shall not prevail against it. I will give you the keys of the kingdom of heaven, and whatever you bind on earth shall be bound in heaven, and whatever you loose on earth shall be loosed in heaven."*[8]

What is promised in these words is promised to Peter *alone* and to Peter himself immediately. Christ addresses Peter alone. He expressly adds his own name, Simon, and that of his father, Jona. He uses the singular while before He had used the plural. It is not true that Peter proclaimed Christ's divinity in the name of the apostles, i.e., as their delegate, or at least as one who knew their mind in the matter. And even if this were true, it would still not make the whole apostolic college the beneficiary of our Lord's promise.

The metaphors of the foundation stone and of the keys indicating the power of binding and loosing show clearly that primacy of real jurisdiction is promised.

a. *"You are Peter* (Kepha', rock), *and upon this rock* (kepha') *I will build my Church, and the gates of hell shall not prevail against it."*

Christ's Church, simply and without qualification (*mou tēn ekklēsian*), is of necessity the *whole* Church of Christ. Simon is now given the name of *Boulder* or *Rock* because he is to be the rock on which the Church will be built, i.e., because he will be for the Church of Christ what a rock foundation is for a house. What does such a foundation do for a house? It assures the permanent connection of all its parts and consequently its solidity.[9] Peter will make Christ's Church cohesive, or *one* and *whole,* and indeed to such an extent that it will never crumble under any enemy attack.[10] Now the Church is a society. What must a man have in order to assure the unity and stability of any society? Real authority, full and supreme authority; for just as in a building all the parts are supported by the foundation, so in a society everything depends on authority.

46 b. *"I will give you the keys of the kingdom of heaven, and whatever you bind on earth will be bound in heaven,"* etc.

To hand over to someone the keys of a house or a city is the same as to give him supreme authority therein, to make him the administrator of the whole house or city. Therefore with His promise of *"the keys of the kingdom of heaven,"* i.e., of the Church here on earth, Christ again promises Peter full and supreme authority over His whole Church.

The meaning of the metaphor of the keys is given fuller explanation in the words which follow.[11] Since Peter is to be given supreme jurisdiction in the Church, then whatever he binds or looses on earth will be ratified in heaven, i.e., by God. Of course it is a question of bonds in the moral order; and so "to bind" means to impose an obligation, and "to loose" means to remove an obligation. This power is to be universal: "whatever," always keeping in mind, of course, the character of the Church and the purpose for which it was founded. Therefore Peter will be able to provide all that will be necessary or useful for the governing of the whole Church.[12]

That the "kingdom of heaven" is in truth the Church here on earth is obvious. Certainly Peter is not promised authority over the realm of glory; besides, our Lord explicitly adds that whatever Peter binds or looses *on earth* will be ratified.

NOTE. *To have the keys* means more than *to have the power of binding.* He who holds the keys is supreme in the kingdom, and consequently enjoys (*a*) the power of binding, but (*b*) supremely and independently. Perhaps others too will be able to bind within the same kingdom, but they will do so only in dependence upon him who holds the keys.

47 2. Proof from the *words of the fulfillment of the promise.* Appearing to His disciples shortly before the Ascension, *Jesus said to Simon Peter: "Simon, son of John, do you love me more than these*

others do?" "Yes, my Master," he replied; "you know that I really love you." "Then," Jesus said to him, "feed my lambs." He asked him a second time: "Simon, son of John, do you love me?" "Yes, Master," he replied, "you know that I really love you." "Then," he said to him, "be a shepherd to my sheep." For the third time he put the question to him: "Simon, son of John, do you really love me?" It grieved Peter that he had asked him the third time: "Do you really love me?" and he replied: "Master, you know everything; you know that I really love you!" "Then," Jesus said to him, "feed my sheep. . . . " (John 21:15-17).

Evidently these words were addressed to Peter *alone*, who three times is called by his own name and that of his father,[13] and is clearly singled out from the other apostles: *"Do you love me more than these others do?"*

Christ bestows upon him supreme jurisdiction over the whole Church. The *lambs and sheep* of the Lord indicate nothing other than the Church, which is elsewhere compared to a sheepfold (John 10:11-16), and indeed the universal Church: *tà arnía mou, tà próbata* (or *probátia*) *mou*.[14]

To feed (*bóskein* and *poimaínein* are, for all practical purposes, synonymous), where it refers to rational sheep, means the same as to rule. In this sense kings are sometimes called shepherds of their people.

Now if Peter alone, apart from the rest of the apostles, is given the office of ruling the universal Church of Christ, it follows that he is invested with real jurisdiction over all who belong to the Church. For how could he fulfill his duty without this jurisdiction? But real jurisdiction over all is just another way of saying supreme jurisdiction.

3. This proposition is corroborated by *many instances in which Peter is given preference over the other apostles or in which he acts as their head.*

a. The bestowal of a new name. When Christ saw Peter for the first time, He said to him, *"You are Simon, the son of John. Your name shall be 'Cephas' [Rock]"* (John 1:42); He actually gave him this name when he selected him as an apostle (Mark 3:16). Now when God gives a man a name, it is not without a purpose,[15] and our Lord Himself explained what was behind the giving of this name when He said, *"and upon this rock [kepha'] I will build my Church."*

CHRIST'S CHURCH

b. Special honor given to Peter. Christ teaches from Peter's boat, and after the miraculous catch of fish He says in a special way to Peter alone, *"You have nothing to fear. Hereafter you will be a fisher of men"* (Luke 5:1–10). He directs that the stater found in the fish's mouth be paid for Himself and Peter (Matt. 17:27); Peter's feet are the first He washes (John 13:6); the Lord's resurrection is to be announced particularly to Peter (Mark 16:7); the risen Christ appears to Peter before He appears to the other apostles (Luke 24:34; I Cor. 15:5).

c. First place given to Peter. Andrew had thrown in his lot with Jesus even before Peter, but in all the lists of the apostles Peter is given first place, and is explicitly referred to as the *first* by St. Matthew, even though no one else is called second or third: *The names of the twelve apostles are as follows: First, Simon, surnamed Peter; then Andrew, his brother; James, the son of Zebedee, etc.*[16] The same order is observed almost always, whenever several apostles are named together;[17] what is more, the college of the apostles is referred to as follows: *Peter with the eleven; Peter with the Apostles.*[18]

49   *d. The task of strengthening his brothers* is entrusted to Peter. *"Simon, Simon, mark my words: Satan has demanded the surrender of you all in order to sift you like wheat; but I have prayed for you personally, that your faith might not fail. Later on, therefore, when you have recovered, it is for you to strengthen your brethren."*[19] The devil sought to shake all the apostles as grain is shaken in a sieve, in order to shake the faith out of their hearts. What was Christ's reaction? He did not ask that the shaking be prevented, but He efficaciously prayed for Peter alone that he might stand immovably firm in faith. And now he directs that Peter, once he has *"recovered,"* make his brethren staunch and immovable. The *brethren* are primarily the apostles; secondarily, and *a fortiori,* the other disciples too.

This method of insuring the staunchness of the others through the personal efforts of Peter is especially fitting if Peter is one day to be head of the whole Church and of the apostles themselves, the Vicar of Christ on earth.[20] In fact, it would otherwise have been quite unseemly and inadequate an arrangement. For how could Peter have efficaciously strengthened his brethren if he had not been given real authority over them; if a real, strict obligation of listening to and of obeying Peter had not been imposed upon the brethren?

*e. Peter's activity after the Lord's Ascension.*²¹ Peter takes the lead in the election of Matthias (Acts 1:15 ff.); on Pentecost Day he is the first to proclaim the gospel (2:14 ff.); he is the first to corroborate its truth by performing a miracle (3:6); he deals with Ananias and Sapphira as head man in the apostolic college (5:3, 8); he is the first to learn—and that by revelation—that the time has come to admit Gentiles, too, directly into the Church, and he himself issues the order for the baptism of the first of them (10); at the Council of Jerusalem, *"after a long debate,"* he is the first to give an opinion, and all acquiesce in it (15:6 ff.); he visits all the faithful throughout Judea, Galilee, and Samaria (9:31–32). Finally, Paul is anxiously concerned about meeting only one apostle —Peter.²²

Real primacy of jurisdiction is not of course strictly proven by each of the instances cited in this number (3); but it cannot be denied, especially if one considers their cumulative force, that they argue for the considerable pre-eminence of Peter. And this pre-eminence fits neatly the notion of real primacy. Indeed, without the latter, it is hard to account for the former.

4. Further corroboration is found in the *testimony of the ancients*. Just a few samples from tradition will suffice, since the arguments from tradition completely clinch the matter, and the testimonies of the fathers to be cited below (PROPOSITION 3) strongly favor this thesis also, either directly or indirectly.

Tertullian: "Was anything hidden from Peter, from him who was called the rock on which the Church would be built, from him who received the keys of the kingdom of heaven?" (*De praescriptione* 22).

Origen: "When Peter was given full charge of feeding the sheep, and when the Church was founded upon him as on solid ground, he was required to admit to just one virtue—charity."²³

St. Cyprian, after citing Matthew 16:18–19, remarks, "It is on one man that He builds the Church" (*De unitate ecclesiae* [2nd ed.] 4; ACW trans.).

St. Aphraates: "Simon, the prince of the disciples . . . the Lord took him, made him the foundation and called him the rock, the foundation of the Church" (*Demonstrationes* 7. 15).

St. Ephraem hymns St. Peter as follows: "Blessed art thou, thou whom the Son of God chose and appointed head of His disciples, and to whom He gave the power and authority to bind and to loose" (*Hymni disputati* 3. 2).²⁴

CHRIST'S CHURCH

St. Cyril of Jerusalem: "Peter, the most (!) foremost [*koruphaiótatos*] and chief of the apostles" (*Catecheses* 2. 19).

St. Optatus: "Peter merited to be put above all the apostles, and he alone received the keys of the kingdom of heaven to be handed on to others" (*De schismate Donatistarum* 7. 3).

St. Jerome: "Of the twelve, one is chosen so that with the appointment of a head the seeds of schism may be suppressed" (*Adversus Jovinianum* 1. 26).

St. John Chrysostom: "Peter, then, was director of that choir, the mouth of all the apostles, the head of that family, the governor of the whole world, the foundation of the Church."[25]

St. Augustine mentions the chief "of the apostles, Peter, in whom primacy over the apostles shines with such brilliant beauty. . . . Who is unaware that that apostolic primacy of his is to be preferred to any other episcopate?" (*De baptismo* 2. 2).

St. Peter Chrysologus: "Just before His return to heaven, He entrusts His sheep to Peter, that he may feed them in His stead" (*Sermones* 6).

Note that all the evidence set forth above proves at the same time that the keys were given to Peter personally, *directly and immediately.* "Remember," said Tertullian, "that here the Lord left the keys to Peter, and through Peter to the Church" (*Scorpiace* 10), but not to Peter through the Church.

51 *Objections:*

1. No special power is promised Peter by the words of Matthew 16, for:

a. elsewhere all the apostles are similarly called the foundation of the Church: *You are fellow citizens with the saints, and members of God's household. You are an edifice built on the foundation of the apostles and prophets with Christ Jesus himself as the chief cornerstone* (Eph. 2:20); besides,

b. if it is a question of the Church's real foundation in the strict sense, then this foundation is Christ alone: *Of course no other foundation can anyone lay than the one already laid, and that is Jesus Christ* (I Cor. 3:11). Furthermore,

c. each and every one of the apostles received the power to bind and to loose whatever they thought fit: "*Whatever you bind on earth shall be bound in heaven,*" etc. (Matt. 18:18).

Answer to a: The metaphor of the foundation can be used in more than one sense, and so one has to determine from the context the precise sense in which it is being employed. Now the context of Matthew 16 shows that Peter is called the foundation of the Church by reason of the supreme authority which he is to receive. Likewise, the context shows that in the Epistle to the Ephesians the apostles are called the foundation of the Church *by reason of their faith and preaching.* In fact, the apostles are called the foundation of the faithful along with the prophets of the Old Testament, and the latter certainly exercised no jurisdiction over the Church of the New Law.[26]

52 *Answer to b:* Again the meaning of the metaphor must be decided on the basis of the context. The meaning of the passage cited is this: Christ, or rather faith in Christ, is the true and unique foundation *of the whole Christian dispensation and of the whole Christian life.* This foundation Paul, *"like a skilled master builder,"* had laid in Corinth; and upon it subsequent teachers were to build. Besides, if this text actually did deal with the question of supreme authority over the Church, it would still prove nothing against the Catholic doctrine, for Peter's power is only a sharing in the power of Christ. "Now although he [Peter] is the rock, he is not the rock in the way Christ is; he does not cease to be Peter. For when Jesus gives out positions of authority, He does not impoverish Himself, but keeps the very things He bestows. He is a priest and makes others priests; He is the Rock and makes another the rock; and so He gives His servants what He Himself has."[27]

53 *Answer to c:* It may be readily granted that the power of binding and of loosing *anything whatsoever* implies fulness of power, but the words *"whatever you bind,"* etc. are addressed not to each of the apostles individually, but to all of them together as a group. And so one cannot legitimately conclude that each of the apostles was promised fulness of jurisdiction. The conclusion is rather that this power was promised to the whole apostolic college, including Peter. A comparison of Matthew 16 with Matthew 18 shows that there will be in Christ's Church a twofold subject, not too sharply distinct, of full and supreme jurisdiction: Peter alone, and the Petro-apostolic college. And this is the Catholic teaching, as Innocent III, among others, testifies:

> But should you discover that it was spoken to all the apostles together, still you will recognize that the power of binding and

loosing was bestowed not upon the others without him [Peter], but that it was given to him apart from the others, so that what the others could not do without him he could do without the others, and this by reason of the privileges conferred upon him by the Lord and by reason of the fulness of power which had been granted him.[28]

Does it not follow, then, that the other apostles did not have each personally the power to bind and to loose? No, for they did indeed have it, but each of them did not have the full and unlimited power that Peter had.

54 *Objection 2.* The rock upon which, according to Matthew 16, the Church is going to be built, is not the person of Simon, but must or at least can be understood as:

a. Christ Himself, as appeared probable to St. Augustine.

> I said somewhere regarding the apostle Peter that the Church was founded upon him as upon a rock. . . . But I am also aware that subsequently I very frequently explained our Lord's words, *"You are Peter,"* etc., as referring to Him whom Peter had confessed. For Christ did not say to him, "You are a rock (*petra*)," but "You are Peter (*Petrus*)." Christ, then, was the rock. . . . But I leave it to the reader to choose which of these opinions seems the more probable.—*Retractationes* 1. 22.

or it can be understood as:

b. Peter's faith or his profession of Christ's divinity, as several fathers have explained this text.

55 *Answer.* As for the proper and directly literal meaning, there can be no doubt that the words *"upon this rock"* refer and can refer only to Simon personally. Christ spoke in Aramaic and used the same word in both instances: *"Thou art* Kepha', *and upon this* kepha' *"*; it is consequently undeniable that the *"kepha' "* of the Church indicates that same person who has immediately before been called *"Kepha'."* The escape device of some Protestants who claimed that Christ pointed to Himself when He uttered the words, *"upon this rock,"* is of antiquarian interest only. The remaining difficulties are those occasioned by some remarks of the fathers.

a. St. Augustine, as the passage quoted shows, made this mistake. Not knowing Aramaic, he thought he saw a real distinction between *Petrus* and *petram*. Had he known that Christ used the same word, *kepha'*, in both instances, he would never have doubted the truth of the explanation which even then, as he himself testifies (*loc. cit.*), was being sung "by the mouth of the multitude" in the verses of St. Ambrose: "At cock-crow, the very Rock of the Church atones for his sin." But even if he did question the truth of the common explanation, he never had any doubts about the objective truth of this statement: Peter is the foundation of the Church. For otherwise he could not have given his readers their choice of either explanation.

b. It is true that many fathers offered this explanation after the rise of the Arian heresy.[29] But they did so in such a way as not at all to exclude the proper and direct explanation of the words as referring to Peter himself, personally. In fact, they expressly include this interpretation, and in other passages give explicit expression to it. The full mind of these fathers was as follows: Peter was the foundation of the Church because of his faith (meritorious cause), and by his unshakable faith (formal but only partial cause). The reason these fathers extolled Peter's faith in such a special way was the attack leveled against Christ's divinity by the Arian heresy.

In the words of Natalis Alexander:

> Therefore the Catholic explanation of these words, "*upon this rock*," is twofold: one refers them to the very faith of Peter, and the other to Peter personally. There is this difference between the two interpretations: the latter gives the direct meaning, while the former gives the indirect or mediate. The latter is the original, constant interpretation, while the other came later and is not so constant. The latter goes back to the beginning of the Church and was for four centuries the only one proposed, while the former came into being only because of particular circumstances.[30]

One last word. Lest certain peculiar interpretations advanced by the ancients shock anyone, attention should be drawn to the fact that the holy fathers, especially in their sermons and spiritual writings, often resorted to mystical and accommodated interpretations, setting aside for the moment, but by no means, excluding, the literal sense.

Objection 3. There are no traces of Peter's primacy to be found in the primitive Church. In fact, several things are recorded in the New Testament writings which militate against any such primacy.

a. Peter is sent to Samaria by the other apostles: *Now when the apostles in Jerusalem heard that Samaria had accepted the word of God, they sent Peter and John to them* (Acts 8:14).

b. Paul puts himself forth as Peter's equal: *On the contrary, when they saw that to me was committed the preaching of the gospel to the uncircumcised, just as to Peter the apostolate to the circumcised . . . James and Cephas and John . . . extended to me and to Barnabas their right hand in token of perfect accord* (Gal. 2:7-9).

c. This same Paul dares to resist Peter to his face: *But when Cephas came to Antioch, I resisted him to his face, because he was in the wrong* (Gal. 2:11).

Answer: It is simply not true that the history of the primitive Church shows no traces of Peter's primacy (see no. 49e). But if the evidence alleged above strikes anyone as unimpressive in itself, let him weigh it in the light of the attendant circumstances and compare it with the personal prerogatives of the other apostles (see no. 33). As for the instances cited as objections, it is easy to reconcile them with the Catholic doctrine already demonstrated.

a. A mission given "according to command" is quite different from one given "according to counsel, as an adviser may be said to send the king to battle."[31] The president's personal physician can "send" the president to bed, and the diocesan consultors can "send" their bishop to Rome for a decision on an extremely important matter. Peter and John were sent to Samaria not by the command, but by the common and brotherly counsel of the apostles.

b. Paul claims equality with Peter not on the grounds of fulness of pastoral power, but on the basis of the apostolate itself (see no. 57), and of a direct divine mission. The meaning then is that Paul had been especially selected by God for the evangelization of the Gentiles, while Peter's special mission was the evangelization of the Jews.

c. Peter's fulness of jurisdiction did not prevent him from acting a bit imprudently on occasion. Since in the case at hand Peter's conduct was proving an obstacle to the faith and the conversion of the Gentiles, Paul, even though inferior in point of jurisdiction, had every right to correct him with due reverence, especially since *"the preaching of the gospel to the uncircumcised"* [32] had been entrusted to Paul by God in a very special way. For the subject of their altercation was more a matter of the material expansion of the Church than of its government. Consider further the context. St. Paul, eager to show his Galatian converts how zealous he was for their rights as Gentiles, tells them that in defense of those rights he made bold to resist *even Peter.* In the light of the circumstances, this interesting little scene argues more in favor of Peter's primacy than it does against it.[33]

Scholion. The relationship of St. Peter to the other apostles and to St. Paul. 57

1. It was pointed out above (no. 33) that a twofold sort of office can be distinguished in the apostles, namely, the *apostolic* and the *pastoral* (episcopal). St. Peter's primacy pertains to the pastoral office, since it is nothing other than the full power to teach and to rule the Church, once the latter has been established. And so, as far as the *apostolate* itself goes, the other apostles were not inferior to Peter. (This explains, by the way, the meaning of the fathers' frequent assertion that the apostles were on an equal footing.) But in the pastoral office they were subordinate to Peter.[34]

It is true that many theologians teach that each of the apostles received from Christ indefinite or negatively universal jurisdiction.[35] By virtue of this jurisdiction they could exercise episcopal authority over individual churches even though these churches had been founded by another apostle. But even if one accepts this opinion, the jurisdiction of the apostles was on several counts inferior to the fulness of power granted St. Peter. For (*a*) it was not positively universal, and as a result, they, unlike St. Peter, could not exercise authority over all the churches at once, by issuing, for example, universal laws; (*b*) it did not extend to the *other apostles personally*, but these latter were subject to Peter; finally (*c*) it could not be exercised *without* reference to Peter, to whom they all had to subject their churches as to the root and foundation of unity.

And anyway, not all theologians accept this teaching on the negatively universal jurisdiction of the apostles. There are those who teach that Christ gave each of the apostles episcopal jurisdiction (under Peter) over only those churches which they themselves had founded. And in the case where one of the apostles may have engaged in activity beyond the limits of this ordinary power, he could have done so as a delegate of Peter and in accordance with Christ's provisions for the needs peculiar to this first stage of the Church's development.[36]

Finally, if it comes right down to the question of the *exercise of primacy*, it is reasonable to assume that Peter rarely—maybe not even rarely—exercised his power over the other apostles, not because he had no right to do so, but because the outstanding qualities of the apostles gave him little occasion to use that right. In fact, the frequency of charisms and the extraordinary circumstances of this early period must have made it quite unnecessary for him to use his power of primacy very frequently.

58   2. The Catholic doctrine on the primacy is not weakened by the fairly common custom of calling Peter and Paul together the *princes of the apostles;*[37] for (*a*) custom itself shows that when Paul is linked with Peter as a "prince of the apostles," he is *not* so called in the same sense, for while Peter alone is very often called *the Prince of the Apostles*,[38] Paul alone is hardly ever so called; (*b*) Venantius Fortunatus has explained *the sense in which* the title "princes of the apostles" is used: "Peter is the prince *of the keys*, and Paul is foremost *in dogma*" i.e., in the preaching of the truth.[39] Since in fact St. Paul worked harder than all the others in the establishment of the Church,[40] i.e., in the exercise of the apostolate in the restricted sense, he is rightfully called a prince in the apostolate and the apostle *par excellence*. Furthermore, Innocent X adjudged and declared heretical the proposition of Antoine Arnauld, who affirmed the "absolute equality of St. Peter and St. Paul, without any subjection or subordination of St. Paul to St. Peter in the supreme power and rule of the universal Church" (DB 1091).

59   PROPOSITION 2: *It was Christ's will that the primacy, begun with St. Peter, should continue forever.*

It is true that the primacy can be called in a certain sense the personal prerogative of St. Peter, since it was conferred on him alone rather than on the other apostles. But it is not a personal prerogative in the sense that when Peter died, it died with him; it is a permanent office which must, in accordance with Christ's will, go on forever, as long as the Church itself continues to exist.

This thesis is a *dogma of faith*. The Vatican Council declared: "If anyone says that it is not by the institution of Christ the Lord

THE CHURCH'S NATURE

Himself or of divine right that St. Peter has an everlasting line of successors in the primacy over the universal Church, let him be anathema" (Constitution *De ecclesia Christi,* chap. 2; DB 1825).

Proof:

1. From the *nature and purpose of the primacy,* assuming as proven the Church's indestructibility.

Primacy *by its very nature* is a permanent or ordinary office, for it is connected, not with the establishment of the Church, but with its conservation and government. Besides, it is intimately bound up with the very constitution of the Church, and this constitution was certainly not to be changed once the apostles had died.

The *purpose* of primacy, as can easily be proved by the words of our Lord in Matthew 16, is to secure and preserve the Church's unity.[41] But this purpose must always be pursued; after the apostolic age its realization is harder because charisms have ceased and the Church is more widespread. The conclusion is evident.

2. From *the words of Christ.* The whole question can be summed up as follows: When Christ promised and conferred the primacy, did He address His words to Peter as to an individual who was soon to die, or to that same Peter as to a man who was to go on living in an unending line of successors? Not the former but the latter alternative is definitely the one to be maintained.

   a. The *words of promise.* Peter is to do for the Church what a foundation does for a house. But the foundation supports a house not only when it is first built, but continuously: *as long as the house lasts.* In like manner, Peter is to support the Church by his authority as long as the latter shall last. But Peter as a physical person cannot do this; so he must do it as a juridical person living on in his successors.

   Again, by his authority, Peter is to make the indestructibility of the Church a reality; for the words, *"and the gates of hell shall not prevail against it"* are joined in a causal relationship with the preceding words. But it is impossible for anyone to make a society indestructible simply through the influence of his rule, unless he unceasingly exercises that influence.

   b. The *words of bestowal.* Peter is charged with the duty of feeding Christ's lambs and sheep, and this means *all* His lambs and sheep. But the faithful and the bishops of succeeding generations certainly belong to the flock of Christ just as truly as those who were living at the time of the apostles. And so, Peter is to feed them too, by living on in his successors.[42]

3. The *testimony of the ancients* corroborates this conclusion. They say, for example,

a. That Peter lives, rules, and teaches in the person of his successors. Thus wrote Philip, a priest and delegate of the See of Rome at the Council of Ephesus, referring to Peter as "he who lives and exercises judicial power to the present day and forevermore in the person of his successors" (*Acta concilii Ephesini* 3).

b. They affirm that they have received the power of the keys in or through Peter. By speaking thus they indicate that the primacy was given to Peter not as a private person, but as a public person, to serve the interests of the Church and to remain in the Church as long as the latter lasts. Tertullian: "Remember that on this occasion the Lord left His keys [of the kingdom of heaven] to Peter and through Peter to the Church" (*Scorpiace* 10).[43]

c. They attest that Peter's primacy continues on in the bishop of Rome. St. Peter Chrysologus: "Whatever the question may be, we urge you to give obedient heed to the writings of the most holy pope of the city of Rome, for St. Peter, who lives on and governs in his own See, offers the truth of the faith to all who seek it" (*Epistula ad Eutychen* 2).

PROPOSITION 3. *Peter's primacy lives on in the Roman pontiff.*[44]

The object of this proposition is to determine precisely where the primacy, once conferred on Peter with a view to its perpetual continuance, is now factually preserved.

Strictly speaking, the primacy could have been preserved without being tied to an episcopal see, in such a way, for example, that the whole business of selecting a successor in the primacy, each time that this should prove necessary, would be the task of the whole episcopal college. But such a procedure, aside from the fact that it would be quite awkward, is in fact not followed. As matters actually stand, the primacy is connected with a particular see, that of Rome, so that whoever is legitimately elected bishop of Rome receives, by that very fact, primacy over the universal Church. It will be indicated later by what right this bond was effected and whether it could ever possibly be undone (nos. 165–166).

THE CHURCH'S NATURE

The present proposition has often been defined by the Church's infallible teaching authority. For example, the Vatican Council asserted: "If anyone says that the Roman pontiff is not St. Peter's successor in the same primacy [as was his], let him be anathema" (Constitution *De ecclesia*, chap. 2; DB 1825; see the Council of Florence, DB 694).

Proof:

1. *Argument of exclusion:* by a process of elimination. Since Christ decreed that Peter should have a never-ending line of successors in the primacy, there must always have been and there must still be someone in the Church who wields his primacy. But aside from the Roman pontiff, no one has ever seriously, or with any semblance of truth, put himself forward as Peter's successor; and no one else has ever been acknowledged as such. Therefore one must admit either that the Roman pontiff wields Peter's primacy, or else that this primacy, contrary to Christ's will, has passed out of existence.

2. *Genealogical argument:* by tracking down the source of Roman primacy; i.e., by showing the route along which the primacy came to the bishops of Rome. Church history proves that Peter came to Rome, became the bishop of its church, and exercised this office until his death. Even non-Catholics now generally admit that he was in Rome and suffered martyrdom there during the Neronian persecution.[45] They usually deny that he was bishop of the church at Rome, but the fact stands irrefutably established by the abundant testimony of early writers.[46] Really, for Peter to have been bishop of Rome, nothing else is required than that he have habitually taken special care of this church throughout the last period of his life. He may even have gone elsewhere occasionally—even for quite a while—to preach the gospel to other peoples, and may even have appointed an auxiliary bishop. Accordingly, anyone who admits that Peter stayed at Rome for some years, either continuously or intermittently, implicitly admits that he functioned as bishop of Rome. Obviously he would have had no reason to stay at Rome or to keep on returning thither if it were not for the fact that he had chosen to watch over the church of that city in a special way.

If it be granted, then, that Peter died as bishop of Rome, it must be granted also that his successor in the episcopal see of

Rome was his successor in the primacy also, unless the contrary be proven on other evidence. It is clear that the primacy was to continue. Now, as a general rule, the rights connected with a see are transmitted along with the see, and this must be presumed to have happened in the present instance, unless it can be shown that either Christ or Peter made some other provision for handing on the primacy. But no trace, not even the slightest, of any other arrangement has ever been discovered. The conclusion is evident.[47]

63   3. *Historical argument:* by citing testimony and facts from the first centuries. Both testimony and facts show clearly that the Roman pontiff always claimed the primacy for himself, and that the Church acknowledged this primacy.[48]

However, it is not necessary—nor could one reasonably expect—to find the primacy of the Roman pontiffs as intensely active and as perfectly understood right at the beginning as it was in ensuing centuries. The doctrine and the institutions of Christianity are like the grain of mustard seed whose natural potentialities neither unfold all at once nor are easily and fully grasped by all at the moment it is planted. If anyone gives due consideration to the condition of the infant Church and to the violence of the times in which it was born, he will readily understand why Peter's successors exercised their rights over far distant churches neither frequently nor solemnly. As a consequence, these latter did not often advert to the fact of Rome's primacy, of the influence of which they had as yet had little practical experience. In fact, when the occasion arose, they felt little difficulty in resisting it.[49] Suffice it, then, to show that the seed was truly there right from the beginning, and that it fructified, growing with the passing of the years into a massive tree.

a. Towards the end of the *first century*, while the Apostle John was still alive, the church of Rome—or, more specifically, St. Clement of Rome—dispatched a letter to the church of Corinth, which St. Paul had founded. In this letter he sharply scolded the Corinthians and proved that he had real authority over them.

> Disgraceful, beloved, indeed, exceedingly disgraceful and unworthy of your training in Christ, is the report that the well-established and ancient Church of the Corinthians is, thanks to one or two individuals, in revolt against the presbyters.—47. 6. You, therefore, the prime movers of the schism, submit to the

presbyters, and, bending the knees of your hearts, accept correction and change your minds.—57. 1.
But should any disobey what has been said by Him [Christ] through us, let them understand that they will entangle themselves in transgression and no small danger. But for our part we shall be innocent of this sin. . . . —59. 1–2.
You certainly will give us the keenest pleasure if you prove obedient to what we have written through the Holy Spirit, . . . We are sending trustworthy and prudent men, . . . that they may be witnesses between you and us.—63. 2–3.[50]

Now this "very powerful"[51] letter was reverently received by the Corinthians; and it was the custom for a long time after that to read it in the public assemblies of the faithful both in Corinth and in many other churches.[52]

b. From the *second century*, St. Ignatius Martyr starts his *Epistle to the Romans* in this fashion: "Ignatius, . . . to the Church that has found mercy . . . which also presides in the chief place of the Roman territory; a church worthy of God . . . and presiding in love" (ACW translation). This salutation is altogether different from those which St. Ignatius used in his other letters, and it intimates the primacy of the Roman church. The verb *prokathêsthai* (to preside) in this context can mean nothing other than "to have pre-eminence or authority." Elsewhere Ignatius uses the same verb to indicate the relationship of a bishop to his priests and deacons (*Epistula ad Trallianos* 6. 1). And so the church which is "in the chief place of the Roman territory" has or exercises authority.[53] But over whom? *prokathēmené tês agápēs* (*presiding over love*). The word *agápē* Ignatius also uses elsewhere (*ibid.* 13. 1) to mean the assembly of love, the assembly of the brethren, the Church. The meaning, then, is that the church of Rome is in command of the Church, and indeed of the universal Church: *tês agápēs* without any restriction.[54] This meaning jibes neatly with what he says later of the Roman church: "You have taught others. All I want is that the lessons you inculcate in initiating disciples remain in force" (*Epistula ad Romanos* 3. 1.), as well as with what he goes on to say about his own soon-to-be-widowed church: "Jesus Christ alone will be her Bishop, together with your love" (*ibid.* 9. 1).

During the reign of Pope Eleutherius (174–189), St. Irenaeus taught that there were two ways to learn the truth. One is to ascertain the common opinion of the churches, whose bishops trace their episcopal lineage back to the apostles through an unbroken line of succession. The other, and easier, way is to seek out the traditional teaching of "the greatest, most ancient, and well known Church, founded by the two most glorious Apostles, Peter and Paul at Rome."[55] Then he goes on to tell why it suffices to consult the church of Rome: "For with this Church, because of its more efficient leadership, all Churches must agree, that is to say, the faithful of all places, because in it the apostolic tradition has been always preserved by the (faithful) of all places."[56] The Roman church, then, enjoys unique pre-eminence over all the others, and consequently all other churches must be of one mind with this one church in believing.

Pope St. Victor (189–199) urged that episcopal synods convene in many provinces to discuss the Quartodeciman question.[57] He ordered the bishops of proconsular Asia under threat of penalties to abandon the Quartodeciman practice and was in fact ready to excommunicate those who would not comply. It seems, however, that he was prevailed upon, particularly by St. Irenaeus, to refrain from carrying out this harsh measure.[58]

Again, throughout the second century, St. Polycarp (Eusebius HE 4. 14), St. Irenaeus while still a priest (*ibid.* 5. 4), Hegesippus (*ibid.* 4. 22), and Abercius of Hieropolis came to Rome with questions concerning faith and discipline. Visits of this kind tie in very nicely with the doctrine of primacy, and apart from it are hard to explain, especially since we never read of a Roman bishop going elsewhere to seek advice.

65   c. In the *third century:*[59] Tertullian had already become a Montanist when he quite clearly attested to the teaching of Catholics on the primacy of the Roman pontiff. He inveighed against Pope Callistus (217–222) as follows: "I also hear that an edict, indeed a peremptory one, has been issued. The sovereign pontiff, that is, the bishop of bishops, issues an edict: 'I forgive the sins of adultery and fornication for those who have done penance.'"[60] Even though these words do not perhaps prove that the bishop of Rome was at that time dignified by the title "Bishop of bishops," they show at least that in this matter Callistus acted as head of the bishops, i.e., that he exercised primacy.[61]

St. Cyprian called the church of Rome the "parent-stem and root of the Catholic Church." He is of the opinion that to be in communion with Cornelius the bishop of Rome is the same as "to esteem and maintain the unity of the Catholic Church" (*Epistula* 44. 3). He writes to this same Cornelius (251–253) on the subject of some African schismatics:

> They have the audacity to set sail and to carry letters from schismatic and profane people to the throne of Peter and to the chief church, the well-spring of priestly unity, and to ignore the fact that these were the Romans whose faith was extolled in the preaching of the apostles, men to whom faithlessness could have no access.[62]

Then he urges Pope Stephen to excommunicate Marcian of Arles, who had gone over to Novatian, and to appoint another bishop in his stead:

> Let letters be dispatched by you to the province and to the people residing at Arles for the purpose of excommunicating Marcian and of appointing another to take his place. . . . Let us know clearly who has been appointed at Arles in the place of Marcian, so that we may know to whom to direct our brethren and to whom we should address our correspondence.—*Epistula* 67. 3–5.[63]

Pope St. Stephen (254–257) forbade Firmilian[64] and other bishops of Asia Minor, under threat of excommunication, to repeat a baptism which had been administered by a heretic (Eusebius HE 7. 5). He issued the same decree against St. Cyprian and very many bishops of Africa, reminding them of the "rank of his episcopate" and insisting that he was "the successor of Peter, upon whom the foundations of the Church were placed." In fact, when St. Cyprian and his partisans refused to obey, he refused to have anything more to do with them.[65]

Dionysius, Bishop of Alexandria, while engaged in controversy with Sabellius, made some rather careless remarks, and was accused of heresy before Pope Dionysius (259–268). He lost no time in "sending a letter to the bishop of Rome, in which he exonerated himself and insisted that the charge was trumped up and false."[66]

d. In the *fourth century:* When the Eusebians had forced St. Athanasius, Bishop of Alexandria, from his see, both Athanasius and Eusebius appealed to Pope Julius I (337–352). Julius insisted that Athanasius be restored to his see and at the same time upbraided the Eusebian bishops for having, without his authority, dared to depose bishops, indeed the bishop of Alexandria himself: "Do you not know that the usual procedure is that letters be first sent to us and that a just decision be passed from here? If, then, any such suspicion fell upon the bishop there, notice of it should have been sent to the bishop of this place."[67] According to Socrates,

> At the same time, Paul, the bishop of Constantinople, Asclepas of Gaza, Marcellus of Ancyra, and Lucius of Adrianople, all having been charged with various offences and evicted from their churches, arrived in the imperial city. There each presented his case before Julius, bishop of the city of Rome, and he, in accordance with the church of Rome's special prerogative, sent them back to the East backed up by commendatory letters. He restored to each of them his see and at the same time reprimanded those who had been so rash as to depose them [the aforementioned bishops].[68]

St. Jerome wrote to Pope Damasus (366–384):

> As I follow no leader save Christ, so I communicate with none but your blessedness, that is, with the chair of Peter. For this, I know, is the rock on which the Church is built. This is the house where alone the Paschal Lamb can be rightly eaten. This is the ark of Noe, and he who is not in it will perish when the flood prevails. . . . He who gathers not with you scatters; he that is not of Christ is of antichrist.—*Epistulae* 15. 2.

Elsewhere he wrote: "When I was helping Damasus, bishop of the city of Rome, with the records of the Church, and was replying to requests for advice from synods in the east and in the west . . ." (*Epistulae* 193. 10).

In 385, Pope Siricius wrote to Himerius, bishop of Tarragona:

> We do not refuse to give a suitable answer to your request for advice, since, considering the office we hold, we have no right to dissemble, we are not free to keep silence. . . . We bear the burdens of all who are heavy laden, or rather St. Peter the apostle bears them in our person—he who, we trust, protects us in all the affairs of his office, and watches over all his successors.—ML, 13, 1133.

THE CHURCH'S NATURE

St. Augustine extols the church of Rome, "in which the ruling power of the apostolic see has always flourished" (*Epistula* 43. 7).

e. In the *fifth century:* St. John Chrysostom, having been unjustly deposed by Theophilus of Alexandria in a council composed of many bishops, wrote to Pope Innocent I (402–417): "I beg you to write that these deeds so unjustly perpetrated have no force— as, in fact, they have no force by their very nature—and that they who have been caught acting in this unjust fashion be subjected to the penalties prescribed by ecclesiastical law" (*Epistula prima ad Innocentem* 1).

The history of the Council of Ephesus (431) furnishes brilliant testimony in favor of the primacy of the Roman pontiff. Pope Celestine had previously (430) condemned Nestorius. He appointed St. Cyril of Alexandria to preside over the council as his proxy. He ordered his legates to be mindful of the dignity of the Roman see and not to become embroiled in arguments, but to pass objective judgment on the opinions expressed by others. He wrote to the synod that he was sending delegates "to be present at the proceedings and to put into execution our previous decisions."[69] One of the delegates, Philip, a priest, explained to the synod in person by what right Celestine took all these steps, and no one raised an objection:

> No one has the slightest doubt—in fact, everyone has known it for centuries now—that our most blessed St. Peter, prince and chief of the apostles, pillar of faith and foundation of the Catholic Church, received the keys of the kingdom from our Lord Jesus Christ. He continues to live and to rule to this very day, and always will, in the person of his successors. It is his present successor and vicar, our holy and most blessed Pope Celestine, bishop, who has sent us to this holy synod to make up for his absence.[70]

The primacy was no less evident in the Council of Chalcedon (451). The fathers followed the previous decision of Pope St. Leo I regarding Eutyches, and in so doing, cried out, "Peter has spoken through Leo!"[71] They openly proclaimed that Leo, in the person of his delegates, presided over them "as the head over the members." On the subject of Dioscorus, the deposed bishop of Alexandria, they said that "he raved insanely against even him to whom the care of the vineyard has been entrusted by the Saviour, i.e., against even your Apostolic Holiness, and considered excommunicating you who are intent upon uniting the body of the Church." Finally, they asked explicitly—but to no avail—that the bishop of Rome approve the privileges which they (in Canon 28) had decreed for the see of Constantinople over the opposition of the Pope's legates: "We ask, therefore, that you approve our decision with decrees of your own, and that as we have tried to be in harmony with our Head wherever the good was involved, so your Headship may grant your sons whatever is fitting."[72] It is worthy of note that among the fathers at Ephesus and Chalcedon there were very few from the West.

68 The above testimonies will suffice, for no one in the ensuing centuries denied the fact of the primacy of the Roman pontiff.

Objection: As an objection, some cite canon 28 of the Council of Chalcedon, in which the fathers assert that the privileges enjoyed by the Roman see spring from a concession made by the Church itself:

> In thorough accord with the decrees of the saints, and in acknowledgment of the previously read canon of the 150 bishops,[73] we too make the same decisions and decrees regarding the privileges of the church of Constantinople, the New-Rome. For it was with full right that the fathers granted privileges (*tà presbeîa apodedōkasi*) to the see of ancient Rome, since it was the imperial city. But the same consideration has led the 150 bishops to grant equal privileges (*tà ísa presbeîa*) to the see of New-Rome. They rightly judge that a city which has been enriched with both empire and a senate, and [in secular affairs] enjoys equal privileges with the ancient queen Rome [should] be like her given a position of prestige in ecclesiastical affairs, too, and take rank second to her alone (*deutéran met' ekeínēn hypárchousan*).[74]

Answer. Worthy of note above all is the fact that this canon, passed, first of all, while the delegates of the Roman see were absent, and over their subsequent protests, was expressly vetoed by St. Leo I;[75] and canon 3 of Constantinople, to which Chalcedon appeals, had never been approved by the Roman pontiff, and had not even been sent to him for study.

Secondly, the privileges which, in the opinion of Chalcedon, the "fathers" had granted the see of Rome, are apparently to be understood not as touching upon primatial jurisdiction, but rather as those rights which the bishop of Rome enjoys as Patriarch of the West. Obviously those "equal privileges" which the synods of Constantinople and Chalcedon were trying to get for the Byzantine see, were simply patriarchal prestige and jurisdiction. For the rest, it is clearly false and contrary to factual history to say that the Roman see received either its primatial or patriarchal rights as the result of any decree of the "fathers," i.e., as the result of a concession made by the Church. No other reason can be found for the fathers of Chalcedon having made this assertion—at least as regards patriarchal rights—than that they could find no other way to increase the prestige of the Byzantine see.

Scholion. Why do the Roman pontiffs often profess to be acting **69**
"on the authority of the holy apostles Peter and Paul"?

Peter alone was bishop of Rome, in the strict and ordinary sense, and the Roman pontiffs succeed only to the Chair of Peter. That is why they claim just as constantly that they alone are the successors of Peter.[76] But since St. Paul worked with St. Peter in founding and instructing the church at Rome, and together with him honored the city by his martyrdom there, it is not at all surprising that the church of Rome has, from earliest times, honored both apostles as its founders, fathers, and principal patrons. That is why the images of both are affixed—not always, but often—to pontifical documents; and that is why the popes, when taking some solemn action, often appeal to the authority or threaten the wrath of both alike.[77] But expressions of this sort do not at all signify that the pope is related to both apostles in the same way, or that he derives from St. Paul another type of authority different from that which he has as the successor of Peter. St. Paul is mentioned rather on grounds of honor and patronage. Furthermore, it is not unseemly for the pope, who enjoys the absolute fulness of power entrusted by Christ to the Petro-apostolic college, to call upon, in a special way, those whom universal tradition has called— though for different reasons—"the princes of the apostles."

III. Epilogue 70
The Roman Catholic Church is the true Church of Christ.[78]

From the points thus far treated, it is clear as day that the true

Church of Christ is none other than the Roman Catholic Church. Surely, if Christ entrusted His universal Church to Peter and to Peter's successors in perpetuity, and if the Roman pontiffs are Peter's successors, then the true Church of Christ is the one which gives steadfast obedience to the Roman pontiffs. There may be also other societies which glory in the name of Christ; there may even be some which are governed by bishops claiming apostolic succession; but they do not have the Chair of Peter, on whom Christ founded the Church. Therefore they do not belong to the household of Christ; they do not follow him to whom Christ entrusted the feeding of His lambs and of His sheep; and so they do not belong to the flock of Christ.

Even the early fathers employed this criterion for distinguishing Christ's true Church from spurious counterfeits:

St. Cyprian:

> The proof is simple and convincing, being summed up in a matter of fact. The Lord says to Peter: *'I say to thee, that thou art Peter and upon this rock I will build my Church'* . . . And He says to him again after the resurrection: *'Feed my sheep.'* It is on him that He builds the Church, and to him that He entrusts the sheep to feed.[79]

St. Ambrose tells this story in praise of his brother, Satyrus. When the latter had been shipwrecked upon a foreign shore, esteeming above all else the grace of the true faith, he asked the local bishop "whether he was in union with the Catholic bishops, i.e., with the Roman Church" (*De excessu Satyri* 1. 47).

St. Optatus says to the Donatists:

> You cannot disclaim knowledge of the fact that in the city of Rome the episcopal see was entrusted first to Peter . . . in order that in this one see unity might be preserved by all. As a result, anyone who would set up another see in opposition to the unique see would become automatically a schismatic and a sinner. Peter was the first to occupy this see, and his successor was Linus. To Linus succeeded . . . Siricius, our contemporary and colleague, with whom the whole world, through the interchange of letters of peace, is in accord with us in one bond of communion.—*De schismate Donatistarum* 2. 2–3.[80]

St. Epiphanius, after having listed the series of Roman bishops, went on, "Let no one wonder at the fact that we have given such an accurate, detailed list, for it is through these men that we can always find out what is true and sure" (*Haereses* 27. 6).

St. Jerome: "The Church is split into three factions [he is referring to the situation in the East, where party spirit was rife], and each of them is anxious to seize me for its own.... Meanwhile I cry out insistently, 'Anyone in union with the Chair of Peter has me on his side'" (*Epistula ad Damasum* 6).

St. Augustine:

> Come, brethren [he is addressing the Donatists], if you want to be grafted on to the vine. It is a shame to see you lopped off and lying there like that. Make a list of the priests who trace their origin back to the see of Peter itself, and in that list of fathers see who succeeded whom. That Rock [the see of Peter] is the very one which cannot be vanquished by the haughty gates of hell.—*Psalmus contra partem Donati* "S."

Now in truth if history attests to the fact, and it does, that the Roman Catholic Church is identical with the Church of Christ, then again we have a most valid confirmation of the conclusion at which we arrived in the treatise on *The True Religion*—to wit, the divine truth of the Catholic religion. For Christ's Church cannot fail, and this is true also in the sense that it cannot cease to preach and to practice the divine religion of Christ (no. 19). Consequently, if the Roman Catholic Church is the true Church of Christ, it doubtless has in its possession the religion of Christ, genuine and unsullied.

Notes

1. See, however, V. Soloviev, *Russia and the Universal Church*, translated by Herbert Rees (London, 1948), p. 107:
   > The perfect circle of the Universal Church requires a unique center, not so much for its perfection as for its very existence. The Church upon earth, called to gather in the multitude of nations, must, if she is to remain an active society, possess a definite universal authority to set against national divisions; if she is to enter the current of history and undergo continual change and adaptation in her external circumstances and relationships and yet preserve her identity, she requires an authority essentially conservative but nevertheless active, fundamentally unchangeable though outwardly adaptable; and finally, if she is set amid the frailty of

man to assert herself in reaction against all the powers of evil, she must be equipped with an absolutely firm and impregnable foundation stronger than the gates of hell. Now we know on the one hand that Christ foresaw the necessity of such a monarchical principle and therefore conferred on a single individual supreme and undivided authority over this Church; and on the other hand we see that of all the ecclesiastical powers in the Christian world there is only one which perpetually and unchangingly preserves its central and universal character; and at the same time is especially connected by an ancient and widespread tradition with him to whom Christ said: "Thou art Peter, and it is upon this rock that I will build my Church; and the gates of hell shall not prevail against it." Christ's words could not remain without their effect in Christian history and the principal phenomenon in Christian history must have an adequate cause in the word of God. Where then have Christ's words to Peter produced a corresponding effect except in the chair of Peter? Where does that chair find adequate cause except in the promise made to Peter?

2. See P. Batiffol, *Catholicisme et Papauté, Les difficultés anglicanes et russes* (1925).

3. See Journet, *Church of the Word, op. cit.,* p. 422, where this significant quote from Cajetan appears:

To understand her regime, you have only to look at her beginnings. She did not emerge from any collectivity or community whatever. She was formed around Jesus Christ her Head, her Ruler, from whom all her life, perfection and power came to her. *You have not chosen me,* He said, *but I have chosen you.* Thus from the birth of the Church her constitution clearly appears. Authority does not reside in the community; it never passes, as in the civil order, from the community to one or to several heads. By its very nature, and from the very outset, it resides in a single recognizable prince. Since this prince is the Lord Jesus, who is to live and to reign yesterday, to-day, and for ever, it results that in natural right it was for Him and not for the ecclesiastical community to choose for Himself a vicar, whose role it would be not to represent the ecclesiastical community, born to obey not to command; but to represent a Prince, the natural Lord of this community. That, then, was what Our Lord Himself deigned to do when, having risen, before ascending to heaven, He chose, as St. John tells us, the Apostle Peter alone for His Vicar. And just as in natural right the Prince of the Church does not draw His authority from the Church, so neither does His Vicar, who depends upon Him and not upon the Church (*Apologia de comparata auctoritate Papae et Concilii,* chap. 1, nos. 450–452).

4. The primacy does not imply by its very nature the power of *orders.* That is why if a layman were to be elected supreme pontiff, he would immediately have full teaching and ruling authority over the universal Church, but would enjoy no power of orders until he was ordained.

5. See J. C. Fenton, *"Vicarius Christi,"* AER, 110 (1944), 459 ff.

6. See DB 1503.

7. Constitution *De ecclesia Christi,* chap. 1 (conclusion); see chap. 3 (conclusion); DB 2145.

8. Matt. 16:13–19. This passage will be studied thoroughly in an appendix. For the present, the following remarks are directed against Harnack and others who claim that this passage is a later interpolation (and see H. Dieck-

THE CHURCH'S NATURE

mann, "Neuere Ansichten über die Echtheit der Primatstelle," Bibl. [1923], p. 189). The text is found in all the MSS and early translations, and so Schanz could write with perfect justification: "This powerful passage is critically as incontestable as any passage in the first Gospel" (*Apologie*, 3rd ed., III, 486. See A. Sloet, *Heeft Christus het Pausdom niet gesticht?* [1913]; H. Dieckmann, *De ecclesia*, 1, no. 350 ff.) And the fact that the other evangelists, notably SS. Mark and Luke, omitted this promise of our Lord is not proof to the contrary. For in the light of the special purpose for which they wrote, this text was not so important to them. Anyway, SS. Luke and John do testify to St. Peter's primacy, but in a different way (Luke 22:31; John 21:15). Plausible reasons for the omission are to be found, e.g., in A. Michiels, *op. cit.*, p. 36 ff.; A. Mertens, *op. cit.*, p. 35; T. Zapalena, *op. cit.*, I, 216, 217.

9. See Matt. 7:24–27.

10. *The gates of hell* (*pýlai hádou*) are taken by many as referring to the abode of the dead or to *death* itself, and would thus mean that death, the common lot of all other things, will not destroy the Church. But the more common opinion is that the gates of hell signify the city or *stronghold of the devil*, i.e., whatever the devil may devise against the Church either by himself or through the agency of wicked people. See Knabenbauer on this passage, and the article of Holzhey in *Theol. Prakt. Quartals.* (Linz), 12, 311; CCHS, 704c.

11. See K. Adam, "Zum auszerkanonischen und kanonischen Sprachgebrauch von Binden und Lösen," ThQ, 49 (1914), 161.

12. For *governing*, since Peter will get the keys not for the purpose of establishing but of ruling the kingdom of heaven on earth. That is why it will not be within his competence to change anything pertaining strictly to the constitution given the Church by its divine Founder.

13. *Son of John:* this is a popular rather than a scientific equivalent of the Aramaic *bar yona'*. "Son of Jonas" would be closer to the original. *Ioannes* (John) was a very common Greek name, and was chosen perhaps because of its phonetic similarity to *yona'*. An analogous case might be that of Saul-Paul, also influenced apparently by phonetic rather than etymological considerations. See D. Buzy on this passage in Pirot's *La Sainte Bible*, 9 (Paris, 1946).

14. Some commentators hold that the *lambs* indicate the less perfect Christians and the *sheep* the perfect. Others understand the *lambs* of the ordinary faithful and the *sheep* of the rulers, i.e., apostles, bishops. Still others are of the opinion that both metaphors embrace all Christians without distinction. See Knabenbauer on this passage; J. B. Bauer, " 'Oves meae' quaenam sunt?" VD, 32 (1954), 321 ff.

15. See Gen. 17:5 (Abraham); 32:38 (Israel); Num. 13:17 (Josue); Matt. 1:21 (Jesus).

16. Matt. 10:2–3; Mark 3:16–19; Luke 6:14–16; Acts 1:13.

17. With the exception of just two passages: John 1:44 and Gal. 2:9. As for the latter passage, the situation which forms the setting for St. Paul's remark may well explain the inverted order. He is assuring the Galatians that his "Gospel" received full approval of the apostles at Jerusalem. Since he stressed in his preaching the freedom of Gentile converts from the observance of the Mosaic Law, it was quite significant for his special purpose to point

out that *even James,* who was personally much attached to that Law, had extended to him the right hand of amicable agreement. He expressed this nuance by mentioning James ahead of Peter in this instance. I Cor. 1:12 and 3:22 are not to be considered as exceptions to the general procedure, for here the order is from the lesser to the greater, and so Peter is most fittingly named last of all.

18. Mark 1:36; Acts 2:14; 5:29.
19. Luke 22:31–32. This passage will be studied more thoroughly in the section dealing with the infallibility of the Roman pontiff.
20. See J. A. Fitzmyer, S.J., "The Function of the Papacy," AER, 121 (1949), 34 ff.
21. See CCHS, 819d–e.
22. Gal. 1:18; see X. Roiron, "Saint Paul témoin de la primauté de Saint Pierre," RSR (1913), 489. The Greek verb used here by St. Paul is very interesting: *historēsai.* It means more than just "to see" and connotes making the personal acquaintance of an *important* person; and, in employing it here, St. Paul pays subtle homage to the authority wielded by St. Peter over the primitive Church. See M.-J. Lagrange, *Saint Paul: Epître aux Galates* (Paris, 1950), p. 17.
23. *Commentarium in epistulam ad Romanos* 6. 5 (towards the end); see *Homilia in Exodum* 5. 4.
24. In the edition of Lamy, IV, 684.
25. Homily on the phrase *Hoc scitote* 4. Worth reading are the following: N. Card. Marini, *Il primato di S. Pietro e dei suoi successori in San Giovanni Crisostomo* (1922); M. Jugie, "St. Jean Chrysostome et la primauté de S. Pierre," EO (1908), p. 5 ff.
26. However, it is the view of the majority of modern exegetes that the prophets mentioned here are those of the *New Testament* exclusively: those charismatics who assisted in the preaching of the gospel and the consolidation of the faith. Similarly, the better view seems to be that which sees in the "apostles" of this passage not the twelve apostles in the strict sense, but those early missionaries who, assisted by charismatic gifts, helped spread the Church. At any rate, it is clear from both the context and the meaning of the words involved that there is here no question of *jurisdictional authority,* but simply of the *evangelization* upon which the faith of the Christians rests as on a solid foundation. See J. Huby, S.J., *Les épîtres de la captivité* (Paris, 1947), p. 187; Eph. 4:11.
27. Homily *De poenitentia,* in the *Opera* of St. Basil. Msgr. Journet seems to touch the heart of the matter with this remark:
> On a more metaphysical plane we may see the opposition [Catholic vs. Protestant] as one between a dogmatic view of the analogy of being, in accordance with which the divine privileges, especially divine sanctity, can be communicated analogically to creatures—as existence once was—without affecting adversely the divine transcendence, but rather manifesting it. On the other hand we have a dogmatic view of the uniqueness of being, which can only safeguard the divine transcendence by denying any possibility for the divine privileges to be communicated, especially divine sanctity: either (a) to the humanity of Christ because of the fear

of Monophysitism; or (b) to creatures because of the fear of idolatry.—*The Primacy of Peter, op. cit.,* p. 36–37; see also p. 57.

28. *Epistle to the Patriarch of Constantinople* ML, 214, 760.

29. Even now we still pray as follows on the Vigil of the Feast of SS. Peter and Paul: "We beseech Thee, almighty God, that Thou suffer no disturbance to unsettle us whom Thou hast founded on the confession of Thine apostles as on a rock."

30. *Historia Ecclesiastica Saec. I,* diss. 4. 3, 2. A full discussion of the difficulties occasioned by some passages in the fathers may be found in Palmieri, *De Romano Pontifice,* Thesis 1 (second edition), p. 317 ff.; see the short but excellent study of J. Crehan, S.J., "Scripture, Tradition and the Papacy," *Scripture,* 7 (1955), 6 ff.

31. S.Th., I, q. 43, a. 1, *corpus.*

32. Of the early fathers, Clement of Alexandria thought that the Cephas reproved by St. Paul was someone other than St. Peter. Others, following Origen's lead, thought that the reproach was just an act put on for the benefit of the faithful with St. Peter's consent. Both are, of course, groundless assumptions. But these very obvious attempts to safeguard the prestige of the prince of the apostles show what a deep conviction the fathers had of Peter's prerogatives.

33. See J. W. Moran, S.J., "The Two Pillars of Rome," AER, 130 (1954), 1–8.

34. According to Cajetan, the apostles were equal *as apostles;* but *as Christ's sheep,* deprived here below of His visible presence, they were entrusted to the care of Peter, the sole pastor (*op. cit.,* cap. 3, no. 23). See C. Journet, *Church of the Word, op. cit.,* p. 144 ff.

35. See Suárez, *De fide,* disp. 10, sect. 1, nos. 2, 25; St. Robert Bellarmine, *De romano pontifice,* lib. 1, cap. 9; Cavagnis, *op. cit.,* II (3rd ed.), no. 20, and see also no. 6. *Jurisdiction* is used here in the sense of ruling or governing power, for we are not now considering the constitutive power or apostolate in its strict sense.

36. Billot, *De ecclesia Christi* (Rome, 1927), p. 563 ff. He adds that there is nothing to prevent the jurisdiction which each one *received directly* from Christ from being considered as *derived* from Peter's fulness:

> Since Peter's power clearly depended on Christ, there was nothing to prevent Christ from personally making the apostles as really and truly *sharers* in *this* power as if by Peter's own will and act jurisdiction had been imparted to them. We have in fact a clear example of this when the sovereign pontiff personally appoints someone vicar-general or personally appoints a pastor with the ordinary jurisdiction proper to this office. For then the pastor's jurisdiction is as really and truly a share in the power proper to the bishop as if it had been received from the bishop himself.—*Loc. cit.,* p. 578.

For various views on this matter, see C. Journet, *Church of the Word, op. cit.,* p. 384; J. C. Fenton, "St. Peter and Apostolic Jurisdiction," AER, 120 (1949), 500 ff.

37. See J. W. Moran, S.J., *loc. cit.*

38. See P. Batiffol, "Princeps Apostolorum," RSR (1928), p. 31.

39. *Miscellanea* ix. 2.

40. See I Cor. 15:10; St. Augustine:
When you see a reference to the Apostle, if there is no specification as to which apostle, then no one but Paul is meant, since he is better known than the other apostles because of his epistles and because he worked harder than all of them.—*Contra duas epistulas Pelagianorum* iii. 4.

41. In the words of the Vatican Council:
That the episcopate itself might be one and indivisible, and that the whole vast multitude of the faithful might be preserved in oneness of faith and of communion by a closely knit body of priests, He [Christ] gave Peter charge over the other apostles and thereby established in his person the unfailing principle and visible foundation of both unities.—*Loc. cit.*, Preamble.
When we say that Christ established the primacy of one physical person so that His Church might be one, we do not mean that it would be absolutely impossible for the Church to be one apart from a monarchical primacy. It is just that factually Christ preferred this arrangement. Furthermore, "one person is a more fitting basis of unity than many persons [an aristocracy] would be" (ScG, IV, 76).

42. Some non-Catholics mistakenly attack the perpetuity of the primacy by pointing out that the primacy seems to have been promised and granted to Peter personally as a reward for his faith (Matt. 16:16) and love (John 21:15). They fail to see the distinction between the purpose for which the office was established and the reason for its having been given to Peter rather than to another, say, James.

43. St. Augustine expresses the same opinion when he asserts that the keys were given to Peter as to the *vicegerent of the Church* (*Tractatus CXXIV in Joannis Evangelium* 1. 12; cxxiv. 5; *De agone Christiano* 30, and elsewhere). And indeed he was the vicegerent of the Church, inasmuch as he was its juridical representative, not as a result of any delegation to that office, but "because of the primacy of his apostolate," i.e., after the manner of a father who represents his family or of a king who represents his realm. St. Augustine had a special reason for using this particular terminology quite frequently. It was the Novatian heresy, which denied that the Church had the power to forgive sins, and taught that the keys given to Peter had gone out of existence with him. See Palmieri, *De Romano pontifice*, Thesis I, p. 345.

44. See J. C. Fenton, "The Apostolicity of the Roman See," AER, 118 (1948), 444 ff.; *idem*, "The Local Church of Rome," AER, 122 (1950), 454 ff.

45. Harnack freely admitted that:
Peter's martyrdom at Rome was attacked at one time as the result of the a priori prejudices of the Protestants and later as a result of the a priori prejudices of the critics. . . . But that both were in error is now clear as day to every scholar who doesn't deliberately blind himself to facts.—*Chronologie der altchristlichen Litteratur bis Eusebius*, I, 244; 709.
See also H. Lietzmann, *Petrus und Paulus in Rom* (2nd ed., 1927).

46. See Kneller, "S. Petrus Bischof von Rom," ZkTh (1902), p. 33; P. Hughes, *op. cit.*, I, 75–84; J. Finegan, *Light from the Ancient Past* (Princeton,

1947), p. 374–379; C. Journet, *The Primacy of Peter*, p. 122; S. Lyonnet, S.J., "De ministerio Romano S. Petri ante adventum S. Pauli," VD, 33 (1955), 143 ff. Recent excavations beneath the Basilica of St. Peter have served to corroborate the ancient tradition. They attracted world-wide attention and the literature on them is extensive. The best study of their archaeological significance is J. M. C. Toynbee's "The Shrine of St. Peter and its Setting," *Journal of Roman Studies* (1953), p. 1 ff. The official report fills two large folio volumes entitled *Esplorazioni sotto la Confessione di San Pietro in Vaticano* (Vatican, 1951). See also C. Journet, *loc. cit.*, p. 127–129; R. T. O'Callaghan, S.J., "Recent Excavations Underneath the Vatican Crypts," *The Biblical Archaeologist*, 12 (1949), 2 ff.; "Vatican Excavations and the Tomb of Peter," *ibid.*, 16 (1953), 70 ff.; L. Cristiana, "Excavations at the Vatican," ThD, 2 (1954), 33 ff. The March 27, 1950 issue of *Life* has several pages of excellent photographs taken on the site of the excavations.

47. A distinction must be made between the principal and the secondary questions in the matter. The *principal* question is: does the bishop of Rome have the primacy which was Peter's? The *secondary* one is: how did it come about that the primacy devolved upon the bishop of Rome in preference to all others? These two questions are not at all identical, for it is certain that God could have arranged either directly or through Peter that the primacy continue after Peter in the see of Rome—even if Peter had never held that see. But although the *secondary* question, *the fact of Peter,* must be distinguished (logically) from the fundamental one, it seems advantageous not to separate the two in practice. For by pointing out the route by which Peter's primacy was transmitted to the bishops of Rome, one anticipates the difficulties raised by those adversaries who try to weaken the earliest testimonies regarding the primacy of the Roman pontiffs by saying: "We grant that the Roman Church exercised some sort of primacy from earliest times, but we are not at all sure *what title* it had to such primacy."

48. See J. Chapman, *Studies on the Early Papacy* (1928).

49. See C. Journet, *The Primacy of Peter, op. cit.,* p. 109–110; *Church of the Word, op. cit.,* p. 470 ff.:

> We have seen that, although Peter alone had the power to rule the universal Church, the other Apostles had, equally with him but in an extraordinary way, the power to found local Churches. On one point therefore they were his equals, and his right could seem to be limited and neutralized by theirs. That explains not only why St. Paul could act with so great a freedom, but also why the jurisdictional primacy, which rested first with Peter and was handed on to his successors in the Chair of Rome, was unable to bring all its virtualities to bear at the outset. It was only after the death of the Apostles that it could begin to express itself fully....
> Rome, once more, could not be unaware of the privileges she had inherited from Peter. But in the Churches that lay beyond her immediate influence there appears, after the death of the Apostles, a certain lack of co-ordination. The whole life, the whole immediate unity of each of these Churches, was gathered instinctively round the bishop whose authority therefore stood out clearly, as the letters of St. Ignatius witness, and later, those of St. Cyprian. This instinct was of course right and infallible. But how then would the unity of the universal Church be understood? The in-

sight here was less penetrating. Everything seemed at times to happen as if it were believed that the bishops, being successors of the Apostles, had only to be in agreement with each other to create by their intercommunion, and dispense to the universal Church, the holy unity which was assured her by the Apostles themselves as long as they lived. There precisely lay the loophole for illusion. For the Apostles had received, besides the simple episcopal jurisdiction, an extraordinary power of government which was not to be continued in the bishops their successors, but which, after their decease, would leave full scope to the jurisdictional primacy of Peter and his successors. It was not possible to pass from the government of Apostles to that of the bishops without stepping down to another level; and the thing destined by providence to restore the equilibrium needed for the life and unity of the great Church, was precisely the full exercise of the Roman primacy. Rome never forgot this truth; but it might perhaps be said that she wished the Churches less immediately under her dependence to have time enough to rediscover its divine importance by experience.—p. 470–471.

See *below,* nn. 61–63.

50. ACW translation. See QP, I, 42–53; T. Zapalena, *op. cit.,* I, 279 ff.; J. Crehan, S.J., *op. cit.,* p. 7–10.

51. So wrote St. Irenaeus *Adversus haereses* iii, 3. 3: *hikanotáte.* And Harnack himself admitted:

This letter proves that already at the end of the first century the Roman community . . . watched over the far distant communities with motherly concern, and that at the time it knew how to use language which is an expression all at once of duty, of love, and of authority.—*Dogmengeschichte,* I (3rd ed.), 444.

52. Eusebius HE 3. 16; 4. 23.

53. See QP, I, 69.

54. See LZ, I, 425–426; J. Crehan, S.J., *op. cit.,* 10–11; Dr. Quasten, however, writes as follows:

The reader of the Epistles will soon realize that the word *agápē,* as used in them, has various meanings. F. X. Funk, basing his solution on the fact that in several instances (*Phil.* 11,2; *Smyrn.* 12,1; *Trall.* 13,1 and *Rom.* 9,3) Ignatius makes the term *ágapē* a synonym for the respective Churches, turned the passage in the letter to the Romans by, 'presiding over the bond of love'—'bond of love' being merely another way of saying 'the Church universal'. But more recent investigations by J. Thiele and A. Ehrhard have proved that this translation is scarcely correct, given the context and the trend of Ignatius' thought. Moreover, the old Latin, Syriac, and Armenian versions of Ignatius' Epistles do not favor such a rendition. Rather convincing is the suggestion of J. Thiele, namely, to give the word in this passage a wider and profounder meaning, and to understand by 'agape' the totality of that supernatural life which Christ enkindled in us by his love. Then Ignatius would by the phrase 'presiding in love' assign to the Roman Church authority to guide and lead in that which constitutes the essence of Christianity and of the new order brought into the world by Christ's divine love for men. But, aside from the problem presented by so difficult an expression, the Epistle to the Romans, taken in its entirety, shows beyond cavil that the position of honor accorded the Roman Church is acknowledged by Ignatius as her due, and is founded not on the extent of her charitable influence but on her inherent right to universal ecclesiastical supremacy.—QP, I, 69–70.

55. *Adversus haereses* iii. 3. 2; see J. C. Fenton, "The Apostolicity of the Roman See," AER, 118 (1948), 444 ff.

56. *Ibid.*; the translation is that of J. Quasten (QP, I, 303), who, especially for the translation of the key phrase *propter potentiorem principalitatem*, "because of its more efficient leadership," follows A. Ehrhard, *Die Kirche der Märtyrer* (Munich, 1932). Other translations of this phrase are possible. J. C. Fenton, *art. cit.*, p. 447, seems to prefer "preeminent authority"; another plausible rendering would be "authoritative leadership." The basic meaning is, in any case, quite clear. See G. Schneemann, "De ecclesiae romanae principatu testimonium s. Irenaei," *Coll. Lac.*, 4 (Appendix); J. Forget, "Le témoignage de saint Irénée en faveur de la primauté romaine," ETL (1928), p. 437; T. Zapalena, *op. cit.*, I, 295 ff.; P. Batiffol, *L'église naissante*, p. 251-252; C. Dawson, *The Making of Europe*, p. 33, n.

57. See Hefele, *Conciliengeschichte*, I (2nd ed.), 92. *Quartodeciman:* from the Latin for *fourteenth:*

The actual date of the death and resurrection of Our Lord formed no part of the Church's traditional faith. From very early on the different Churches followed each their own judgment in the matter. By the end of the second century the majority of the Churches, Rome amongst them, had come to celebrate the Resurrection on the Sunday which followed the 14th day of the Jewish month of Nisan. The Churches of the Roman province of Asia (*Asia proconsularis*) celebrated the commemoration of Our Lord's death rather than His resurrection, and kept it on the 14th of Nisan whether that day fell on a Sunday or not. This difference of observance was felt as a serious inconvenience, and, in 154, the pope of the time, Anicetus, made an effort to win over to the Roman and more general practice the bishop whose prestige might have brought in the rest of the Asiatics—St. Polycarp of Smyrna. St. Polycarp invoking the great name of the apostle St. John as the source of the Asiatic tradition, would not be persuaded and endeavoured in his turn to win over Anicetus. But Anicetus, too, had his tradition—the tradition of his predecessors in the Roman see. There the matter rested—the harmony of charity between the two bishops in no way disturbed.

In 167 this difference of practice again came to the fore. . . . Twenty-four or twenty-five years later, . . . the question came up once more and speedily developed into a crisis of the first magnitude.—P. Hughes, *op. cit.*, I, 122–123.

58. Eusebius HE 5. 24. The extent of authority which Victor claimed for himself in this affair is clear from the remark of Lightfoot (*Clemens Romanus*, I, 70), who called him for this very reason the prototype of Hildebrand and Innocent III. See P. Hughes, *op. cit.*, I, 123 ff.

59. See G. Bardy, "L'autorité du siège romain et les controverses du IIIe siècle," RSR (1924), 255; 385.

60. *De pudicitia* 1. 6; see chaps. 13 and 21. In the matter of penitential discipline, there was in the second century a school of thought which sought to limit drastically the power of the Church to forgive sins. Tertullian expressed such views in his *De pœnitentia*. For him an involved process of public penance, the so-called *Exomologesis*, was necessary for the forgiveness of post-baptismal sins, and pardon could be thus obtained once and once only.

The sinner who relapses must thereafter negotiate his own pardon with the mercy of God. Nor is the Exomologesis available for every kind of sin. Three sins notably are excluded—idolatry, murder, and fornication. The Church does not teach that these sins are unforgivable. Merely she will not take it upon herself to forgive those who commit them. They may be admitted to the ranks of the penitent there to remain for the rest of their life. Their penance will avail them much in the sight of God, but the Church does not formally receive them back into her communion. It was with this reservation in the discipline of the Exomologesis that the action of Calixtus I is concerned.—P. Hughes, *op. cit.*, I, 134–135.

61. See J. C. Fenton, "The Apostolicity of the Roman See," AER, 118 (1948), 444 ff.; D. Van den Eynde, *Les normes de l'enseignement chrétien dans la littérature patristique des trois premiers siècles* (Gembloux, 1933), p. 203 ff. J. Quasten, however, is of a different mind:

> The question is, who was this bishop? Many identify him with Pope Callistus (217–222). No grounds for doubting this would exist, if Tertullian were pointing to the same case as caused the schism of Hippolytus, or if it were certain, that the precedent mentioned in *De pudicitia* could have been set only at Rome. Neither the former nor the latter can be established, as pointed out above. The titles *pontifex maximus* and *episcopus episcoporum* do not prove the contrary, because they are employed ironically, like the others, *benignissimus Dei interpres, bonus pastor et benedictus papa*. Moreover, they were unknown at that time as specific designations of the bishop of Rome.—QP, II, 313.

Since such eminent authorities are divided on the relevance of this text, it would seem wise not to press it as an element in the proof of the present thesis.

62. *Epistula* 59. 14. For the expression "the chief church," see C. Kneller, "Cyprian und die römische Kirche," ZkTh (1911), p. 674; A. d'Alès, "Ecclesia principalis," RSR (1921), p. 374.

> Thus the *cathedra Petri* is to him the *ecclesia principalis* and the point of origin of the *unitas sacerdotalis*. However, even in this letter he makes it quite clear that he does not concede to Rome any higher right to legislate for other sees because he expects her not to interfere in his own diocese 'since to each separate shepherd has been assigned one portion of the flock to direct and govern and render hereafter an account of his ministry to the Lord' (*Epist.* 59. 14). It is precisely this same idea which led him to oppose Pope Stephen in the question of rebaptism, but it cannot be called his consistent attitude. M. Bévenot has recently and rightly pointed to his reaction to Pope Cornelius' inquiries about the consecration of Fortunatus, which Cyprian had performed without first consulting Rome. In his reply, the African prelate recognizes his obligation to report to the Pontiff any matter of major importance: . . .
> This answer makes no protest about responsibility to God alone but, by actually rendering an account of the incident, recognizes Cornelius' right to expect submission of any 'matter of enough importance or gravity.' The same reason explains exactly the same behaviour when, during the vacancy following the death of Pope Fabian (250), the mere clergy of the capital city expressed their disapproval of Cyprian's going into hiding; in this case also, he yields a report of his conduct, and, over and beyond that, adopts the Roman line of action with regard to the *lapsi*; in short, he feels an obligation, not only to the ordinary, but, in his absence, to the very see.—QP, II, 376–377.

63. The year before, in the matter of some deposed bishops in Spain, Cyprian refused Rome any right to interfere. It was for the people to depose sinful bishops. They were the competent judges. And now, in this incident of Marcian of Arles,

> St. Cyprian, in his indignation, has forgotten his own theory of the year before. He contradicts it. He is appealing, once more, in the traditional manner to the *potentior principalitas* of the *ecclesia principalis*. A year later, and in conflict with Rome on a question of policy, he once more involves himself in novelties and contradiction.—P. Hughes, *op. cit.*, I, 143.

Hughes' sketch of St. Cyprian's temperament and background throws no little light on this whole matter:

> It has been well said of St. Cyprian that "He was a practical man without any philosophy or theology." He repeats the tradition, he borrows very largely from Tertullian, he writes a highly cultivated Latin, but there is nowhere evidence that he possessed any power of seeing general principles in the learning he had, nor of deducing thence, in his day to day application of it, further general truths. The one subject which he ventures to explore is this question of the Church and its nature. He explores it simply because exploration of it is forced on him by the controversies he cannot escape. And it is in the spirit of a practical controversialist, eager to find arguments and confirmation of his policy that he explores it. The pitfalls to which such a character is exposed in such a work are very easy to imagine. St. Cyprian was to experience them in full measure.—*Ibid.*, p. 141.

64. See P. Hughes, *loc. cit.*, p. 145.

65. St. Cyprian *Epistula* 74. 1; *Epistula Firmiliani ad Cyprianum* 17. It is not hard to see how our adversaries infer from the actions of St. Cyprian (and Firmilian) that he did not acknowledge the primacy of the Roman pontiff. But it is one thing to resist legitimate authority from time to time in particular cases, and quite another to refuse absolutely to recognize that authority. It must be granted that St. Cyprian neither wrote nor acted as he should have in this business. But who is the preferable witness, a Cyprian in the heat of anger or a Cyprian calm and objective, acknowledging in the clearest of terms the primacy of the Church of Rome? The latter, certainly. We are sure that peace was soon restored between the see of Rome and St. Cyprian, but it is not quite clear how this came about. The more probable explanation seems to be that Sixtus II, the successor of Stephen, at the urging especially of Dionysius of Alexandria, did not press the decree of Stephen (which was only disciplinary, not doctrinal), and that he re-established actual communion with Cyprian, a communion which had been broken in fact only. See J. Ernst, "War der hl. Cyprian excommuniciert?" ZkTh (1894), 473; "Der angebliche Widerruf des hl. Cyprian in der Ketzertauffrage," *ibid.* (1895), 234. Moreover, the outcome of the whole controversy argues in favor of the primacy of the Roman pontiff. For although Cyprian and others defied him, and although they had reasons on their side which could not be ignored, still the universal Church followed the opinion of St. Stephen. See *above*, nn. 49, 62; J. C. Fenton, *loc. cit.* (n. 61, *above*); T. Zapalena, *op. cit.*, I, 313 ff. Hughes sums the matter up well:

> St. Cyprian, it is not hard to understand why, has been the chosen patron of the modern sects whose ideal is a Catholicism without the Roman

primacy. But so to esteem him is to do him serious injustice. The theological impasse into which at the end of his career his untheological mentality led him must be judged in the light of his whole life, the mood which found expression when storms provoked his gallant soul set side by side with those calmer hours when, free from the necessity to justify a policy, "he recognized in the Roman See an altogether special importance because it is the See of that Apostle upon whom Christ conferred the primacy of apostolic authority."—*op. cit.*, I, 146–147.

66. St. Athanasius *Epistula de decretis Nicaenae synodi* 25.

67. St. Athanasius *Apologia contra Arianos* 20; 35.

68. HE 2. 15; see *Concilium Serdicense* can. 3–5; Hefele, *Conciliengeschichte*, I (2nd ed.), no. 64; DB 576 ff.

69. See Hefele, *op. cit.*, II (2nd ed.), 164, 180, 184.

70. Labbe, III, 626.

71. See F. K. Murphy, C.SS.R., *Peter Speaks through Leo: The Council of Chalcedon, A. D. 451* (Washington, 1952).

72. See Hefele, *loc. cit.*, p. 440; 545–547.

73. The reference here is to canon 3 of the First Council of Constantinople (381); "The bishop of Constantinople ought to have primacy of honor (*tà presbeía tês timês*) after the bishop of Rome, since it is New-Rome." See Hefele, *loc. cit.*, p. 17.

74. See Hefele, *loc. cit.*, p. 527; T. Harapin, *Primatus pontificis Romani in concilio Chalcedonensi et Ecclesiae dissidentes* (1923); P. Hughes, *op. cit.*, I, 318 ff.

75. See T. Harapin, *op. cit.*, p. 549; P. Hughes, *ibid.*

76. See De Groot. *Summa de ecclesia* (3rd ed.), p. 539, for the peculiar opinion of Papebroch, who appealed especially to St. Epiphanius (*Haereses* 27. 6) to support his contention that the Church of Rome had two bishops at once, Peter and Paul, "but in such a way that Peter, head and prince of the apostolic college, safeguarded his prestige" (*Paral. ad Conatum in catal. pontif.*, in Acta Sanctorum, vol. XIII, *Propylaeum ad Acta SS. Maji*, 33).

77. See, for example, the bull *Ineffabilis* (DB 1641), and the apostolic letter of Leo XIII, *Properante ad exitum*, May 11, 1899 (conclusion).

78. See J. C. Fenton, *loc. cit.* (n. 61, *above*). In the words of Msgr. Duchesne:

> Thus the Churches of the whole world, from Arabia, Osrhoene and Cappadocia to the ends of the West, felt in everything, in faith, in discipline, in government, in ritual, in charitable works, the ceaseless action of the Roman Church. She was everywhere known, as St. Irenaeus says, everywhere present, everywhere respected, everywhere followed; without parallel, without rival. There was none to put herself on the same footing. Later there were to be patriarchates and other local primacies. Their first lineaments are hardly to be detected in the third century, and then only more or less vaguely. Above these organisms in course of formation, as above all the isolated Churches, rose the Roman Church in sovereign majesty, the Roman Church represented by her Bishops whose long line went back to the two leaders of the Apostolic choir, the Roman Church who thought herself, called herself, and was held by all the world to be the centre and organ of unity.—*Eglises séparées* (Paris, 1896), p. 155; quoted by Journet, *Church of the Word, op. cit.*, p. 442, note 2.

79. *De unitate ecclesiae* (1st ed.) 4. ACW trans. On the authenticity and integrity of this work, see C. A. Kneller, "Der hl. Cyprian und die Idee der Kirche," *Stimmen*, 65 (1903), 498; C. Journet, *Church of the Word, op. cit.*, p. 398; QP, II, 349–352; J. C. Fenton, *loc. cit.*, p. 451; T. Zapalena, *loc. cit.*, p. 393.

80. See J. C. Fenton, *loc. cit.*, p. 454.

CHAPTER III

The Properties of the Church

Article I

THE CHURCH'S INFALLIBILITY

I. *Meaning of the Term*

II. *Errors:*
   1. Protestants
      a. Pistoians
      b. Jansenists
   2. Modernists

III. *The Fact of Infallibility:*

   PROPOSITION: When the teaching office of the Church hands down decisions on matters of faith and morals in such a way as to require of everyone full and absolute assent, it is infallible.
   Proof: 1. from the promises of Christ;
   2. from the testimony of the Apostle;
   3. from the testimony of the early fathers;
   4. theological argument.
   Corollary: The infallibility of the Synagogue.

IV. *The Object of Infallibility:*

   PROPOSITION 1: The primary object of infallibility is each and every religious truth contained formally in the sources of revelation.
   Proof: 1. from the words of Christ;
   2. from the express purpose of infallibility.

Sequel

   PROPOSITION 2: The secondary object of infallibility comprises all those matters which are so closely connected with the revealed deposit that revelation itself would be imperilled unless an absolutely certain decision could be made about them.

Assertion 1: The Church's infallibility extends to theological conclusions.

Proof: 1. from the purpose of infallibility;
2. from the mind of the Church.

Assertion 2: The Church's infallibility extends to dogmatic facts.

Proof: 1. from the purpose of infallibility;
2. from the practice of the Church.

Objection: The *Three Chapters*.

Corollary: The Church does not usually pass judgment directly on the dogmatic fact itself, but on the proposition which, through the medium of a dogmatic fact, is deduced from a revealed premise.

Assertion 3: The Church's infallibility extends to the general discipline of the Church.

Proof: 1. from the purpose of infallibility;
2. from the official statement of the Church.

Corollary: Lex orandi est lex credendi (The law of prayer is the law of belief).

Assertion 4: The Church's infallibility extends to the approval of religious orders.

Proof: 1. from the purpose of infallibility;
2. from the solid conviction of the Church.

Assertion 5: The Church's infallibility extends to the canonization of saints.

Proof: 1. from the solid conviction of the Church;
2. from the purpose of infallibility.

Corollary: Equivalent canonization.

Scholion: Is the fact of the Church's infallibility in matters related to revealed truth itself a revealed truth?

V. *The Nature of Infallibility:*

1. Not merely actual absence of error, but the impossibility of erring.

2. A privilege which depends for its exercise on some objective, external help.
3. Its efficient cause is the assistance of the Holy Spirit.
4. The divine assistance does not render superfluous human industry.
5. This assistance extends to the threefold function of the Church's rulers as:
   a. witnesses of revelation;
   b. teachers of religious truth;
   c. arbiters of controversy.

Sequel: The Rule of Faith:
   1. established by Christ Himself;
   2. nicely accommodated to people's needs.

CHAPTER III

The Properties of the Church

The Church's properties are those qualities which flow from its very essence and are a necessary part of it. Authors differ somewhat in enumerating these properties; and some distinguish between properties and endowments. But the difference seems to concern method and terminology rather than the matter itself. Seven properties, then, can be listed: *visibility, indestructibility, infallibility, unity, holiness, catholicity,* and *apostolicity.* Since visibility and indestructibility have already been considered, there remain for discussion only the last five.

Article I

THE CHURCH'S INFALLIBILITY

77* I. Meaning of the Term

The word infallibility itself indicates a necessary immunity from error. When one speaks of the *Church's infallibility,* one means that the Church can neither deceive nor be deceived in matters of faith and morals. It is a prerogative of the whole Church; but it belongs in one way to those who fulfill the office of teaching and in another way to those who are taught. Hence the distinction between *active* infallibility, by which the Church's rulers are rendered immune from error when they teach; and *passive* infallibility, by which all of Christ's faithful are preserved from error in their beliefs.

Passive infallibility depends on and is caused by active infallibility: for the faithful are kept free from error in religious matters only by loyally following their rulers. Consequently, it is limited by the same restrictions as is active infallibility, and it will there-

* Nos. 71–76 of the Latin edition are 150a-h in the present edition.

fore suffice to treat only the latter. Active infallibility may be defined as follows: *the privilege by which the teaching office of the Church, through the assistance of the Holy Spirit, is preserved immune from error when it defines a doctrine of faith or morals.*

The words *through the assistance of the Holy Spirit* indicate that this freedom from error is something derived; the words *when it defines a doctrine of faith or morals* limit this inerrancy to definite subject matter.

II. Errors 78

1. **Protestants** in general ascribe infallibility to no church, at least to no visible church. The *Puseyists* were willing to grant it to some sort of ideal Church made up of the Roman Catholic, Greek, and Anglican communions. The *Pistoians* asserted that infallibility, like all sacred power, had been given principally and directly to the whole body of the faithful, but to rulers only as agents of that body. The *Jansenists* of Holland seem to follow the same opinion, since they demand for an infallible decree: (*a*) that delegates or representatives of the whole "Church" be gathered together for a ecumenical council; (*b*) that these delegates agree that the doctrine belongs to the deposit of faith and that it has always been accepted by the whole Church; (*c*) that their judgment be ratified universally by the Church throughout the world.

2. **Modernists,** since they acknowledge not even a divinely established teaching office, naturally do not admit that the privilege of infallibility was granted this office. The doctrinal or dogmatic authority which they themselves grant the Church's rulers means only this: that these rulers are to be watchfully alert for what may, at any given period, be going on in the Christian consciousness, so that they may give it apt formulation. Of course the formulae must be modified as soon as they no longer correspond with the new mentality and the evolution of religious consciousness. In fact, in the Modernist system, the duty of doctrinal authority is *not* to see to it that there is never any change in the believing or in the understanding of the absolute and immutable truth preached from the beginning by the apostles. This authority is rather to take care that that be maintained which may seem best adapted to the cultural level of each generation.[1]

The first step in the treatment to follow will be a demonstration of the *fact* of infallibility. Next in order will be a study of its *object* or extent, and finally an investigation into its *nature*. The special discussion of the *subject* of infallibility fits more conveniently into the second section of this treatise. Suffice it to mention here, in anticipation of the fuller discussion, that that subject is both the body of the Church's rulers together with its head, in other words, the *Roman Catholic college of bishops,* and the supreme ruler of the whole Church, the *Roman pontiff*.

III. The Fact of Infallibility [2]

79 PROPOSITION: *When the teaching office of the Church hands down decisions on matters of faith and morals in such a way as to require of everyone full and absolute assent, it is infallible.*

This is a *dogma of faith.*

The teaching office of the Church or, as they say, "the teaching Church," is made up of those to whom God entrusted the right and the duty to teach the Christian religion authoritatively. The words "in matters of faith and morals *in such a way as to require of everyone full and absolute assent*" are included in the proposition because, according to Catholic teaching, the Church's rulers are infallible not in any and every exercise of their teaching power; but only when, using all the fulness of their authority, they clearly intend to bind everyone to absolute assent or, as common parlance puts it, when they "define" something in matters pertaining to the Christian religion. That is why all theologians distinguish in the dogmatic decrees of the councils or of the popes between those things set forth therein by way of definition and those used simply by way of illustration or argumentation. For the intention of binding all affects *only the definition,* and not the historical observations, reasons for the definition, and so forth. And if in some particular instances the intention of giving a definitive decision were not made sufficiently clear, then no one would be held by virtue of such definitions, to give the assent of faith: a doubtful law is no law at all.

Although this proposition has never been defined in the precise form in which it is here stated, it is a *dogma of faith* by reason of the universal teaching of the Church. Moreover, the Vatican Council did define that the Roman pontiff "enjoys that infallibility with which the divine Redeemer wished His Church to be equipped in defining a doctrine of faith or morals."[3]

THE PROPERTIES OF THE CHURCH

Proof:

1. From the *promises of Christ.* (*a*) Christ said to the apostles in the Last Supper discourse, "*And I will ask the Father, and he will grant you another Advocate to be with you for all time to come, the Spirit of Truth . . . he will make his permanent stay with you and in you. . . . but the Advocate, the Holy Spirit, whom the Father will send in my name, will teach you all things, and refresh your memory of everything I have told you*" (John 14:16–17, 26). "*But when he, the Spirit of truth, has come, he will conduct you through the whole range of truth*" (John 16:13). Then, after His Resurrection, He added, " *. . . you shall be baptized with the Holy Spirit not many days hence . . . you shall receive power when the Holy Spirit comes upon you, and you shall be my witnesses in Jerusalem and in all Judea and Samaria and even to the very ends of the earth*" (Acts 1:5, 8).

Two things are promised in these texts: the Holy Spirit, as the Teacher of truth (*a*) will come upon the apostles to imbue them with an exceedingly rich knowledge of the Christian religion; (*b*) He will remain with them forever. The purpose and the result of both these aids is that the apostles will preach Christ's religion pure and unabridged "*even to the very ends of the earth.*"

The former promise has in view especially the first communication of the Christian religion and, furthermore, at least in the strict and full sense, refers to the apostles alone. The latter promise, which is concerned more directly with the practice and preservation of this religion, cannot, in view of the words themselves [4] and of the purpose intended, be limited to the apostles personally; but embraces the apostolic college as it is to continue forever. But if the Holy Spirit is to remain with the successors of the apostles forever, and is to be in them that they may be witnesses of Christ to the ends of the earth, He will doubtless keep them from error when they define Christian doctrine. For would they really be witnesses of Christ if they corrupted His doctrine in even one point and unjustifiably demanded the assent of all to a falsehood?

(*b*) "*Absolute authority in heaven and on earth has been conferred upon me. Go, therefore, and initiate all nations in discipleship . . . and teach them to observe all the commandments I have given you. And mark: I am with you at all times as long as the world will last*" (Matt. 28:20). These words contain a promise to the apostolic college, as to a perpetual institution, of continuous and effective aid in teaching all nations the religion of Christ (see no. 20). But this aid certainly includes infallibility, for if they could err at times in defining Christian doctrine, the purpose of the aid would not be realized.

Furthermore, the force of Christ's promise is highlighted in an extraordinary manner by the obligation enjoined on all men to accept the doctrine preached by the apostles and by their successors throughout all ages: *"He that believes . . . will be saved, but he that does not believe will be condemned"* (Mark 16:16). Could our Lord have imposed this obligation without any limitation or restriction, and under the threat of eternal damnation, if He had left to posterity a teaching authority which was liable to error?

82   2. From the *testimony of the Apostle*. St. Paul: *I write these instructions to you, so that . . . you may know what your conduct should be in the house of God which is the Church of the living God, the pillar and bulwark of truth* (I Tim. 3:14–15). Truth purely and simply is the whole body of truth leading to eternal salvation: Christian doctrine in its entirety. The Church considered absolutely, i.e., the universal Church, is called a thoroughly solid pillar of this truth,[5] because it bears and supports the truth as an unshakably solid pillar supports a building. But it would not be the pillar and bulwark of the truth if it could shift from the truth in even one matter. Therefore we have here a direct statement of the infallibility of the Church as a whole; but one can immediately deduce from this the infallibility of the teaching office, since the whole Church depends on this office for its knowledge and profession of the truth.

83   3. From the *testimony of the early fathers*. They have left, in unmistakably clear or at least equivalent terms, testimony to their belief in the infallibility of the teaching office or, what actually comes down to the same thing, of the Church itself. St. Ignatius:

> Live in harmony with the mind of God. Surely, Jesus Christ, our inseparable life, for His part in the mind of the Father, just as the bishops, though appointed throughout the vast, wide earth, represent for their part the mind of Jesus Christ.—*Epistula ad Ephesios* 3. 2; ACW translation.
>
> Now, if those who do this to gratify the flesh are liable to death, how much more a man who by evil doctrine ruins the

faith in God, for which Jesus Christ was crucified! Such a filthy creature will go into the unquenchable fire, as will anyone who listens to him. The Lord permitted myrrh to be poured on His head that He might breathe incorruption upon the Church. Do not let yourselves be anointed with the malodorous doctrine of the Prince of this world.—*Ibid.* 16. 2–17. 1; ACW translation.

St. Irenaeus:

One should obey the presbyters [bishops] of the Church, for they are the successors of the apostles and along with episcopal succession have received the sure charism of truth according to the good pleasure of the Father.[6]

Tertullian makes sport of the thesis that

the Holy Ghost sent by Christ and asked of the Father for this very purpose, *viz.*, to teach the truth, neglected His duty by allowing the Church to understand and to believe otherwise than what He Himself taught the apostles.—*De praescriptione* 28.

St. Athanasius: "The only words you need for answering those [paradoxes of the heretics] are the following: 'This is not the teaching of the Catholic Church'" (*Epistula ad Epictetum* 3).

St. Jerome: "I was able to dry up all the rivulets of false assertions with the one sun of the Church" (*Altercatio luciferiani et orthodoxi* 28).

St. Augustine:

Many tongues and various heresies speak in opposition . . . hasten to the tabernacle of God, hold fast to the Catholic Church, depart not from the rule of truth, and you will find in this tabernacle asylum from the tongues which wag in opposition.—*Enarrationes in Psalmos* 30. 3. 8.

The Catholic Church wages war against all heresies. It can give battle, but it can never be vanquished. All heresies have gone forth from it [the Church] like useless branches pruned from a vine; but it remains itself firmly fixed in its roots, in its vine, in its love. The gates of hell will not prevail against it.[7]

4. *Theological argument.* The Church, according to Christ's

promises, is indestructible (no. 19); but it would fail through corruption if it strayed from the true teaching of Christ; and it would so stray, indeed inevitably, if its teaching authority were to err at any time in defining points of doctrine.

84 Corollary

Since even in the Old Testament period the revealed religion was to be piously safeguarded, theologians usually bring up at this juncture the question of the *infallibility of the Synagogue*. Opinions vary, but, here, in sum, is that of Cardinal Franzelin.[8] (*a*) The Aaronic priests undoubtedly exercised authoritative teaching power in sacred matters; but there is no sufficient proof that the charism of infallibility was granted this ordinary teaching body. However, (*b*) even at that time God was watching over the preservation of sacred doctrine, and He did so in a manner suited to the special character of that stage of religious development, when revelation was not only to be safeguarded but also to be steadily increased. He effected this increase through new revelations made to the prophets, whose mission, however, was directed no less to the safeguarding of already promulgated revelation than to its further unfolding. Consequently the teaching office of the Old Testament comprised two elements, the ordinary teaching office of the priests and the extraordinary teaching office of the prophets; and so, *considered in its entirety*, it guarded the deposit of faith with infallible sureness, inasmuch as the prophets corrected any mistakes which the ordinary teachers might possibly have made.

IV. The Object of Infallibility

85 In the definition given above the object of infallibility was expressed in these words borrowed from the Vatican Council: "when it defines *a doctrine of faith or morals*." It remains now to fix more accurately the meaning and the scope of this formula. This will be done on the basis of the words of Christ and of the apostles cited in the course of the proof; and on the basis, too, of the purpose for which the privilege of infallibility was granted.

It is important to pay attention above all to the word *doctrine;* for infallibility concerns the teaching office and so has as its special object doctrines, or at least doctrinal decisions by which some truth is presented to be believed or maintained by everyone.

The formula, "a doctrine of faith or morals," comprises all doctrines the knowledge of which is of vital concern to people if they are to believe aright and to live uprightly in accordance with the religion of Christ. Now doctrines of this sort have either been revealed themselves or are so closely allied with revelation that they cannot be neglected without doing harm to the latter. Consequently the object of infallibility is twofold: there is a primary and a secondary object.

PROPOSITION 1: *The primary object of infallibility is each and every religious truth contained formally in the sources of revelation.* 86

By a religious truth is meant anything (doctrine or fact) which pertains to religion, i.e., to faith and morals, and insofar as it does pertain to it. The various ways in which a truth can be formally contained in the sources of revelation will be explained in the treatise on Faith. According to all Catholics, the present proposition is a *dogma of faith.*

Proof: That religious truths *contained formally in the sources of revelation* are the object of infallibility calls for no explicit demonstration.

That infallibility extends to each and every one of these truths, whether they be matters of intellectual concern or of practical action, is clear: (1) from the words of Christ, who promised His assistance to the apostles and sent them forth to teach the nations *"to observe all the commandments I have given you,"* and who promised them the Spirit of truth who *"will teach you everything."* (2) from the express purpose of infallibility. If the latter did not embrace all these truths, one could be doubtful about almost any single truth; for where could one find a criterion for distinguishing fundamental from not-so-fundamental truths?

Sequel

To the primary object of infallibility belong *specifically:*

1. Decisions on the *canon,* or the material extent, of Sacred Scripture, or on its true meaning in passages dealing with faith or morals.

2. Decisions acknowledging and explaining the *records of divine tradition.*

3. Decisions on the *selection of terms* in which revealed truth is to be presented for belief (dogmatic terminology, creeds, dogmatic decrees).

4. Decisions on doctrines *directly opposed* to revealed truth (condemnation of heresies). For he who knows with infallible certainty the truth of a proposition knows with the same infallibility the falseness of a contradictory or contrary proposition.

87 PROPOSITION 2: *The secondary object of infallibility comprises all those matters which are so closely connected with the revealed deposit that revelation itself would be imperilled unless an absolutely certain decision could be made about them.*

The charism of infallibility was bestowed upon the Church so that the latter could piously safeguard and confidently explain the deposit of Christian revelation, and thus could be in all ages the teacher of Christian truth and of the Christian way of life. But if the Church is to fulfill this purpose, it must be infallible in its judgment of *doctrines and facts* which, even though not revealed, *are so intimately connected with revelation that any error or doubt about them would constitute a peril to the faith.* Furthermore, the Church must be infallible not only when it issues a formal decree, but also when it performs some *action which, for all practical purposes, is the equivalent of a doctrinal definition.*

One can easily see why matters connected with revelation are called the *secondary* object of infallibility. Doctrinal authority and infallibility were given to the Church's rulers that they might safeguard and confidently explain the deposit of Christian revelation. That is why the chief object of infallibility, that, namely, which *by its very nature* falls within the scope of infallibility, includes only the truths contained in the actual deposit of revelation. Allied matters, on the other hand, which are not in the actual deposit, but contribute to its safeguarding and security, come within the purview of infallibility not by their very nature, but rather *by reason of the revealed truth* to which they are annexed. As a result, infallibility embraces them only secondarily. It follows that when the Church passes judgment on matters of this sort, it is infallible only insofar as they are connected with revelation.

When theologians go on to break up the general statement of this thesis into its component parts, they teach that the following *individual* matters belong to the secondary object of infallibility: 1. theological conclusions; 2. dogmatic facts; 3. the general discipline of the Church; 4. approval of religious orders; 5. canonization of saints.

THE PROPERTIES OF THE CHURCH

Assertion 1: The Church's infallibility extends to theological conclusions. This proposition is *theologically certain.*

88

A *theological conclusion* is a *proposition which by genuinely discursive reasoning is deduced with certainty from two premises, one of which is formally revealed, the other known with natural certitude.* It can be *strictly a matter of intellectual knowledge,* like the fact that the Son proceeds from the Father by a process of intellectual generation; or it can be a *matter of practical knowledge,* like the fact that one may not directly abort a foetus to save the life of the mother. To assert that the Church is infallible in decreeing these conclusions is to affirm implicitly that it is infallible in rejecting *errors opposed thereto;* the principle is the same for both.

Proof:

1. From the *purpose of infallibility.* The Church is infallible in matters so closely connected with revelation that any error in these matters would constitute a peril to the faith. But theological conclusions are matters of this type. The conclusion is obvious.

Major. It is evident from Christ's promises that the teaching office of the Church was endowed with infallibility so that it might be able to carry out its mission properly: to safeguard reverently, explain confidently, and defend effectively the deposit of faith. But the realization of this purpose demands the extension of infallibility to related matters, in the sense explained above. Here is the reason. The security of the deposit requires the effective warding off or elimination of *all* error which may be opposed to it, even though only indirectly. This would be simply impossible without infallibility in related matters. If the Church were infallible only in the field of revealed truth and not in that of matters annexed thereto, it would be like a general who was assigned to defend a city but was given no authority to build up defenses or to destroy the materiel which the enemy had assembled. It would be like a caretaker to whom the master of the house had said, "Take care that my house doesn't burn down; but don't put out any flames as long as they remain merely nearby"!

Minor. Every conclusion is so connected with its premises that a denial of the conclusion involves necessarily the denial of at least one of those premises. Now one of the premises upon which every theological conclusion rests is a truth evident from reason, and since no one can very well deny such a premise, there is danger that an error in the conclusion may give rise to an error about the revealed premise.

2. From the *mind of the Church*. The Church surely makes no mistake when it determines the force and extent of its infallibility, for the greatest of harm would result if the Church, by stretching infallibility beyond its limits, could force everyone to give unqualified assent to a matter about which it is liable to be mistaken. But the fact is that the Church has often and openly expressed its conviction of being infallible in the matter of theological conclusions. It has expressed this conviction at least in an active, practical way, by irrevocably repudiating doctrines which, while not directly opposed to revealed truths, are opposed to theological conclusions. See, e.g., DB 602, 679, 1542, 1748.

89 *Assertion 2: The Church's infallibility extends to dogmatic facts.* This proposition is *theologically certain*.

A *dogmatic fact* is a *fact* not contained in the sources of revelation, *on the admission of which depends the knowledge or certainty of a dogma or of a revealed truth*. The following questions are concerned with dogmatic facts: "Was the Vatican Council a legitimate ecumenical council? Is the Latin Vulgate a substantially faithful translation of the original books of the Bible? Was Pius XII legitimately elected bishop of Rome?" One can readily see that on these facts hang the questions of whether the decrees of the Vatican Council are infallible, whether the Vulgate is truly Sacred Scripture, whether Piux XII is to be recognized as supreme ruler of the universal Church.

From the time of the Jansenist controversies, theologians have understood by the term "dogmatic fact" especially the following question: "Is such and such a doctrine (orthodox or heretical) really contained in such and such a book?" The Jansenists in fact admitted the Church's infallibility in a *question of right* or of dogma, i.e., the Church could decide whether this or that doctrine (considered in itself and prescinding from the book in which it was said to be expressed) was heretical. But at the same time they denied its infallibility in a *question of fact*, e.g., whether this (heretical) doctrine was really stated in such and such a book, as, e.g., Jansen's *Augustinus*.[9] One can readily see that a determination of this fact would determine whether one could or could not maintain and defend the doctrine of this book.

Proof:

1. From the *purpose of infallibility*. The Church is infallible in those related matters in which an error would constitute a danger to the faith. But dogmatic facts are matters of this kind. The reason should be obvious from the examples alleged above. What good would it do to proclaim in theory the infallible authority of ecumenical councils if one could licitly doubt the legitimacy of a specific council? What good would it do to acknowledge the inspiration of the Sacred Books in their original forms—forms long ago extinct—if one could not definitively establish the substantial fidelity of copies of the original, and of the translations which the Church has to use? Could Christians be effectively protected against errors in their faith if the Church could not warn them against poisonous fare, such as are books which contain heresy or errors in religious matters?

2. From the *practice of the Church*, which (*a*) often resolutely and officially repudiated heretical writings as e.g., the *Thalia* of Arius in the Council of Nicaea and the works of Nestorius in the Council of Ephesus; (*b*) declared the Vulgate to be authentic at the Council of Trent,[10] and the Canon of the Mass to be free of any error;[11] (*c*) asserted specifically in the case of Jansen that "reverent silence" about a dogmatic fact is not at all adequate, "but that all faithful Christians must condemn as heretical in their hearts as well as with their lips the opinions [which the Church has] condemned in the five aforementioned propositions of Jansen's book, opinions which the very words of those propositions quite clearly state."[12]

A famous objection is that concerned with the *Three Chapters* (Theodore, bishop of Mopsuestia and his *works; some of the works* of Theodoret, bishop of Cyrrhus, and the *letter* of Ibas, a priest of Edessa, to Maris of Persia, all of which works favored Nestorianism). The Council of Chalcedon is said to have approved these works and the Second Council of Constantinople and Pope Vigilius subsequently to have condemned them. Consequently, they say, at least one of them was in error about a dogmatic fact. But this conclusion is not justified, for although the fathers of Chalcedon, *after having expressly condemned Nestorianism*, accepted Theodore and Ibas as members of the Council, they passed no explicit decision regarding the *Three Chapters*.[13]

90 Corollary

The Church does not usually pass judgment directly on the dogmatic fact itself; but on the proposition which, through the medium of a dogmatic fact, is deduced from a revealed premise (either through a true reasoning process or through a merely explanatory syllogism). Of course, whatever the Church declares directly must be maintained by everyone, e.g., that the Vulgate contains the word of God; that Pius XII is head of the Church; that the doctrine of this or that book is heretical. It arrived at these decisions in the following manner: every faithful translation of the inspired books contains the words of God; but the Vulgate is a faithful translation; therefore, . . . Anyone legitimately elected bishop of Rome is head of the Church; but Pius XII was legitimately elected; therefore, . . . Any book containing this doctrine is heretical; but such and such a book contains this doctrine; therefore, . . . Since then, the Church's decision is concerned more directly with the conclusion deduced from revelation with the help of a dogmatic fact, rather than with the dogmatic fact itself (which is assumed in the decision rather than directly affirmed), dogmatic facts can rightly be called not only secondary but also *indirect* objects of infallibility.

It may help to mention that several theologians treat this question a bit differently. For they understand by the term "dogmatic fact" not a premise drawn from history, on which the conclusion would depend, as in the examples above, but *the conclusion itself*, e.g., that the Vulgate contains the word of God or that such and such a book is heretical. If one prefers this view of the matter, he will then define a dogmatic fact, in the words of the illustrious de Groot, as "a fact in which a doctrine is expressed."[14]

One may wonder what name is to be given the conclusion, following the view proposed above. To answer that, a distinction is necessary. If the conclusion is the result of a real reasoning process, it is to be called a *theological conclusion*. But if the syllogism is merely explanatory, then it expresses a truth *formally but implicitly revealed*. The precise meaning of this distinction will be explained in the treatise on Faith (no. 200).

91 *Assertion 3: The Church's infallibility extends to the general discipline of the Church.* This proposition is *theologically certain.*

By the term "general discipline of the Church" are meant those *ecclesiastical laws passed for the universal Church for the direction of Christian worship and Christian living.* Note the italicized words: *ecclesiastical* laws, passed for the *universal* Church.

The imposing of commands belongs not directly to the teaching office but to the ruling office; disciplinary laws are only indirectly an object of infallibility, i.e., only by reason of the doctrinal decision implicit in them. When the Church's rulers sanction a law, they implicitly make a twofold judgment: 1. "This law squares with the Church's doctrine of faith and morals"; that is, it imposes nothing that is at odds with sound belief and good morals.[15] This amounts to a *doctrinal decree*. 2. "This law, considering all the circumstances, is most opportune." This is a *decree of practical judgment*.

Although it would be rash to cast aspersions on the timeliness of a law, especially at the very moment when the Church imposes or expressly reaffirms it, still the Church does not claim to be infallible in issuing a decree of practical judgment. For the Church's rulers were never promised the highest degree of prudence for the conduct of affairs. But the Church is infallible in issuing a doctrinal decree as intimated above—and to such an extent that *it can never sanction a universal law which would be at odds with faith or morality or would be by its very nature conducive to the injury of souls.*

The Church's infallibility in disciplinary matters, when understood in this way, harmonizes beautifully with the *mutability* of even universal laws. For a law, even though it be thoroughly consonant with revealed truth, can, given a change in circumstances, become less timely or even useless, so that prudence may dictate its abrogation or modification.

Proof:

1. From the *purpose of infallibility*. The Church was endowed with infallibility that it might safeguard the whole of Christ's doctrine and be for all men a trustworthy teacher of the Christian way of life. But if the Church could make a mistake in the manner alleged when it legislated for the general discipline, it would no longer be either a loyal guardian of revealed doctrine or a trustworthy teacher of the Christian way of life. It would *not be a guardian of revealed doctrine,* for the imposition of a vicious law would be, for all practical purposes, tantamount to an erroneous

definition of doctrine; everyone would naturally conclude that what the Church had commanded squared with sound doctrine. It would *not be a teacher of the Christian way of life,* for by its laws it would induce corruption into the practice of religious life.

2. From the *official statement of the Church,* which stigmatized as "at least erroneous" the hypothesis "that the Church could establish discipline which would be dangerous, harmful, and conducive to superstition and materialism."[16]

92 Corollary

The well-known axiom, *Lex orandi est lex credendi* (The law of prayer is the law of belief), is a special application of the doctrine of the Church's infallibility in disciplinary matters. This axiom says in effect that formulae of prayer approved for public use in the universal Church cannot contain errors against faith or morals. But it would be quite wrong to conclude from this that all the historical facts which are recorded here and there in the lessons of the Roman Breviary, or all the explanations of scriptural passages which are used in the homilies of the Breviary must be taken as infallibly true.[17] As far as the former are concerned, those particular facts are not an object of infallibility since they have no necessary connection with revelation. As for the latter, the Church orders their recitation not because they are certainly true, but because they are edifying.

93

Assertion 4: The Church's infallibility extends to the approval of religious orders. This proposition is *theologically certain.*

The religious state is essentially the observance, under obligation of a vow, of the evangelical counsels recommended by our Lord Himself. But every congregation or order *follows its own constitution, its own laws for living the evangelical counsels and for attaining its own special purposes.* The present discussion, therefore, has to do *with the approval of this constitution,* and furthermore, with that solemn and definitive approval which is reserved for the sovereign pontiff and by which a congregation is established as a religious *order* in the strict sense of the word.[18]

Practically the same thing is to be said about the approval of orders as was said about the general discipline of the Church: it is an indirect object of infallibility by reason of the doctrinal judgment which it implies. No one claims that the Church is infallible in the decree of practical judgment—as, for instance, whether, in view of the circumstances, it would be expedient to allow the foundation of the new order—but only in the *doctrinal judgment*— as, for instance, *whether such and such a constitution is an apt instrument for the acquiring of Christian perfection.*

Proof:

1. From the *purpose of infallibility*. The Church was endowed with infallibility that it might be forever a trustworthy teacher of Christian truth and perfection. But it would certainly not be, if it could approve, by a definitive decision, a constitution opposed to the gospel or to the natural law. It is useless to object that an error in this sort of affair would harm not the universal Church, but only the members of this particular order. Of course it would harm the latter immediately and most of all, but indirectly it would affect the whole Church; for when an order is solemnly approved, it is recommended to the whole Church as a fit means for acquiring perfection, so that no one may licitly impugn it from this point of view.

2. From the *solid conviction of the Church*, which, when approving orders, expresses itself in such a way as to make it sufficiently clear that it considers decisions of this type to be infallible. For an example of such a decision, see Pesch, *Praelectiones dogmaticae*, I, 545.

Assertion 5: The Church's infallibility extends to the canonization of saints. This is the *common opinion* today.[19]

Canonization (formal) is the *final and definitive decree by which the sovereign pontiff declares that someone has been admitted to heaven and is to be venerated by everyone*, at least in the sense that all the faithful are held to consider the person a saint worthy of public veneration. It differs from *beatification*, which is a provisional rather than a definitive decree, by which veneration is only permitted, or at least is not universally prescribed. Infallibility is claimed for canonization only;[20] a decree of beatification, which in the eyes of the Church is not definitive but may still be rescinded, is to be considered morally certain indeed, but not infallible. Still, there are some theologians who take a different view of the matter.

Proof:

1. From the *solid conviction of the Church*. When the popes canonize, they use terminology which makes it quite evident that they consider decrees of canonization infallible. Here is, in sum, the formula they use: "By the authority of our Lord Jesus Christ and of the apostles Peter and Paul and by our own authority, we declare that N. has been admitted to heaven, and we decree and define that he is to be venerated in public and in private as a saint."

2. From the *purpose of infallibility*. The Church is infallible so that it may be a trustworthy teacher of the Christian religion and of the Christian way of life. But it would not be such if it could err in the canonization of saints. Would not religion be sullied if a person in hell were, by a definitive decree, offered to everyone as an object of religious veneration? Would not the moral law be at least weakened to some extent, if a protégé of the devil could be irrevocably set up as a model of virtue for all to imitate and for all to invoke? But it cannot be inferred: therefore the Church must also be infallible in authenticating the relics of the saints; for (*a*) the Church never issues so solemn a decree about relics; and (*b*) the cases are not parallel, for in the case of relics, it is a question of relative cult, while in that of the saints it is one of absolute cult.[21]

95 Corollary

Several considerations urge the conclusion that the Church's infallibility extends also to *equivalent canonization*, formerly quite common. By this means, without any formal decree of canonization, a deceased person gradually came to be venerated by the universal Church. However, formal and equivalent canonizations are not at all on the same plane; in the latter the consent of the supreme pontiff can be taken as purely permissive, in much the same way as the veneration of a beatified person is sometimes permitted the universal Church. Some scholars are led by this observation to think that it is not absolutely impossible that someone who is not a saint might appear among those who, without being formally canonized, have a commemoration or even a full office in the Breviary. The papal approval of the Breviary, they say, as far as they who have not been formally canonized are concerned, amounts to nothing more than an order that no change be made therein.

This is not a definitive decree, but rather permission to continue the traditional cult.²²

Scholion: Is the fact of the Church's infallibility in matters related to revealed truth itself a revealed truth?

In each instance we have proved the infallibility of the Church's teaching office in matters related to the deposit of revelation from the express purpose of infallibility and from the mind of the Church. It is, consequently, clear that this infallibility is at least a conclusion from revelation; indeed a conclusion whose validity the Church itself has sanctioned at least by its practical attitude and mode of action. But serious reasons incline us to state that this extension of infallibility—not of course to each of the items considered individually above, but to related matters in general—is a *formally revealed truth*. There is no doubt that our Lord promised His Church the *"Spirit of truth"* (John 14:17), who would teach *"the whole range of truth"* (John 16:13); the apostle calls the Church *the pillar and bulwark of truth* (I Tim. 3:15).²³ What, then, does the word "truth" or the phrase "the whole range of truth" mean in these texts: just revealed truth, or all the truth which the Church, in view of its special purpose, must know with certainty? The answer seems to be that since the terms are general, and the purpose of the Church militates against their being restricted to revealed truths, they must doubtless be understood as referring to all doctrines which concern Christian faith and morality either directly or indirectly. In other words, they must include also matters connected with revealed truth.

This is why Cardinal Franzelin could in the following way describe the general proposition of infallibility in related matters: this assertion, "as all theologians agree, is so certain that its denial would be an error, or even, in the opinion of many, a heresy, even though it has not as yet been explicitly condemned as heretical."²⁴

V. The Nature of Infallibility

1. The privilege of infallibility is **not** merely actual absence of error, but the *impossibility of erring*. It is of course a *supernatural gift*, and since it works not to the advantage of the recipients themselves but to that of the whole Church, it is a *gratia gratis data* or charism. It is often called "the charism of truth."

2. Infallibility must **not** be thought of as a habit permanently

residing in the minds of the Church's official teachers, a habit which would express itself in the making of a dogmatic definition, as e.g., the habit of faith expresses itself in an act of supernatural faith. It is rather a *privilege which depends for its exercise on some objective external help.* This privilege can be called habitual in the sense that it was promised by a definite divine decree. But it is in *actual* existence only when something is being defined.

98   3. **The efficient cause of infallibility is the assistance of God or of the Holy Spirit.** This assistance:

a. is a help inferior in nature to revelation and inspiration; furthermore,

b. it can involve any kind of influence which God may choose to use in order to turn away the teacher's mind from what is false and to lead him to a sure knowledge of the truth.

As for *a:* this assistance differs from *revelation,* through which some *new* doctrine is received from God. "For," says the Vatican Council,[25] "the Holy Spirit was promised to Peter's successors [and the same holds good for the Roman Catholic episcopate] not that they might, as a result of His revelation, make known a new doctrine, but that with His assistance they might reverently safeguard and faithfully explain the revelation handed down by the apostles, i.e., the deposit of faith."

It is different from inspiration, through which a document is written in such fashion as to be the Word of God and comes from the mouth of God in such a way that God is its principal author and man the instrumental author only. A decree issued under divine assistance, however, is the word of the Church, and its principal author is the pope or a council. It is a question here of inspiration in the strict sense, such as that which the sacred authors enjoyed; any divine assistance could be loosely referred to as inspiration.

As for *b:* God *assists* at least *negatively* by preventing an arrival at an erroneous definition. But it seems that we must go further and say that whenever, and to the extent that it is necessary, God also *positively guides* the Church's teachers to a correct knowledge and presentation of the truth He has entrusted to the Church. The means, natural or supernatural, which divine Providence selects for this purpose, can be quite varied, and can operate internally or externally.[26]

99   4. **The divine assistance does not render at all superfluous**

the hard work and study of men, the investigation of the sources of revelation, etc.; it rather supposes and includes these elements. In actual practice, the usual preamble to doctrinal definitions includes not only the request for divine light, but also the most careful theological research. Consequently, those who object that the promise of divine assistance fosters indolence do so without justification. However, infallibility (or the inability to err) does not depend formally on human industry, but on divine assistance. And so no one can spurn a definition of the Church on the pretext that it is not backed up by adequate research; when a definition has once been issued, one can be sure that the Church's official teacher did not act precipitously, but did all the necessary preliminary research; or else, if he did act rashly, that his rashness did not adversely affect at least the truth of the definition. All this is, of course, only a supposition, for it seems much more reasonable to hold that the Holy Spirit would never allow the Church's rulers to act rashly in issuing doctrinal definitions.

5. The assistance promised the Church's rulers extends to the threefold function which they must fulfill with regard to religious truth. (*a*) They are infallible *witnesses* of revelation, in that they always reverently safeguard the deposit entrusted to the Church; (*b*) they are infallible *teachers* of religious truth, in that they always faithfully interpret and explain revealed doctrine; (*c*) they are infallible *arbiters of controversies,* in that they always decide without error questions which have arisen on matters of religion.

Sequel 100

The rule of faith. It seems timely to add here a few remarks on the rule of faith. This term signifies the standard or *norm according to which each individual Christian must determine what is the material object of his faith.*

Protestants claim that the written Word of God, Holy Scripture, and that alone, is the one rule of faith. Catholics, on the other hand, even though they, too, admit that our faith must be regulated in the final analysis by the Word of God—including tradition as well as Scripture—hold that the proximate and immediate rule of faith—that rule to which each of the faithful and each generation of the faithful must look directly—is the preaching of the Church. And so, according to Catholics, there exists a twofold rule of faith: one remote and one proximate. The *remote rule of faith* is the

Word of God (handed down in writing or orally), which was directly entrusted to the Church's rulers that from it they might teach and guide the faithful. The *proximate rule of faith*, from which the faithful, one and all, are bound to accept their faith and in accordance with which they are to regulate it, is the *preaching of the ecclesiastical magisterium*.[27] The following assertions concern the proximate rule of faith.

1. The Church's preaching was established by Christ Himself as the rule of faith. This can be proved from Matthew 28:19-20 and Mark 16:15-16; the command to teach all nations certainly implies a corresponding duty on the part of the nations to believe whatever the apostles and their successors teach. On the other hand, there is no notice anywhere of Christ's having commanded the apostles to give the people the doctrine of salvation in writing, and never did He command the faithful as a whole to seek their faith in the Bible.[28]

2. The Church's preaching is a rule of faith which is nicely accommodated to people's needs. For (*a*) it is an *easy* rule, one that can be observed by all alike, even the uneducated and unlettered. What could be easier than to give ear to a magisterium that is always at hand and always preaching? (*b*) It is a *safe* rule, for the Church's teaching office is infallible in safeguarding and presenting Christ's doctrine. (*c*) It is a living rule, in accordance with which it is possible in any age to explain the meaning of doctrines and to put an end to controversies.

Notes

1. See the decree *Lamentabili*, propositions 6, 62-64; encyclical *Pascendi* (DB 2093); *Oath against Modernism* (DB 2147).

2. See J. C. Fenton, "The Church and Catholic Dogma," AER, 120 (1949), 123 ff.

3. Constitution *De ecclesia*, chap. 4.

4. It is with utter improbability that some have tried to interpret the words of John 14:16, "*for all time to come*" (*eis tòn aiôna*) and those of Matt. 28:20, "*as long as the world shall last*"—as "to the end of *this* age," i.e., the apostolic age.

5. In vain some Protestants, basing themselves on no good reasons, but forced by the need to bolster their position, have tried to refer the words "*the pillar and bulwark of truth*" either to Timothy or to the mystery of the Incarnation. They would read as follows: " . . . the Church of the living God. The pillar and bulwark of truth and something clearly great is the sacrament of piety which has been manifested in the flesh."

THE PROPERTIES OF THE CHURCH

6. *Adversus haereses* iv. 26. 2; see iii. 24. 1.
7. *De symbolo ad catechumenos* 1. 6.
8. *De ecclesia*, Thesis 3, 2.
9. It was, then, not a question of this fact, *viz.*, whether the five condemned propositions (DB 1092 ff.) can be found *verbatim* in the book *Augustinus;* much less whether Jansen maintained *in the secret of his soul* and intended to teach the doctrine expressed in the five propositions. Obviously the "mind of the author" which is condemned is nothing other than the meaning which the words of the author objectively express according to the usual norms of interpretation.
10. Session 4.
11. Session 22, chap. 4; and canon 6.
12. Constitution *Vineam Domini* of Clement XI (DB 1350).
13. See Hefele, *Conciliengeschichte* (2nd ed.), II, 798 ff.; Hergenröther-Kirsch, *Kirchengeschichte*, I, 602 ff. See P. Hughes, *op. cit.*, I, 342 ff.; H. M. Diepen, O.S.B., *Les trois chapitres au Concile de Chalcédoine* (Oosterhout, 1953).
14. *De ecclesia* (3rd ed.), p. 318.
15. An example may help to clarify the matter. If the whole Christ were not present under the appearances of bread alone, the law forbidding lay people to drink from the chalice would offend against the faith. Or if the words *increase and multiply* (Gen. 1:28) constituted an ordinance binding every individual man, then the law of celibacy would be opposed to right morals. The same conclusion would hold if virginal purity were morally impossible for men.
16. The bull *Auctorem fidei* (DB 1578).
17. See Benedict XIV, *De servorum Dei beatificatione*, lib. IV, pars II, chap. 13, nos. 7–8. Very many bishops asked the Vatican Council for an appropriate revision of the Breviary on some points "which seem not at all to square with established historical fact and sound scriptural exegesis" (*Coll. Lac.*, VII, 874; see VII, 844, 882). There should be nothing surprising about this. At the time the Roman Breviary was edited, the critical apparatus now at our disposal was simply not available.
18. On a lower plane than this solemn approbation, there are also: (*a*) *episcopal* approbation; (*b*) *permissive* papal approbation; (*c*) *commendatory* papal approbation. These are all treated in works on canon law.
19. See N. Scheid, "Die Unfehlbarkeit des Papstes bei der Heiligsprechung," ZkTh (1890), p. 599; F. Spedalieri, *De Ecclesiae infallibilitate in canonizatione sanctorum quaestiones selectae* (Rome, 1949); for a critique of this latter work see TS, 12 (1951), 249.
20. The names of canonized saints are inserted in the *Roman Martyrology*, but this work contains other names besides. That is why scholars, following the lead of Benedict XIV, warn us that the presence of a person's name in the *Martyrology* is not conclusive proof that that person is enjoying the bliss of heaven. See N. Paulus, "Martyrologium und Brevier als historische Quellen," *Der Katholik*, I (1900), 355.
21. *Absolute* cult or worship is directed to a *person; relative* cult is directed to some object or other, not because it possesses any intrinsic worth

in itself, as a person would, but because it *is* connected in some way with a sainted person. See A. Aldama, S.J., *Sacrae theologiae summa*, III (Madrid, 1953), 469.

22. See N. Paulus, *art. cit.*, p. 359; A. Spaldak, "Zur geplanten Emendation des römischen Breviers," *Der Katholik*, I (1905), 290; Bainvel, *De magisterio*, p. 111.

23. See J. C. Fenton, "New Testament Designations of the Church and of its Members," CBQ, 9 (1947), 286.

24. *De Traditione et Scriptura* (3rd ed.), p. 123.

25. Constitution *De ecclesia*, chap. 4.

26. See Heinrich, *Dogmat. Theol.* II, par. 90.

27. The *Symbols* (Creeds, i.e., those formulae in which the Church's teaching authority sums up the chief points of its preaching in view of the needs of different ages), are also called rules of faith. But they are *material* rules of faith, while the *formal* rule of faith is the preaching itself.

28. An appeal to John 5:39 is in vain: (*a*) from the context, the verb *ereunâte* seems to be the indicative rather than the imperative (Kleist-Lilly: *You have the Scriptures at your finger ends;* Confrat. NT: *You search the Scriptures*); (*b*) even granting that it is the imperative, the text still proves nothing. From the fact that Christ refers the unbelieving Jews, the Scribes and Pharisees, to the sacred books of the Old Testament that they may learn therein of His divine mission, it does not at all follow that He intends every individual Christian to draw his faith directly from the Scriptures.

Article II

THE CHURCH'S UNITY

Preliminary Remarks

PROPOSITION: Christ willed that His Church enjoy unity of faith and of profession (credal unity) which consists in this, that all the members of the Church hold and make profession of the same doctrine as it is presented for belief by the teaching office of the Church.

Proof: 1. from the words of Christ and of the apostles;
2. from the solid conviction of early Christianity.

Scholion 1. What unity of faith does and does not mean.
Scholion 2. The Fundamentalist system.

PROPOSITION: Christ willed that His Church enjoy unity of communion or of (social) charity which consists in this, that all members of the Church, whether as individuals or as particular groups, mutually cohere like the finely articulated parts of one moral body, one family, one single society.

Proof: 1. from the metaphors used by Christ and the apostles in describing the Church;
2. from Christ's prayer after the Last Supper;
3. from the solid conviction of early Christianity.

Scholion 1. The diversity of liturgies and disciplinary laws.

Scholion 2. The opinion of some Anglicans.

PROPOSITION: Christ willed that His Church enjoy unity of rule which consists in this, that all members of the Church obey one and the same visible authority.

Scholion: The Western Schism.
Corollary: Unity of worship.

Article II

THE CHURCH'S UNITY

Preliminary Remarks

101   It was demonstrated above (no. 9) that Christ founded just one Church; so, the present article is concerned not with the unity of the Church as opposed to plurality, but rather with internal unity as opposed to division within the Church itself. This will involve a study of the bonds of unity which hold together the true Church of Christ.

All Christians agree that the true Church of Christ is unified in one way or another, but non-Catholics acknowledge only a spiritual principle of unity. If they occasionally acknowledge external bonds also, they make them quite elastic.

Catholic teaching has it that the Church, by the institution of its Founder, and hence necessarily and essentially, enjoys a threefold unity which is external and visible, namely, unity of *doctrine* and *profession*, unity of *communion*, and unity of *government*.[1] The Vatican Council says: "Our eternal Pastor willed to build a holy Church in which . . . all the faithful would be bound together by the bond of the one faith and of charity. And in order that the universal fold might be kept in oneness of faith and communion by priests who would themselves be joined in close union, He gave St. Peter charge over the other apostles and thereby established in his person the unfailing principle and visible foundation of both unities."[2] And Leo XIII: "Since the Church's divine Founder had determined that it should be one in belief, in rule, and in communion, He selected Peter and his successors to be the principle and, as it were, the focal point of unity."[3]

102   PROPOSITION: *Christ willed that His Church enjoy unity of faith and of profession (credal unity) which consists in this, that all the members of the Church hold and make profession of the same doctrine as it is presented for belief by the Church's teaching office.*

THE PROPERTIES OF THE CHURCH

Note the phrase "make profession of"; for a purely internal assent of the mind to truth does not satisfy the requirements of a visible society such as the Church is. This assent must be given clear outward expression as well: *Because with the heart a man believes and attains holiness, and with the lips profession of faith is made and salvation secured* (Rom. 10:10).

Proof: That our Lord so set up His Church that it must needs be one in oneness of faith is proved:

1. From the *words of Christ and of the apostles,* which clearly and unqualifiedly demand that everyone profess the faith preached by the apostles and their successors. Read Matt. 28:18-20; Mark 16:15-17; Gal. 1:8; I Cor. 1:10; Eph. 4:5, 13-14; Tit. 3:10-11.

2. From the solid *conviction of early Christianity.* According to St. Justin, real Christians are "disciples of the genuine and unsullied doctrine of Jesus Christ," and are "one mind, one congregation, one Church." On the contrary, "those who claim to be Christians but do not hold His doctrine" are heretics.[4] Hegesippus stigmatizes as heretics those "who have, each of them, privately introduced their own pet opinions," because "by introducing strange doctrine . . . they have rent asunder the unity of the Church."[5] St. Irenaeus:

> Just as the sun is one and the same all throughout the world, so too the preaching of the truth shines everywhere and enlightens all who desire to arrive at a knowledge of the truth . . . for the universal Church has the one and the same faith all throughout the world.[6]

St. Augustine lists eighty-eight heresies, and then concludes: "There may be or there may arise other heresies, but if anyone espouses one of them, he will not be a Catholic Christian."[7]

Scholion 1. What unity of faith does and does not mean.   103

The unity of faith which Christ decreed without qualification consists in this, that everyone accepts the doctrines *presented for belief by the Church's teaching office.* In fact our Lord requires nothing other than the acceptance by all of the preaching of the apostolic college, a body which is to continue forever; or, what amounts to the same thing, of the pronouncements of the Church's teaching office, which He Himself set up as the rule of faith. And

(127)

so, (*a*) the essential unity of faith definitely requires that everyone hold each and every doctrine clearly and distinctly presented for belief by the Church's teaching office; and that everyone hold these truths explicitly or at least implicitly, i.e., by acknowledging the authority of the Church which teaches them. But, (*b*) it does not require the absence from the Church of all controversy about religious matters. For as long as there does not exist a clear and explicit statement of the Church about some point or other, even though it may perchance be contained objectively in the sources of revelation, it can be freely discussed without any detriment to the unity of the faith, provided that all the disputants are ready to bow to a decision of the Church's teaching office, should one be forthcoming. Obviously the unity of faith does not extend beyond the limits of the rule of faith.

104 *Scholion 2. The Fundamentalist system.*

Towards the end of the eighteenth century, Pierre Jurieu, a Calvinist minister in France, developed the *system of fundamental articles.* According to this system, agreement on fundamental doctrines would suffice for the required unity of faith, and people could hold a variety of opinions on other truths, just as surely revealed, but less fundamental. And so even within the limits of the true Church there would be room for an assortment of creeds. This system, to which nearly all Protestants adhere, if not by explicit profession, then at least in practice, is altogether untenable; for, (*a*) Christ demanded faith not just in some doctrines, but in all those doctrines which the authority set up by Him should teach. Consequently, any distinction between fundamental and nonfundamental articles of belief is contrary to the mind and will of Christ. Furthermore, (*b*) it is impossible to determine a sure standard for distinguishing fundamental from nonfundamental articles; this system thus paves the way—and a broad way it is—to indifferentism.

105 PROPOSITION: *Christ willed that His Church enjoy unity of communion or of (social) charity which consists in this, that all members of the Church, whether as individuals or as particular groups, mutually cohere like the finely articulated parts of one moral body, one family, one single society.*

It follows from this that they all share the same common benefits: sacrifice, sacraments, intercession.

THE PROPERTIES OF THE CHURCH

Proof: That Christ so instituted His Church that it should of necessity be one in oneness of communion is proved:

1. From the *metaphors which Christ and the apostles used to describe the Church.* They compared it to a house,[8] a kingdom,[9] a sheepfold,[10] an organic body.[11] All of these imply social unity.

2. From *Christ's prayer after the Last Supper,* in which He asked without qualification that, just as He and the Father are one in the oneness of perfect love, so the apostles and all the disciples might be united as perfectly as possible in love and social harmony:

> *"May they be one as we are one . . . All are to be one; just as you, Father, are in me and I am in you, so they, too, are to be one in us. The world must come to believe that I am your ambassador . . . I in them and you in me. Thus their oneness will be perfected"* (John 17:21-23).

3. From the solid *conviction of early Christianity,* which abhorred schisms above all else, and precisely because they destroy unity of communion. St. Ignatius Martyr: "If a man runs after a schismatic, he will not inherit the Kingdom of God."[12] St. Irenaeus:

> Those who foster schisms for petty or personal reasons rip and tear the great and glorious body of Christ, and—as far as in them lies—they kill it. For they can never make amends in such measure as to match the wickedness of their schism.[13]

St. Cyprian:

> If man does not hold fast to this oneness of the Church, does he imagine that he still holds the faith? If he resists and withstands the Church, has he still confidence that he is in the Church?[14]

St. Chrysostom: "I say in private and in public that to tear the Church apart is no less an evil than to fall into heresy."[15] St. Augustine: "There is nothing more serious than the sacrilege of schism . . . there can never be any just need for severing unity."[16]

Scholion 1. The diversity of liturgies and of disciplinary laws.

The diversity of rites in different parts of the Church does not break up the required unity of communion. This variety does not affect the substance of Christian worship, i.e., those rites which

Christ personally determined, but only the external ceremonies instituted by the Church. Ceremonies are simply declarations of faith that are expressed in deeds rather than in words. Therefore, as long as the same faith is expressed by these different ceremonies and the necessary submission to legitimate pastors is observed, the communion is not sundered. It is the same with *disciplinary laws,* i.e., particular regulations by which the divinely established laws of right living are applied in different ways and given specific determination to correspond to varying circumstances of times, locales, and persons.

107 *Scholion 2. The opinion of some Anglicans.*

Some Anglicans (Pusey, Palmer, and others) pervert completely the genuine notion of the Church by admitting that unity of communion is indeed desirable but not absolutely necessary; and by claiming that the true Church of Christ actually comprises three distinct communions: Roman, Greek, and Anglican, which should be joined in an amicable association without destroying their individual independence. Whatever they are in fact, these three societies most certainly do not form one fold, one body. And even should such an association be effected, they would still remain simply several Churches; this is clear from the case of nations which, although they often enter into mutual alliances, still remain several distinct nations. And Gladstone's[17] position is hardly tenable, namely, that Christ did at the beginning will the unity of the Church, but that now that circumstances have changed, He no longer requires it!

108 PROPOSITION: *Christ willed that His Church enjoy unity of rule (hierarchical unity) which consists in this, that all the members of the Church obey one and the same visible authority.*[18]

This authority rests in the Catholic episcopate with the Roman pontiff at its head, yet in such wise that it is found full and entire in the latter all by himself.

That Christ so built His Church as to make it necessarily one in oneness of rule is proved by what has already been said about the institution by Christ of the hierarchy and of the primacy and about their permanent continuity.

The Vatican Council called the supreme pontiff the "principle and foundation" of unity, because by his influence he establishes and preserves unity. Leo XIII called him the "principle and focal point" of unity, especially because all, faithful and bishops alike, must look up to him and stand faithfully by him. This latter description expresses the relationship of the Church to the pope, the former the relationship of the pope to the Church.

Scholion. The Western Schism. 109

It might seem that unity of rule suffered a setback in the Church at the time of the Western Schism, when for forty years (1378–1417) two or three men claimed to be sovereign pontiff. But with the preservation of unity of faith and communion, hierarchical unity was *only materially,* not formally, interrupted.[19] Although Catholics were split three ways in their allegiance because of the doubt as to which of the contenders had been legitimately elected, still all were agreed in believing that allegiance was owed the one legitimate successor of Peter, and they stood willing to give that allegiance. Consequently, those who through no fault of their own gave their allegiance to an illegitimate pope would no more be schismatics than a person would be a heretic who, desirous of following the preaching of the Church, would admit a false doctrine because he was under the impression that it was taught by the Church.

Corollary

Several popular catechisms and quite a few theologians speak of a *unity of worship,* or liturgical unity, in addition to unity of faith and rule (and communion), in line with which all share in the same sacraments. This unity does of course obtain and is absolutely necessary to the extent that the worship was determined by Christ Himself. However, liturgical unity is already included in the other unities: in unity of faith, since faith includes also the revealed doctrine on the sacrifice of the Mass and the sacraments; in unity of communion, since this involves the sharing in the same spiritual benefits. This is perhaps the reason that neither the Vatican Council nor Leo XIII in his encyclical on the unity of the Church make any specific mention of liturgical unity.

Notes

1. See J. C. Fenton, "Our Lord's Presence in the Catholic Church," AER, 115 (1946), 50 ff.; I. Salaverri, *op. cit.,* p. 884 ff.; C. Journet, *Church of the*

Word, op. cit., p. 493 ff.

2. Constitution *De ecclesia Christi*, Preamble. See J. A. Fitzmyer, S.J., "The Function of the Papacy," AER, 121 (1949), 34 ff.

3. Encyclical *Satis cognitum* (June 29, 1896); *Leonis XIII allocutiones* (Desclée edition), VI, 183.

4. *Dialogus cum Tryphone* 63 and 35.

5. Cited in Eusebius HE 4. 21.

6. *Adversus haereses* i. 10. 2–3.

7. *Liber de haeresibus* concl.

8. Matt. 16:18; I Tim. 3:15.

9. Matt. 16:19.

10. John 10:16.

11. Rom. 12:4–5; I Cor. 10:17; 12:12 ff.; Eph. 4:16.

12. *Epistula ad Philadelphenses* 3. 3 (ACW trans).

13. *Adversus haereses* iv. 33. 7.

14. *De unitate ecclesiae* (2nd ed.) 4; ACW trans.

15. *Homilia in Epistula ad Ephesios* 11. 5.

16. *Contra epistulam Parmeniani* ii. 11. 25.

17. Writing in *The Nineteenth Century;* cited by Wilmers, *De ecclesia*, p. 518.

18. Unity of rule and of communion are not at all identical. The former implies the submission of everyone to one head, the latter the mutual cohesion of all the members. Now submission to a single head can occur apart from the mutual cohesion of all the members, as is clear in the case of two countries under one ruler. However, the aforementioned unities are intimately related, for unity of communion cannot exist apart from unity of rule. In fact, to be perfectly accurate, it may be said that they do coincide, for where there is not only just one person in authority, but in addition a regime or authority which is formally one, submission to one head necessarily involves mutual cohesion. In view of this, it is easy to see why authors sometimes suggest a threefold division of the Church's unity: unity of *faith*, of *communion*, and of *rule*, and sometimes a twofold division: unity of *faith* and of *communion*, or unity of *faith* and of *rule*.

19. See Salaverri, *op. cit.*, p. 931.

Article III

THE CHURCH'S HOLINESS

I. *Preliminary Remarks:*
   PROPOSITION: Christ willed that His Church be holy as to its means (or principles).
   Proof: 1. from the purpose for which He founded the Church;
   2. from the metaphors which He used in describing the Church;
   3. from an enumeration of the means of sanctification at its disposal:
   PROPOSITION: Christ willed that His Church be holy as to its members (or its effects).
   Assertion 1. A harvest of outstanding holiness can never be wanting in the Church.
   Proof: 1. from Christ's purpose in founding the Church and the aid He promised;
   2. from the fact that the Apostle calls the Church the *body of Christ,* which Christ *nourishes and cherishes;*
   3. from the fact that Christ wanted His Church to be recognizable by its abundant holiness;
   4. from Old Testament prophecies.
   Assertion 2. The harvest of holiness, to the extent that it is a minimum requisite to justify one's pointing to the Church's members as holy, does not extend beyond the limits intimated in the above PROPOSITION.
   Proof: 1. one has no right to expect all members of the Church to be actually holy.
   2. one cannot expect either that of those who are actually brought to holiness, very many will reach a heroic degree of sanctity.

Corollary. The Church can be called unqualifiedly holy.

PROPOSITION: Christ willed that His Church be holy as to its charisms, that is, that the Church in every age be enriched with certain miraculous gifts through which God manifests its holiness.

Article III

THE CHURCH'S HOLINESS

I. Preliminary Remarks 110

Holiness consists in union with God, the supreme Norm of rectitude. It implies two things: being cleansed of anything that can sully, and adhering staunchly to God through love.[1]

Sanctity has unlimited degrees, for everyone is capable of yet greater holiness. For the present discussion it will suffice to distinguish just two degrees: *ordinary,* by which one is habitually free of mortal sin, and *heroic,* by which one surpasses in a notable way the common run of people who live virtuous lives.

Holiness is taken here in its strict sense, such as applies to rational creatures alone. Holiness can, however, be predicated analogously of irrational things like churches and altars, inasmuch as they are set apart for divine worship; or, inasmuch as they have some power to make men holy, like the sacraments, or are signs of inner holiness, like miracles.

Christ's Church is holy on several counts: e.g., because of its Founder and Head, who is the only-begotten Son of God; because of its purpose, which is the glory of God and the sanctification of mankind; about these there is no difficulty. Catholic teaching states in addition that the Church, by the institution of Christ and therefore necessarily and irrevocably, is adorned with a threefold external and visible holiness: that of its *means* of sanctification, that of its *members,* and that of its *charisms.*

PROPOSITION: *Christ willed that His Church be holy as to its means* 111
(or principles).

That is, that the Church possess means suitable to produce moral holiness in people, even perfect and outstanding or heroic holiness.

Proof: That Christ endowed His Church with means of this type is proved:

1. By the *purpose for which He founded the Church: He gave*

himself for us, to redeem us from every kind of iniquity and cleanse a people for his very own, zealous for good deeds (Tit. 2:14–15). *Christ loved the Church, and delivered himself for her, that he might sanctify her by cleansing her in the bath of water with the accompanying word, in order to present to himself the Church in all her glory, devoid of blemish or wrinkle or anything of the kind, but that she may be holy and flawless* (Eph. 5:25–27). It makes little difference whether one understands *the Church in all her glory, devoid of blemish or wrinkle* as applying to the Church of this present world, which sparkles with perfect holiness in at least some of its members, or as applying to the Church in the glory of heaven. For the Church Triumphant is made up only of those who were sanctified while here on earth. Now, if it was Christ's will that people be guided to even outstanding holiness by the Church, He certainly must have endowed it with effective means for the attainment of perfect holiness.

2. By the *metaphors which Christ used* when He called the pastors of His Church *"the salt of the earth"* (Matt. 5:13), and compared the Church itself with yeast (Matt. 13:33). Both of these figures indicate the sanctifying influence which the Church, by the institution of its Founder, is to exercise.

3. By an *enumeration of the means of sanctification* entrusted to the Church. Our Lord entrusted to the apostles and their successors: (*a*) sound doctrine, containing both precepts and counsels; (*b*) sacraments, the instruments of abundant grace, chief of which are baptism (Eph. 5:26–27) and the Eucharist (John 6:54–59); (*c*) sacred authority, the purpose of which is to instruct all men in Christian perfection:

> *He established some men as apostles, and some as inspired spokesmen, others again as evangelists, and others as pastors and teachers, thus organizing the saints for the work of the ministry, which consists in building up the body of Christ, until we all attain to unity in faith and deep knowledge of the Son of God. Thus we attain to perfect manhood, to the mature proportions that befit Christ's fullness* (Eph. 4:11–13).

The *perfect manhood* of Christ signifies the fulness of Christian perfection.

112 PROPOSITION: *Christ willed that His Church be holy as to its members (or its effects).*

THE PROPERTIES OF THE CHURCH

That is, *that in every age very many of the Church's members be brought to a state of ordinary holiness, and at least some be shining examples of outstanding or heroic holiness.* This harvest of holiness may be quite abundant at one time, less satisfying at another.

There are two points to be proved: 1. that a harvest of even outstanding holiness can never be wanting in the Church; and 2. that the harvest of holiness required to justify one's pointing to the holiness of the Church's members does not, for all practical purposes, have to exceed the limits just determined.

Assertion 1. A harvest of even outstanding holiness can never be wanting in the Church.

Proof:

1. From *Christ's purpose in founding the Church and the aid He promised.* He founded the Church that it might lead men to even perfect holiness; besides, He promised it effective and perpetual help (Matt. 28:20) for the attainment of this purpose. Therefore the Church can no more fail in producing holiness than it can in preaching truth.

2. From the fact that the Apostle calls the Church the *body of Christ,* which Christ *nourishes and cherishes* (Eph. 5:23, 29). But if the Church is always animated and made fruitful by the Spirit of Christ, it must at all times produce a harvest of holiness which will be proportionate to such a Spirit; this must include even perfect holiness.

3. From the fact that Christ wanted His Church to be *recognizable by its abundant holiness:*

> *"You are the light of the world. It is impossible for a city to escape notice when built on a mountain top. . . . Just so let your light shine before your fellow men, that they may see your good example and praise your Father who is in heaven"* (Matt. 5:14–16; see 7:16–17).

This demands that the Church be resplendent with holiness, even outstanding and striking holiness.

4. From the *Old Testament prophecies,* which describe the Church as a kingdom of surpassing holiness: *Justice shall flower in his days, and profound peace* (Ps. 71:7). *And they shall call*

them, the holy people, the redeemed of the Lord (Isai. 62:12). *And the nations shall know that I am the Lord the sanctifier of Israel, when my sanctuary shall be built in the midst of them forever* (Ezech. 37:28).

113   *Assertion 2.* The harvest of holiness, to the extent that it is a minimum requisite to justify one's pointing to the Church's members as holy, does not extend beyond the limits intimated in the above PROPOSITION.

Proof:

1. One has no right to expect *all the members* of the Church to be actually holy, for Christ Himself forewarned us that there might be and in fact would be very many sinners in His kingdom. Read the parables of the cockle, of the net, of the wise and foolish virgins.[2] Besides, it is clear from the writings of the apostles that even in the primitive Church not all were holy (I Cor. 5; 11:18 ff.; II Cor. 12:20–21). It is enough, then, that there are many in the Church who actually attain holiness.

2. One cannot expect either that of those who are actually brought to holiness, *very many will reach a heroic degree of sanctity.* Even ordinary holiness is quite a difficult attainment, won only by relentless striving. That is why it is so truly remarkable that so many men and women from every class of mankind, through the influence of the Church, actually do attain it. But heroic sanctity is a sublime state reached only by supreme effort and the most gruelling work. In any field of endeavor those who rise to any notable extent above the common level are usually quite rare. Again, heroic sanctity, at least in the strict sense, is a miracle on the moral plane, involving a very special assistance from God. But miracles are something out of the ordinary in the realm of grace as well as in the realm of physical nature. The conclusion should be evident.

Corollary

Granted the holiness of the means at its disposal, the Church, even though perhaps it clasps to its bosom more sinners than saints, can be with justification called *unqualifiedly holy.* For the saintly members of the Church, since they have been formed through its influence, belong to it *precisely* because they are holy, but this can not at all be said of sinners. The latter are what they are for the simple reason that they do not follow the standard of life set up by the Church and neglect the means that it provides for them. It would be ridiculous to stigmatize a society because of those members who shun the influence of that society's principles. Even should they be in the majority, they would by no means be representative members.

114 PROPOSITION: *Christ willed that His Church be holy as to its charisms, that is, that the Church in every age be enriched with certain miraculous gifts through which God manifests its holiness.*

Charisms have an essential relationship to holiness, both because they are signs that the Holy Spirit dwells in the Church, and because ordinarily they are enjoyed by those who are outstanding for perfect holiness.

Proof: That Christ willed His Church to be favored with charisms in all ages is proved by *His unqualified promise:*

> "*Go into the whole world and preach the gospel to all creation. . . . And in the way of proofs of their claims, the following will accompany those who believe: in my name they will drive out demons; they will speak in new tongues; they will take up serpents in their hands, and if they drink something deadly, it will not hurt them; they will lay their hands on the sick, and these will recover*" (Mark 16:15–18; see John 14:12; I Cor. 12:4–11).

This promise is general, restricted by no time limit, and therefore it cannot be confined to the apostolic age. And Christ added nothing about the measure in which the promise (which was made to the Church, not to individual Christians) should be fulfilled. Consequently there can be a profusion of miraculous gifts in one age and a relative scarcity of them in another, in accord with the needs of the Church or with the decrees of divine Providence, but they will never be totally lacking. As a matter of fact, they abounded in the Churchs' infancy, and the chief reason for this was suggested in the treatise on *The True Religion* (no. 114, 3).

Notes

1. See S.Th. II-II, q. 81, a. 8; Salaverri, *op. cit.*, p. 895.
2. Matt. 13:24–30; 48–50; 25:1–12. At the same time, note that the

wicked people found in the Church are there not as a result of the Church's influence, but in spite of it, and as the result of *completely extraneous circumstances:* '*Sir, was it not good seed that you sowed in your field? How, then, is it overrun with weeds?*' '*That is the work of an enemy!*' *he replies.* Furthermore, all the people in the Church have at least one foot on the path to holiness: they profess the true faith, they are subject to legitimate rulers, and they partake of the sacraments at least to some extent. See C. Journet, *Church of the Word, op. cit.*, p. xxvii; p. 95 ff.; R. H. Benson, *op. cit.*

Article IV

THE CHURCH'S CATHOLICITY

I. *The Notion of Catholicity:*
  1. Etymological meaning.
  2. As applied to the Church, the term may describe its:
     a. doctrine
     b. personnel
     c. duration in time
     d. geographical diffusion.
  3. In strict, apologetic usage, catholicity may be defined as *the diffusion of the one and undivided Church throughout the entire world.*
     a. catholicity *by right:* the Church's aptitude for world-wide diffusion.
     b. catholicity *in fact:* the actual spread of the Church throughout the world.

II. *Catholicity is an Essential Quality of Christ's Church:*

  PROPOSITION 1: The Church is endowed with absolute catholicity: it will some day reach literally all nations.
  Proof: 1. from the Messianic prophecies;
  2. from the words of Christ.

  PROPOSITION 2: The Church is endowed with moral catholicity: Christ's Church, after its beginnings, should always be conspicuous for its morally universal diffusion.
  Proof: 1. from the Messianic prophecies;
  2. from the words of Christ and St. Paul.
  Corollary: Large numbers alone do not satisfy the requirements for catholicity.

PROPOSITION 3: The morally universal diffusion, characteristic of the Church in all ages, should be a progressive expansion.

Proof: 1. from the Messianic prophecies;
2. from Christ's own words.

Article IV

THE CHURCH'S CATHOLICITY

I. The Notion of Catholicity

1. The term catholic (kata holon = throughout a whole) means something complete, whole, or entire. Even etymologically, then, catholicity suggests some sort of universality.

2. As applied to the Church[1] the term catholic may take on various shades of meaning since a number of facets in its makeup fit the notion of totality or universality. For example, it may be called catholic in reference to:

>   *a)* doctrine
>   *b)* personnel
>   *c)* time
>   *d)* place

The Church is catholic in *doctrine* because it teaches Christ's religion in its completeness or entirety; in *personnel* because it welcomes people of every sort of temperament and condition in life and erects no racial, national or social barriers; with reference to *time* because it covers the whole era from the time of Christ until the end of the world; with reference to *place* because it is spread throughout the entire world.

Even though the first three meanings do turn up occasionally in the writings of the fathers,° they occur far less frequently than

---

° As an example, St. Cyril of Jerusalem: The Church "is called catholic because it is diffused throughout the entire world from one extremity to the other; because it teaches everywhere in their completeness all the truths which men should learn, whether those truths be concerned with things visible or invisible, earthly or heavenly. Again [it is called catholic] because it brings men of all sorts to correct worship: princes and private citizens, learned and unlearned; and, finally, because it cures and heals every sort of sin that can be committed in body or soul. It possesses, in fact, all gifts of holiness, of whatever name, whether holiness in deeds, words, or spiritual gifts of any kind whatsoever" (*Catechesis* 18. 23). See St. Thomas, *In symbolum apostolorum expositio*, a. 9.

(143)

the fourth, which is the correct usage and the best known. In the present discussion the term will be used exclusively in that sense.[2]

3. By the term catholicity, then, is meant the diffusion of the one and undivided Church throughout the entire world. Notice the phrase, *one and undivided Church*. Catholicity necessarily implies that the Church in its world-wide diffusion retains the triple unity (doctrinal, social, governmental) explained earlier (see nos. 101–109). Finally, it is customary to distinguish between what is called catholicity *by right* and catholicity *in fact*.

a. Catholicity by right (i.e., destined or intended to be such) means that the Church has the aptitude, right, and duty to spread throughout the world.

The Church has the *aptitude* to spread over the whole world because there is nothing in its structural principles which bind it to one nation or a few nations rather than to any other. The Church has both the *right* and the *duty* to spread throughout the world because its Founder endowed it with the power and the obligation of spreading to all regions.

These facts are clearly proven by Christ's words: *"Go, therefore, and initiate all nations in discipleship."*[3]

The new-born Church possessed only catholicity by right; but that is, of course, the root and foundation for catholicity in fact.

b. Catholicity in fact.[4] Catholicity in this sense means the actual spread of the Church throughout the world. If that diffusion actually extends to all people, it is called *absolute* catholicity; if it reaches only a great number of people, it is called *moral* catholicity.

II. Catholicity is an Essential Quality of Christ's Church

After its first beginnings, then, Christ's Church *should always enjoy a morally universal and progressive diffusion until finally one day it reaches all nations*. This is the genuine notion of the catholicity God promised His Church. Each part of this notion bears explaining. We begin with the last, the eventual, complete diffusion of the Church.

PROPOSITION 1: *The Church must finally one day reach literally all nations.*

Proof:

1. From the *Messianic prophecies: And in thy seed shall all the*

THE PROPERTIES OF THE CHURCH

nations of the earth be blessed (Gen. 22:18); *Ask of me and I will give you the nations for an inheritance and the ends of the earth for your possession* (Ps. 2:8); *In him shall all the tribes of the earth be blessed; all the nations shall proclaim his happiness* (Ps. 71:17); *All the nations you have made shall come and worship you, O Lord, and glorify your name* (Ps. 85:9).

2. From the *words of Christ*: "Go, therefore, and initiate all nations in discipleship" (Matt. 28:19); "*This gospel of the kingdom must be preached throughout the whole world, so that all nations may have valid evidence. And then will come the end.*" (Matt. 24:14); "This," he said to them, "is the gist of the Scriptures: *the Messias must suffer and on the third day rise from the dead. Furthermore, in his name the need of a change of heart and forgiveness of sins must be preached to all the nations*" (Luke 24:46–48); "*You shall be my witnesses in Jerusalem and in all Judea and Samaria and even to the very ends of the earth*" (Acts 1:8).

These texts should not be interpreted as meaning only a moral universality among some nations; there is no justification for restricting their meaning in such a fashion. Actually reason itself urges that if a Church is destined for all nations, and is supported by God's help for all time, it should one day actually reach all nations. The only sensible conclusion is, then, that Christ and His Church were promised an *absolute* universality: one which would embrace all nations. We say, "all nations," or what amounts to the same thing, "all regions," of the earth; we do not say all "individuals"; that is nowhere promised.[5] Indeed a universal reign over all individuals is rather emphatically excluded by the prophecies about the continual persecutions of the Church and the great defection to take place near the end of the world.[6] That is why Augustine observed in his own day:

> For all nations were promised, but not all the individual men of all nations . . . for otherwise how would that other prophecy be fulfilled: "you shall be hated by all nations for my name's sake," unless in all nations there would be found both those who hate and those who are hated.[7]

If it be asked "*just when* will the Church be spread throughout all the regions of the world?" we can only reply: sometime rather

CHRIST'S CHURCH

close to the end of the world: *"This gospel of the kingdom must be preached throughout the entire world, . . . And then will come the end."*[8] The calendar date is a secret of God's providence.

117 PROPOSITION 2: *The Church is endowed with moral catholicity: Christ's Church, after its beginnings, should always be conspicuous for its morally universal diffusion.*

In other words, the Church should always include in its membership *a vast number of men from many different nations.*

Proof:

1. From the *Messianic prophecies.* The Messianic prophecies constantly speak of the universality or diffusion of the Messianic kingdom among all peoples.[9] Now a quality which is described, without any time-limitation, as an essential characteristic of the Church, must always belong to it in *at least some degree.* Since this quality could not always belong to it in an *absolute* degree, as should be obvious from what has been already discussed, it must belong to it in a more restricted degree. In other words, the Church should be *morally everywhere* in any given age and throughout all ages.

2. From the *words of Christ and the testimony of St. Paul.* Christ unconditionally willed His Church to spread among all nations. To attain this goal He promised it His perpetual assistance. The Church, then, must of necessity always actually fulfill its destiny *at least in some measure.* The conclusion is clear. Again, no one doubts that Christ's words: *"You shall be my witnesses in Jerusalem . . . and even to the very ends of the earth,"* were to be fulfilled at least in some sense, though very imperfectly, even by the apostles themselves. As a matter of fact the events matched the prediction: according to St. Paul's testimony, the gospel, even in his day, was being preached and bearing fruit *throughout the whole world*[10]—morally speaking, that is to say.

Corollary

To satisfy the requirements of moral catholicity in fact—a quality belonging to Christ's Church perpetually and necessarily—we stated there was required: "a great number of men from many *different nations.*" For catholicity (which is directly opposed, not to fewness of numbers, but to nationalism or any other sort of provincialism) strictly implies diffusion throughout various regions of the world, and consequently diffusion among different peoples. Such diffusion, obviously, cannot be had without a really large number of adherents; but large numbers alone do not satisfy the requirements of catholicity. For example, if all the adherents, no matter how vast their number, were to belong to only one nation or one racial stock, they would still never constitute a church which was truly *Catholic*. Four hundred million Chinese converts would not make a Catholic Church.

Again, a *merely successive* diffusion in which the Church would spread around the world in such fashion as to gather in a new people only by relinquishing its former adherents, would never fulfill the requirements for the essential catholicity of the Church. Just suppose the Church were to have traveled around the whole world moving from new people to new people in the fashion just described—winning the Germans only at the expense of the Italians, or the Italians only at the expense of the English—at no one time would it ever have been actually Catholic.

PROPOSITION 3: *The morally universal diffusion, characteristic of the Church in all ages, should be a progressive expansion.*

Proof: The statement hardly needs proving. If the Church was designed to start from small beginnings and a short time thereafter to be quite widespread and finally was to reach literally all parts of the world; if, furthermore, the Church was destined to spread by God's help, but at the same time, dependently on human resources, it follows quite naturally that its diffusion was to be effected by continuous additions. As a matter of fact, both the Messianic prophecies and Christ's own words point to such a progressive expansion.

1. From the *Messianic prophecies*. For example: *Enlarge the place of thy tent and stretch out the skins of thy tabernacles. Spare not: lengthen thy cords and strengthen thy stakes. For thou shalt pass on to the right hand and to the left: and thy seed shall inherit the Gentiles and shall inhabit the desolate cities . . . and thy Redeemer, the Holy One of Israel, shall be called the God of all the earth* (Isai. 54:2–5).

2. From *Christ's own words:* "The kingdom of heaven reminds me of a mustard seed. . . . This is the tiniest of all seeds; but the full-grown plant is larger than any garden herb and, in fact,

becomes a tree, so that the birds of the air come and settle in its branches" (Matt. 13:31-32).

Please note, however, that the *continuity* of this progressive expansion should not be pressed too hard. The texts cited do not rule out the possibility of the Church's being notably decreased in this or that century due to schism or heresy (whose occurrence was foretold[11] in the Sacred Scripture), without its being able to recoup immediately. Still, theologians usually reject the hypothesis that the Church might ever be so besieged with heresy that it would—even for a brief period—be restricted to just one region.[12] Neither should one interpret the scriptural prophecies about the great defection at the end of the world in such a sense.[13]

Notes

1. The term *catholic* as applied to the Church appears for the first time in the writings of St. Ignatius Martyr *Epistula ad Smyrnaeos* 8. 2. Next, it is found in the *Muratorian Fragment* (ML, 3, 191) and in Tertullian, St. Cyprian, St. Cyril of Jerusalem, and in other fathers mentioned in *The True Religion*, p. 197.

2. For a theological analysis of the concept of catholicity, stressing especially the Church's catholicity of *doctrine,* see H. de Lubac, *Catholicism* (London, 1950).

3. Against the assertion of Harnack that Christ never gave a command to preach the gospel throughout the world, see, e.g., *Der Katholik*, I (1903), 240; Meindertz, *Jesus und die Heidenmission* (1908).

4. See Poulpiquet, "Essai sur la notion de catholicité," RSPT (1909), p. 19.

5. Maldonatus, commenting on the words of Christ (John 10:16), *"and there will be one flock, one shepherd,"* has this to say:

> The error that perhaps some time before the end of the world all men, both Gentiles and Jews, will become Christians and thus there will be one flock and one shepherd takes its origin from a bad and unscientific interpretation of this passage. For its meaning is not that all men will enter the Church; but rather, there will be no discrimination between those of Jewish origin who shall become believers, and those of Gentile origin who shall become believers; for the wall which formerly divided these two groups will have been broken down.

6. Ps. 2:1-4; Isai. 54:17; Zach. 12:3; Matt. 24:9; II Thess. 2:3.

7. *Epistulae* 199. 48.

8. Matt. 24:14; see 10:23, *"you will not make the round of the towns in Israel before the Son of Man comes."* See also Rom. 11:25.

9. See, for example, Dan. 2:35, 44-45; Mich. 4:1-2; Mal. 1:10-11.

10. Rom. 1:8; Col. 1:6, 23.

11. I Cor. 11:19.

12. Melchior Cano (*De locis*, IV, 6. ad 13) and Bellarmine (*De ecclesia*, IV, 7) were of the opinion that even in this hypothesis the Church could still be called catholic; namely, insofar as it could be clearly proved to be the same Church as that Church which was once diffused throughout the whole world. But the point at issue is whether the Church, if confined in that fashion, would still be catholic *in the sense indicated by the Scriptures*.

13. Luke 18:8, II Thess. 2:3; see St. Augustine [?] *De unitate ecclesiae* 15. 38.

Article V

THE CHURCH'S APOSTOLICITY

I. *The Notion of Apostolicity:*
   1. according to Protestants.
   2. according to Schismatics and Anglicans.
   3. according to Roman Catholics.

II. *Christ's Church is Apostolic in Doctrine, Government, and Membership:*
   1. Apostolicity of *doctrine:*
      Christ willed His Church to preserve unadulterated the doctrine taught it by His apostles.
   2. Apostolicity of *government:*
      By Christ's mandate the Church will always be ruled by pastors who are legitimate successors of the apostles.
      Scholion 1. How can one prove that this or that bishop is a legitimate successor of the apostles?
      Scholion 2. The early Protestant theory of having an "extraordinary mission" supply for the lack of apostolic credentials.
   3. Apostolicity of *membership:*
      Christ's Church in any given age is and remains *numerically* the same society as that originally planted by the apostles.

Article V

THE CHURCH'S APOSTOLICITY

I. Notion of Apostolicity

The term *apostolic* normally means something originating with the apostles. Everyone grants that the Church is in some sense apostolic.

1. **Protestants usually mean by apostolicity, apostolicity of doctrine.** That is all that is required, they say, and it suffices.

2. **But Greek schismatics and Anglicans**—at least a large number of them—**require in addition to apostolicity of doctrine some sort of apostolicity of government.** They do not, however, specify legitimacy of the mode of succession.

3. **According to Catholic teaching, Christ's Church essentially and necessarily enjoys a triple sort of apostolicity:** apostolicity of *doctrine, government,* and *membership.*

II. Christ's Church is Apostolic in Doctrine, Government, and Membership

1. **Apostolicity of doctrine** means the Church always retains and teaches the very same doctrine which it received from the apostles. Doctrine, as the term is used at this point, includes also the sacraments.

That Christ unequivocally willed His Church always to preserve the same doctrine taught by His apostles scarcely needs proving. It was the apostles and *no one but* the apostles that Christ commissioned to teach all nations. It was to those very apostles He promised the Holy Spirit so that they might clearly understand all the truths of salvation.[1]

2. **Apostolicity of government**—or mission, or authority—means the Church is always ruled by pastors who form one same juridical person with the apostles. In other words it is always ruled by pastors who are the apostles' legitimate successors.

It has already been proved that Christ Himself founded a living organization, a visible Church. Granted that fact, it should be obvious that an essential part of that Church's structure is apostolicity of government. For on no one but the apostolic college, under the headship of Peter, did Christ confer the power of teaching, sanctifying, and ruling the faithful until the end of the world.[2] This triple power, therefore, necessarily belongs, and can only belong, to those who form one moral person with the apostles: their legitimate successors.

120 *Scholion 1. How can one prove that this or that bishop is a legitimate successor of the apostles?*

It has already been established (see no. 34) that bishops succeeded to the position in the Church originally filled by the apostles. But as was pointed out, this succession does not mean that a particular bishop succeeded to the job of a particular apostle—say that the bishop of Bridgeport has taken over the job of St. Bartholomew. Rather, it means that the college of bishops, viewed collectively, succeeded the apostolic college, viewed collectively. It may be asked then: "How can you be sure that this or that bishop should be counted as a *legitimate* successor of the apostles?" Obviously a man does not become a genuine successor to the apostles merely by arrogating to himself the title of "bishop," or by carrying on in some fashion a function once performed by the apostles. Neither is it enough for a man merely to possess some one, individual power, say for example, the power of *orders*.—The power of orders can be acquired even illicitly, and once acquired can never be lost.—What is required for genuine apostolic succession is that a man enjoy the *complete* powers (i.e., ordinary powers, not extraordinary) of an apostle. He must, then, in addition to the power of orders, possess also the power of *jurisdiction*. Jurisdiction means the power to teach and govern.—This power is conferred only by a legitimate authorization and, even though once received, can be lost again by being revoked.—Now two methods suggest themselves for proving that this or that bishop is a legitimate successor of the apostles.

a. The *first method* is to demonstrate by historical documents that the man in question is connected with one of the original apostles by a never-interrupted line of predecessors in the same office. One must also prove that in this total line no one of his predecessors either acquired his position illicitly, or even though he may have acquired it legitimately, ever lost it. For a purely physical succession proves nothing at all. To move into the White House by physical force would not make a man president of the United States. It is easy to see how lengthy and extremely complicated such a method of procedure would be. Christianity is nearly 2,000 years old. Indeed, in many cases it would be quite impossible to proceed along these lines because of a lack of documentary evidence.

b. The *second method* is quite brief. First one locates the legitimate successor of the man whom Christ Himself established as the head and leader of the entire apostolic college. Once that has been done we can find out whether the particular bishop under scrutiny is united to Peter's successor and is acknowledged by him as a genuine successor in the apostolic office. It is easy enough to investigate these two points; it is also a perfectly satisfactory method of procedure.

It is certainly not a backbreaking job to find the legitimate successor of Peter. First, it is a fact beyond question that Christ's Church can never fail to have a successor to Peter; secondly, no one ever seriously claims to hold Peter's office except the Roman pontiffs (see no. 61). To find out which men are acknowledged by the Roman pontiff as the legitimate successors of the apostles is as easy as looking up a number in a telephone directory.

This method of procedure is *perfectly satisfactory*. Christ conferred the government of His Church on the apostles collectively, or insofar as the apostles formed a kind of college under Peter as head. In other words, none of the apostles shared in the sacred power of governing the universal Church except as a member of the Petrine, apostolic college. If that held true for the apostles themselves, it holds true all the more obviously for the apostles' successors. How could a man belong to the college of the successors of the apostles unless he were united to the head of the college and acknowledged by him as belonging to it? A man could hardly be a cabinet member if the president refused to accept him. Any man, then, who boasts of apostolic succession but is not united to the Roman pontiff, may indeed actually possess the power of orders; he may even by purely physical succession occupy a chair formerly occupied by an apostle—at least he could do so— but he would not be a genuine successor of the apostles in their pastoral office. He would be a usurper.

121 *Scholion 2. Theory of an extraordinary mission.*

Since the original Protestants obviously lacked apostolicity of government, they took refuge in an appeal to the theory of an "extraordinary mission." To put it briefly, they maintained that God could at some time raise up a group of men by an extraordinary vocation and confer on them apostolic functions if current apostolic pastors should become viciously corrupt. This was the case, they asserted, with Luther and the other reformers.

It is clear, however, if any such extraordinary mission were ever to be granted by God, it would have to be proven by miracles, or other clearly divine trademarks. The plain truth is, however, that Christ's own promises completely rule out the possibility of any such extraordinary mission. Understand now, we are talking about a mission by which a man *absolutely apart from and utterly independent of apostolic succession* would receive from God the power to rule (or reform)* the Church. Christ conferred sacred powers on His apostles and their successors *until the end of the world.* Further, He promised them His perpetual and unfailing assistance.[3] Consequently Christ would be contradicting Himself were He ever to deprive the legitimate successors of the apostles of their authority.

Granted that fact, it would be a further contradiction for God to confer the same power or a similar power on other men who were not in union with the ordinary successors. In that hypothesis there would be two separate and independent sources of authority, both demanding, by divine right, obedience from the same subjects. The only thing that could result in such an hypothesis would be confusion and schism in Christ's Church. And in that event, one would imply that God Himself, who willed His Church to be unified, was Himself sowing the seeds of necessary division. From another point of view, God has no need of extraordinary legates, in the sense claimed above, to preserve His Church from corruption.

122 **3. Apostolicity of membership** means that the Church in any given age is and remains numerically the same society as that planted by the apostles.

It was stated above that the Church's government is neces-

---

* Many saints have arisen from time to time to reinvigorate the moral life of Catholics (a Bernard, a Francis of Assisi, a Catherine of Siena, a Charles Borromeo, etc.), but they have always done so in a spirit of perfect obedience to the Church's legitimate pastors.

sarily apostolic: in brief, the college of bishops who rule it always forms one and the same juridical person with the apostolic college (see no. 119, 2). Here it is asserted that the entire membership of the Church is likewise apostolic. Apostolicity of membership follows as an inescapable consequence of apostolicity of government. A moral body, despite the fact that it constantly undergoes change and renovation in its personnel, remains *numerically the same moral body* so long as it retains the same social structure and the same authority. This should be clear from the fact that corporations like General Motors, or RCA Victor, or nations like the United States, France, or Switzerland, remain the same corporate or political entities, and are represented before national or international tribunals as the same moral body even though there is vast fluctuation in their personnel.

Please note the word, *numerically* the same society. A mere *specific* likeness would never satisfy the requirement of apostolicity. Just for the sake of argument—even though it can not actually happen—let us conjure up some church which would bear a merely specific likeness to Christ's Church; a church which would be like it in all respects except numerical identity. Imagine, now, that the Church planted by the apostles has perished utterly. Imagine— whether you make it the year 600, 1500, or 3000—that all its members have deserted. Imagine, furthermore, that out of this totally crumpled society a fresh and vigorous society springs up and then, after a time, is remodeled perfectly to meet the blueprints of the ancient but now perished apostolic structure.

Such a process would never yield a church that was genuinely apostolic, that is, numerically one and the same society which actually existed under the apostles' personal rule. There would be a brand new society, studiously copied from a model long since extinct. The new church might be a decent imitation. It might be a caricature. One thing it definitely would not be— apostolic.

Notes

1. John 16:13.
2. Matt. 28:18–20; 16:18–19; John 21:15–17.
3. Matt. 28:17–20.

CHAPTER IV

The Marks of the Church

I. *What Marks Belong to the Church Founded by Christ?*
II. *Which Christian Society Verifies Those Marks?*

Article I

THE MARKS OF THE CHURCH FOUNDED BY CHRIST

I. *The Purpose of this Article*
II. *Notion of a Mark:*
   1. Definition.
   2. Requisites for a quality to serve as a mark.
III. *The Marks of the Church Laid Down by Non-Catholics:*
   1. Photian Churches.
   2. Early Protestant Churches.
IV. *The Marks of the Church Laid Down by Catholics:*
   1. Unity.
   2. Holiness.
   3. Catholicity.
   4. Apostolicity.

Corollaries

CHAPTER IV

The Marks of the Church

123 Christ founded only one Church. He founded one Church so that He might *unite in one body all the scattered children of God* (John 11:52). Unfortunately, there have come into existence many religious societies which claim the name of Christ and "every single group of heretics considers its members to be the best Christians of all and its church to be the Catholic Church."[1] It is absolutely necessary, then, for priests and all who have a duty to rescue souls in error, to have a thorough knowledge of the ways in which the genuine Church of Christ can be recognized and distinguished from all heretical or schismatic societies.

That Christ's Church is distinguishable from all counterfeits and can be clearly and surely recognized, no Christian will doubt: if Christ wanted all mankind to enter His Church, and to obtain salvation through His Church, He certainly must have made it easily recognizable. As a matter of fact, He Himself compared it to a city seated on a mountain top (Matt. 5:14).

Christ's own Church can be distinguished from all man-made imitations by its essential qualities, or properties. When these properties are used as criteria for distinguishing the true Church from all counterfeits, they are called *marks*.

First we shall investigate abstractly what marks belong to the Church founded by Christ; secondly, we shall scrutinize the various Christian societies to see which one of them verifies these marks.

Article I

THE MARKS OF THE CHURCH FOUNDED BY CHRIST

1. The Purpose of this Article

124 The purpose of this Article is not to inquire, "Of all the religions in the world, including the non-Christian, which is the true religion?" Rather, it is to point out which of the many "Chris-

(158)

tian" societies is actually Christ's own. For this reason the treatment of the marks of the Church is often labeled the *Catholic* demonstration, for it demonstrates the claims of the Catholic Church against heretics and schismatics. Three things are presupposed at this point: (1) that Christ was truly a messenger from God;[2] (2) that Christ founded a society really deserving the name, Church; that is, a visible society, in fact a society which is numerically one; (3) that this Church founded by Christ, since it is indestructible, still exists in the present-day world.

II. Notion of a Mark 125

1. Definition. Everyone is familiar with the general notion of a mark from such terms as laundry-marks, postmarks, trademarks, etc. A *mark* is a quality which distinguishes a thing from all other things.

Marks may be either *negative* or *positive*. A *negative* mark shows that nothing prevents a particular object, bearing the mark, from being the article we are looking for; but does not identify it in positive fashion. A *positive* mark is one which proves unmistakably that the thing possessing it is the genuine article sought for. Here only positive marks of the Church will be discussed.

2. Requisites for a quality to serve as a mark. The very purpose of marks—to identify—shows what characteristics are required for a quality to serve as a mark. A mark ought to be *essential* to the thing sought for, *easier to recognize* than the thing itself, and it ought to be *visible or obvious*.

a. Essential to the thing. If a mark really belongs to a thing, it will never be missing from it. Men are always rational. Again, it will never be found in anything but the genuine article—at least not in the same way.

b. Easier to recognize. In other words the mark should be known to exist even before the marked article itself is discovered. That is why infallibility, for example, which could not be known to exist in this or that society until one had first found out whether that society was the genuine Church of Christ, can not be described as a mark of the Church.

c. Visible or obvious. Granted that a mark should be easier to recognize than the article sought for, it follows that a mark should be something visible or fairly obvious. Notice, however, that if an article is endowed with a *variety* of marks, all the marks need not be conspicuous to exactly the same degree. It is enough, for example, if one or two of them are easily recognizable by all men; while the rest may be clear only to those who are more learned in the matter.

126 III. The Marks of the Church Laid Down By Non-Catholics

1. **The Schismatic, Oriental Churches** (which may be labeled *Photian* Churches since they take their origin from Photius the author of the schism in 857) hold for only one mark of the Church. Though they constantly insist that the true Church of Christ is one, holy, catholic, and apostolic, they nonetheless specially insist that the one really distinctive mark of Christ's Church is its *unchanging preservation of the doctrine of the first seven ecumenical councils*. To put it another way, the really distinctive mark is the identity of today's Church with the Church of the first nine centuries.[3]

To bypass all other considerations, it should be obvious that doctrinal identity between a present-day Church and the first seven councils proves nothing more than that the present-day Church—on the score of *doctrine* at least—is the same as the eighth or ninth century Church. Suppose it is. One must still find out whether the Church of the eighth century was truly the Church of Christ or not. The mere preservation of the doctrine of the first seven councils cannot suffice to prove that point. Furthermore, static preservation of doctrine, in the sense that the Greeks understand the phrase—as ruling out not only any reversal of doctrine, but even any organic exposition of it—simply cannot be characteristic of that Church which, under the aid of the Holy Spirit, constantly progresses in its understanding and exposition of the apostles' teachings. But this matter will be discussed *ex professo* in the treatise *on Faith* (see volume III of this series).

2. **Early Protestants** assigned as distinguishing marks of the Church, *the gospel preached in its purity* and *the rightful use of the sacraments*. According to Calvin's dictum:

> Wherever we find the word of God preached sincerely, and sincerely listened to, and those sacraments Christ Himself instituted being administered, there we have a church of God about which there can be no ambiguity.[4]

Unfortunately the criteria just mentioned are clearly unsuitable to fulfill the functions of marks. This is true whether the criteria be understood in the sense the words themselves indicate, or whether they be understood according to the mentality of the original Protestants. The original* Protestants by the phrase "the gospel preached in its purity," really meant the doctrine of "justification by faith alone" as proven exclusively from Scripture. By the phrase, "the rightful use of the sacraments," they meant the use of the chalice by the laity.

The reason the above described criteria fail to meet the requirements of genuine marks is this: if the words are taken according to their obvious meaning, these factors are *no easier to recognize* than the very thing sought for. It is impossible to know what the "pure gospel" is (that is, the *full* gospel) and what the "rightful use of the sacraments" is (that is, of *all* the sacraments) unless you already know which is the true Church of Christ. If you take the above described criteria in the special sense understood by the ancient Protestants, they are not qualities proper to the thing we are searching for; they are completely arbitrary criteria. It was only to meet the exigencies of their own position that early Protestants advanced the idea that Christ's Church is distinguishable by the doctrine of "justification by faith alone," and that His Church was inescapably bound to the practice of receiving Communion under both species.

IV. The Marks of the Church Laid Down by Catholics

Catholics unanimously † lay down *four* marks of the true Church. They take those marks from the Niceno-Constantinopolitan

---

* It is extremely important to distinguish between "original" or "ancient" Protestants and twentieth-century Protestants. Relatively few of the latter would care to subscribe to the major tenets of the early reformers. In fact, as will be mentioned below, many of them are unaware of original Protestant doctrines.

† Even though some of the older theologians frequently list more than four marks, they do not really differ from recent theologians on this point; they differ merely in the way they distinguish and present the same marks. All the rest of the characteristics they mention—when viewed from the aspect of acting as criteria, or marks—are ultimately reducible in one way or another to the four listed above. The marks of the Church ought to be drawn from the Church's essential properties; that is why qualities like visibility, indestructibility, and infallibility cannot serve to function as marks. There remain then only the four listed above.

Creed which states: "I believe in the *one, holy, catholic,* and *apostolic* Church."

These four qualities, unity, holiness, catholicity, and apostolicity, must be examined to see if they meet all the requirements of genuine marks. That those four qualities are *necessary* and *inseparable* "properties" of the true Church of Christ has already been established in the preceding chapter. All that remains to do, then, is to see if they meet the remaining requisites for genuine marks: *a.* Are they visible? *b.* Are they easier to recognize than the thing sought?

128 1. **Unity.** It should be clear that unity of creed, membership and government is something visible, and consequently easier to recognize than the true Church itself. Furthermore, if one examines this unity, not in abstract fashion, but concretely—that is, as a unity which is *perpetually present* in a society *spread practically over the entire world;* as a unity which arises *spontaneously and connaturally,* and not as the artificial product of terroristic activities or military might—one finds something miraculous, something which can only be adequately explained on the basis of God's help.[5] If this be true, something further follows: such unity could not be found outside of the true Church of God. Christ Himself pointed out that His own divine mission, as continued by His Church, can and should be recognized by that Church's miraculous unity:

> "*However, I do not pray for them alone* [the apostles]; *I also pray for those who through their preaching will believe in me. All are to be one; just as you, Father, are in me and I am in you, so they, too, are to be one in us. The world must come to believe that I am your ambassador.*"—John 17:20-21.

129 2. **Holiness.** Not everything that has been said about holiness, insofar as it is a property of the Church, can be applied in exactly the same way when we consider holiness as a *mark*. For example, if our discussion be limited to the means to holiness—and exclusively to the bare possession of such means—it must be admitted that some of the means to holiness can be found in a false church. Nothing prevents some sect, which has split off from the true Church, from holding on to the doctrine, sacraments, laws, and most of the devotional activities of that Church. Such a sect—not rightfully, of course, but physically nonetheless—might continue to possess some of the means to holiness. Contrariwise, any church holding even one doctrine or one institution which is clearly contradictory to holiness stands convicted as a counterfeit. A church, for example, which would espouse euthanasia would betray an erroneous moral sense.

Holiness of members which does not reach heroic proportions can also be found in some fashion in a false church. That happens, however, purely accidentally; God, who wills all men to be saved, does not deprive men, who are innocently enmeshed in error, of His normal graces. Furthermore, most of the sacraments can be validly administered even outside the true Church. If the recipients be in good faith, these sacraments can be fruitfully received and produce some harvest of holiness even outside the house of God. Doubtless even this ordinary type of holiness occurs far more frequently within the true Church than outside of it, but since that greater frequency is not discernible except by difficult investigation,[6] and is not something obvious, its incidence lies open to much quibbling. If, then, holiness is to serve as a distinguishing mark of the true Church, we must limit our investigation, if not exclusively at least principally, to *heroic holiness of the members* and to *the holiness of charisms.**

Extraordinary or heroic holiness, by the very fact that it is far beyond the normal measure, is readily perceived. Furthermore, heroic holiness can be acknowledged to be a mark of the true Church even before one actually locates the true Church. Finally, such extraordinary holiness will never be found outside the true Church; such holiness requires an extraordinary abundance of graces that is not granted to those in error. Even though Christ does not deprive anyone of necessary graces, He does nourish and cherish His own flesh, His Church, with an altogether special love. Otherwise God Himself would lead mankind into error, were He to raise up, outside the road to salvation, heroes of sanctity. The same thing holds true with even greater force of *charisms* which attest either to the holiness of the Church itself or to the holiness of its finest members.

---

* *Charisms* (gratiae gratis datae) are extraordinary gifts of God, such as miracle-working, prophecy, speaking or interpreting strange tongues, etc. (see I Cor. 12:4, 7-11; Rom. 12:6). They are usually bestowed not for the sake of the individual recipient so much as for the edification of the Church as a whole. For a discussion of this matter see Garrigou-Lagrange, *The Three Ages of the Interior Life*, II, 575 ff.

Christ Himself, at least in some fashion, referred to the mark of holiness when He said: *"Just so let your light shine before your fellow men, that they may see your good example and praise your Father who is in heaven"* (Matt. 5:16).

130 3. **Catholicity.** *Catholicity by right* is not a mark of the Church, but rather a necessary preliminary to the mark itself. The mark of catholicity, then, means exclusively that *catholicity in fact* which should always be found in the true Church: its *morally universal diffusion*. That this sort of catholicity when viewed *concretely*—that is, as comprising genuine unity and the unbroken preservation of that unity throughout many centuries without recourse to force or military might—amounts to a moral miracle, no one of good sense will doubt. Such God-given unity, therefore, cannot be a property of a false religion. That the other requirements of a mark are verifiable in the criterion of *catholicity in fact* should be obvious.

OBSERVE. Some theologians incorrectly, at least in our opinion, claim that the true Church of Christ, because of this mark of catholicity, should always possess a larger number of members than any sect. But catholicity does not consist merely in numbers. It also requires diffusion throughout the world. That is why no sect, however numerous its adherents, can ever be morally universal; in other words, there could never exist in addition to the true Church of Christ some other religious society which, while retaining genuine unity, would be spread among a great number of diverse peoples for a long time.

131 4. **Apostolicity.** Apostolicity *of doctrine* should not be listed as a mark of the Church because it is not something obvious. Furthermore, it is not something easier to recognize than the true Church herself. For it is extraordinarily difficult, in fact impossible, to have certitude about the entire body of doctrine taught by the apostles without the testimony of Christ's Church. It presumes, then, that that Church is already identified. That is why the rule of faith has always been: find out who are the successors of the apostles, and which *society* is a continuation of the Church planted by the apostles, then you will be able to receive the pure and complete doctrine taught by the apostles. Notice, too, that apostolicity of doctrine, taken all by itself would be only a negative mark of the Church; for there is nothing intrinsically contradictory in the notion of having some sect retain the doctrine of the apostles in its entirety. This point alone is guaranteed by that negative criterion:

if it be proven that a Christian denomination has departed from even one point of doctrine taught by the apostles, by that very fact it is convicted of being a counterfeit.

The mark of apostolicity, then, is found in *apostolicity* of both *membership* and *government*. These two factors are, of course, only inadequately* distinguished from one another. Even though this double sort of apostolicity is not obvious to all men, but only to those who are fairly well versed in history, it clearly fulfills all the requirements for a genuine mark.

OBSERVE. If one considers apostolicity in purely abstract fashion, it is simply an historical fact; if one views it concretely, that is, as including the *unconquerable stability* of that same Church which has existed as a world-wide organization throughout nineteen hundred years, it is at the same time a moral miracle as we have demonstrated in the treatise, *The True Religion* (see no. 124).

Corollaries 132

1. After the foregoing considerations, it should be easy to answer the following question: "To identify the true Church, is it enough to verify only one mark, or must one verify all four marks simultaneously?" Any one of the four marks suffices to identify the true Church provided the mark be applied in its complete and concrete meaning. But the marks of unity and catholicity are so inextricably interwoven, that they can not be separated from one another. That is why the Vatican Council, in enumerating the marvelous signs which distinguish the Church, does not speak of unity *and* catholicity, but speaks of *"catholic unity."*[8]

2. It was stated at the beginning of this article that the real purpose of the study of the marks is to distinguish the genuine Church of Christ from all other societies using the name Christian. But even in our purely abstract discussion of the marks we have seen that each of these marks actually involves something miraculous—something beyond the power of creatures to produce. Unless there were some such external manifestations of the Holy Spirit who breathes life into Christ's Church, there would really be no reason why founders of merely human sects could not imitate those marks in their own societies.[9] A merely human mark can always be counterfeited. Precisely because those marks of the Church are

---

* That is, the rulers of the Church are also part of its membership.

miraculous qualities, or moral miracles, they are not only suitable for identifying the church which possesses them as the genuine Church founded by Christ, but, even apart from the necessary presuppositions discussed above (see no. 124), they directly prove that a church possessing those marks—and the religion preached by that church—is a work of God. That is why a little deeper consideration of those same marks is sufficient to demonstrate the divine origin of the Catholic religion over all the religions in the world including the non-Christian religions.[10]

Notes

1. Lactantius, *Divinae institutiones* 4. 30.
2. See *The True Religion*, p. 127 ff. for an *ex professo* demonstration of Christ's Divine Mission.
3. See J. B. Baur, *Argumenta contra orientalem Ecclesiam*, part I (1897). —The seventh ecumenical council is the Second Council of Nicaea held in the year 787. Even though the Fourth Council of Constantinople (870) was held in the East and took place long before the completion of the Photian schism (1054), it is not accepted by the Greeks because it contains a condemnation of Photius and professes in unmistakable terms the primacy of the Roman pontiff. See Hefele, *Conciliengeschichte* (4th ed.), IV, no. 493.
4. *Institutes of the Christian Religion*, IV, 1, 9; see *Confessio Belgica*, article 29, which, nevertheless, goes on to add a third distinctive mark: the observance of right discipline. The marks of the Church as laid down by the Protestants are also admitted by the Anglicans according to Murray (see Billot, *De ecclesia* [5th ed., 1927], I, 126, note 1).—Notice in the quotation from Calvin the word "*a* church of God." In the Protestant system, the marks serve the purpose of distinguishing a visible church which is, indeed, purely human in origin but which is in conformity with the principles of the gospel and, as a consequence, also forms some part of the *invisible* Church which is hidden within it. See above, p. 5–6.
5. See *The True Religion*, p. 211 ff.
6. About the only procedure one could follow would be to compile some sort of *statistics of morality* and that would be highly unreliable. For, (*a*) it is impossible to select all points of comparison in such a way that all circumstances would be equal on both sides with the sole exception of religion. Then, (*b*) even granted absolutely fair and absolutely accurate statistics, only a very limited number of virtuous acts would be capable of being statistically analyzed. Practically all that could be examined would be works of piety or charity performed *in public*; but the motivating reasons behind the deeds, on which morality depends to a large extent, completely escape the reach of statistics. Finally, (*c*) as for sins, again statistics can reach only the smallest portion of them, and one can not justly divide the shadows from the light by such a method. A woman who becomes pregnant by a sinful act

would throw statistics out of gear completely, if in addition to the sin already committed she would not be afraid to add another sin by having an abortion. Her sins would be in no danger of detection by the birth of illegitimate children. Again, the sin of a man who gets angry and uses insulting language to another would be easily detectable and he would receive a black mark against his name. But another chap who is busily engaged in lecturing and writing about overturning the foundations of religion, morality, and public peace—so long as he does so with an air of objective gravity—would not find a place in a statistical table of sinners. A philosopher who advocates perversity with an air of sweet reasonableness is often classified as a sort of humanitarian saint rather than as a sinner. Finally, all that statistics can measure in morality is the physically perceptible side of moral actions, and the attempt to adjudicate morality on that basis is valueless.

7. See *The True Religion*, p. 211 ff.

8. Constitution *De fide catholica*, chap. 3.

9. The case is a bit different with the mark of apostolicity. For the mark of apostolicity, even if we prescind from the miraculous stability which is now factually implied by it (i.e., after the passing of so many centuries), fully proves the truth of the Church it belongs to because it rests upon an historic fact which once demonstrated can never be changed: the fact that the apostles planted *this* Church and no other.

10. This method of demonstration was actually used in the volume, *The True Religion* (Section II, ch. 3), to prove the divine origin of the Christian-Catholic religion by arguing from its *stability*—which notion presupposes and includes the mark of *catholic unity* (article 2)—and by arguing from its *holiness* (articles 1, 3, 4).

Article II

WHICH CHRISTIAN SOCIETY VERIFIES THE MARKS OF CHRIST'S CHURCH?

I. *A Brief Sketch of All Christian Societies:*
 1. Ancient Eastern Christian sects:
    a. Nestorian Churches
    b. Monophysite Churches
 2. The Orthodox Churches
 3. The Reformation Churches:
    a. Lutheranism
    b. Calvinism
    c. Anglicanism
 4. The Roman Catholic Church

II. *Application of the Mark of Unity and Catholicity to the Various Churches:*
 PROPOSITION 1: The mark of unity and catholicity cannot be verified in either the Eastern or the Reformation Churches
  Proof: 1. considered collectively they lack unity both of membership and of government
  2. considered singly they lack catholicity
 PROPOSITION 2: The Roman Catholic Church possesses the mark of unity
  Proof: 1. it has unity of *doctrine*
  2. it has *social* unity
  3. it has unity of *government*
 PROPOSITION 3: The Roman Catholic Church possesses the mark of catholicity
  Proof: 1. vindicated by its very name
  2. its vast membership
  3. its geographical diffusion
  4. its constant growth

III. *Application of the Mark of Apostolicity to the Various Churches:*
   PROPOSITION 1: Both the Photian and Protestant Churches lack the mark of apostolicity
      Proof: 1. they lack apostolicity of membership:
         a. Photian Churches did not exist as such till 1054
         b. Protestant Churches did not exist before the sixteenth century
      2. they lack apostolicity of government:
         a. Michael Caerularius' claim to independence was something brand-new; and consequently not apostolic
         b. Same argument applies to the Schismatic and Protestant bishops
         c. Lay rulers are not successors to the apostles
   PROPOSITION 2: The Roman Catholic Church does possess the mark of apostolicity
      Proof: 1. it has apostolicity of membership
      2. it has apostolicity of government
   Corollary

IV. *The Application of the Mark of Holiness to the Various Churches:*
   PROPOSITION 1: Neither the Photian nor the Protestant Churches possess the mark of holiness
      Proof: 1. neither group exhibits extraordinary or heroic holiness
      2. they lack miracles and charisms
      3. they are deprived of many of the means to holiness
   PROPOSITION 2: The Roman Catholic Church possesses the mark of holiness

Preliminary Suasions:
   1. Christ prophesied His Church would be hated
   2. History and motives of conversions
      Proof: 1. the Catholic Church possesses many means to holiness:

       a. Doctrine
       b. Disciplinary laws
       c. Institutions
   Corollary: Bad Catholics vs. Church's Holiness
   Proof: 2. the Church produces an immense harvest of holiness:
       a. Vast number of people dedicated to the state of holiness
       b. Vast number of genuine saints
       c. The Church has always been ornamented by miracles and charisms
   Scholion: On Temporal Prosperity

Conclusion to First Section:
1. Roman Catholic Church is clearly marked as being the Church founded by Christ
2. Why do so many non-Catholics fail to reach this truth?
   a. Not due to lack of sincerity
   b. Many are imbued with such prejudices from childhood that they do not bother to examine its claims
   c. Such innocent prejudices can be dissipated only gradually

Article II

WHICH CHRISTIAN SOCIETY VERIFIES THE MARKS OF CHRIST'S CHURCH?

In this discussion the following churches must be investigated: (1) some ancient Eastern Christian sects far older than the Photian Schism; * (2) the Photian Churches; (3) the Reformation Churches; (4) the Roman Catholic Church. Here we present a very brief sketch of these churches.

I. A Brief Sketch of All Christian Societies

1. **The ancient Eastern Christian sects** † include the following:

a. The Nestorian Church. "Of all the existing churches which in the course of the centuries have separated from the unity of the Catholic Church, the oldest is the Church of the Nestorians" (Algermissen, *op. cit.*, p. 687). The Nestorians separated from Rome in the year 431 after the Council of Ephesus condemned Nestorius, patriarch of Constantinople, for Christological heresy.‡ The Nestorian Church spread widely and created a high culture.

In its period of greatest flowering in the thirteenth century, the Catholics of the Nestorian Church had jurisdiction over 27 metropolitans, each of whom had from 6 to 12 bishops under him. Nestorianism was spread through all of Asia, numbered

---

* The first schism occurred under Photius himself in the year 867. After his deposition by Emperor Leo VI in 886, the break with Rome was temporarily mended. The permanent break occurred in 1054 under Michael Caerularius. For the causes of this schism see Algermissen, *Christian Denominations* (St. Louis, 1945), p. 560–85.

† Most of the following information about the individual Eastern Churches is condensed from Algermissen, *op. cit.* The statistics on church membership are for the most part based on Attwater, *The Christian Churches of the East*, 2 vols. (rev. ed., Milwaukee, 1947).

‡ Catholic doctrine teaches that Jesus Christ is one person—a divine Person who unites in Himself two distinct, complete, and unconfused natures: divinity and humanity. Nestorius considered Christ two persons: one, the man Jesus Christ; the other, the Word, or Son of God. The union between them was purely a moral one. For a brief, accurate analysis of Nestorianism see Parente, *op. cit.*, p. 199–200.

230 dioceses, had millions of adherents, and created a comprehensive theological literature. The domain of the Nestorian Church stretched from Egypt to China, and from Lake Baikal to Cape Comorin.—Algermissen, *op. cit.*, p. 688.

In the fourteenth century vast numbers of Nestorian Christians were wiped out in the terrible persecutions under Tamerlane. During succeeding centuries large numbers of the surviving Nestorian Christians returned to the Roman Catholic Church and, with papal approval, were allowed to retain many of their ancient customs. The remaining Nestorians today are found mainly in Iraq and Syria. Their patriarch is called the *Catholicos of the East*. A much smaller group is found in Malabar (India) under the headship of the metropolitan of Malabar. All told, the Nestorian Christians today number around 50,000.

b. The *Monophysite* (Eutychian) *Church*. The Monophysite Christians include a series of national churches which separated from the universal Catholic Church around the sixth century. They are all called Monophysites because they all more or less * fell into the heresy of Eutyches condemned by the Council of Chalcedon in 451. Eutyches held Christ had only one nature: a mixed nature compounded of divinity and humanity. The Monophysite Churches include the following:

1. *The Syrian Jacobite Church.* The Syrian Jacobites today are found mainly in Syria and Iraq. They number roughly 90,000 members and are under the control of the patriarch of Antioch.

2. *The Malabar Jacobite Church* (Christians of Thomas the Apostle) is found today in Malabar, India. The Thomist Christians number roughly 363,000 and are ruled over by the catholicos of India.†

3. *The Armenian Church.* The Armenian Christians number

---

* We say "more or less" for some of them like the Armenians and Jacobites expressly reject any "mingling" of natures in Christ and expressly condemn Eutyches as a heretic. But they are all in error concerning the humanity of Christ either by denying it a human will (Monotheletism) or at least by depriving the human nature of its own normal activity (Monergism). These heresies are in the last analysis simply a subtler or milder form of Monophysitism. For the exact Christology of each of these Monophysite Churches see Algermissen, *op. cit.*, pp. 694–712.

† "In 1930 the Jacobite metropolitan Ivan and his suffragan came over to the Catholic Church and thus started a strong movement for union with Rome. In 1932 Pope Pius XI erected for those converted Thomas Christian Jacobites,

perhaps as many as 2,500,000, about half of whom live in the Russian Soviet Republics of Armenia and Azerbaijan. Outside of Russia, groups of Armenians are found in Turkey (almost exclusively at Constantinople), Persia, Syria, Palestine, Greece, Cyprus, China, and North America. They are ruled over by several patriarchs. The principal one, known as the catholicos of Echmizdzin, resides in the city of Echmizdzin at the foot of Mount Ararat in Russian Armenia. He bears the title of *Supreme Patriarch and Catholicos of all the Armenians.*

4. *The Coptic Church* traces its origin back to one of the most venerable sees in Christendom: the patriarchate of Alexandria. Originally it belonged to that portion of the universal Catholic Church planted by St. Mark. It fell into the Monophysite heresy under the patriarch Dioscurus, successor to St. Cyril of Alexandria. A violent champion of Monophysitism, Dioscurus was deposed by the Council of Chalcedon in 451. Large numbers followed him into heresy. By the year 640 when the Arabs conquered Egypt, the Copts had become a full-blown national church. At present the Egyptian Coptic Christians number about 1,000,000 members and are under the rule of the patriarch of Alexandria.

5. *The Ethiopian Church* (Abyssinian Copts) numbers roughly 4,000,000 members. They are ruled by a metropolitan who lives in Addis Ababa and bears the title, *Abuna* ("our father"). Throughout the centuries this church has always been extremely dependent on the Coptic Church. Not until as late as 1937 did any Ethiopian succeed in becoming head of the church, and he has since been excommunicated by the Coptic synod.

2. The Photian Churches (The Orthodox Church). Out of the Photian Schism, brought to the final rupture point under Michael Caerularius in the year 1054, sprang up, with the passing of time, a number of "sister" churches. Even though these sister churches agree in large measure in their creed and liturgy, they do not constitute one, single church:

134

> Unlike the Catholic Church, the Orthodox Church does not constitute a closed, centrally governed Church community, but

---

numbering about 35,000, the archbishopric of Trivandrum with the suffragan see of Tiruvalla. These together with about 68,000 Uniate Syrians and 375,000 Maronites form the Syro-Malankar Church" (Algermissen, *op. cit.*, p. 704, note 15).

consists of the union of a number of entirely *equal, independent, autonomous* Church associations, which are held together by unity of faith, similarity of liturgy, and their mutual relationship, so that they appear to be one.—Algermissen, *op. cit.*, p. 586; italics ours.

Consequently it is only by an abuse of terminology that they are referred to as though they were one, for each actually claims our Lord Jesus Christ as its only "head," and though they grant a pre-eminence of honor to the patriarch of Constantinople they are really independent churches and self-governing. Among these autonomous churches we find the following distinct groups:

a. The Patriarchate of Constantinople. This church has its own patriarch who bears the title of *Ecumenical Patriarch.* He rules approximately 80,000 Christians who are located in Constantinople, and the four metropolitan cities of Derkos, Imbros, Chalcedon, and Prikipo.

b. The Patriarchate of Alexandria is ruled by its own patriarch who bears the title, *Most Blessed and Holy Father and Patriarch of the great city of Alexandria and of all Egypt, Pentapolis, Pelusium, Libya, and Ethiopia.* This church numbers roughly 125,000 souls.

c. The Patriarchate of Antioch, next to Alexandria, was the most illustrious see in the ancient Eastern Catholic Church. At present the only reminder of its ancient glory is the title borne by its patriarch: *Most Blessed and Holy Patriarch of the great city of God, Antioch, and of the entire East.* He resides in Damascus and has under his jurisdiction some 220,000 Christians.

d. The Patriarchate of Jerusalem was established as a separate patriarchate from Antioch by the Council of Chalcedon. Although it remained true to the Catholic faith during the Monophysite heresies, it lapsed into the Greek schism about the end of the eleventh century. Its patriarch bears the title: *Most Blessed and Holy Patriarch of Jerusalem and all Palestine.* Today under his jurisdiction are some 45,000 Arabic-speaking Syrians in Palestine and Jordan.

e. The Church of Cyprus is governed by its own archbishop. It ranks fifth in prestige among the autocephalous churches of the East. It has roughly 280,000 members.

f. The Russian Church. The main portion of Russian Orthodox

Christians belong to the patriarchate of Moscow. Orthodox Russians living outside Russia are divided into four metropolitan jurisdictions: the Balkans, Western Europe, the Far East, and North America. In addition to its orthodox members a number of strange, heretical, mystical sects,* with their own peculiar doctrines and esoteric rituals have been found in the Russian Church: the *Raskolniky*, the *Khlysty* (Flagellants), the *Skoptsy* (Self-castrated), the *Dukhobory* (Spirit-wrestlers), the *Molokany* (Milk-drinkers), the *Stunda* (Baptists), and the *Paskovites*. Prior to the Communist enslavement the orthodox members of the Russian Church were numbered somewhere between 105 to 115 million.† The mystical sects numbered around 15 million. At present it is impossible to get reliable figures about either the Orthodox Russians or these various sects.

g. *The Greek Church* is ruled by a synod of seven bishops under the presidency of the archbishop of Athens. It numbers about 6,000,000 members.

h. *The Serbian Patriarchate*. This independent Orthodox Church is ruled by a patriarch. It numbers about 7,000,000 Yugoslavian Christians.

i. *The Church of Bulgaria* has no particular patriarch of its own: it is ruled by an exarch. It numbers about 4,500,000 souls.

j. *The Patriarchate of Rumania* established itself as an independent, national orthodox Church in 1865. It is ruled by its own patriarch and numbers some 10,000,000 Christians.

k. *The Polish Orthodox Church* became an independent church in 1924. At that time it numbered about 4,000,000 members—mostly Ukranians and White Russians. It was ruled over by a synod whose president was the metropolitan of Warsaw. With the Russian occupation of 1945 most of its members were reabsorbed into the Russian Church. At present there is reputedly still an independent Polish Orthodox Church composed of about 350,000 members, headed by the metropolitan of Warsaw. There are other "groups of Orthodox refugees from Poland in Great Britain, Germany, the Near East, and other places. They are the ecclesiastical charge of an archbishop, whose headquarters is in London and who has an auxiliary bishop to help him" (Attwater, *The Christian Churches of the East*, op. cit., II, 145).

---

* For details of their doctrines see Algermissen, *op. cit.*, pp. 599–604.
† *Life* magazine gives 150,000,000 (*Life*, Dec. 26, 1955, p. 105).

l. The Catholicate of Georgia has a very ancient history, traceable back as far as the first quarter of the fourth century. Though at first part of the patriarchate of Antioch, it acquired complete independence in the eighth century. Only gradually did it defect from the ancient Catholic faith and slip into the Orthodox Schism. In 1811 Russia suppressed the catholicate of Georgia. After the Bolshevist revolution in 1917 the catholicate was re-established. It numbers some 2,000,000 members. Its present status is difficult to ascertain, as is the case with all religious groups in the U.S.S.R.

m. The Albanian Church became autonomous in 1929. It is ruled by a synod and has some 185,000 members.

n. The Church of Finland declared its independence in 1923. It is ruled by a synod and comprises roughly 60,000 souls.

o. The Church of Estonia was declared autonomous in 1923. At that time it numbered roughly 300,000 members under its own metropolitan. "When Russian troops occupied Estonia in 1940 and the country was annexed to the U.S.S.R., the aged Metropolitan Alexander renounced the autonomy of his church, and brought the faithful once more into the jurisdiction of Moscow" (*Ibid.*, p. 79).

p. The Church of Latvia was declared autonomous in 1936 with the consent of the ecumenical patriarch of Constantinople. At the time it numbered about 150,000 members. Its independence was short-lived. With the occupation of the country in 1940 it became a part of the patriarchate of Moscow.

q. The Church of Lithuania was declared an autonomous eparchy in 1924 under the *Metropolitan of All Lithuania and Vilna.* It numbered about 55,000 members. Since the majority of the Lithuanian Orthodox were of Russian descent—the rest of the population were mainly Roman Catholic—and its first metropolitan was "a zealous supporter of the canonical jurisdiction of the Patriarchal church in Russia" (Attwater), there was little difficulty in restoring the Lithuanian Orthodox to the jurisdiction of Moscow when Russia occupied the country in 1940.

r. The Church of Czechoslovakia became partially autonomous in 1921, but was affiliated with the Serbian patriarchate. At present the Orthodox Czechs have been transferred to the jurisdiction of Moscow. There is a patriarchal exarch at Prague and displaced persons and others have increased his flock to some 146,000.

s. The Orthodox Church of Japan is a relic of an old Russian mission established by Father Nicholas Kasatkin in 1871. In 1939 when the Japanese government brought the Christian bodies there under rigid control it was decided to make the church autonomous. It numbered about 41,000 members in 1939.

t. The Orthodox Church of America dates from 1794 when a small band of monks built the first Orthodox church on Kodiak Island. The Orthodox in the United States number roughly 2,000,000 members (*Life, loc. cit.*) from various racial backgrounds: Russian, Syrian, Greek, Rumanian, Serbian, Bulgarian, and Albanian. Attempts have been made (in 1927 and then in 1943) to unite all the Orthodox in America into one independent church, but so far they have not succeeded.*

u. The Church of Sinai is the smallest independent Orthodox church in the world. It is ruled by an archbishop who is abbot of the monastery of St. Catherine, possibly the oldest monastery in the world. It became an independent church in 1575. From that year on the archbishops received their consecration from the patriarch of Jerusalem. Total membership of the church is about 120; about a third † are monks, the rest, laymen.

3. The Reformation Churches. Even though these churches are autonomous groups they are usually grouped together under the term of Protestantism.¹ The name arose at the Diet of Spires in 1529. Until a future council could be held to iron out quarrels between the Reformers and their Catholic opponents, the diet temporarily issued an edict (March, 1529) to preserve the religious *status quo*. The princes who favored Luther at the diet "protested" against this edict on April 19, 1529. From this formal protest they received the name "protestants." Later on the name became attached to all adherents of the Reformation.‡

The most important branches of early § Protestantism are *Lutheranism, Calvinism,* and *Anglicanism*. From one or another of

---

* For details about the various groups of Orthodox in the United States, see Attwater, *loc. cit.*, pp. 148–55.

† Algermissen mentions some thirty monks at St. Catherine plus twenty more in Cairo who belong to this church (p. 592); Attwater gives the figure of 26 monks and 100 laymen in the year 1936.

‡ Actually the Lutherans called themselves from the very beginning, "evangelists."

§ Please note the adjective *early*. Many contemporary Protestants, in America at least, are unaware of the doctrinal teachings of the early Reformers. They would indignantly repudiate any such ideas as, that human nature was totally depraved by original sin; that good works are useless; that the Holy Spirit guarantees His infallible assistance to every Bible reader; that God these original branches multitudinous Protestant groups (Methodists, Baptists, Congregationalists, Quakers, Mennonites, etc.), ultimately evolved.[2]

a. Lutheranism, in addition to the dogmas it retained from Catholicism, historically subscribed to the following tenets as a basic part of its creed: justification by faith alone, the intrinsic corruption of human nature by original sin, the Bible as the only norm of faith, the existence of only two sacraments (baptism and the Lord's Supper), the rejection of a sacramental priesthood in favor of the common priesthood of all believers. In church government Lutherans historically conferred supreme power over its churches on secular rulers, under whom they were governed in Germany by *consistories* and in Scandinavia by bishops. Since the First World War, however, the system of a state Lutheran Church has been changed even in Germany.[3]

In the United States the Lutheran Church government is democratic in nature: the pastors are elected by the people and presided over by a *synod*.[4]

b. Calvinism, while agreeing with many fundamental tenets of Lutheranism, such as justification by faith alone, the complete sufficiency of the Bible as a norm of faith, the retention of only two sacraments, the corruption of human nature by original sin, the invisible character of the Church, etc., differed radically in its interpretation of some of these doctrines and also introduced other beliefs peculiarly its own.[5] For example, Luther found the Scriptures clear and obvious; Calvin found them obscure and intricate:

---

arbitrarily precondemns some men to hell; that sins are not really forgiven, but merely cloaked with the merits of Christ, and so forth. Other contemporary Protestants, aware of the original Reformation teachings, either expressly repudiate the more exaggerated doctrines or palliate them to such an extent as to make them harmless. Many contemporary Protestants have actually accepted, consciously or unconsciously, many Catholic viewpoints. Their hospitals and many splendid charities are testimony enough to their belief in good works. Their interest in missions is a sign of a more Catholic perspective. Their recent ecumenical movements testify to a hunger to regain something of that Catholic unity which was torn asunder at the Reformation. Billy Graham's syndicated religious column, *My Answer,* is a good example of the infiltration of Catholic perspectives into Protestant thinking. Apart from the heavy emphasis he lays on Bible reading, and the insistence on justification by faith alone, a great number of the solutions Graham offers to problems raised by his readers could appear in any popular Catholic *Question Box* without causing an eyebrow to quiver.

he offered as the only real key to their understanding, the immediate assistance of the Holy Spirit enlightening the mind of the individual believer.[6] For Luther, Christ was really and substantially present in the Eucharist;[7] for Calvin, dynamically present.[8] In addition to these disagreements in interpretation, Calvin himself introduced his own doctrine of absolute predestination.*

Calvinism has generally excluded secular rulers from church government and reserved such ruling power to the churches themselves. It has consequently always been characterized by a democratic constitution in its churches. From its very beginnings it was extremely practical and zealous about promoting both good moral behavior and social works. This positive side of Calvinism was a natural corollary to the doctrine of election: one who was conscious of his election was anxious to transform not merely himself but the whole world into the kingdom of God. And since good works were the *result* of, and confirmation of election by God, men were spurred to find such signs of their election in their everyday economic and political lives.[9]

Lutheranism, because of its more mystical character, had a less popular appeal and was restricted largely to Germanic peoples; Calvinism, because of its practicality and its democratic temperament, appealed to a wide variety of peoples. It flourishes in Switzerland, Holland, Scotland, and the United States.

c. *Anglicanism* at the beginning of its separation from Rome under Henry VIII, rejected practically nothing more than the primacy of the Roman pontiff. Later on, under Edward VI, it submitted to the influence of Lutheranism; still later, under Elizabeth, it yielded yet more to the influence of Calvinism. Anglicanism retained the hierarchical strata of the episcopacy, but turned over supreme spiritual authority to the king.† Anglicanism is made up of three main groups: the *High Church* which believes that the episcopacy is of divine origin, holds it in great esteem, and has a horror of being dubbed "Protestant." To the High Church group belong Puseyites or Ritualists ("Anglo-Catholics") who both in doctrine and in worship resemble the Catholic Church quite

---

* Most of the Reformed Calvinistic Churches expressly repudiate in their creeds Calvin's original doctrine that God arbitrarily precondemns some men to hell and others to heaven irrespective of their merits. See Algermissen, *op. cit.*, p. 906–907.

† To this day the English monarch is still nominally the head of the Anglican Church.

closely. The *Low Church* leaned heavily in the direction of Calvinism, and is much more concerned with justification by faith alone than with any episcopal rank. The *Broad Church* opened its doors widely to rationalism and treats major Christian dogmas as debatable questions.

Finally, until very recent times Lutheranism, Calvinism, and Anglicanism had become divided into so many independent churches and tiny coteries that it was discouraging to even enumerate them, let alone analyze their doctrines. Fortunately, with the growth of the modern ecumenical movements,* starting in the 1920's, a large number of these Protestant Churches have federated. This makes the task of the outsider attempting to understand them sympathetically far less difficult than formerly. *The total number of Protestants in the world* today is estimated at 199,672,321.†

---

* Father Tavard's remarkable little book, *The Catholic Approach to Protestantism*, has been highly applauded both by many non-Catholics and Catholics. There the interested reader will find a brief, readable, and very charitable resume of the modern, Protestant ecumenical movement. The movement poses some delicate problems for the Roman Catholic Church which must counterbalance in their proper proportion truth, charity, and prudence. Rome looks on the movement with sympathy insofar as it bespeaks a hunger for that Catholic unity torn apart at the Reformation, and insofar as she views these Protestant Christians as her own wandering children. At the same time she cannot compromise the truth that she is the one, only, true Church founded by Jesus Christ. To be sympathetic to the ecumenists without misleading them into thinking that she is becoming doctrinally indifferent; or on the other hand, to point out her uniqueness without appearing to them to be harsh or arrogant calls for exquisite tact. Father Tavard's little book, it seems to us, both faithfully represents Rome's position and is a small reflection of it. He does not compromise the truth; yet it would be difficult for any non-Catholic to take offense at the way he presents that truth. If he is a bit hard on some of his fellow Catholic theologians they will probably be charitable enough to ignore it for the sake of the many fine points in his book.

† Church	U. S. Membership	World Membership
Roman Catholic	33,574,017	484,077,000
Baptist	18,274,088	20,680,478
Methodist	11,688,002	13,391,034
Lutheran	6,818,283	71,000,000 est.
Presbyterian	3,703,021	13,330,000
Episcopalian	2,757,944	40,000,000
Eastern Orthodox	1,500,000 est.	30,000,000 [1]
Disciples of Christ	1,897,736	2,029,963
Churches of Christ	1,600,000 [2]	—
Latter Day Saints	1,319,155	1,500,000 est.
Congregationalists	1,298,205	1,838,108

THE MARKS OF THE CHURCH

4. **The Roman Catholic Church.** Juxtaposed to all the Photian and Protestant Churches just enumerated, we find the Roman Catholic Church. In sharp distinction from Orthodox and Protestant Christianity, Roman Catholicism is not composed of a series of autonomous churches: it is one vast, world-wide church. Structurally this single Church is stratified into 2,057 ecclesiastical jurisdictions throughout the world: 713 in Europe, 492 in Asia and Oceania, 295 in North and Central America, 310 in South America, and 247 in Africa. These jurisdictions are broken down into the following ecclesiastical categories: 374 archdioceses (including 10 residential and 7 titular patriarchates), 1,238 dioceses, 205 vicariates apostolic, 119 prefectures apostolic, 84 abbacies and prelacies nullius, 19 apostolic exarchates, 11 apostolic administrations, and 7 missions.°

The total membership of the Roman Catholic Church is estimated [10] at somewhere between 421,340,901 and 484,077,000.

After this preliminary sketch of the various Christian societies we must now apply the marks of Christ's Church to see which Christian society verifies those marks. For the sake of clarity we shall apply the marks in this order: *first,* the mark of "catholic unity," or unity and catholicity considered together; *secondly,* apostolicity; *finally,* holiness.

II. Application of the Marks of Unity and Catholicity to the Various Churches

PROPOSITION 1. *The mark of unity and catholicity can not be verified in either the Eastern or the Reformation Churches.*

Proof: The Photian and Reformation Churches may be considered either collectively or singly.

1. If either group of churches be considered *collectively,* they

Adventists	270,079	924,822
Church of Christ, Scientist	268,915 [3]	– [4]
Jehovah's Witnesses	187,120	642,000
Unitarians	90,398	92,600
Universalists	70,000 est.	– [4]
Friends (Quakers)	119,000	200,000

[1] Excluding U.S.S.R.   [2] U.S. and world.   [3] 1936 U.S. Census.
[4] Unavailable.
– Based on J. Hardon, S.J., *The Protestant Churches of America* (Westminster, Md., 1956).
° These figures are taken from *The National Catholic Almanac* (1957), p. 332; the original source for the figures is *Annuario Pontificio* (1956).

(181)

evidently lack *unity:* both unity of *membership* and unity of *government;* for they are made up of many churches which are completely independent. If they do not possess unity, they necessarily lack that kind of *catholicity* with which Christ ornamented His Church (see above nos. 101–109).

2. If all these churches be considered *singly* (that is, each individual Photian Church, and each individual Protestant Church) they obviously lack *catholicity;* for each of these churches is for the most part confined within the boundaries of a single country. If they do not possess catholicity, by that very fact they necessarily lack that kind of *unity* which Christ bestowed upon His Church (see nos. 116–118).

Unity of doctrine is again quite obviously missing in Protestantism considered as a totality. In fact unity of doctrine can not be found even in the individual Protestant churches: each of them, at least the large Protestant bodies, has always been split by internal divisions—divisions and subdivisions which have increased with time. There is nothing strange in this fact, seeing that the fundamental principle of Protestantism—private judgment—is a principle which by its very nature militates against unity.*

Neither should one overestimate the doctrinal unity of the "Orthodox Church." While historically the Photian Churches have been substantially agreed in doctrine, in recent times they have shown some wavering tendencies:

> It is extremely remarkable that they have retained so much unity as in fact they display. This unity of faith, morals, and

---

* This fact is not gainsaid, but emphasized by the modern Protestant ecumenical movement. Protestants themselves have grown weary of the fracturing process induced by the very principles of the Reformers and are hungry to restore Christian unity. While viewing the ecumenical movement sympathetically one must not confuse the external unity achieved by federating churches or by practical cooperation between various sects with the internal, organic unity we are here discussing. Such confusion evidently existed in the mind of the journalist who naively captioned his article on the United Church of South India (a merger of Anglican, Methodist, Presbyterian, Congregational, and Reformed Churches in 1947): *Lesson in Unity,* (*Life,* Dec. 26, 1955, pp. 148–153). Actually this kind of unity has threatened to cause a crisis in the Anglican Church. Ronald Knox long ago envisioned the possibility of this type of Christian unity in a witty, devastating essay entitled: "Reunion All Round." It showed how one might hope to unite in the Church of England "all Mahometans, Jews, Buddhists, Brahmins, Papists and Atheists" (*Essays in Satire* [1930] pp. 47–77). To achieve such unity all one has to do is eviscerate Christianity.

worship is undoubtedly due in some measure to lack of precision in definition and to a willingness to differ; in theory the unity is complete; in fact it is a substantial agreement which today shows some tendency to weaken (there are currents of opinion trickling toward Rome, toward Protestantism, toward Modernism), and the weakening is due not a little to the close association of many of the churches with the civil power.— Attwater, *loc. cit.*, p. 6 f.; see p. 158; also Algermissen, *op. cit.*, pp. 222–3.

As a matter of fact in the Photian Churches in the nineteenth century a fair number of the more educated clergy were imbued with both Protestantism and Rationalism:

No wonder. For it is a well known fact that many of those who are called to direct and occupy the chairs of theological schools, or to hold episcopal and metropolitan sees, were educated in Protestant universities (especially the Protestant universities of Germany).[11]

Again, it is a note of real *catholicity* to have a constant interest in the conversion of pagans by preaching the gospel to them. But the "Orthodox Church" has never bothered about the conversion of pagans: "it feels no desire to convert them."[12]

Protestantism, on the other hand, while it was still a youthful and vigorous movement did not even think about converting the pagans and, generally speaking, before the beginning of the nineteenth century hardly moved a hand seriously to establish foreign missions. We must admit, however, that later on, and particularly after the middle of the nineteenth century, Protestants did establish foreign missions and did send a vast number of men and vast sums of money to found them. Some feel, however, that inasmuch as their missionaries—prescinding from a few noteworthy exceptions *—were not outstanding for real zeal and self-denial, their harvest of genuine conversions has been relatively modest.[13]

* The world-famous Albert Schweitzer has been hailed as a kind of Protestant saint in recent years. With all due tribute to his genius and undoubted sincerity it is difficult to classify him as a Protestant in any traditional sense of the word. He still seems caught up in the misty world of liberal Protestantism into which he was born. He still distinguishes between the "Jesus of faith" and the "historical Jesus." Such a man, however great or noble he is, with his own special views of "reverence for life," should rather be classified as a "mystical humanitarian" than as a Christian.

138 PROPOSITION 2. *The Roman Catholic Church possesses the mark of unity.*

Proof:

1. It has *unity of doctrine.* All Roman Catholics throughout the entire world, ordinary laymen and professional theologians alike, no matter what theological school they belong to, profess the doctrine proposed to them by the Roman Catholic bishops. Even though they may disagree on some minor questions which have not yet been clarified by the teaching Church, they all confess that they are ready to accept immediately whatever decision the Church will hand down on these questions.

2. It has *social unity.* All Roman Catholics belong to one single society; they worship God with one and the same sacrifice, and they partake of the same sacraments and other spiritual goods, and obey the same universal laws.

3. It has *unity of government;* for both the laity and the clergy obey the bishops, and all the bishops of the world together with their flocks are under the rule of the Roman pontiff so that the whole Church is indeed: *like an army drawn up in battle formation* (Cant. 6:13).

This unity of the Roman Church, which is not brought about by secret police or terroristic tactics or by military might, but by the free submission of the faithful and by the powerful operation of the Holy Spirit, is so obvious a fact that all men acknowledge it either by their admiration or by their envy. Still this remarkable unity in nowise destroys the legitimate use of personal liberty; neither does it hamstring the native genius of individual men or nations by forcing on them a rigid and artificial uniformity. The Church, wise mother that she is, in all matters which do not conflict with God's rights, freely accommodates herself to the varying characteristics of different nations and different ages, granting liberty without license and preserving unity without tyranny.

139 PROPOSITION 3. *The Roman Church possesses the mark of catholicity.*

Proof:

1. This fact is in a sense vindicated by its very name. Other Christian societies are usually designated by names indicating something localized;[14] while the Church presided over by the

THE MARKS OF THE CHURCH

Roman pontiff is the only society which, by the common consent of the whole world, is called *catholic* or universal. Since it is everywhere so called, it is immediately and without ambiguity recognizable. St. Augustine says:

> There are many things which quite rightly keep me within the Catholic Church.... For she possesses the very name *catholic*—something which is no mere accident when amid so many heresies that Church alone so rightly deserves the name catholic, that even though the heretics might prefer to have themselves called catholics, yet when any traveler inquires where he can find the Catholic church, no heretic would dare to point out his own church or his own meeting place.[15]

As a matter of record, heretics not only in Augustine's day but in later ages have constantly tried to snatch this name away from us, referring to us as "papists," "romanists," "ultramontanes" and so on. Strangely, they have always been frustrated in their attempts to pin another label on us:

> Whether they like it or not, even the heretics and schismatics when they are discussing the Catholic Church, not simply among themselves but with outsiders, always refer to it as the Catholic Church. Unless they did refer to it by that name no one would understand what they were talking about, since the whole world calls it by that name.[16]

How truly the Roman Church deserves the name "catholic" becomes quite clear if you stop to consider its vast membership, its geographical diffusion, and its continuous growth.

2. Its *vast membership*. The number of Roman Catholics not only vastly exceeds the membership of any other individual Christian church considered alone, but her membership equals or surpasses even their total combined membership. According to the most recent poll, almost 20 per cent or one-fifth of all the inhabitants of the world are Catholics.

```
Total Christian population..............817,530,926
                                        32.4 per cent
                                        of world pop.
Total Roman Catholic...................484,077,000
Total Protestant ......................204,566,009
Total Schismatic ......................128,887,917
```

3. Its *geographical diffusion*. The Roman Church is spread *practically over the entire world*. In Europe it is spread through every country; 39 per cent of all Europeans are Catholic: 230,000,000 Catholics out of a total European population of 590,000,000. In Central and South America the Roman Church has practically no rivals, and in North America it is widely spread in all parts of the region. There are 190,000,000 Roman Catholics in the Americas, or 56 per cent of the combined total population of 337,000,000. The Roman Church is spread through a great number of Asiatic countries and adjacent islands, and though its membership is proportionally considerably less than elsewhere it is still quite striking: 31,000,000 or 2.3 per cent of the total Asian population of 1,300,000,000. It has considerable membership in Africa and in Oceania. Africa has 17,000,000 Catholics or 8.5 per cent of the entire population of 198,000,000. In Oceania there are 2,800,000 Catholics, or 20 per cent of the total population of 14,000,000.*

This geographical diffusion of the Roman Catholic Church—which definitely includes the conservation of its unity in the midst of diffusion—quite easily surpasses the diffusion not merely of any other *Christian* church, but far surpasses the diffusion of every other religion including the non-Christian. For the *Mohammedans* are not found in America or Australia; neither are they found in Europe (with the exception of Turkey and Serbia). *Buddhists* and *Hindus* find their membership confined within the boundaries of Asia alone. Incidentally, no one should harbor the illusion that Mohammedans, Buddhists, and Hindus are not divided against one another, or that they somehow form one united society; let alone a Church of Pagans!

4. Its *constant growth*. Another striking feature of the catholicity of the Roman Church is that it *keeps spreading constantly ever wider.** Just as at its very beginning it obeyed the command of Christ to preach the gospel to all nations, so it continues to obey

---

* The countries with the largest Roman Catholic populations are the following:

Brazil	53,149,500
Italy	47,426,600
France	35,690,000
United States	34,563,841
Spain	28,659,000
Germany	27,696,564
Mexico	27,696,000
Argentina	16,993,320

THE WORLD'S RELIGIONS

CHRISTIAN

	North America	South America	Europe	Asia	Africa	Oceania	Total
Roman Catholic	90,582,000	111,922,000	230,338,000	13,276,000	18,608,000	19,351,000	484,077,000
Eastern Orthodox	2,466,000	—	112,447,000	8,106,000	5,868,000	—	128,887,000
Protestant	65,189,000	2,427,000	113,572,000	8,837,000	6,278,000	8,262,000	204,565,000
Total	158,237,000	114,349,000	456,357,000	30,219,000	30,754,000	27,613,000	817,529,000

NON-CHRISTIAN

	North America	South America	Europe	Asia	Africa	Oceania	Total
Jewish	5,430,000	638,000	3,439,000	1,629,000	678,000	58,000	11,872,000
Mohammedan	33,000	343,000	12,425,000	318,341,000	85,325,000	102,000	416,569,000
Taoist	15,000	17,000	12,000	50,000,000	1,000	8,000	50,053,000
Confucian	86,000	95,000	50,000	300,000,000	8,000	52,000	300,291,000
Buddhist	165,000	135,000	10,000	150,000,000	—	—	150,310,000
Hindu	10,000	275,000	—	315,314,000	300,000	100,000	315,999,000
Primitive	50,000	1,000,000	—	45,000,000	75,000,000	100,000	121,150,000
Miscellaneous	76,541,000	9,803,000	82,491,000	185,685,000	12,639,000	5,363,000	372,522,000
Total	82,330,000	12,306,000	98,427,000	1,365,969,000	173,951,000	5,783,000	1,738,766,000
Grand Total	240,567,000	126,655,000	554,784,000	1,396,188,000	204,705,000	33,396,000	2,556,295,000

Him—and in very energetic fashion. For to all lands, however remote or however barbarian, it ceaselessly sends missionaries.

III. Application of the Mark of Apostolicity to the Various Churches

140 PROPOSITION 1. *Both the Photian and Protestant Churches lack the mark of apostolicity.*

Proof:

1. First it should be clear that both of them lack *apostolicity of membership*.

   a. No amount of tortuous reasoning can ever hide the fact that the church of Constantinople (from which the rest of the Eastern Churches sprang up) simply did not exist *as such* (that is, as a self-governing and independent church) before the schism of Michael Caerularius in 1054. The church which flourished in those regions before the schism was simply a portion of the Roman Catholic Church. Before the schism it freely acknowledged the primacy of the pope, as is clearly borne out by the very history of Photius and the acts of the Fourth Council of Constantinople (870).[17]

   b) It is even more obvious that the Lutheran, Calvinist, and Anglican Churches simply did not exist before the sixteenth century. How could a "reformed" church exist before there was a "reformation"? Clearly, then, none of these churches which began to exist only hundreds and hundreds of years after the death of the apostles can be said to be numerically the same as that Church which existed under the apostles' personal rule.

2. Similarly it is quite easy to show that both the Eastern and the Protestant Churches lack *apostolicity of government*.

   a. The patriarchs of Constantinople before the time of Michael Caerularius simply did not possess supreme and independent power over their church. They possessed only a limited and derivative authority as is clear from their own earlier acknowledgment of the primacy of the Roman pontiff.[18] Consequently, when Michael Caerularius claimed independent authority he was claiming something which did not accrue to him by the mere succession to the see of Constantinople. His claim was something brand new; and if new, not apostolic.

   Again, by claiming independent authority Caerularius *ipso facto* ceased to be a member of the college of bishops to which he formerly belonged;* one can hardly be a subordinate member of a corporate body and at the same time utterly independent of it. Now if Caerularius ceased to be a member of the episcopal college, he necessarily lost such apostolic power as he possessed precisely in virtue of his membership in that college.† Consequently, even though Caerularius continued physically to occupy a see which was (indirectly) apostolic, he was no longer a legitimate successor of the apostles.

b. The same argument applies to the rest of the schismatic patriarchs; and, on the other side of the ledger, to all bishops who occupy a see which was originally Catholic: all Orthodox, Anglican, and Scandinavian Lutheran bishops. All of these men, by refusing to acknowledge what their own predecessors acknowledged—that the Roman pontiff is the head of the episcopal college—by that very fact departed from the apostolic body of pastors.

c. Finally, it should not take too much brow-furrowing to realize that political rulers, lay synods and lay consistories, whether Photian or Protestant, cannot possibly be considered legitimate successors of the apostles. Christ did not hand over the government of His Church to Caesar; He handed it over to Peter and the apostles.

We can, then, justly dismiss all such apostolic pretenders, eastern or western, with these words of Tertullian:

> Let them show, then, that the line of their bishops descends in such fashion through successions right back to the beginning; that their first bishops had as their consecrators or immediate predecessors either one of the apostles themselves, or one of those men of the apostolic era who at the same time persevered [in unity] with the apostles.[19]

If Tertullian could issue that challenge back in the second century and no heretic could take it up, it should be limpidly clear how little chance any schismatic or heretical bishop of 1000, or 1600 years later could have to lay claim to apostolic succession.

---

* We are here taking for granted something admitted by both the Eastern Schismatics and the Roman Catholic Church; namely, that Michael Caerularius' predecessors in the see of Constantinople truly belonged to the body of apostolic pastors.

† He lost, in other words, such apostolic power as is losable: the power of *jurisdiction*. He did not lose, what is unlosable, the power of *orders*.

141 PROPOSITION 2. *The Roman Catholic Church does possess the mark of apostolicity.*

Proof:

1. It has *apostolicity of membership*. First, it should be evident that the Roman Catholic Church is older than all the other Christian societies, since they only came into being by separating from it. This fact itself implies, by the argument of exclusion, that the Roman Church is the continuation of that Church which existed under the apostles' personal rule. The Church of the apostles was certainly promised indestructibility and consequently must still exist. Since the rest of the Christian societies did not spring up till long ages after the apostolic era, the only thing one can conclude is that the Catholic Church alone is that society which was planted by the apostles.

Even more startling is the fact that no one can assign any plausible date later than the apostolic era for the beginning of the Catholic Church. So striking is this fact that Rationalists have dreamed up various theories to try to account simply for its origin through some sort of natural evolution.[20] These theories simply have no plausibility to them. Actually they are completely ruled out in positive fashion by what was discussed at length in *chapters I and II*.

2. The Roman Church has *apostolicity of government*. It is united to the bishop of Rome, who by a never-interrupted series of predecessors reaches back to Saint Peter upon whom Christ built His Church. This succession of the Roman pontiffs right back to the prince of the apostles, despite the quibblings of a few hardheaded people, is a fact so plain as to be beyond cavil.*

Once this fact has been established, it follows that the bishops of the Roman Catholic Church are the genuine successors of the apostolic college. Why? Because they are united to Peter's successor and are acknowledged and honored by him as the sole lawful inheritors of apostolic power (see no. 120).

With good reason then can we echo Augustine's words: "What holds me [in the Catholic Church] is that succession of priestly bishops which descends from the very chair of Peter the apostle, on whom our Lord bestowed the office of feeding his sheep, right down to the present day."[21]

---

* A list of popes from the present pope back to St. Peter can be found in any almanac. See, for example, *The World Almanac* (1957), p. 725.

Corollary

Since all the other Christian societies took their origin by separation and desertion from the Catholic Church, all men who are converted to the Church—however numerous they may be from any particular sect—are correctly said *to return* to the household of the Church. For they return to that house from which either they themselves or their forefathers had gone out.

IV. The Application of the Mark of Holiness to the Various Churches

PROPOSITION 1. *Neither the Photian nor the Protestant Churches possess the mark of holiness.*   142

Proof:

1. No harvest *of extraordinary or heroic holiness* * appears in either the Eastern or Protestant Churches. It is a fact that until recent times of persecution,† religion in the *Photian* Churches had grown rather feeble. Their organizations and societies lacked both vigor and a spirit of piety; many times they became devoted to political rather than religious purposes.[22] After their separation from Rome, they ceased to produce any genuine saints whose sanctity can be historically documented.

As for the *Protestant* Churches, we do not at all deny that many of their members worship God sincerely and lead good moral lives. But the point here is that these people do not possess holiness to a *heroic* degree. By abolishing religious orders, the Protestant

---

* It is extremely important to note here what was treated above in the theoretical exposition of the marks of the Church. The only type of holiness which can serve as a mark, as an obvious or easily detectible sign, is *heroic* holiness: great sanctity. To state then that these churches lack the *mark* of holiness is not in any sense to deny that large numbers of both Schismatics and Protestants may lead excellent, normally holy lives. Ordinary holiness is, of course, very praiseworthy, but it cannot serve as a mark of the true Church. All the marks, as we have seen, involve something truly remarkable, something indeed miraculous—that is why they are so useful in spotlighting the only genuine Church of Christ. For a respectful, sympathetic description of the real piety to be found among the Orthodox, see Algermissen, *op. cit.*, pp. 684–6; see also, L. Bouyer, *The Spirit and Forms of Protestantism* (Westminster, Md., 1956), pp. 177–92.

† The persecutions by the Communists seem to have revived a very deep spirit of piety among the Russians (see *Newsweek*, 44 [October 18, 1954], pp. 59–62). A recent book, however, takes a rather pessimistic view, indicating that the present patriarch of Moscow is seeking to control all the Orthodox Churches and to bring them under the sway of the Kremlin; see Matthew Spinka, *The Church in Soviet Russia* (Oxford, 1956).

Churches totally uprooted a very way of life dedicated to the pursuit of perfection. They have never emphasized the practice of the evangelical counsels—poverty, chastity, obedience. Consequently, relatively few Protestants dedicate their entire lives and energy exclusively to works of religion and charity. Nowhere can they point to genuine heroes of sanctity. More striking still, the history of original Protestantism brings us face to face with two hard facts:

a. The very founders of Protestantism (Luther, Calvin, Henry VIII) would hardly be classified by disinterested observers as outstandingly holy men.*

b. The immediate results of the Reformation, according to the testimony of the Reformers themselves, was not an increase in holiness and morality, but just the reverse.[23]

As a matter of fact, present-day Protestants, who are well-versed historically in the facts of the Reformation era, tend to emphasize, not the holiness of the original Reformers, but their contributions to the development of the spirit of liberty, the free-

---

* See, for example the descriptions of Luther and Calvin by Paul Hutchinson, himself a Protestant:

Martin Luther was a great bull of a man, bursting with animal spirits, whose sermons and tracts seemed to erupt from him in an undammable flood. His voice could summon to spiritual battle with a power that still reaches across the years as one reads his greatest writings. In his home, sitting at his table drinking "good Wittenberg beer" while he regaled his innumerable guests with the *Table Talk* that still makes good reading, playing his flute in the orchestra he formed with his children, visiting like a good pastor the sick and the poor—this is a Luther of infinite fascination. But there was another Luther, also a full-fledged German—a Luther who could flame into towering rages, who could vilify his opponents with a disgraceful abuse dredged from the gutter, who could command the princes who had protected him to crush with unbridled ferocity the social uprising of what he called "the Murderous and Thieving Rabble of the Peasants." . . .

The other "father of the Reformation" was about as different from Luther as a mortal could be. John Calvin was a wispy French intellectual with an introspective, syllogistic mind like that of Thomas Aquinas. . . .

Calvin's great contribution was to reduce the Protestant revolt to theological coherence. . . .

But the figure of Calvin himself remains cool, remote and as repellent of familiarity as was the living man when, accosted on a Geneva street by an enthusiastic refugee as "Brother Calvin," he frostily answered that he was to be correctly addressed as "Monsieur."—"The Onward March of the Christian Faith," *Life*, 39 (Dec. 26, 1955), 41-2.

ing of men from authoritarian control, the recognition of the dignity of the individual conscience, and so forth.

2. *Miracles and charisms* which Christ promised would emblazon the holiness of His Church are totally lacking among both the Eastern[24] Churches and the Protestant. In fact, Protestants are so keenly aware of this that they often state blandly that miracles no longer happened after the apostolic era.*

3. When discussing the *means to holiness* one must make one judgment with regard to the Orthodox and another with regard to the Protestant Churches.

The *Orthodox* are not lacking in the means to holiness: when they departed from the Catholic Church, they retained practically its entire doctrine, the seven sacraments, and many of its organizations and pious practices. None of these means are, however, the rightful property of the Orthodox; hence the fruitful use of the means to holiness is merely accidental to this church. Again, we must not forget the fact that because of their lack of apostolicity, the Orthodox schismatics lack the sacred power of jurisdiction † which was conferred on the true Church "for the *complete* development of the saints." Finally, many of these Eastern Churches, and particularly the Russian Church, historically handed themselves over, bound hand and foot, to the civil government. This slavery, until recently, hindered even their natural vigor. From these facts it should be clear why the Photian Churches have had a difficult time exercising any great sanctifying influence.

The *Protestant Churches* are far more destitute of *means* to holiness than the Orthodox.

In *doctrine* the original Reformers did not simply reduce the contents of the Catholic faith: they distorted it. Along with the doctrines they retained correctly, they blended a caricature of other Catholic teachings and introduced some new doctrines which were peculiarly their own creation. Among these caricatured teachings, and newly-minted ones, some were completely contrary to

---

* Oddly enough, one of the best books to appear about the famous Catholic shrine of Lourdes is by a Protestant woman, Ruth Cranston, *The Miracle of Lourdes* (1955). It is a well-documented study by an on-the-spot observer. Miss Cranston seems quite convinced of the genuineness of many of these miracles. What is of pertinence here is that the miracles occur at a Catholic shrine. Perhaps the first *photographed* miracle in history took place in recent times at the same shrine. See the pictures and article in *Le Match* (September, 1954).

† See *above*, p. 189, footnote †.

holiness. For example, justification by faith *alone*,* the uselessness of good works, denial of free will, the impossibility of losing justification,† and so forth. Since all these doctrines entered into the one system, the original doctrine of Protestantism should strictly be called *unholy*, in accord with the axiom: a thing is morally good only if completely good; bad if even partially defective.

The *institutions and laws* of the original Protestants did little to promote holiness in a positive fashion. They rejected most of the sacraments. They had a special loathing for the sacrament of penance. This sacrament, even if one considered it merely psychologically (i.e., prescinding from the grace it produces by the very working of the sacrament), is a powerful remedy for controlling vicious tendencies and promoting sound morality.[25]

Early Protestants also outlawed nearly all religious rites and ceremonies in their search for a purely spiritual religion. They forgot that man is an organic unity of body and soul; and not to be conceived as a soul *inside* a body. Consequently they failed to see the importance of religious rites and ceremonies which act like visual aids in stimulating men's minds to a consideration of spiritual

---

* The Catholic Church has always stressed that faith is "the beginning, and root, and foundation of all holiness" (Council of Trent, Session 6, chap. 8), but it never leapt to the strange conclusion that nothing but faith is needed for holiness. It continues to agree with the Apostle James that: *You see, a man is justified by deeds, and not merely by faith. . . . Really, just as the body without the soul is lifeless, so also faith without deeds is lifeless.* (Jam. 2:24–26). It is one thing to say a man is justified by faith: quite another to say he is justified by faith *alone*.

† According to Catholic doctrine a man's sins are really wiped out by the process called justification; he is rendered innocent internally. According to the Reformers a man's sins were not really wiped out; they were merely cloaked by the merits of Christ much the way a rubbish heap might be covered over by a lovely, white blanket of snow. Calvin added to the general Reformation premise of a purely extrinsic justification his own special conclusion that a man once justified was justified forever. Catholic doctrine teaches that a man once justified can become a sinner again through his own bad will. In other words the grace of justification is losable by mortal sin. If the Calvinistic doctrine were correct then Christ's warning: *"Keep awake and pray, all of you, that you may not succumb to temptation"* would be unnecessary and useless. So, too, would be St. Paul's warning: *whoever believes he is standing firm, should beware lest he fall.* Catholic doctrine on this matter is summed up in these words of the Council of Trent: "If anyone says that a man who has once been justified cannot sin again or lose grace, and consequently that he who does slip and sin was never really justified, let him be anathema" (DB, 833, 837).

and divine realities. With the advent of modern psychology, however, modern Protestants have begun to appreciate more and more man's need for tangible realities to help him in the practice of religion. That is why many of their present-day churches are beginning to exhibit beauty and color, stained glass windows, statues, and, even occasionally, altars. Such items would have filled many of their forebears with horror.

The original Protestants did away with religious orders and congregations—those specialized schools for the pursuit of holiness. In fact, until quite recent times Protestants did not much bother to see that the very ministers of God's word received special training in spirituality. By abrogating the law of celibacy, they subjected their ministers to all the worries and distractions of worldly life. Finally Protestants, early or modern, have very few disciplinary laws that govern the worship that is to be offered to God, and practically none that foster penance or mortification.

The one means to stimulate holiness retained by Protestants, early and modern, is the Bible. Many of them are faithful and devout readers of the Scriptures and there can be no doubt that a reverent reading of God's word does much to stimulate many Protestants to lead upright and exemplary lives.*

PROPOSITION 2. *The Roman Catholic Church possesses the mark of holiness.* 144

Before we offer direct proofs, here are two general indications which testify at least indirectly to the Church's holiness.

Preliminary Suasions

1. Christ prophesied that His Church would be *hated by the world;* hated precisely because, under the life-giving impulse of the Holy Spirit, it would not *belong* to this world:

---

* We do not include in this category those Protestants, however scholarly, who regard the Bible as simply an interesting collection of Jewish religious myths and pore over it in antiquarian fashion; nor those Protestants, however sincere, who are fanatical Bible-readers and are sure that the Holy Spirit guarantees them His infallible assistance whenever they interpret any chapter or verse. This latter type of reader, lacking both scientific knowledge of the Bible and the guidance of the Church, is apt to do himself more spiritual harm than good. The snake-bite cults are a good example of what can result from such reading. The Protestants we refer to here are good, normal people who accept the Bible as being truly God's word and use it as a form of spiritual reading.

"If the world hates you, bear in mind that it has hated me first. If you were children of the world, the world would cherish its own flesh and blood. But you are not children of the world; on the contrary, I have singled you out from the world, and therefore the world hates you. Remember what I told you: a slave is not better than his master. If they persecuted me, they will persecute you also; if they treasure my teaching, they will treasure yours also."—John 15:18–20; see Matt. 24:9.

Now it is a strange as well as a notorious fact that of all the Christian societies none experiences this hatred of the world so strongly as the Catholic Church. Something further, it is the only Church which is *continuously* attacked by that amorphous multitude which rises age after age under the leadership of evil men. By their very persecutions, then, the children of this world identify that Church which is vivified by the Spirit of Christ.[26]

2. Another general indication of its holiness is found in *the history of conversions.*[27] It frequently happens that some of the very best men found in other Christian societies become converted to the Catholic Church. It is quite clear that these people are not motivated by any hope of worldly advantage; they do not enter the Church to grow wealthy, or to embrace an easier moral code. In fact they usually have to make painful sacrifices to gain the treasure hidden in the field of the Church.*

Contrariwise, what Catholic, because of the pressure of his conscience and at painful sacrifice to himself, ever joined a non-Catholic sect in order to become holier, purer, more intimately united to God? What Catholic, on his deathbed, ever said goodbye to the Church? What Catholic who was both chaste and pious was ever haunted by the thought that perhaps some other Christian society might be preferable to the Catholic Church? The normal rule is that when Catholics leave the Church they are prompted by either wounded pride; hope of business, social or political advancement; or, above all, some marital difficulty or struggle over purity. What accounts for this difference in the *motives* of conversion? Is it not that God's grace frequently deserts those who have first deserted Him, and at the same time with exquisite guidance leads sincere and religious souls to the sheepfold of Christ?

* A simple perusal of the conversion stories of Newman, Chesterton, Ronald Knox, Claire Booth Luce, Rabbi Zolli, Karl Stern and Jacques Maritain will indicate something of the painful sacrifices normally made by converts entering the Church.

THE MARKS OF THE CHURCH

Enough for preliminary observations and suasions. Now the direct proofs for the Church's holiness need to be examined.

Proof:

1. The Catholic Church possesses *many means to holiness* which it ceaselessly dispenses and uses.

   a. Its *doctrine* not only does not run counter to norms of holiness, but it embraces in their entirety the gospel ideals, including the evangelical counsels of poverty, chastity, and obedience. This extremely holy doctrine, the Church, with both apostolic liberty and authority, inculcates in all men by tireless teaching. It adapts that same holy doctrine to the comprehension and needs of every age-level—from childhood to mature manhood.

   b. The Church has many *disciplinary laws* by which it constantly and earnestly instructs men in the keeping of divine laws. Think of its commandments governing the hearing of Mass, Sunday rest, the reception of the sacraments; its laws on fast and abstinence, on marriages and particularly on mixed marriages; its laws about religious education; its prohibition of membership in subversive societies; its index of forbidden books; its moral guidance in the matter of entertainment and so forth.*

   c. The Church is rich in *institutions* that are powerful stimulants to holiness. Think particularly of the seven sacraments which link the main events of human life with religion, and irradiate a man's entire life with a religious aura.[28] Think, too, of the various religious devotions: missions, retreats, Forty Hours devotions, novenas, jubilees. Think of the confraternities and societies: the St. Vincent de Paul Society, the Holy Name Society, Ladies Sodalities, Altar boy Societies, Catechetical Organizations, Cana Conferences, Legion of Mary and a host of other societies which the Church uses to stimulate and strengthen the spirit of religion and fraternal

---

* The last two items often infuriate non-Catholic Americans who view such legislation as an infringement of personal liberty. It is one thing to protest against the classification of a particular book or stage show or movie as immoral, or dangerous to faith; it is quite another matter to protest *in principle* against *any* such classification as subversive of personal liberty. The latter viewpoint is taken by those who confuse liberty with license. Liberty is a very precious thing, but it is not an absolute; it carries with it corresponding social obligations. Any rightly ordered society has laws for the common good; and such laws for the common good necessarily place limits to the rights of individuals. The Church, too, as a genuine society has its laws to safeguard the spiritual common good of all its children.

charity. Think of what seminaries and the law of celibacy contribute to the sanctification of its clergy. Think, finally, of that mighty array of religious orders and congregations (Benedictines, Carmelites, Cistercians, Dominicans, Franciscans, Jesuits, Maryknoll Fathers, Vincentians, Trappists, and so forth) with which the Church fosters the observance of the evangelical counsels.

The Catholic Church has never, like a miser, concealed those talents which it received from its Founder—doctrine, sacraments, authority—in a napkin, nor buried them in the ground.* Heaven forbid! It uses those talents with vast ingenuity to irrigate the dry souls of the faithful with the living waters of sanctity. It battles courageously to be a ferment in all walks of human life: it pervades domestic, social, and political life and tries to sanctify them all.[29]

Corollary

Bad Catholics versus the Church's holiness.

If, in spite of the holiness of the doctrine, laws, and institutions of the Church, one encounters individual Catholics, clerical or lay, who are perverted or evil, any fair-minded man can see that their evilness results not from following, but from betraying, Catholic principles. It is Judas, not Christ, whom we blame for the betrayal; likewise, it would be irrational to blame the Church for the bad behavior of some of its children. Bad Catholics refuse to follow the way of life proposed by the Church: they disobey its laws and ignore the means to sanctity it offers them. In short, the sinners found in the Church are there only accidentally.†

We can justly repeat what St. Augustine said to the Manicheans when they raised the same muddleheaded objection against the Catholic Church back in the fourth century:

> My advice to you now is that you ought at least to cease slandering the Catholic Church by loudly denouncing the morals of men whom the Church itself condemns and whom it constantly strives to correct as wicked children. For if any of them undergo a change of heart and are corrected by God's grace, they regain by repentance what they had lost by sin. And if any of them continue in their old vices along with the wicked,

---

* See Christ's parable of the talents, Matthew 25:14–30.

† "It is true to say that although the Church is not without sinners, it is without sin, for we belong to her by reason of the supernatural gifts we possess and not by reason of the sins we have committed" (Charles Journet, *The Wisdom of Faith* [Westminster, Md., 1952], p. 148).

or even add worse vices to their present ones, they may indeed be allowed to remain in God's field and to grow side by side with the good wheat—but the time for separating the tares [from the wheat] will [finally] come.*

2. The Church produces an *abundant harvest of holiness*. We shall not discuss here the millions of Catholics in every state of life who, with strong courage and ceaseless struggle, maintain the ordinary level of holiness. This is something noble in itself—in fact, quite wonderful. But, as was mentioned above, ordinary holiness is not suitable to act as a *mark* of the Church. What interests us here is that the Catholic Church glitters with *heroic* holiness. This is clear from:

146

a. *The vast number of those who are consecrated to the state of perfection* and spend their entire lives worshiping God and serving their neighbor. No one drafts this huge army of heroic men and women: they rise spontaneously generation after generation. How many over the centuries choose that glorious type of life and persist in it may be gauged in some degree by the following statistical table for 1954 covering simply the priests and brothers of religious orders throughout the world: †

1.	Jesuits	32,008
2.	Franciscans (Friars Minor)	25,438
3.	Salesians	17,356
4.	Christian Brothers	14,832
5.	Franciscans (Capuchins)	14,198
6.	Benedictines	11,100
7.	Dominicans	8,543
8.	Marist Brothers	8,050
9.	Redemptorists	7,819
10.	Oblates of Mary Immaculate	6,264
11.	Vincentians	5,096
12.	Holy Ghost Fathers	4,500
13.	Divine Word Missionaries	4,287
14.	Franciscans (Conventuals)	3,650
15.	Augustinians	3,565
16.	Passionists	3,500

* *De moribus ecclesiae catholicae* i. 34. 76. (ML 32: 1342). This treatise was written in 388 not long after Augustine became converted to Catholicism. All of it is worth reading. A fair English translation can be found in *Basic Writings of St. Augustine* (New York, 1948), I, 319–57.
† See *The National Catholic Almanac* (1956), p. 430–1.

17. Discalced Carmelites 3,433
18. Trappists 3,420
19. White Fathers 3,020
20. Missionaries of the Sacred Heart........ 2,916
21. Claretians 2,800
22. Marianists 2,600
23. Brothers of the Sacred Heart............ 2,568
24. Fathers of the Sacred Heart............ 2,530
25. Piarists 2,300
26. Holy Cross Fathers 2,246
27. Christian Brothers of Ireland........... 2,226
28. La Mennais Brothers 2,200
29. Carmelites 2,187
30. Hospitallers of St. John of God.......... 2,149
31. Presentation Brothers 1,915
32. Marists 1,889
33. Assumptionists 1,880
34. Sons of Divine Providence.............. 1,766
35. Pallottines 1,750
36. Scheut Fathers 1,658
37. Viatorians 1,650
38. Fathers of the Sacred Hearts
    (Picpus Fathers) 1,634
39. Cistercians 1,600
40. Premonstratensians 1,551
41. Brothers of Charity 1,548
42. Servites 1,511
43. Brothers of Christian Instruction......... 1,450
44. African Mission Fathers................ 1,437
45. Montfort Fathers 1,427
46. Blessed Sacrament Fathers 1,250
47. Camillians 1,107
48. Salvatorians 1,076
49. Augustinian Recollects 1,009
50. Verona Fathers 1,005

Communities under 1,000 members.......... 34,568

Total male religious 271,482

To this figure must be added perhaps some 400,000 religious sisters whose various groups are too numerous to enumerate here.*

* A list of religious orders of women just for the U.S.A. covers 20 pages in *The National Catholic Almanac* (1956), p. 432–52.

And although they are not bound by the three religious vows, to this number of heroic servants of Christ should be added 256,152 *diocesan or secular priests* (*The National Catholic Almanac*, p. 431) whose lives are expressly dedicated to ministering to the spiritual needs of the laity in parish life. Their way of life, though not canonically classified as a "state" of perfection actually demands a high degree of personal sanctity or perfection if they are to fulfill their sublime calling in a fitting fashion.

b. From the *vast number of genuine saints* the Church continually produces. No one can compute the exact number of men and women saints the Catholic Church has brought forth from apostolic times until the present day.* Something of the vastness and continuousness of that production is witnessed by the *Martyrology*, and by that huge, scholarly collection of the Bollandists, the *Acta Sanctorum*.[30] The recently revised (1956) edition of Butler's *Lives of the Saints* contains some 2500 entries. There is hardly a nation in which Catholicism flourishes, or formerly flourished—in fact, hardly a diocese—which does not have its own saints.

We adduce one fact, merely as a sample of many other facts the like of which can be found nowhere in the world, save in the Catholic Church. The Church possesses, *as a normal part of its life,* public legislation (CIC, nos. 1999–2141) and standard tribunals to examine the cases for the servants of God whose sanctity is proposed for official recognition. These tribunals act with such accuracy and strictness that, even though they discuss cases of canonization publicly, no learned man has ever protested their decisions. Despite their severity, it is by no means a rare event for these tribunals to hand down a decision raising some servant of

---

* The canonization of St. Ulrich in the year 993 by John XV is the first instance of *papal* canonization. Since that time, there have been about 250 solemn proclamations of sainthood (*The National Catholic Almanac*, 1956, pp. 272–3). These statistics on *papal* canonizations, of course, give us no information about the vast number of saints who lived during the first 1,000 years of the Church's history. The simple fact that thousands of *unnamed* people suffered martyrdom for the faith during the Roman persecutions of the first three centuries should be enough to help us understand why it is impossible to have mathematical precision in this matter. The additional sobering fact that, at a conservative estimate (see *Time's* report on the study of the "efficiency" of the Catholic Church by the Anglican managerial expert, Martindell, vol. 67 [January 30, 1956], 39–40), at least some 5 billion people have been baptized into the Roman Catholic Church over its long history, should point out the staggering difficulties confronting anyone who naïvely hopes to compute, to the decimal point, the incidence of sanctity over the centuries.

God to the honor of the altar. Since the start of the nineteenth century, more than 400 people have been declared *blessed* and more than a hundred declared *saints*.

This harvest of heroic sanctity has not ceased even in modern times. For example, the following illustrious confessors have been declared *venerable:* Vincent Pallotti, priest (d. 1850); Francis Liebermann, a Jewish convert (d. 1852); Father Peter Donders, C.SS.R., (d. 1887); and Father Damien "the Leper" (Damien de Veuster, d. 1889). The following have been canonized *saints:* John Baptist Vianney, "the curé of Ars" (d. 1859); Gabriel of the Sorrowful Virgin (d. 1862); John Bosco (d. 1888); Thérèse of the Child Jesus (d. 1897); Gemma Galgani (d. 1903); Pius X (d. 1914); Frances (Mother) Cabrini (d. 1917).

An impressive number of martyrs underwent death to spread the faith in barbaric regions, as attested in *Mission Annals*. To these should be added the martyrs of Poland, Siberia, Mexico, and Russia whose deaths were brought about by persecution, hunger, and cold during the earlier stages of Marxist world revolution. In addition to the current, well-publicized cases of Cardinal Mindszenty, Archbishop Stepinac, and Cardinal Wyszynski, literally hundreds of heroic priests, nuns, and laymen are at present suffering imprisonment for the faith in Iron Curtain countries. Their "dry" martyrdom is, perhaps, even more difficult than that of actual execution.

Study the history of the Catholic Church a little more deeply and find that it has not only produced saints in every century, but that it is truly the Church which *belongs to the saints*. In other words, it is especially by the works of its saints that the Catholic Church has been spread, consolidated, defended, and supported in a hundred different ways. Those who planted the Church in the very beginning (the apostles and first Christian bishops) and who later planted it in individual countries (Augustine, Patrick, Boniface, Cyril and Methodius, Francis Xavier, and so forth) were for the most part saints and martyrs. Who took the lead in refuting heresies? Who defended most vigorously the Church's liberty against the assaults of secular power? Who founded the great religious orders? Who developed the science of theology, constructed the Church's worship and liturgy, and who revived its spirit of religion and piety whenever it threatened to collapse? Was it not before all others the saints themselves? It is Christ

Himself, of course, who builds and ornaments His Church: He is the Head of His Mystical Body—"*I am the vine, you are the branches.*" Small wonder, then, if He uses as His principal instruments the people who are most imbued with His spirit. Christ is the perfect model of utterly sublime holiness and He is the Head of the Church; what wonder, then, if He makes the saints, as it were, the very bones of His body?

c. The Catholic Church, finally, sparkles with the *holiness of charisms*. That miracles have never ceased to occur in the Catholic Church, even in the blackest periods of its history, is plain from the very decrees of beatification and canonization. Since the time of Urban VIII (1625), with the exception of some martyrs, no one is beatified until it has been conclusively established that at least two miracles have occurred through his intervention. And no one is canonized until two more irrefutable * miracles have been proven. Finally, it is no secret how many miraculous cures occur even to the present day at the shrine of Lourdes in France.†

147

Scholion. On Temporal Prosperity.

148

In discussing the mark of holiness, strange as it may seem, non-Catholics often introduce the subject of the influence of the true religion in promoting prosperity, and the alleged superiority of Protestant nations in this regard. In so complex a question—since this is not a dissertation on economics—one can only indicate a few points which may help save confusion. It is one thing to inquire about genuine happiness in this life; and quite another matter to inquire about *temporal prosperity* in the sense of an abundance of material comforts.

1. The *real source of earthly happiness* does not depend either uniquely, or principally, on material goods or secular culture. It depends much more on the soul's moral dispositions, on what is currently termed, "peace of mind." America, for example, which is the world's wealthiest nation, has seen in the past 10 years a perfect rash of best sellers designed to help unhappy people find

---

* A lively description of the type of miracle required is given in *Time* magazine's account of the miracles worked in behalf of Peter Smith through the intercession of Mother Cabrini (July 15, 1946), p. 76.

† The non-Catholic author, Ruth Cranston, has recently (1955) written an absorbing book on this subject: *The Miracle of Lourdes*. She has been impressed by the evidence for physical miracles, but even more impressed by the "moral" cures effected at the shrine.

such interior peace. Many people who struggle hard for their daily bread and who are not possessed of much secular culture, frequently seem to lead happier lives than others who are quite wealthy and highly cultured. We do not deny in the least that worldly goods, both of body and mind, can contribute to happiness in this life; but we do maintain that nothing contributes so much to this life's happiness as does the following of the true religion and the serious pursuit of and progress in moral goodness. Happiness and real holiness go hand in hand; so much so that it has become a truism: "a saint who is sad, makes a sad sort of saint." That is why there is no doubt at all that Catholic men who strive to live up to the rules of their religion—all else being equal—even in this life enjoy far greater happiness than other men. This is true not only of individuals but of nations. But please note the restrictive clause: *all else being equal.*

2. *Temporal prosperity* considered strictly as such, i.e., as distinct from morality, may be summed up in the following points: a plentiful supply of material goods, intellectual cultivation of native talents, political peace, and political power. Now, these things, even though they can receive an indirect stimulus from religion, *do not directly or necessarily depend upon religion.* They depend on other and purely natural causes—causes which are quite varied and complex. Thus it is ridiculous to try to use such things as criteria for solving questions about the truth or holiness of any religion. Passing over the question of purely material goods, the arts and sciences flourished widely in ancient Greece; the Roman people, during the era of the Emperors, enjoyed complete domination of the entire known world. May we then conclude that the ancient Greek or Roman religions were so excellent? On the other side of the ledger, during Old Testament times the Jews alone worshipped the true God, yet at the same time they were far below the Egyptians and Babylonians by standards of wealth, secular culture, and political power. Christ Himself was poor. He worked as a carpenter and lived in a backward village. Shall we conclude: *therefore,* His religion is untrue?

If someone raises the question of the *indirect* influence on temporal affairs, as contrasted in Catholicism and Protestantism, one might fairly concede that Protestantism, by the very fact that it does less to focus attention on heavenly things, does perhaps favor the production of material wealth more than Catholicism.

But there is no doubt at all that Catholicism by its teachings on the necessity of good works, does more to foster the *equitable distribution* of material goods.* Again, one might concede that Protestantism by its principle of private judgment (this is even truer of Rationalism) does perhaps give more stimulus to investigations in the field of the physical sciences.† At the same time, however, that very same principle has produced the giddiest sort of errors in some sciences, particularly the philosophical. Catholicism is definitely more favorable to the development of the arts. Catholicism by its very nature strikingly promotes political tranquility (i.e., in principle). The fact that some so-called "Catholic nations" have been split into multitudinous factions in recent times stems, not from Catholicism, but from principles which are diametrically opposed to the principles of the Catholic religion; namely, Rationalism and a spirit of rebellion. Rationalism and a spirit of rebellion were the genuine offspring of early Protestantism; and it is precisely these principles which agitate political matters in the very nations alluded to. As a matter of fact, few would maintain that modern France, Italy, Spain and so forth are Catholic insofar as they are *political* units. Certainly, during the early years of the twentieth century, it was quite clear that the governments and ruling classes in those nations were not animated by Catholic principles. In more recent days, the advent of men like Adenauer or De Gasperi has witnessed the attempt to infiltrate the political arena with Christian, rather than rationalist principles.

As for *political superiority,* the modern world has tasted bitterly the fact that it is often not the result of moral goodness, but of military might and injustice. Can anyone forget Hitler's Germany, Stalin's Russia, or Chou En-lai's Red China?

For these and other reasons, which this is definitely not the place to discuss in detail, the temporal superiority of some Protestant nations, when it is genuinely present, should not be attributed to Protestantism as such, but to altogether different factors; just

---

* That is, Catholicism by its *principles* inculcates the necessity of social justice (see, for example, the papal encyclicals); this is not to deny that factually there are wealthy Catholics who disregard the Church's teaching and have little care for the underprivileged.

† On this point see the provocative essay by Julian Pleasants, "Catholics and Science," analyzing the reasons why American Catholics have not pulled their proportionate weight in contributions to science in this country. See *Catholicism in America* (New York, 1954), p. 165–79.

as the collapse of some Catholic nations is due not to their religion, but either to their abandoning Catholic principles, or to various causes in the purely natural order.[31]

Finally, the tremendous good various nations, and particularly European nations, owe to the influence of the Catholic Church is a fact that educated Protestants admit.[32]

149 Conclusion

1. It has been proven that the Roman Catholic Church alone is that Church which "God founded through His only begotten Son, and endowed with obvious marks of its [divine] origin."[33] Actually, the Catholic Church does stand out with *obvious* marks. Those who have even a fair amount of education realize that it is far more ancient than all the other Christian societies; and that it is like a mighty tree whose lopped off branches these societies are. Finally, it is almost impossible for anyone to live long among good Catholics and not to glimpse at least some manifestation of the holiness of the Catholic Church. Who, for example, among our non-Catholic countrymen does not realize that Catholic priests usually exhibit a strikingly different care for the sick and dying than Protestant ministers, even though many of the latter are fine, upright men? Which of them has never marveled at the modesty, self-denial, and charity exhibited to the sick by our hospital nuns! Abraham Lincoln, for example, wrote this moving tribute in his Civil War diary:

> Of all forms of charity and benevolence seen in the crowded wards in the hospitals, those of some Catholic Sisters were among the most efficient. I never knew whence they came or what was the name of their order. More lovely than anything I have ever seen in art . . . are the pictures that remain of those modest sisters, going on their errands of mercy among the suffering and the dying. Gentle and womanly, yet with the courage of soldiers leading a forlorn hope, to sustain them in contact with such horrors. As they went from cot to cot . . . they were veritable angels of mercy.—Cited in the *Philadelphia Catholic Standard and Times* (Feb. 10, 1956).

Thus it is that nearly all men, educated and uneducated alike, perceive something in the Catholic Church which they cannot help admiring and cannot help realizing is lacking in their own sects.

In a word, nearly all of them are struck and amazed by at least some one ray of Catholic truth.

2. Why is it, then, that many of them—whose sincerity can not be doubted—fail to arrive at an acknowledgment of the truth? Because *the light shines in the darkness, and the darkness does not lay hold of it;* because, that is to say, they are enveloped by so many and such great prejudices that a suspicion that the Catholic Church is the true and only Church of Christ can hardly arise in their minds. Such prejudices, it seems, can be dispelled from their minds only very gradually, and without their being conscious of the fact. But those prejudices vanish the more quickly, the more Catholics, both in their private and public lives, unconsciously exhibit religion, charity, and tranquility. They vanish the more quickly, the more priests are resplendent with moderation, chastity, devotedness, and a prudent but tireless zeal. Those prejudices vanish more quickly, the more diligently and fully Catholic doctrine is explained in both oral instruction and popular writing;° and above all, the more frequently and fervently all Catholics pour forth prayers to the Father of Lights to snatch away the veil that covers the hearts of those in error.

° See, for example, the excellent little series of pamphlets issued by the Knights of Columbus and designed solely to refute the caricatures of Catholic doctrine so often accepted in all innocence by non-Catholics as genuine Catholic doctrine.

Notes

1. The following observation made by J. de Maistre remains true today: "If Protestantism always bears the same name, no matter how immensely varied its creed may be, the reason is that its name is something purely negative and does not signify anything else but a rejection of Catholicism. The less it shall believe and the more it shall protest, so much the more will it true to itself: its name becoming truer day by day" (*Du Pape,* IV, 5).

2. For a good historical sketch of all these churches see Algermissen, *op. cit.,* pp. 764–880. For a very brief, but accurate and sympathetic sketch of the same matter see George H. Tavard, *The Catholic Approach to Protestantism* (New York, 1955). Tavard, in attempting to give a logical grouping of multitudinous Protestant "sects" which differ radically from classical Protestantism, classifies them into three categories: *pietist, millenarist,* and *gnostic* sects. The last named category (*gnostic*) includes such groups as Jehovah's Witnesses, Christian Scientists, and Mormons. It is a mistake to classify such groups as "Protestant." Strictly speaking, they are non-Christian religions (*op. cit.,* p. 43–44).

3. See *American Encyclopedia*, article, "Lutheranism."
4. Tanquerey, *Synopsis theologiae dogmaticae*, "De ecclesia," no. 10 ff.— For a good summary of the *original* doctrinal tenets of early Protestantism, see Algermissen, *op. cit.*, p. 892–935. For a survey of the development and changes in original Reformation doctrines up to and into the nineteenth century, see *ibid.*, p. 936–60. For a brief sketch of present-day Protestant theology see Gustave Weigel, S.J., *Survey of Protestant Theology in Our Day* (Westminster, Md., 1953); George H. Tavard, *op. cit.*, p. 45–56.
5. See Algermissen, *op. cit.*, p. 792–96.
6. See Tavard's neat delineation of this point, *op. cit.*, p. 27–8.
7. See Volume VIII, *Christ's Sacraments*, part 1, no. 270.
8. *Ibid.*, no. 271.
9. See Algermissen, *op. cit.*, p. 794; Tavard, *op. cit.*, p. 28.
10. The first figure is that of the *Encyclopedia Brittanica*; cf. *Information Please Almanac* (1957), p. 447. The second is that of the "CSMC World Mission Map, 1956"; cf. *National Catholic Almanac* (1957), p. 332 and 343.
11. So Baur: *Argumenta contra orientalem ecclesiam*, p. 15; see also *Kirchenlexikon* under the entry, *Russen*, X, 1396.
12. Baur, *loc. cit.*, p. 3; see *Kirchenlexikon*, under the entry, *Mission*, VIII, 1635.—Algermissen finds the explanation for this lack of missionary effort in a too mystical view of the Church: "The wholly insufficient missionary activity of the Orthodox Church is intimately connected with its extravagantly mystical view of the Church, as Bulgakow plainly states: 'The Orthodox Church places its hope not upon human efforts and not upon the missionary efforts of its members, but it places its reliance upon the Spirit of God who abides in the Church and leads her to unity'" (*op. cit.*, p. 641).
13. See *Kirchenlexikon*, under the entry, *Mission*, VIII, 1610–35; P. Charles, "L'activité missionaire protestante," NRT (1932), p. 324.

It may be helpful to add a few testimonies by *non-Catholic* authors on this subject: Sainton, a pastor of the Reformed Church, wrote in the year 1880:

> There is no reason to wonder, when Protestantism, with such enormous sums of money, sends forth in every direction—not only to the pagans but also to France, Italy, Austria, Spain, and especially to the Far East— its emissaries, its itinerant preachers, its Bible salesmen, who have honeyed tongues and money-filled hands—if poor Catholics and Schismatics, oppressed by bitter want, often allow themselves to be converted to Protestant beliefs; the real cause for wonder is the fact that they obtain such meager results among the pagans.—*Kirchenlexikon*, *loc. cit.*, p. 1630.

The Anglican Canon, Taylor, wrote in the year 1888: "I believe our methods are not only unsuccessful, but altogether wrong" (quoted in A. Tanquerey, *De ecclesia*, no. 146).

Von Wiszmann, the German Commissar in Africa,

> felt constrained to lavish the highest praise on the good works, the Christlike influence, the culture-and-morality promoting efforts of the self-sacrificing and indefatigably working Catholic missionaries. While he extolled the latter as pillars of civilization, he stated without reservation that the English and German Protestant missionaries actually made his work more difficult and obstructed it, so that the great sums expended on Protestant

missionary work were in fact thrown away, and further that these people have, by reason of their political agitation, been more of a hindrance than a help.

Emin Pacha wrote in the year 1890:
There is a peculiar contrast between the Catholic and Protestant (English) missions here in East Africa. In the case of the former, there is a lack of means and of personnel, in fact real need; in the case of the latter, abundance of money and men, in fact, overabundance. In the case of the former, hard work and earnest striving to educate their pupils in useful, purposeful living; in the case of the latter, psalm-singing, and the eye-rolling of complacent self-sufficiency. Much might be said on this subject.

Dr. Peters, after visiting the missions in Uganda wrote in the year 1890: "What I have seen of English (Protestant) installations falls far short of the French (Catholic) in every respect."

Scavenus, a Dane, after visiting the Negro missions in East Africa wrote in the year 1894:
Here in Tanga there is a German Protestant mission; in Usambona there are two English missionaries; none of these stations can point to any result worth mentioning. . . . In this connection one cannot help comparing the invariably ineffectual Protestant missionaries and the Catholic missionaries, who are making ever greater conquests.

Von Bulow, around the year 1884, wrote as follows about the missions in the islands of Samoa:
Further, it is a fact that the missionaries of the Protestant sects are concerned first of all with furnishing living quarters for the missionary before they even think about building a church. In this they are in direct contrast to the Catholic priests, who build first a beautiful and substantial church before they give any thought to their own comfort. In the later instance we have devotion to one's calling, and in the former, desire for gain and easy living. But if one now asks whether the life of the Protestant natives has already taken on a Christian hue—the answer to this must be a positive "No."

Senator West in the year 1884 stated in the Congress of the United States:
I certainly hold no brief for the Jesuits; I was brought up in the sect of the Presbyterians, who consider every Jesuit a devil; but I declare that nowhere in North America can be found a single tribe of Indians which holds a candle to the Jesuit-civilized Flatheads. In the eleven Protestant missions which I visited—and I speak as a Protestant—the missionaries in these places were unable to bring the Indians one step forward.

All the preceding quotations are taken from V. Hammerstein, *Das Katholische Ordenswesen* (1896), pp. 145–158.

14. We mean the names as consecrated by common usage: *Oriental* Church, *Greek* Church, *Russian* Church, *Anglican* Church, *Lutherans, Calvinists, Reformed* Church, The Greeks call themselves *Orthodox*, others wish to be called *Evangelical*, or *Apostolic*, yet despite that fact they are called by everyone else: *Greeks* and *Protestants*. "All the sects have two names: one which they give themselves, and the other which other people give them. . . . Each one being free, of course, to give itself the name which pleases itself . . . but the big job is to make other people call them by this or that name. But that is not quite so easy as to deck ourselves out with a name by our

own authority; and yet there is no real name unless the name is recognized or acknowledged" (J. de Maistre, *Du Pape*, IV, 5.)

15. *Contra epistulam Manichaei quam vocant fundamenti* 4. 5.
16. Augustine *De vera religione* 7. 12.
17. See Algermissen, *op. cit.*, p. 560–85.
18. *Ibid.*, p. 689.
19. *De praescriptione* 32.—How keenly Luther himself felt about this lack of apostolicity:

> You can rescue a wheel from the wagon and frighten someone that the pope and those who boast of being his are the Christian Church. The term *Sancta Ecclesia* alarms one; then they stand up and say: Preach and do what you want and as you can, still here is the *ecclesia Christiana*. Here is the bark of St. Peter which may indeed flounder on the sea—but it will not sink and be drowned; we are the true people of God, the Christian Church; what will you do about it? . . . Then such thoughts as these rage in one's heart: Now I see that I am wrong! Oh that I had not started it and had never preached a word . . . it is hard to stand here and preach against such an excommunication.—Cited in Hettinger, *Lehrbuch*, 2nd ed., p. 544.

20. Holding first place among all such rationalistic theories stands the explanation of F. Ch. Bauer (d. 1860), developed by others (Neander, Rothe, Ritschl, Pierson and Naber, *Verisimilia*). According to this theory, the Catholic Church arose about the middle of the second century as an amalgam of the Petrinism of the Jewish-Christians (justification through the *works* of the Law) and the Paulinism of the Pagan-Christians (justification through *faith* in Christ) fermenting together in the bosom of Joaninism (justification through faith *and* works) through the efforts of harmonizers. See De Groot, *De ecclesia* (3rd ed.), p. 175.

21. *Contra epistulam Manichaei quam vocant fundamenti* 4. 5.
22. See Chotkowski, "Die katholischen Glaubenszeugen in der Verbannung am Uralgebirge," in *Hist. pol. Blätter* (1889), p. 103; see also *ibid.* (1890), p. 893. In those articles the gist of his book entitled, *Russischen Christenthum, dargestellt nach Russischen Angaben* (Paderborn, 1889), is synopsized in the following words:

> This church since its origin has contributed simply nothing at all to the moral education of the people; it has, on the contrary, made of the Russian people a creation bearing no resemblance to any other Christian people, and precisely because its Christian-ecclesiastical spirit got simply lost in the surrender to Czarist despotism. It was and is nothing other than a division of the State Police set up for worldly and political purposes. This is the explanation of the thousand-year old *rigor mortis* of the Russian Church.

23. See V. Hammerstein, *Katholizismus und Protestantismus* (1894), p. 65 ff.: "When W. Wengel (so writes Schanz, *Apologie* III [3rd ed.], p. 383), "said that with the Reformation a completely new barbarism entered the courts and universities of the Protestants, people found his judgment biased. When Janssen collected such original reports, they censured his works as a prejudiced fabrication. But at the present the chorus of voices is swelling which characterizes a general decay as the direct result of the Reformation:

Droysen, Roscher, Meitzen, Paulsen, and others." On this point, in English, see the quotations from the original Reformers cited in J. Maritain, *Three Reformers* (New York, n. d.).

24. Numerous miraculous healings are related of John Serguieff, popularly known as *Father John of Croonstadt*, a Russian orthodox priest. The facts alleged are not thus far historically established with certitude; yet even if they be genuine, they at least prove nothing in favor of the schism, but simply in favor of those doctrines and practices which the Russian Church has retained from true Christianity. See A. Staerk, *Le père Jean de Cronstadt*.

25. Voltaire: "The enemies of the Roman Church who have rebelled against so salutary an institution [auricular confession] appear to have deprived men of the greatest restraint which could be put upon their secret crimes." Marmontel: "There is no better means of preserving the moral purity of youth than the practice of monthly confession" (quotations taken from De Groot, *op. cit.*, p. 254).

26. On this point J. de Maistre comments aptly: "No enemy of the faith is ever deceived. They all strike in vain because they are battling against God; but they all know where to strike" (*Du Pape*, IV, conclusion).

27. See A. Räsz, *Die Convertierten seit der Reformation*, 13 vols., 1866–80. In English see the several collections of convert autobiographies edited by John C. O'Brien: *The Road to Damascus, Where I Found Christ*, etc.

28. Even A. Harnack admits: "It cannot be denied that Catholicism has created in its seven sacraments what is pedagogically a very effective and impressive institution. . . . No one will be able to deny how useful is this collection of seven sacraments which escort one through life" (*Lehrbuch der Dogmengeschichte*, III, p. 462 and 465).

29. See, for example, P. Pourrat, *Christian Spirituality* (4 vols., Westminster, Md., 1953–55); H. Bremond, *Histoire littéraire du sentiment religieux en France* (10 vols., 1929–32).

30. See also K. Kirsch, *Helden des Christentums* (12 vols., 1921–); A. Ehrhard, *Die Kirche der Märtyrer* (1932).

31. Worth reading on this point are: Bougaud, *Le Christianisme et les temps présents* (6th ed.), IV, 318 ff.; Yves De La Brière, *Nations protestantes et nations Catholiques* (1905); H. Krose, *Die Einfluss der Confession auf die Sittlichkeit*; H. Rost, *Die Kulturkraft des Katholizismus* (1919). In English see Christopher Dawson, *The Making of Europe*, and *Religion and Culture*; G. Schnürer, *Church and Culture in the Middle Ages*, 3 vols. (Paterson, N.J., 1957–).

32. For example, Dr. K. Sell:
The Catholic Church illumined the twilight of the moribund ancient world with a gentle glow; she rescued its precious cultural values for posterity. As the great mother of modern civilization she educated and instructed the most powerful nations and races of modern history: Germans, Romans, Slavs. Never can these young European nations deny that from the eighth to the eleventh century the Christian Christmas song of the Church resounded over their cradle, the song which consecrated them to a higher existence than the merely earthly. The greatest achievement of Catholicism is the centuries-long development of that consistent world-view which tied

biblical religious concepts with ancient sciences and philosophy and with the half-Christian-ascetic, half-pagan-Germanic ideals of life into a cohesive whole which even today forms the basis of European culture and holds sway especially over our whole esthetic experience, our world of imagination. Not only dogma, liturgy, and ecclesiastical organization, but also "here" and "hereafter," our logic and our ethics has Catholicism given us; our system of politics, too, finds its origin therein.—In *Preussischen Jahrbücher* (Oct., 1899).

33. Vatican Council, constitution *De fide catholica*, chap. 3.

SECTION II

The Church Viewed from Inside
(Dogma)

150 *Thus far the Church has been discussed mainly from a historical and apologetical viewpoint. Since it has been completely established in the whole first section of this book that the Roman Catholic Church is the one true Church of Christ and God, and that it enjoys the prerogative of infallibility in religious matters, in this second section proof will be based not simply on historic evidence, but also and especially on the Church's own infallible authority. Briefly, this second section of the book is strictly dogmatic theology.*

The matters to be treated are the following:
1. The Church: the Mystical Body of Christ .... Chapter I
2. The Members of the Church .... Chapter II
3. The Roman Pontiff .... Chapter III
4. The Bishops .... Chapter IV
5. Church and State .... Chapter V
6. The Promise of the Primacy Analyzed Exegetically .... Appendix

CHAPTER I

The Church: The Mystical Body of Christ

I. *Introduction:*

The Roman Catholic Church is not merely the embodiment of the religion of Christ; it is the very body of Christ.

PROPOSITION: The Church is the Mystical Body of Christ.

Proof: 1. our Lord personally promised to establish and maintain a unique, intimate union between Himself and His members.
2. St. Paul calls Christ the *Head of the Church,* and the Church the *body* of Christ.
3. the earliest fathers are fond of repeating this doctrine in their writings.
4. the Church's magisterium.

II. *Explanation of the Analogy*

III. *The Term "Mystical Body":*

PROPOSITION: Sanctifying grace holds first place among the supernatural gifts which come down to the Church from Christ its Head.

PROPOSITION: The Holy Spirit is the Soul of this body which is the Church.

PROPOSITION: The soul and the body of the Church are not two Churches, the one invisible and the other visible, but together they form one Church, which is at once visible and endowed with interior life.

Corollary: The Church is a continuation of Christ in the world

Scholion: The Coextension of the concepts "Church" and "Mystical Body."

Special Bibliography

CHAPTER I

The Church: The Mystical Body of Christ

150a I. Introduction

The Roman Catholic Church is not merely the embodiment of the religion of Christ; it is, in a very real sense, the body of Christ Himself.¹ In a certain very real sense, it is Christ Himself living and acting in the world. This doctrine has been a treasured part of the deposit of faith right from the beginning. It came from the lips of the Master Himself during His earthly ministry. It was the first truth He revealed to His "vessel of election," St. Paul, and he in turn expressed it over and over again in his writings. It is to him that we owe the analogy which best expresses it—the analogy of the head and the body—and the Church teaches this same truth today as the doctrine of the Mystical Body. Unfortunately, the demands of Reformation polemics forced ecclesiologists to focus attention almost exclusively on the external, juridical aspects of the Mystical Body, and the rich supernatural depths of the doctrine received scant attention, if any.² This situation obtained until quite recently, when theologians once more subjected the notion to searching scientific analysis.³ The results were not always happy; confusion developed on several important points. Finally, however, on June 29, 1943, Pope Pius XII issued the encyclical *Mystici Corporis,* and gave the world a clear and authoritative explanation of the Church's teaching.⁴

150b PROPOSITION: *The Church is the Mystical Body of Christ.*

This is *proximate to divine faith.**

This proposition may be expressed more analytically as follows: *the Church is united in an intimate and indissoluble union with Christ, its invisible Head.* Even though Christ, just before His Ascension into heaven, provided His Church with a visible head,

---

* That the Church is Christ's *body* is formally and explicitly revealed in Scripture. That it is His *mystical* body is a further theological precision.

(216)

still He Himself by no means abandoned it, but maintains an invisible union with it and exercises a constant influence on it.

Proof:

1. Our Lord personally promised to establish and maintain this union. The following eloquent statements are recorded in John 6:

> "*I am the bread of life*" (48) . . . "*He who eats my flesh and drinks my blood is united with me, and I am united with him. As the living Father has appointed me his ambassador, and I live because of the Father, so, too, he who eats me will have life because of me*" (57–58).

Most expressive of all is His figure of the vine and the branches:

> "*I am the real vine, and my Father is the vinedresser. . . . Remain united with me, and I will remain united with you. . . . One bears abundant fruit only when he and I are mutually united; severed from me, you can do nothing. If one does not remain united with me, he is simply thrown away like a branch, and dries up*" (John 15:1, 4–6).

2. St. Paul informs us of the existence of this bond and of its nature as well, when he calls Christ the *Head of the Church*, and the Church the *body* or *fulness* (complement) of Christ:

> *He has subjected every single thing to his authority and has appointed him sovereign head of the Church, which is truly his body, the complement of him who fills all the members with all graces* (Eph. 1:22–23).[5] *Further, he is the head of his body, the Church, in that he is the beginning, the first to rise from the dead, so that he may have pre-eminence over every creature. For it pleased God the Father that in him all fullness should dwell, and that through him God should reconcile to himself every being, and make peace on earth and in heaven through the blood shed on the cross* (Col. 1:18–20).

Jesus had revealed this sublime doctrine to Paul, at least in germinal form, on the occasion of the latter's conversion. When He asked him, "*Saoul, Saoul, why do you persecute me?*" He intimated quite clearly that He considered Himself and His disciples as one.

CHRIST'S CHURCH

That this revelation left a strong and abiding impression on Paul's mind is made abundantly clear by the way in which it colors all his writings and by the way in which it is developed in those same writings. In a summary treatment such as this must be, a few representative samples will have to suffice:

For example, just as the body is a unit, although it has many members, and all the members of the body, many though they are, form but one body, so too is the Christ. In fact, by a single Spirit all of us, whether Jews or Greeks, slaves or free men, were introduced into the one body through baptism, and were all given to drink of a single Spirit. The body, I repeat, is not formed of one but of many members. . . . You are Christ's body and individually its members (I Cor. 12:12–14, 27). *Rather by professing the truth, let us grow up in every respect in love and bring about union with Christ who is the head. The whole body is dependent on him. Harmoniously joined and knit together, it derives its energy in the measure each part needs only through contact with the source of supply* (Eph. 4:15–16).[6] *I rejoice now in the sufferings I bear for your sake, and what is lacking to the sufferings of Christ I supply in my flesh for the benefit of his body, which is the Church* (Col. 1:24).

3. *The earliest fathers* were fond of repeating this doctrine in their writings:

St. Ignatius Martyr:

You must all follow the lead of the bishop, as Jesus Christ followed that of the Father; follow the presbytery as you would the Apostles; reverence the deacons as you would God's commandment. Let no one do anything touching the Church, apart from the bishop. Let that celebration of the Eucharist be considered valid which is held under the bishop or anyone to whom he has committed it. Where the bishop appears, there let the people be, just as where Jesus Christ is, there is the Catholic Church.—*Epistula ad Smyrnaeos* 8. 1–2; ACW trans.

According to St. Ignatius, it is impossible for anyone to obtain a share in the divine life of grace apart from Christ, who lives a hidden life in the Church as its vivifying principle and a visible life in that body which is composed of the members of the hierarchy. There is in the Church a visible and an invisible unity, just as in its divine-human Head.

Most striking is St. Irenaeus' theory of *recapitulation,* according to which the entire universe, the whole range of being, is summed up in Christ as under one head (see also Eph. 1:10). This summing up, this *recapitulation,* has in view a universal restoration, and Christ, the Word, effects this in and through His Church, of which He is the Head. The Church is, as it were, Christ continued:

> . . . one Christ Jesus our Lord, who comes by a universal dispensation and recapitulates all things in Himself. But in "all things" man also is comprised, a creature of God; therefore He recapitulates man in Himself. The invisible has become visible, the incomprehensible has become comprehensible, and the impassible passible; and the Logos has become man, recapitulating all things in Himself. Thus, just as He is the first among heavenly and spiritual and invisible things, so also is He the first among visible and corporal things. He takes the primacy to Himself and by making Himself the Head of the Church, He will draw all things to Himself at the appointed time.—*Adversus haereses* iii. 16. 6.
>
> Where the Church is, there is the Spirit of God; and where the Spirit of God is, there is the Church and every kind of grace; but the Spirit is truth. Those therefore who do not partake of Him are neither nourished in the life from the mother's breasts, nor do they enjoy that most limpid fountain which issues from the body of Christ.—*Ibid.* iii. 24. 1; see also i. 10. 2; iii. 12. 7; iii. 36. 7.

The writings of Tertullian and St. Cyprian are rich on this subject also, but those of St. Augustine are richest of all. He wrote, for example: "A head and a body go to make one man; Christ and the Church combine to make one man, a perfect man: He is the Groom, she the bride" (*Enarrationes in psalmos* 18:2.10; see also *ibid.* 101:1,2. 137; 18:2. 10; *Tractatus CXXIV in Joannis evangelium* 14; *Epistula* 23).

Quite evidently, then, in the minds of our Lord, of St. Paul, and of ecclesiastical writers from the earliest years,[7] practically the same relationship exists between Christ and the Church as between a man's head and the rest of his body.

4. The *Church's Magisterium.* Pius XII, in the *Mystici Corporis,* teaches this doctrine in unmistakably clear terms:

If we would define and describe this true Church of Jesus Christ—which is the One, Holy, Catholic, Apostolic, Roman Church—we shall find no expression more noble, more sublime or more Divine than the phrase which calls it "the Mystical Body of Jesus Christ."—17.

150c II. **Explanation of the Analogy** [8]

1. A person's head: (*a*) is *of the same nature* as the rest of his members, for it is itself a member of his body; (*b*) is *superior* to his other members in *dignity, position,* and in the *perfection of sensory activity*—for it is in the head that all the other senses are actively coordinated; (*c*) is so intrinsically connected with the other members as to form with them but *one totality*.

In like manner: (*a*) Christ has the *same nature* as the members of the Church, for He is Head of the Church in His human rather than in His divine nature. (*b*) Christ is *superior in dignity* to all the members of the Church, and this because of the hypostatic union of His human nature with the Word. He is superior *in position,* seated as He is at the right hand of the Father. He is superior in the *perfection of supernatural life,* because it pleased God the Father that in Him all fulness should dwell, and that through Him God the Father should reconcile to Himself every being (see Col. 1:19). (*c*) Christ is so intimately conjoined with the Church and its members as to form with them *one totality* (see I Cor. 12:27); for the Church is called Christ's fulness for no other reason than that it is a sort of extension in time of Christ Himself, and forms together with Him one mystical person. *You are all one in Christ Jesus.*[9] That is why Holy Scripture says that Christ is formed in His faithful (Gal. 4:19), that He lives (*ibid.,* 2:20), hungers (Matt. 25:35–45), and is persecuted (Acts 9:4–5) in them. The faithful in their turn are said to complete in their lives the work left unfinished by Christ (Col. 1:24). In fact, the Church is called "Christ" without any qualification (I Cor. 12:12).

2. A person's head—or better, his soul using the head as an instrument—exerts a twofold *influence* over his other members: (*a*) an *internal* influence, by communicating feeling and motion to the members; (*b*) an *external* influence, by watching over the safety of the body through the eyes and ears, etc., and by guiding its steps and directing its movements.[10]

In like manner Christ—strictly speaking, the Word using His

humanity as an instrument (*instrumentum conjunctum*)—exerts a twofold influence over His Church; (*a*) internally, by imparting supernatural gifts to people, as Scripture tells us: *And of his fullness we have all received a share—yes, grace succeeding grace* (John 1:16); (*b*) externally, by governing (teaching and ruling) the Church. Of course, He does not visibly exercise this latter function of external government, since He is an invisible Head. But He does so through visible pastors to whom He has imparted His own authority, and, of course, in a special way through the Roman pontiff, who is for this reason called the visible head of the Church. Pius XII has given eloquent expression to these truths:

> Because Christ is so exalted, He alone by every right rules and governs the Church; and herein is yet another reason why He must be likened to a head. . . .
> Moreover, He conferred a triple power on His Apostles and their successors, to teach, to govern, to lead men to holiness. This triple power, defined by special ordinances, by rights and obligations, He made the fundamental law of the whole Church. But our Divine Saviour governs and guides His community also directly and personally. For it is He who reigns within the minds and hearts of men and bends and subjects to His purpose their wills even when rebellious. . . .
> But we must not think that He rules only in a hidden or extraordinary way. On the contrary, our Divine Redeemer also governs His Mystical Body in a visible way and ordinarily through His Vicar on earth. You know, Venerable Brothers, that after He had ruled the "little flock" Himself during His mortal pilgrimage, when about to leave this world and return to the Father, Christ Our Lord entrusted to the chief of the Apostles the visible government of the entire community He had founded. He was all wise; and how could He leave without a visible head the body of the Church He had founded as a human society?
> Nor against this may one argue, that the primacy of jurisdiction established in the Church gives such a Mystical Body two heads. For Peter in virtue of his Primacy is only Christ's Vicar; so that there is only one chief Head of this body, namely Christ. He never ceases personally to guide the Church by an unseen hand, though at the same time He rules it externally, visibly through him who is His representative on earth.[11]

The influence mentioned is exercised by the divinity through the instrumentality of the (conjoined) humanity. It is quite true that God alone is the principal cause of all supernatural gifts, but still Christ's humanity is an instrumental cause. Consequently, He is Head of the Church not in His divine nature, for it is not characteristic of a head to influence a body as the principal agent. Even in the case of a human being, the head communicates sense activity to the other members not as the principal cause, but only as the instrument of the soul. If one looks deeper into this matter, one realizes that the supernatural gifts showered on the Church come from all three divine Persons together. But sometimes they are attributed to the Father, who is the source of all good, sometimes to the Word or to Christ as God, in view of the hypostatic union, and sometimes—in fact, most often—to the Holy Spirit, to whom acts of love are more particularly appropriated. They are even said to come down to the members of the Church from the Holy Spirit through Christ (as man). And there is nothing surprising in this, for that very fulness of grace which is Christ's is commonly attributed to His anointing by the Holy Spirit.[12]

150d III. The Term "Mystical Body" [13]

It must be remarked at the outset that the term "Mystical Body" is an analogy—the expression of a truth based not on the perfect identity of the two analogues or terms of comparison, but on a very real likeness between them.[14] It is, nonetheless, the expression of a deep and sublime truth, and is not to be shrugged off as a "mere figure of speech."[15] As is the case with many other supernatural truths and concepts, the expression of this reality must also be analogical, we being what we are and the supernatural being what it is. The term "mystical," then, distinguishes the Church from the *physical* body of our Lord, and protects us against giving the concept a pantheistic coloring. As Pius XII wrote:

> In a natural body the principle of unity so unites the parts that each lacks its own individual subsistence; on the contrary in the Mystical Body that mutual union, though intrinsic, links the members by a bond which leaves to each intact his own personality.—74.

The term "Mystical Body" serves also to distinguish this unique

THE CHURCH: THE MYSTICAL BODY OF CHRIST

organism from so-called *"moral* bodies." Again, in the authoritative words of the Holy Father:

> But if we compare a Mystical Body to a moral body, here again we must notice that the difference between them is not slight, rather it is very considerable and very important. In the moral body, the principle of union is nothing more than the common end, and the common cooperation of all under authority for the attainment of that end; whereas in the Mystical Body, of which We are speaking, this collaboration is supplemented by a distinct internal principle, which exists effectively in the whole and in each of its parts, and whose excellence is such, that of itself it is vastly superior to whatever bonds of union may be found in a physical or moral body. This is something, as We said above, not of the natural but of the supernatural order. Essentially it is something infinite, uncreated: the Spirit of God, Who, as the Angelic Doctor says, "numerically one and the same, fills and unifies the whole Church."—75.

These distinctions may be represented graphically as follows:

	HEAD AND MEMBERS	
in a physical body	have the same life	are *not* distinct persons
in a moral body	do *not* have the same life	are distinct persons
in the Mystical Body	have the same life	are distinct persons

PROPOSITION: *Sanctifying grace holds first place among the supernatural gifts which come down to the Church from Christ its Head.* 150e

A great variety of gifts flows into the Church from Christ. For, apart from extraordinary charisms, there are: (*a*) the *power of jurisdiction,* including the power to teach (infallible when exercised in its fulness) and to rule; (*b*) the *sacramental character,* to which are joined, in the sacrament of orders, the powers of the priesthood; (*c*) numerous *actual graces,* which are granted as, excepting faith and hope, temporary helps; (*d*) *infused virtues,* which are so intimately tied up with sanctifying grace as to be inseparable from it. But all these things are directed to habitual or *sanctifying grace,* by which we are made strictly and formally holy and just. Since, then, the special purpose of Christ's mission and of the founding of the Church is nothing other than the sanctification of people, it is beyond doubt that the union of Christ with the Church has as its primary and chief aim the imparting of sanctifying grace to its members. In fact, the Apostle gave clear expression to this influence when he wrote:

> *Christ is the head of the Church and also the savior of that body.* . . . *Christ loved the Church, and delivered himself for her, that he might sanctify her by cleansing her in the bath of water with the accompanying word, in order to present to himself the Church in all her glory, devoid of blemish or wrinkle or anything of the kind, but that she may be holy and flawless.*
> —Eph. 5:23, 25–27.

For no holiness or purity can be obtained in this world, no glory or beauty in the next, except through sanctifying grace.[16]

150f PROPOSITION: *The Holy Spirit is the Soul of this body which is the Church.*

Leo XIII stated this truth unequivocally when he wrote in his *Divinum illud:* "Let it suffice to say that, as Christ is the Head of the Church, the Holy Spirit is its soul." Pius XII developed this theme at greater length in the *Mystici Corporis:*

> If we examine closely this Divine principle of life and power given by Christ, in so far as it constitutes the very source of every gift and created grace, we easily see that it is nothing else than the Holy Spirit, the Paraclete who proceeds from the Father and the Son, and who is called in a special way the "Spirit of Christ" or the "Spirit of the Son."—68.
> To this Spirit of Christ, too, as to an invisible principle, is to be ascribed the fact that all the parts of the Body are joined one with the other and with their exalted Head; for He is entire in the Head, entire in the Body, and entire in each of the members. . . . It is He who through His heavenly grace is the principle of every supernatural act in all parts of the Body. It is He who, while He is personally present and divinely active in all the members, also acts in the inferior members through the ministry of the higher members. Finally, while with His grace He provides for the constant growth of the Church, He yet refuses to dwell with sanctifying grace in members that are wholly severed from the Body.—69.

THE CHURCH: THE MYSTICAL BODY OF CHRIST

It is important to note, however, that the analogy comparing the Holy Spirit with the human soul is not perfect, any more than is that comparing Christ with the head of a human body. Analogical knowledge is true knowledge, but it represents truth only indirectly, by means of resemblance or proportionate similarity. In the human composite, it is true, the soul is a spiritual substance, the principle of unity, life, and vital activity. But it is an incomplete substance and enters into a substantial union with the body. The same cannot be said of the Holy Spirit in relation to the Mystical Body. For the Holy Spirit is a complete, independent, incommunicable Person, and His union with the Body can be consequently only accidental, to use the language of philosophy—a language with unfortunate connotations in modern parlance. Accidental in this technical sense does not connote fleeting, loose, impermanent, haphazard. The union of the Holy Spirit with the Church is not the same as that of a person's soul with his body; * but for all that, it is nonetheless real and intimate and vivifying. In the interests of strict accuracy, theologians now frequently refer to the Holy Spirit as the quasi-Soul (*quasi-Anima*) of the Church.[17]

PROPOSITION: *The soul and the body of the Church are not two Churches, the one invisible and the other visible, but together they form one Church, which is at once visible and endowed with interior life.*   150g

According to the doctrine set forth above, there are in the Church just as there are by nature in man two elements, one visible and one invisible. But it by no means follows that there are two Churches, for the Holy Spirit and His works are, by the institution of Christ, the *special property of that visible society which is the Church,* inasmuch as they can never fail to be found therein, and can not, in the ordinary course of events, be obtained outside of it. Pius XII has harsh words for the contrary opinion:

> For this reason We deplore and condemn the pernicious error of those who conjure up from their fancies an imaginary Church, a kind of Society that finds its origin and growth in charity, to

---

* The human soul and the human body are both incomplete substances which unite to form one person. The Holy Spirit *is* a Person, and since one of the constituent elements of personality is incommunicability, He cannot join with the Church in a union of the same type as that of the human soul and body.

(225)

which they somewhat contemptuously oppose another, which they call juridical. But this distinction, which they introduce, is baseless.[18]

Obviously the sanctifying influence of the Head can never fail of effect in the body as a whole, even though it may be blocked in individual members of the Church, considered strictly as individuals. Otherwise Christ would cease to be *"the savior of that body,"* and would no longer nourish and cherish the Church as His own flesh. And this would be at odds with the teaching of the Apostle (Eph. 5:23, 29).

On the other hand, no one who knowingly and willingly strays outside the body of the visible Church receives the life of grace, and that is what Augustine meant when he wrote: "Only the body of Christ lives by the Spirit of Christ. Do you want to live by the Spirit of Christ? Then be in the body of Christ."[19] This should occasion no surprise, for the divinely established order of things prescribes that the life of grace be imparted to people, preserved and increased in them, through the same external ministrations—including those of teaching, of the priesthood, and of ruling—by which people are gathered into the visible Church:

> *He established some men as apostles, and some as inspired spokesmen, others again as evangelists, and others as pastors and teachers, thus organizing the saints for the work of the ministry, which consists in building up the body of Christ, until we all attain to unity in faith and deep knowledge of the Son of God. Thus we attain to perfect manhood, to the mature proportions that befit Christ's fullness. . . . The whole body is dependent on him. Harmoniously joined and knit together, it derives its energy in the measure each part needs only through contact with the source of supply. In this way the body grows and builds itself up through love.*[20]

It is indeed true that those who, through no fault of their own, know nothing of the Church of Christ, can, other things being equal, receive sanctifying grace and so share in the life imparted by the Soul of the Church; but this is quite accidental, and happens quite apart from the usual order of things. For the rest, if anyone who is not an actual member of the Mystical Body is to be justified, it is absolutely necessary that he be related to it by at least an implicit desire.[21] If this condition is fulfilled, then the mercy of God who wills that all men be saved (I Tim. 2:4) will credit his desire as if it were an act.[22]

Corollary 150h

The Church is a continuation of Christ in the world. Pius XII wrote in the *Mystici Corporis:*

> As Bellarmine notes with acumen and accuracy, this naming of the Body of Christ is not to be explained solely by the fact that Christ must be called the Head of His Mystical Body, but also by the fact that He so sustains the Church, and so in a certain sense lives in the Church that it is, as it were, another Christ. The doctor of the Gentiles in his letter to the Corinthians affirms this when, without further qualification, he called the Church "Christ," following no doubt the example of his Master who called out to him from on high, when he was attacking the Church: "Saul, Saul, why persecutest thou Me?" Indeed, if we are to believe Gregory of Nyssa, the Church is often called "Christ" by the Apostle; and you are conversant, Venerable Brothers, with that phrase of Augustine: "Christ preaches Christ."—66.

The Founder of the Church, our Lord Jesus Christ, is the incarnate Son of God, perfect God and perfect man. These two elements of divinity and humanity are verified in the Church also, the mystical Christ, though not, of course, in precisely the same manner.[23]

> As these two aspects are found in Christ's humanity, they will also be found in the mystic perpetuation of that humanity which is the Church. The Church will likewise be an empirical thing and a mysterious reality.
> First, it will be an empirical, concrete, visible, tangible thing, like all human realities that prolong themselves in some form of continuation; for it is a human institution, a human society. And it is a society quite visibly and tangibly; its sociology and canon law can be written down; it has its clearly defined members and its definite seat: it is the Church of Rome, as Jesus Christ was Jesus of Nazareth. As a society it is perfect in its kind, with a firm and well-delineated structure, as befits a thing that is the perpetuation of the God-man.
> Secondly, the Church will be an invisible reality: a life of

thought, love, and grace that is infused into souls, a divinization and adoptive sonship which, in the unity of the only-begotten, incarnate Son is diffused throughout all mankind so deeply as to be inaccessible to natural consciousness, and which, in the depths thus reached, unifies mankind in itself and attaches it to God.
Through this second aspect, that is, the divinization conferred on it, the Church is a theandric[24] reality, a divine-human reality, as many authors aptly put it. The reason is not that the Godhead is one of its elements or aspects, or that the Church has its own union with the Godhead independently of Christ and His hypostatic union, but only that it is the perpetuation of the theandric humanity, the humanity fully divinized * and subsisting in the Word, the humanity of the God-man.[25]

If the Church in its very essence is so remarkable a continuation of the Incarnation, it is in its activity no less remarkable a perpetuation of the whole activity of its incarnate Head. Through the Church, which is His body, Christ continues, in a constantly recurring cycle, to be born, to go into exile, to live His hidden life, to manifest Himself to the world, to teach, to heal, to sanctify, to rule, to forgive sins, to console, to admonish, to be embraced, to be spit upon, to be hailed as a king, to be crowned with thorns, to be loved, to be hated, to be crucified, and to rise from the dead.

> The whole Body of the Church, no less than the individual members, should bear resemblance to Christ. Such is His will. And we see that realized when following in the footsteps of her Founder she teaches, she governs and offers the Divine Sacrifice. Embracing the evangelical counsels she reflects the Redeemer's poverty, obedience and virginal purity. Enriched with institutes of many different kinds as with so many precious jewels, she points out Christ deep in prayer on the mountain, or preaching to the people or healing the sick and wounded and bringing sinners back to the path of virtue, or in a word doing good to everyone. What wonder then if, while she walks this earth, she be persecuted like Christ, hounded and weighed down with sorrows.[26]

Msgr. Robert Hugh Benson gave powerful expression to this truth in his *Christ in the Church*. One should read the whole thing to appreciate its full force, but here is an illustrative passage:

---

* Not, of course, in the Monophysite sense.

THE CHURCH: THE MYSTICAL BODY OF CHRIST

Still, to the eyes of the Catholic, there moves on earth that amazing figure whose mere painted portrait in the Gospels has driven men—artists, seers, and philanthropists—mad with love and longing—and he is part of it. There still sounds on the air the very voice that comforted the Magdalene and pardoned the thief; the same Divine energy that healed the sick and raised the dead is still active on earth, not transmitted merely from some Majesty on high, but working now, as then, through a Human Nature that may be touched and felt. If the Catholic be mistaken in this astounding vision, yet he cannot be accused of substituting a system for a Person, since it is the groundwork of his whole life and hope that what men call a system *is* a person, far more accessible, more real and more effective than one can be who is thought to reign merely in a distant heaven, and no longer in any real sense to be present on earth. The true minister of every sacrament, for example, as every Catholic believes, is none else than the supreme and Eternal High Priest Himself.[27]

Scholion. The coextension of the concepts "Church" and "Mystical Body." 150i

The concepts of both "Church" and "Mystical Body" may be taken in either a broad or a strict sense depending on whether one takes Christ's Church exclusively from the viewpoint of its earthly sojourn, or from the total viewpoint of its existence, and modes of existence, both in time and in eternity. The same is roughly true of the concept, "the kingdom of God," the common New Testament expression for the Church. It is from this total viewpoint (ecclesiological, soteriological, and eschatological), that a number of competent theologians, even after the encyclicals *Mystici Corporis* and *Humani generis*, continue to use distinctions as: "potential members" *vs.* "actual members"; "members *in voto*" *vs.* "members *in re*," etc. Indeed Pius XII himself, after explicitly naming the members of the Mystical Body in the strict sense of the term, seems to employ the term "member" in a broader sense in referring to both catechumens and the souls in purgatory as members of the Mystical Body (see 119).

It is important, then, to remember the precise viewpoint from which the theologians are speaking in order to avoid hopeless confusion in this whole matter. Briefly, the concepts of "Church" and "Mystical Body" are always mutually coextensive *provided* that *both* are used in the same sense. Confusion arises when an author simultaneously employs the one concept in the strict sense and the other in the broad* sense.

150j Special Bibliography for the Doctrine of the Mystical Body

BENSON, R. H. *Christ in the Church*, St. Louis, 1914.
BONSIRVEN, J. *L'évangile de Paul*, Paris, 1948.
CERFAUX, L. *La théologie de l'église suivant saint Paul*, Paris, 1948.
FENTON, J. C. AER, 110 (1944), 48 ff.; 124 ff.; 459 ff.; 113 (1945), 44 ff.; 377 ff.; 115 (1946), 50 ff.; 119 (1948), 202 ff.; 123 (1950), 295 ff.; 129 (1953), 343 ff.; 133 (1955), 258 ff.
GOOSSENS, W., *L'église, corps du Christ, d'après St. Paul*, Paris, 1949.
GRUDEN, J. G. *The Mystical Christ*, St. Louis, 1936.
HASSEVELDT, R. *The Church, A Divine Mystery*, translated by Wm. Storey, Chicago, 1954.
LECLERCQ, J. *La vie du Christ dans son église*, Paris, 1947.
MEINERTZ, M. *Theologie des neuen Testamentes*, Bonn, 1950.
MERSCH, E. *The Whole Christ*, Milwaukee, 1938.
————. *The Theology of the Mystical Body*, St. Louis and London, 1951.
MURPHY, J. L. *The Living Christ*, Milwaukee, 1952.
PARENTE, P. *Theologia fundamentalis*, Rome, 1950.
PIUS XII. *Mystici Corporis*, in the English edition of J. Bluett, *The Mystical Body of Christ*, New York, 1943.
PRAT, F. *The Theology of St. Paul*, Westminster, Md., 1946.

---

* For the subtler question of what theological justification can be given for using the term "Mystical Body" in a *broad* sense, see Zapalena's long, detailed treatment of this problem (*op. cit.*, II, 341–88 and 553–97). Although we disagree with the learned author's conclusions, we have not the space to spare for a detailed examination of his arguments. It seems to us a sufficient justification for the broad use of the term "Mystical Body" that: *1*) its legitimacy is guaranteed by *patristic tradition; 2*) Pius XII in the *Mystici Corporis* seems to use the term in its broad as well as its strict sense; *3*) a too rigid and mathematical approach to this particular point can lead to strange conclusions: if one rules out completely the broad usage of the term "Mystical Body," and restricts it exclusively to the strict sense (i.e., the Church militant —the Church and its members on earth), what shall we conclude about the Blessed Mother, St. Peter, St. John, St. Paul, and the other saints in heaven? They are not living on earth; shall we conclude: therefore they are *not* "members of the Mystical Body of Christ?" An awkward conclusion. See J. C. Fenton, "The Communion of Saints and the Mystical Body," AER, 110 (1944); 378 ff., and especially the conclusions stated on p. 387–88.

THE CHURCH: THE MYSTICAL BODY OF CHRIST

SALAVERRI, I. *Sacrae theologiae summa*, I, Madrid, 1952.
SERTILLANGES, A. *The Church*, London, 1922.
TROMP, S. *Corpus Christi quod est Ecclesia*, Rome, 1937.
TYSZKIEWICZ, S. *La sainteté de l'église Christoconforme*, Rome, 1945.
ZAPALENA, T. *De ecclesia Christi*, pars altera, Rome, 1954.

Notes

1. See Pius XII, encyclical *Mystici Corporis* (June 29, 1943):
If we would define and describe this true Church of Jesus Christ—which is the One, Holy, Catholic, Apostolic, Roman Church—we shall find no expression more noble, more sublime or more Divine than the phrase which calls it "the Mystical Body of Jesus Christ."—17.
All references to the encyclical throughout the chapter will be to the English edition of J. Bluett, S.J., *The Mystical Body of Christ* (New York, 1943). The numbers will refer to the paragraph division of this edition. See also E. Mersch, *The Theology of the Mystical Body*, p. 518, 523, 527; R. H. Benson, *Christ in the Church*. Very much to the point are the following words of C. Journet, *The Primacy of Peter, op. cit.*:
The Church is therefore like Christ; the Body is like the Head. This homogeneity of the Church with Christ, of the Body with the Head, enables Christ to be diffused and communicated in space and time. It assures a continuous presence of Christ in space and time. This is the mystery of the Church's catholicity.
Once this perpetual and real presence of Christ in the midst of space and time has been broken, once the continuity of the Christian mystery has been mutilated, the desire to go on speaking of Catholicism and catholicity at all costs amounts to nothing but insistence upon using a traditional word which has been emptied of all traditional meaning.—p. 11 f.

2. This was not the only important aspect of ecclesiology forced into the background. See J. C. Fenton, "The Church and the World," AER, 119 (1948), 202 ff.; "The Church and God's Promises," *ibid.*, 123 (1950), 295 ff.; "The Church in Adequate Perspective," *ibid.*, 133 (1955), 258 ff.; J. Leclercq, *La vie du Christ dans son église.*

3. See T. Zapalena, *op. cit.*, p. 331.

4. Any work written on the Mystical Body before this date and, unfortunately, even some written subsequently should be read with one eye always on this normative pronouncement. See Zapalena, *op. cit.*, p. 331–597, *passim*.

5. The last phrase, *"who fills,* etc.," is susceptible of several other translations in English, depending on whether one takes the Greek verb as a middle or passive form. One might, for example, translate as follows: *the completion of him who everywhere and in all things is complete.* But none of these possible translations affects the essential meaning of the verse. See Medebielle, "Epître aux Ephésiens," in Pirot-Clamer, *La Sainte Bible* (Paris, 1946), XII, 37–39; A. Feuillet, "L'église plérôme du Christ d'après Ephés., I, 23." NRTh, 78 (1956), 449 ff.; 593 ff.

6. See also Rom. 12:5; I Cor. 6:15; Eph. 4:4, 25; 5:23, 29; Col. 2:9, etc. For a full treatment of the Pauline doctrine on the Mystical Body, and for a careful theological analysis of the pertinent passages, see Zapalena, *op. cit.;* Meinertz, *op. cit.,* F. Prat, *The Theology of St. Paul;* J. Bonsirven, *L'évangile de Paul;* L. Cerfaux, *La théologie de l'église suivant saint Paul;* Werner Goossens, *L'église, corps du Christ, d'après saint Paul;* CCHS, Index, *s.v.* Mystical Body of Christ, The.

7. See QP, indices under *Church.*

8. See St. Thomas Aquinas, S.Th., III, q. 8, a. 1 and 6; *De veritate,* 29,4.

9. Gal. 3:28. *One* in the Greek is masculine: *one person.* St. Augustine: "The whole Christ consists of head and body: the head is the only-begotten Son of God, His body is the Church: Bridegroom and bride, two in one flesh" (*Epistula contra Donatistas de unitate ecclesiae* 4.7).

10. See J. C. Fenton, "Our Lord's Presence in the Catholic Church," AER, 115 (1946), 50 ff.

11. *Op. cit.,* 45–50; see also 61–64; J. C. Fenton, *"Vicarius Christi,"* AER, 110 (1944) 459 ff. Soteriologically speaking, our Saviour is Head of the whole human race, a fact to which the Holy Father alludes when speaking of the holy sacrifice of the Mass:

> In this act of sacrifice through the hands of the priest, whose word alone has brought the Immaculate Lamb to be present on the altar, the faithful themselves with one desire and one prayer offer It to the Eternal Father—the most acceptable victim of praise and propitiation for the Church's universal needs. And just as the Divine Redeemer, dying on the Cross, offered Himself as Head of the whole human race to the Eternal Father, so "in this pure oblation" He offers not only Himself as Head of the Church to the heavenly Father, but in Himself His mystical members as well.—*Op. cit.,* 97.

12. See Isai. 11:2; 61:1; Acts 10:38.

13. See MCC, 18–20, 73.

14. The analogy is one of proper but inadequate proportionality, i.e., one in which the notion common to the two analogues applies properly to both but on the basis of a certain similarity, i.e., it does not apply to both in exactly the same way.

15. See M. Meinertz, *op. cit.,* II, 156.

16. See MCC, 67–70.

17. Christ the Head acts through the Holy Spirit:
                    intrinsically   (grace and gifts)
                    extrinsically   (the hierarchy)
                    in both ways   (sacraments).

See P. Parente, *op. cit.,* p. 159; Salaverri, *op. cit.,* p. 825–7.

18. MCC, 79. See also J. C. Fenton, "The Use of the Terms Body and Soul with Reference to the Catholic Church," AER, 110 (1944), 48 ff.; "The Extension of Christ's Mystical Body," *ibid.,* 124 ff.; "The Church and the Non-Catholic," *ibid.,* 113 (1945), 44 ff.; "The Catholic and the Church," *ibid.,* 377 ff.; "The Invocation of the Holy Name and the Basic Concept of the Catholic Church," *ibid.,* 129 (1953), 343 ff. The Holy Father repeated this truth pointedly and emphatically in a subsequent encyclical, *Humani generis* (Aug. 12, 1950):

THE CHURCH: THE MYSTICAL BODY OF CHRIST

Some say they are not bound by the doctrine, explained in Our Encyclical Letter of a few years ago, and based on the sources of revelation, which teaches that the Mystical Body of Christ and the Roman Catholic Church are one and the same thing. Some reduce to a meaningless formula the necessity of belonging to the true Church in order to gain eternal salvation. . . .

These and like errors, it is clear, have crept in among certain of Our sons who are deceived by imprudent zeal for souls or by false science. To them We are compelled with grief to repeat once again truths already well known, and to point out with solicitude clear errors and dangers of error.—NCWC edition, 27–28.

19. *Tractatus CXXIV in Joannis evangelium* 26. 13.

20. Eph. 4:11–13. St. Cyprian, among others, expressed the same truth when he wrote: "You cannot have God for your Father if you have not the Church for your mother" (*De unitate ecclesiae* 6; ACW trans.). Indeed Scripture itself calls the Church Christ's *bride* (Eph. 5:22) and *wife* (Apoc. 21:9), inasmuch as it is joined forever to Him by a bond like that of marriage, and by Him is made fruitful in giving birth to adoptive sons of God. But note that the Church is a bride who was not merely found by Christ, but actually formed by Him, as St. Augustine wrote: "So has the king desired your beauty. What beauty, if not that which He Himself did create? You are being wedded to a God-king, and it is He who has given you your dowry, adorned you, redeemed you, healed you. Whatever you have that may prove pleasing to Him, you have from Him." (*Enarrationes in psalmos* 44. 12).

21. For the expression "related to," see MCC, 121, and Zapalena, *op. cit.*, 379 ff.

22. See *below*, the Scholion, "Outside the Church no salvation."

23. MCC, 67:

But this noble title of the Church must not be so taken, as if that ineffable bond by which the Son of God assumed a definite human nature belongs to the universal Church; but it consists in this, that our Saviour shares His most personal prerogatives with the Church in such a way that she may portray in her whole life, both external and interior, a most faithful image of Christ. For in virtue of the juridical mission by which our Divine Redeemer sent His Apostles into the world, as He had been sent by the Father, it is He who through the Church baptizes, teaches, rules, looses, binds, offers sacrifices. But in virtue of that higher, interior and wholly sublime communication, with which We dealt when We described the manner in which the Head influences the members, Christ our Lord brings the Church to live His own supernatural life, by His divine power permeates His whole body and nourishes and sustains each of the members according to the place which they occupy in the Body, very much as the vine nourishes and makes fruitful the branches which are joined to it.

24. From the two Greek words, *theós* (God) and *anér* (man).

25. E. Mersch, *op. cit.*, p. 428 ff.; see also P. Parente, *Theologia fundamentalis*, p. 156 ff.; T. Zapalena, *De ecclesia Christi*, pars altera, p. 331; J. C. Fenton, "Our Lord's Presence in the Catholic Church," AER, 115 (1946), 50 ff.

26. MCC, 59; see also 3, 93.

27. R. H. Benson, *op. cit.*, p. 20. The book ends with this moving passage:

For I see through her eyes, the Eyes of God to shine, and through her lips I hear His words. In each of her hands as she raises them to bless, I see the wounds that dripped on Calvary, and her feet upon the altar stairs are signed with the same marks as those which the Magdalene kissed. As she comforts me in the confessional I hear the voice that bade the sinner go and sin no more; and as she rebukes or pierces me with blame I shrink aside trembling with those who went out one by one, beginning with the eldest, till Jesus and the penitent were left alone. As she cries her invitation through the world I hear the same ringing claim as that which called, "Come unto me and find rest for your souls"; as she drives those who profess to serve her from her service I see the same flame of wrath that scourged the changers of money from the temple courts. As I watch her in the midst of her people, applauded by the mob shouting always for the rising sun, I see the palm branches about her head, and the City and Kingdom of God, it would seem, scarcely a stone's throw away, yet across the Valley of the Kedron is the garden of Gethsemane; and as I watch her pelted with mud, spurned, spat at and disgraced, I read in her eyes the message that we should not weep for her but for ourselves and for our children, since she is immortal and we but mortal after all. As I look on her white body, dead and drained of blood, I smell once more the odor of the ointments and the trampled grass of that garden near to the place where He was crucified, and hear the tramp of the soldiers who came to seal the stone and set the watch. And, at last, as I see her moving once more in the dawn light of each new day, or in the revelation of evening, as the sun of this or that dynasty rises and sets, I understand that He who was dead has come forth once more with healing in His wings, to comfort those that mourn and to bind up the brokenhearted; and that His coming is not with observation, but in the depth of night as His enemies slept and His lovers woke for sorrow.

Yet even as I see this I understand that Easter is but Bethlehem once again; that the cycle runs round again to its beginning and that the conflict is all to fight again; for they will not be persuaded, though One rises daily from the dead.

CHAPTER II

The Members of the Church

Article I

CONDITIONS FOR MEMBERSHIP IN THE CHURCH

I. *Preliminary Remarks:*

    PROPOSITION: Members of the Church are all and only those who have received the sacrament of baptism, and are not separated from the unity of profession of the faith, or from hierarchical unity.

    Proof: 1. baptism is the sacrament which incorporates a man into the Church:

        2. membership in the Church can be severed by destroying either the bond of faith or the bond of hierarchical unity.

    Scholion 1: *Who are not members of the Church?*
- a. The nonbaptized
- b. Public heretics
- c. Public schismatics
- d. Total excommunicates

    Scholion 2: *Consequences of baptism in the matter of Church membership.*

II. *Heretical Views on Membership in the Church:*
1. All the predestined and only the predestined are members of the Church.
2. Only those in the state of grace are members of the Church.

Objections

CHAPTER II

The Members of the Church

After the discussion of the Church as the Mystical Body of Christ, the question spontaneously arises: who are members of the Church? This chapter is divided into two articles: the first deals with the *conditions* requisite for *membership* in the Church; the second deals with the *necessity* of belonging to the Church for salvation.

Article I

CONDITIONS FOR MEMBERSHIP IN THE CHURCH

I. Preliminary Remarks

Here we are speaking of the Church, or the Mystical Body, taken only in its *strict* ° and proper meaning: namely, that militant Church of the New Testament which, as has been repeatedly pointed out, is essentially a *visible* society.[1] In the strict sense of the term, the Mystical Body is, as Pius XII informs us in plain words, the Roman Catholic Church:

> If we would *define* and describe this true Church of Jesus Christ—which is the One, Holy, Catholic, Apostolic, Roman Church—we shall find no expression more noble, more sublime, or more Divine than the phrase which calls it "the Mystical Body of Jesus Christ." This title is derived from and is, as it were, the fair flower of the repeated teaching of Sacred Scripture and the Holy Fathers.—MCC 17; italics ours.

The same pontiff reiterated this teaching on the identity of the Mystical Body and the Roman Catholic Church in his encyclical, *Humani generis* (1950), when he explicitly rebuked theologians who had failed to heed the teachings of *Mystici Corporis:*

° See scholion, "Coextension of the Concepts 'Church' and 'Mystical Body'" above p. 229.

THE MEMBERS OF THE CHURCH

Some say they are not bound by the doctrine, explained in Our Encyclical Letter of a few years ago, and based on the sources of revelation, *which teaches that the Mystical Body of Christ and the Roman Catholic Church are one and the same thing*.... These and like errors, it is clear, have crept in among certain of Our sons who are deceived by imprudent zeal for souls or by false science.—NCWC transl., 27–28; italics ours.

PROPOSITION: *Members of the Church are all and only those who have received the sacrament of baptism, and are not separated from the unity of the profession of the faith, or from hierarchial unity.* 151

This proposition is *certain*.

Theological label for the proposition. The proposition viewed *as a whole* and as formulated in *general* terms is regarded as certain by all Catholics. When it comes to a more precise delineation of some of these terms,* there are some divergent opinions.²

We call *members* of the Church only those who unqualifiedly belong to the visible Church. Three facts are required for this: (*a*) that a person have received the sacrament of baptism; (*b*) that he be not separated from the profession of the faith of the Church; (*c*) that he be not separated from union with its hierarchy. These three factors, however, should not receive the same evaluation. Baptism alone is the *cause* which incorporates a man into the Church; the other two factors are *conditions* which must be fulfilled if baptism is not to be frustrated in its effect. Baptism, by Christ's own ordinance, always ingrafts a man into the body of the Church unless its efficacy be impeded; and union with the Church, once it has been caused by baptism, perseveres uninterruptedly so long as it be not severed by either of the separations mentioned above.

Proof:

1. *The sacrament of baptism is the means by which men become members of the Church.* This is *of faith*.

---

* The generic terms of the proposition (particularly the second part of it) cover a variety of categories of people: "formal" and "material" heretics; "public" and "occult"—heretics; "formal" and "material" schismatics; "total" and "partial" excommunicates; etc. Since the theologians are not all of one mind in discussing some of these categories, they differ in some of the theological labels they append to each category considered singly.

a. From *Sacred Scripture: Those who accepted his word were baptized, and there were added that day (to the Church) about three thousand persons* (Acts 2:41). *By a single Spirit all of us, whether Jews or Greeks, slaves or free men, were introduced into the one body through baptism* (I Cor. 12:13).

b. From the *Church's magisterium:* The Council of Florence in its *Decree for the Armenians* states:

> Holy baptism holds the first place among all the sacraments because it is the door of the spiritual life. By it we are made members of Christ and of His body, the Church.—DB 696; TCT 686.

The Council of Trent declares:

> The Church does not pass judgment on anyone who has not already entered her ranks through the gate of baptism. The Apostle says, "For what have I to do with judging those outside?" (I Cor. 5:12). The situation is different with regard to the members of the household of the faith whom Christ our Lord has made members of his body once and for all by the water of baptism.—DB 895; TCT 789.

These words, while directly concerned with the extent of the Church's jurisdiction, at the same time show that according to the mind of the Church there is no other cause of insertion into the body of the Church but baptism.

c. Finally, Pius XII in his encyclical, *Mystici Corporis,* states explicitly:

> Only those are really to be included as members of the Church who have been *baptized* and profess the true faith and who have not unhappily withdrawn from Body-unity or for grave faults been excluded by legitimate authority.—29; italics ours.

2. The fact that *membership in the Church* (meant to be effected by baptism) can be *impeded,* or that even after its accomplishment can be *severed* either by a departure from *unity of faith* or *unity of government,* hardly needs *ex professo* proof. Still, lest there be any misunderstanding of this point, here are a few cita-

tions from the unanimous voice of tradition, and the recent explicit teaching of Pius XII:

*a. Tradition:*³ Tertullian: "If they are heretics, they cannot be Christians" (*De praescriptione* 37). St. Hilary: "I am a Christian, not an Arian" (*Ad Constantium liber II*ᵘˢ 1. 2). St. Augustine: "Neither heretics nor schismatics belong to the Catholic Church" (*De fide et symbolo* 21). St. Jerome: " . . . a schismatic faction, because of the rebellion of its bishop, is cut off from the Church" (*Commentarium in Epistulam ad Titum* 3. 10). Finally, the whole dispute over "rebaptizing" heretics presupposed as a fact that public heretics and public schismatics are not members of the Church. For the crux of the problem centered on this one point: how could a baptism administered to heretics suffice for entrance into the Church if the one baptizing was himself outside the Church?

b. The *Church's magisterium:*

> As, therefore, in the true Christian community there is only one Body, one Spirit, one Lord and one Baptism, so there can be only one Faith. And so if a man refuse to hear the Church, let him be considered—so the Lord commands—as a heathen and a publican. It follows that those who are divided in faith or government cannot be living in one Body such as this, and cannot be living the life of its one Divine Spirit.—MCC 29.

Scholion 1. Who are not members of the Church?

From the principles laid down it is fairly easy to know which classes of men are excluded from membership in the Church. A few exceptional cases, however, pose some difficulties. These will be discussed briefly in the course of dealing with clear-cut cases of nonmembership.

The following classes of men are definitely *not* members of the Church: (*a*) The nonbaptized; (*b*) public heretics;° (*c*) public schismatics; total excommunicates.

° A heretic is one who denies a truth of *divine and Catholic* faith: i.e., a truth which has been revealed by God and proposed by the Church for our belief (see vol. III of this series, nos. 210 and 259). Heretics are classified as "public" or "occult," "formal" or "material." A *public* (notorious) heretic is one whose heresy is known to a large number of people, even if he has not formally joined the ranks of a heretical church; an *occult* heretic is one whose errors in faith are either totally unknown, or known only to a few. A *formal* heretic is one who stubbornly and guiltily adheres to heresy; a *material* heretic is one who innocently and in good faith subscribes to some heretical doctrine.

a. Those who have not received baptism of water are not members of the Church. Jews, pagans, etc., are not members of the Church. Since the cause of incorporation into the Church is strictly baptism insofar as it imprints an indelible character, dedicating us to the worship of God as that is practiced in the Catholic religion, it follows: (1) neither baptism *of desire* ° (act of perfect charity), nor baptism *by blood* (martyrdom) makes a man a member of the Church. Even though they confer sanctifying grace, they do not imprint a character. Consequently catechumens are not members of the Church. (2) For the same reason, according to the more probable opinion, a *putatively valid* baptism (i.e., really invalid) does not suffice for membership. Incorporation in the Church is something *real*.[4] No one becomes a member of any society, or any visible organization, by an invalid act of admission. Those[5] who advance the opinion that a *putatively* valid baptism should suffice argue: "otherwise one could not reach certitude about the Church's membership, since it is possible for the sacrament of baptism to be invalidated even by a hidden defect in the intention of the minister." The answer to that argument is, in our opinion, that most of the time the intention of the minister can be proven with moral certitude—the only type of certitude one should normally expect to have in human affairs. And since the cases of those only "putatively" baptized would certainly be very rare, there is no danger implied for the visibility of the entire Church.

Although some authors, notably Suárez,[6] count *catechumens* as members of the Church, they are not members actually but only

---

These same divisions apply to schismatics. A *schismatic* is one who ruptures the *social bond* of Catholic unity by completely denying obedience to the legitimate rulers of the Church. By definition, a schismatic differs from a heretic in that the former refuses to obey divinely constituted authority, while the latter rejects divinely revealed truth. Usually, however, schisms end ultimately in heresy. An *apostate* is one who rejects the Christian faith totally: not merely this or that doctrine, but the whole of Christianity. Finally, an *excommunicate* is one who is separated from the Church by the action of legitimate authority. Excommunication is a punishment for some serious and usually scandalous crime; it may be total or only partial, depriving one of some or of all his rights as a member of the Catholic Church. For details see CIC.

° As Parente pertinently remarks: "Reason itself suggests the need of some *visible means* for a man's being made a member of the Church which is a visible society. Consequently it is necessary for anyone who wishes to be a member of the body of the Church to receive baptism *actually* and not simply in desire" (*Theologia fundamentalis, op. cit.*, p. 184, no. 3).

in desire and, as it were, by proximate potency. The fact that catechumens have penances imposed on them does not suffice to prove the contrary opinion. No one would maintain that a man was already a member of a given society merely because he freely accepted some of the conditions laid upon him as a *preliminary* to membership. Strictly speaking, then, we should say that the Church does not have power of "government" over catechumens, but only power of "teaching"—a power which extends to all mankind, even those still to be called to the Church. Finally, the fact that Pius XII seems to refer to both catechumens and the souls in purgatory as members of the Church (MCC 119) in requesting prayers to be offered "for all the members of the Mystical Body of Christ" proves nothing in favor of Suárez' opinion. All it proves, in our opinion, is that it is still possible to use the term Mystical Body in a broad as well as a strict sense.[7] But here we are discussing members only in the strict sense of the word.

b. *Public heretics* (and *a fortiori, apostates*) *are not members of the Church.* They are not members because they separate themselves from the unity of Catholic faith and from the external profession of that faith. Obviously, therefore, they lack one of the three factors—baptism, profession of the same faith, union with the hierarchy—pointed out by Pius XII as requisite for membership in the Church (see *above,* p. 238). The same pontiff has explicitly pointed out that, unlike other sins, heresy, schism, and apostasy automatically sever a man from the Church. "For not every sin, however grave and enormous it be, is such as to sever a man automatically from the Body of the Church, *as does schism or heresy or apostasy*" (MCC 30; italics ours).

By the term *public heretics* at this point we mean all who *externally* deny a truth (for example Mary's Divine Maternity), or several truths of divine and Catholic faith, regardless of whether the one denying does so ignorantly and innocently (a merely *material* heretic), or wilfully and guiltily (a *formal* heretic). It is *certain* that public, formal heretics are severed from Church membership. It is the *more common* opinion that public, material heretics are likewise excluded from membership. Theological reasoning for this opinion is quite strong: if public material heretics remained members of the Church, the visibility and unity of Christ's Church would perish.[8] If these purely material heretics were considered members of the Catholic Church in the strict sense of the term, how would one ever locate the "Catholic Church"? How would the Church be one body? How would it profess one faith? Where would be its visibility? Where its unity? For these and other reasons we find it difficult to see any intrinsic probability to the opinion which would allow for *public* heretics, in good faith, remaining members of the Church.

When it comes to a question of *occult* heretics remaining members of the Church, theologians are in sharper disagreement and the intrinsic probability of their respective arguments seems better balanced than in the preceding case. An occult heretic is one who denies a truth of divine and catholic faith *in his heart*, while professing the same truth with his lips. So a man might recite the Nicene creed with the rest of the faithful, but deny the doctrine of the Trinity internally. Even if he were to deny such a truth *externally*, but his defection from the faith was *secret*, known only to one or two intimates, he would also be classified as an occult heretic. The more common opinion [9] is that such heretics remain members of the Church. Occult heresy does not take away their former public profession of the Catholic faith. The authority of Pius IX is raised in objection to this view because he says in his bull, *Ineffabilis Deus*:

> If anyone shall dare to *believe otherwise in his heart* (*corde sentire*) than has been defined by us—which God forbid—let them fully realize, that they are condemned by their own judgment, and have suffered shipwreck in the faith and that they have departed from union with the Church (*ab unitate Ecclesiae defecisse*).—DB 1641.

The usual reply to that objection is: the meaning of the above passage seems to be that internal heresy, since it destroys that interior unity of the faith from which unity of profession is born, separates one from the body of the Church *dispositively*, but not yet formally. Zapalena objects to this interpretation as "an arbitrary and aprioristic exegesis which does injury to the obvious meaning of the words" (*op. cit.*, II, 390). Regardless of whether it is an "arbitrary" exegesis or not, it seems equally arbitrary to attempt to make any argument at all from the passage cited: the pope was defining the Immaculate Conception, not making a definitive declaration in the matter of membership or nonmembership of occult heretics in the Church.

THE MEMBERS OF THE CHURCH

The question comes down to this: how satisfactorily can the theologians on either side of this disputed point square their opinion with the necessary *visibility* of the Church? If true supernatural faith is required for membership in the Church, how can one be sure of the Church's membership? The virtue of faith, like any other supernatural gift, is not discernible by empirical methods. In the hypothesis of the proponents of the other opinion, a pope who was secretly a heretic would cease to be a member of the Church and its head (Lercher, *op. cit.*, no. 419 b, p. 238): and it cannot be demonstrated apodictically that God has promised never to allow a pope to become an occult heretic. One of the best arguments that occult heresy does not deprive one of membership is that heresy is not the gravest of sins. It is not the *gravity* of the sin of heresy which causes one to lose membership, but the antisocial nature of that sin which militates against the unity of the Mystical Body:

> Finally there does not appear any reason why occult heretics more than other sinners should be excluded from the body of the Church. Heresy is not the gravest of all mortal sins: hatred of God is greater. Therefore if other very grave sins do not exclude from the body of the Church, neither does occult heresy. Public heretics are excluded not because of the gravity of their fault, seeing that even material heretics [i.e., innocent] are outside the Church. The reason for their exclusion is the nature of the Church as a society which demands a unity in the profession of the same faith.—Lercher, *op. cit.*, p. 239, e.

 c. *Public schismatics are not members of the Church.* They are not members because by their own action they sever themselves from the unity of *Catholic communion.* The term Catholic communion, as used here, signifies both cohesion with the entire body catholic (unity of worship, etc.), and union with the visible head of the Church (unity of government). Since Catholic communion signifies both the subordination of all members to one head, and the coordination of all the members with one another, a man may become a schismatic in either of two ways: *(1)* by directly withdrawing himself from obedience to the pope—not, of course, by a simple act of disobedience towards some law laid down by the pope, but by such a rebellion that he would really in practice refuse to recognize the pope as the head of the Catholic Church;

(2) by directly rupturing the bonds of cohesion with the body catholic: by setting up a separate, national Church, by following a usurping bishop, etc.

Once again, it makes no difference whether a person who breaks the bonds of Catholic communion does so in good faith or in bad; in either case he ceases to be a member of the Church. The innocence or guilt of the parties involved is purely an internal matter, purely a matter of conscience; it has no direct bearing on the question of one of the external and social bonds requisite for membership. Pius XII in listing the three requisites for membership in the Church makes no distinction between those in good and bad faith and seems [10] to exclude both categories from membership: "Only those are really to be included as members . . . who have not unhappily withdrawn from Body-unity" (MCC 29). Still, in giving a theological label to this particular point—since the pope has not explicitly settled it, and since the same theologians who maintain that a public heretic in good faith remains a member of the Church maintain the same for a schismatic—we should say: (*1*) It is *certain* that a public, *formal* schismatic is not a member of the Church; (2) it is the *more common and more probable* opinion that a public, *material* schismatic is not a member of the Church.

155   d. *Total excommunicates are not members of the Church.* Excommunicated people, unlike schismatics, are separated from the unity of Catholic communion not directly by their own action, but by the judgment of ecclesiastical authority. For the rulers of the Church, like the rulers of any other genuine society, have the right to cut off obstinately rebellious members and to separate them from the social body until they come to their senses again.[11]

This exclusion from the body-unity, brought about by the sentence of ecclesiastical authority, can be *total* or only *partial*. A member may be prevented from exercising a few or even many of the rights which belong to him as a member in that society, without being erased from membership. That is why there have been in the past, and still are, various degrees of excommunication.[12] Excommunicated people are divided into two main classes: *tolerated* excommunicates and *to-be-shunned* excommunicates. The latter are those who have been singled out *by name* by the Apostolic See for exclusion from the rest of the faithful and who have, either by the law itself, or by a public decree and sentence, been denounced as *to-be-shunned* (see CIC, 2257 ff.; and 2343, 1, n. 1).

THE MEMBERS OF THE CHURCH

Concerning membership in the Church, the *more probable* opinion is that *to-be-shunned* excommunicates are excluded from membership in the Church; *tolerated* excommunicates—provided no condemnatory or declaratory sentence has been passed on them —seem to remain members of the Church. One point to be noted is that it must be clearly shown in the decree of the Apostolic See that the Church *intends* to cut off such persons from Church membership.[13]

That the Church has the *right* and the power to deprive men of membership in the Church is clear from the fact of its constitution as a perfect society. The scriptural foundation for this right is solidly founded in Matthew 18:17: *"If he pays no attention to them, then notify the Church; and if he pays no attention to the Church, then treat him as a heathen and tax-collector."* That the Church *intends* to exercise this right is clear from the formula found in the Roman Pontifical: "We cut off from the body of the Church." That such excommunications deprive a man of *membership* in the Church is clearly taught by Pius XII:

> Only those are really to be included as members of the Church who have been baptized and profess the true faith and who have not unhappily withdrawn from Body-unity or for grave faults been *excluded* by *legitimate authority.*—MCC 29.

Scholion 2. Consequences of baptism in the matter of Church membership. 156

From the fact that baptism is properly the cause of engrafting into the Church, two facts follow: *(a) All validly baptized babies*, even if they were baptized by heretics and in the midst of dissident Christian sects, *are members of the Roman Catholic Church.* The baptismal character conjoins them, not to any sect but to the Church of Christ. Moreover, since such children are incapable of rational activity (human acts), they cannot cut themselves off from the Church by acts of heresy or schism; neither can they be separated by the sword of excommunication, for excommunication presumes guilt. Such children, consequently, remain members of the Church until, after reaching the age of reason, they separate themselves from the Church by entering into heresy or schism publicly. And if in so doing, they act in good faith, they are not deprived of all relationship with the Catholic Church. Still, they are not Catholics; they have severed, even though blamelessly, one of the bonds requisite for actual membership in the Church. Should they become converted in mature life it is often a comfort to them to know they are not betraying an ancestral spiritual heritage but simply returning to their Father's house.[14] *(b) All validly baptized persons always (objectively) remain subject to the Church* (CIC, 87). Here it is important to disitnguish between being *subject* to the Church and being a *member* of the Church. The former term has a far wider connotation and extension. Consequently, though all its members are subject to the Church, not all its subjects are members. So, for example, a visitor in a foreign land is temporarily subject to the laws of that land; again, a soldier who is a deserter is legitimately tried and punished by the army authorities. Yet, neither the visitor nor the soldier is, strictly speaking, a member of the society to which he is subject.[15]

Similarly, even though public heretics, public schismatics, and total excommunicates are not actually members of the Church, they are never completely deprived of all relationship to the Church. For the baptismal character, once received by these people is indelible. And although they prevent its unifying force by their own actions—which, considered purely abstractly and objectively, are evil—they do not thereby destroy that character.* That is why, as long as they live, *by law and obligation* they belong to the Church and are subject to its jurisdiction, even though they may be in invincible ignorance on both counts. They are like sheep wandering outside the sheepfold: whether they fled from it of their own accord, or were put out of it for a time because of some disease, they are not exempted from the power of the shepherd. "The Church, however, can—and generally does—excuse them from the observance of ecclesiastical law" (Lercher, *op. cit.*, I, no. 412, p. 234).

157 II. Heretical Views on Membership in the Church

These viewpoints might all be said to stem from an impatience for the Day of Judgment. Disregarding the advice of the Apostle to

---

* The importance of this point for Church membership is this: heresy, schism, and excommunication are said to *impede* union with the Church. In other words they are simply *obstacles* which block the unifying action which the baptismal character possesses by its very nature. Once the obstacles are removed, it itself suffices to restore union with the Church (Salaverri, *op. cit.*, III, no. 1024, p. 837).

THE MEMBERS OF THE CHURCH

work out your salvation with fear and trembling, a certain type of religious mind reappears [16] throughout the ages, that which insists on abolishing the trembling, the uncertainty, and wants to be sure here and now which persons are going to heaven and which are going to hell. The Catholic mentality here might be summed up this way: if one knows with certitude which church is Christ's and enters it, one has a good chance of going to heaven; the heretical mentality is: if one knows now positively which people are going to heaven, one has a good chance of locating Christ's Church on earth. Consequently, the latter's criterion for membership in the Church has always been something invisible and naturally undetectable like the state of grace or predestination.

1. All the Predestined and Only the Predestined Are Members of the Church.

Following in the footsteps of Wycliffe and Huss, Calvin [17] taught that *all the predestined and only the predestined are members of the Church.* This doctrine was condemned by the Council of Constance (DB 627 ff.) and by Martin V. [18] How right it was to condemn such an aberration stands out from the fact that Christ Himself repeatedly and clearly taught that His Church would contain continually even some of those who would eventually end up in hell (*praesciti*): read His parables about the wheat and the tares, about the net enclosing both good and bad fish, about the wise and foolish virgins, [19] about the banquet in which some people would be found without wedding garments, etc. All of these parables, which point out vividly that the good and bad will only be decisively separated in the next life, clearly show that the Church will always contain in her membership some who will be eventually damned. Conversely, even though St. Paul was predestined, there was a time when he was not a member of the Church—when he was the scourge of the Church. The same is true of a number of the Church's early martyrs: they were certainly predestined, but there were long years in which they were not members of the Church.

2. Only Those in the State of Grace are Members of the Church.

Following in the footsteps of the early Novatian and Donatist heretics, the Lutherans, Quesnel, and the Synod of Pistoia taught that any mortal sin separates one from the Church. Consequently, *only those in the state of grace are members of the Church.* This doctrine is likewise heretical and is refuted by: *a.* the parables mentioned above; *b.* by our Lord's own words:

> "*But when your brother does you wrong, go and, between you and him alone, convict him of his fault. If he listens to you, you have won your brother over; but should he not listen to you, then take one or two along with you, so that 'every case may be decided on the testimony of two or three witnesses.' If he pays no attention to them, then notify the Church; and if he pays no attention to the Church, then treat him as a heathen and tax-collector.*"—Matt. 18:15–17.

These words plainly show that in Christ's own Church there can be found hardened sinners, people difficult to correct; at the same time they show that such sinners remain in the Church until they have been definitely expelled from it by the judgment of a superior. Rightly, therefore, does St. Augustine say: "From the viewpoint of God's foreknowledge and predestination, how many sheep are outside [the Church], how many wolves within" (*Tractatus CXXIV in Joannis evangelium* 45. 12).

c. From the fact that the apostles themselves were used to correcting evil-doers and yet continued to regard them as members of the Church. That is why St. Jerome did not hesitate to state: "Noah's ark was a figure of the Church . . . as there were found both panthers and goats, wolves and lambs, so here also are found saints and sinners" (*Altercatio luciferiani et orthodoxi* 22).

d. Pius XII tells us plainly that the Church always has some sinners in its midst and we must not be scandalized by that fact through an unrealistic conception of the conditions under which Christ's Church operates here on earth. Its members are men, not abstractions, and men always are frail. As Christ did not despise sinners, so neither does His Church:

> One must not imagine that the Body of the Church, just because it bears the name of Christ, is made up during the days of its earthly pilgrimage only of members conspicuous for their holiness, or consists of only the group of those whom God has predestined to eternal happiness. It is the Saviour's infinite mercy that allows place in His Mystical Body here for those whom He did not exclude from the banquet of old. For not every sin, however grave and enormous it be, is such as to sever

a man automatically from the Body of the Church, as does schism or heresy or apostasy. . . .

Let everyone then abhor sin, which defiles the members of our Redeemer; but if anyone unhappily falls and his obstinacy has not made him unworthy of communion with the faithful, let him be received with all affection and let eager charity see in him a weak member of Jesus Christ. For, as the Bishop of Hippo remarks, it is better "to be cured within the Church's community than to be cut off from its body as incurable members." "No reason to despair of the health of whatever is still part of the body; once it has been cut off, it can be neither cured nor healed."—MCC 30–31; see also 80–81.

e. Christ Himself instituted the sacrament of penance and left it to His Church precisely to heal His members who would through frailty fall into sin after baptism (John 20:23).

Finally, both these condemned doctrines necessarily destroyed the *visibility* of Christ's Church. Since one cannot normally prove even with moral certitude which men are in the state of grace, or which men are predestined, it follows from these heretical views that one could never know either who are members of the Church, or even who are its rulers.

Objections:

158

Against the Catholic doctrine on Church membership outlined above, our opponents often cite scriptural passages* and statements of the fathers of the Church, particularly St. Augustine, which seem to belie that doctrine. These passages either extol the immaculate sanctity of the Church, or at least seem to exclude sinners, and those whose eventual damnation is foreseen, from Church membership.

About the *scriptural quotations,* one should note that they sometimes view the Church according to its final and perfect mode of existence in heaven (Church Triumphant); or according to its

---

* For example, Eph. 5:25–27: *Husbands, love your wives, just as Christ loved the Church, and delivered himself for her, that he might sanctify her by cleansing her in the bath of water with the accompanying word, in order to present to himself the Church in all her glory, devoid of blemish or wrinkle or anything of the kind, but that she may be holy and flawless.* Other passages cited as objections are: John 10:27–28; Heb. 3:6; (see Salaverri, *op. cit.,* nos. 1083–1086).

earthly mode of existence, indeed, but in that ideal fashion in which it appears only in its holier members.*

The statements of the fathers are in perfect harmony with the Catholic doctrine outlined above, if one keeps in mind that members in the strict sense of the term are not all perfect or exemplary members of the Church.

Members of the Church in the strict sense are those who are bound to the Church by the three bonds of unity: unity of baptism, unity of faith, and hierarchical unity. Still, one must keep in mind that in the traditional usage by both fathers and theologians it has been and still is customary[20] to apply the term "member of the Church" in a *broad* sense to men who fulfill only one or another of the three conditions requisite for membership, or to those who may loosely be dubbed members when considered under some single, special aspect (*membrum secundum quid*). In this broad usage of the term it has been customary to designate the following classes as belonging to the Church in some fashion or other (i.e., at least by *implicit* desire): (1) those who are joined to it by at least the bond of interior, supernatural *faith;* (2) those who are in the *state of grace;* (3) those who are *predestined* to heaven.

Keeping these two facts in mind—the strict meaning of the term "member of the Church," and the custom of also using the term in a wider, loose meaning—we are in a better position to grasp the real meaning of those passages of the fathers which, at first glance, might seem to be at variance with the doctrine outlined above. For example: (*a*) It is customary to say of members belonging to any society that if they fail to exhibit the characteristic spirit of that society or exhibit it very poorly, that they are not "true," "sincere," or "genuine" members of that society. So we might say of an American who has disgraced the United States abroad: "Oh, he

---

* Keep in mind, however, that holiness of members (passive holiness) is only *one* aspect of the multifaceted holiness of the Church. Even during her earthly existence the Church is absolutely holy because of the holiness of her Head and Soul (Christ and the Holy Spirit); she is spotless and holy in her sacraments, in the doctrine she teaches, holy in the sacred laws she promulgates for the entire Church, holy in the evangelical counsels she recommends, holy "in those heavenly gifts and extraordinary graces through which, with inexhaustible fecundity, she generates hosts of martyrs, virgins, and confessors" (MCC 81). In fact we might say it is precisely because she is by nature holy that she can tolerate in her midst, as did Christ, the presence of sinners. It is her exquisite charity, her motherly concern for the feebler children that allows her, unperturbed and unstained, to keep them at her side with but one purpose in mind: to lead them back to the health of holiness (see MCC *loc. cit.*).

is not a *real* American"—not meaning that he has lost his citizenship, but simply that he does not live up to American ideals or standards of behavior. Thus one could speak of Catholics who are lacking in interior faith, or even of those living in a state of sin, as not being members of the Church even though they seem to be—*provided* one understands by such statements: they are not the *kind* of members of the Church they *ought to be*. (*b*) If one considers the actual members of the Church—not from the viewpoint of their present earthly membership in the Mystical Body, but from the *precisive viewpoint* of their eventual fate in the next life—it can be said that those who will eventually be damned are not truly and fully members of the Church, *insofar as* they will not always remain within it and will not arrive with the Church at the goal of heaven for which they were originally conjoined to it.°

That the mind of the fathers should be thus put into proper perspective when examining statements in which they seem to restrict membership in the Church to those who are holy or who will eventually reach heaven is clear from the following statements of Augustine, the one most appealed to by those who subscribe to the notion of an invisible Church:

> Catholics have refuted their [Donatist] calumny about *two* Churches, showing expressly and repeatedly what they have claimed: namely, that the Church which now has bad men in her midst is not something different from the kingdom of God, where there will be no evils, but that one and the same holy Church exists now in one fashion, and in a different fashion in the future; now she has bad people in her midst, then she will have them no longer; just as now she is mortal by the fact of being constituted of mortal men, but then will be immortal because there will then be in her no one about to undergo even corporeal death.—*Breviculus collationis cum Donatistis* iii. 10. 20; cited in Parente, *Theologia fundamentalis, op. cit.,* p. 183.

And finally his definitive viewpoint on this matter is found in his *Retractationes* ii. 18:

> Wherever I have mentioned in these books [*De baptismo contra Donatistas*] that the Church is without stain or wrinkle,

---

° Generally, however, such loose statements should be avoided today: they only generate confusion.

such statements should not be taken to mean that she is already such, but that she is being prepared to be such when she shall appear in her glorious state.[21]

Notes

1. See MCC 84.

2. Parente, *Theologia fundamentalis, op. cit.*, p. 183. Salaverri in presenting this same matter uses a four-part proposition (thesis no. 25) and a variety of labels in making each part more precise (*op. cit.*, IV, 842). He also produces a brief survey of divergent opinions by other theologians: see *ibid.*, no. 1029–32; see also L. Lercher, *Institutiones theologiae dogmaticae*, I (1948), 233, no. 407 ff.

3. See L. Lercher, S.J., *Institutiones theologiae dogmaticae* (5th ed. rev. by F. Schlagenhaufen, S.J.; Innsbruck, 1951), p. 234.

4. See Parente, *loc. cit.*; and Lercher, *loc. cit.*, p. 235, no. 412, scholion 2.

5. Salaverri cites as proponents of this opinion the following theologians: St. Robert Bellarmine, H. Kilber, C. Mazella, A. Straub, Ch. Pesch, L. Lercher; Salaverri's reference to Lercher is to his 1927 edition. In the 1947 edition revised by F. Schlagenhaufen, S.J., this opinion has been deleted and the contrary position is maintained; cf. *loc. cit.*, p. 235, no. 412, scholion 2.

6. Parente calls this a "wandering opinion" (*loc. cit.*, no. 1).

7. Zapalena deals with this passage of the encyclical *ex professo*: (*op. cit.*, pp. 381–383). He admits as a possible solution of the difficulty the fact that the pope may be using the term Mystical Body in the broad sense (p. 383, c). Zapalena's extremely tentative language in broaching this solution is due, we think, to the fact that he has insisted so rigidly on the strict meaning of the concept Mystical Body as being the *unique revealed* concept (p. 384), and criticized so lengthily the views of other theologians who have admitted both a broad and a strict usage of the term as perfectly legitimate; so that to have to admit that the pope himself employs the concept in the broad sense would weaken the whole position he has so laboriously constructed. See his whole treatment of this difficult point, p. 341–88 and 553–74.

8. See Lercher, *loc. cit.*, no. 410 a.

9. Salaverri lists the following theologians as *denying* that occult heretics are members of the Church: Suárez, Billuart, Franzelin, Michelitsch, Stolz, Fraghi, *et alii pauci* (*op. cit.*, I, bk. III, no. 1030 a). For a long list of modern theologians who support St. Robert Bellarmine's opinion that occult heretics *remain* members of the Church see Msgr. Fenton's article, "The Status of St. Robert Bellarmine's Teaching about the Membership of Occult Heretics in the Catholic Church," AER, 122 (1950), p. 215–6. Fenton gives both an excellent analysis of Bellarmine's teaching and a strong defense of the perfect compatibility of that opinion with MCC contrary to the position maintained by Francis Lawlor, S.J. in his article: "Occult Heresy and Membership in the Church," TS, 12 (1949).

10. So Zapalena, *op. cit.*, p. 391.

11. See vol. IX of this series, *Christ's Sacraments*, II, n. 130.

THE MEMBERS OF THE CHURCH

12. It is certain, for example, that that type of excommunication which was used in ancient days to exclude bishops for a time from special association with the rest, ordering them to be content with communion with their own flock, did not strictly (*simpliciter*) cut them off from the Catholic Church (see De Smedt, *Diss. in prim. aetat. hist. eccles.*, [1876], p. 70). And according to the present Code of Canon Law, those who are called *tolerated* excommunicates, so long as there has been no condemnatory or declaratory sentence, seem to remain members of the Church because they retain their jurisdiction and can licitly exercise it when asked to do so by the faithful (CIC, 2261). *Licitly*, that is, considered solely from the viewpoint of their excommunicated status; for if the exercise of their jurisdiction is such that it requires the state of grace, an excommunicate might still perhaps act illicitly from this viewpoint. Furthermore, even without such a request, they can validly exercise certain ecclesiastical actions (see CIC, 2265).

13. So Salaverri, *op. cit.*, no. 1024, p. 837. For a fuller treatment of this whole matter, see *ibid.*, nos. 1049–54.

14. It is interesting to note how often this point is mentioned by converts in sketches of their conversion. See, for example, some of the spiritual biographies in *The Road to Damascus* and *Where I Found Christ* edited by John C. O'Brien.

15. See Lercher, *op. cit.*, I, no. 405, 232.

16. See Ronald Knox's fine presentation of this point in his book, *Enthusiasm*.

17. See *Institutes of the Christian Religion*, IV, c. 1, no. 2–3; *Heidelberg Catechism*, q. 54.

18. See DB 627, 629, 631.

19. Matt. 13:24–30; 47–50; 25:1–12.

20. See, for example, Parente, *Theologia fundamentalis, op. cit.*, p. 182; Salaverri, *op. cit.*, bk. III, no. 998, p. 829 and no. 1063, p. 853; Lercher, *op. cit.*, no. 405, p. 232; and Zapalena, *op. cit.*, II, 342 f. The last named author, by the very length of his exposition on the question of the "coextension of the concepts Mystical Body and Church" (pp. 341–88 and 553–97), gives sufficient witness to the continuity of this customary usage of the terms "Mystical Body" and "member of the Church" in a broad sense, even though he himself vehemently questions its legitimacy.

21. Cited in Lercher, *op. cit.*, I, no. 417, p. 237. The same author gives a succinct summary of the gradual evolution of Augustine's ecclesiology from its rudimentary stage to its mature development, *ibid.*

Article II

NECESSITY OF BELONGING TO THE CHURCH

I. *Preliminary Remarks*

II. *Errors:*
    1. Minimizing the necessity of the Church.
    2. Exaggerating the necessity of the Church.

III. *Terminology:*
    1. Necessity of precept
    2. Necessity of means
    3. Necessity of means may arise from the nature of the case or the positive ordination of God.
    4. Meaning of an implicit desire.

PROPOSITION: By Christ's institution the Roman Catholic Church is necessary for salvation for all men by necessity of means.

Analysis of Proposition

Proof: 1. Church's magisterium
        2. patristic tradition
        3. theological argument

Corollary: Some Union with the Church, at Least in Desire, is Absolutely Necessary for all Men for Salvation.

Scholion 1. "Outside the Church there is no salvation."
Scholion 2. Tolerance.

Article II

NECESSITY OF BELONGING TO THE CHURCH

I. Preliminary Remarks

At this juncture it is customary to inquire: is it necessary, or more precisely, in what sense is it necessary to belong to the Roman Catholic Church in order to be saved? Since the Catholic answer to this question is often caricatured as meaning: "all non-Catholics are automatically damned," it is well to have the precise point at issue clear from the outset. The point here under discussion must not be confused with the question: which men are *actually saved?*[1] For that is God's secret, to be disclosed on the Day of Judgment.* The question here discussed is the Church as a *means* to salvation and the *necessity* of making use of that means.

II. Errors 158a

In discussing the necessity of the Church it is possible to err either by *minimizing*, or by *exaggerating* that necessity.

1. By minimizing. In this category fall all the various shades of opinion favoring religious indifferentism. Those who claim that no revealed religion and no church is necessary for salvation, but simply ethical goodness; those who hold that all churches and all religions equally lead to salvation ("one religion is as good as another"); those who subscribe to the "branch theory" of Christianity (Anglican-Orthodox-Roman). Finally, to be included in this category are those theologians who out of mistaken zeal for the conversion of dissident Christians watered down the doctrine on the necessity of the Church to the point of "reducing it to a meaningless formula," as Pius XII put it.[2]

2. By exaggeration. In this category fall the unfortunate

---

* It should be noted here that the question of "the salvation of infidels" cannot be treated *exclusively* from the viewpoint of ecclesiology. Other tracts of theology discussing "God's salvific will" (vol. IV), "the distribution of actual grace" (vol. VII), "the effects of original sin" (vol. V), etc., would be involved in an adequate treatment.

(255)

Father Feeney[3] and his followers, who hold that only those who are *actually* members of the Roman Catholic Church can be saved, and exclude the possibility of salvation for even those men of good faith neatly dubbed by Msgr. Knox "unconscious Catholics."[4] Knox meant men who, though in invincible ignorance of the unique nature of the Catholic Church, are nonetheless related to it by implicit desire and who, if saved, will be saved because of the Church.[5] To the same category belongs the opinion of Favara, who, apparently misinterpreting St. Augustine, thought that the necessity of belonging to the Roman Catholic Church (at least in desire— *in voto*) extended even to those who lived under the Old Testament dispensation.[6]

159 III. Terminology

In view of the extremes to which one can easily go in discussing the necessity of the Church for salvation, it is of paramount importance, though admittedly wearisome, to make some theological distinctions concerning various types of necessity. Two general types of necessity are distinguished: necessity of *precept* and necessity of *means*.

1. Necessity of precept signifies the type of necessity which arises exclusively from a moral obligation. It is the result of a commandment. It conduces to salvation not so much by positive causal influx as by the removal of obstacles to salvation. If the precept is not observed, serious sin is committed; and sin itself is an obstacle to salvation. Consequently, necessity of precept: (*a*) refers only to adults, since they alone are capable of moral obligations; children and those mentally equivalent to children are not bound by precept; (*b*) ceases just as soon as there is present a cause *excusing* one from a moral obligation so that there is no question of sin; such a cause is blameless ignorance, or the temporary impossibility of fulfilling the commandment. (*c*) The blameless omission of what is necessary by precept does not prevent the attaining of a goal.

2. Necessity of means, signifies that something—abstracting from any question of moral obligation, or sin—is a means requisite for salvation: it is a causal force *positively* leading to salvation in such a way that without that cause salvation simply cannot be attained. So, for example, in the natural order generation is necessary for the beginning of life, food for the maintenance of life.

In the supernatural order priestly power is necessary to consecrate the Eucharist.

Consequently, it follows that: (*a*) the absence of something necessary by necessity of means can prevent the salvation even of babies (i.e., lack of the gift of sanctifying grace); (*b*) salvation does not become automatically assured to a person merely because he is guiltless in failing to use some means requisite for salvation. In the natural order, for example, a lifeboat or a life-preserver is a necessary means to keep afloat if a ship sinks. The mere fact of not being guilty of negligence in securing a life-preserver, or of getting into a lifeboat would not save a man from drowning.

3. A thing may be necessary by necessity of means either by its very nature or by the positive ordinance of God. In the first case there is such an intrinsic relationship between means and end that no substitute can take its place. Such a means is said to be *absolutely* necessary. Such a relationship obtains in the natural order between the human eye and the act of seeing; in the supernatural order between grace and the beatific vision.

Necessity by *positive ordinance* results from an extrinsic bond established between two things by God's fiat: so the sacrament of baptism as a remedy for original sin. Such a means *can have a substitute,* or the means can be supplied for in some other way than its actual use. In the supernatural order baptism of water is a necessary means for the remission of original sin and the reception of sanctifying grace. But a catechumen who is martyred for Christ before he can be baptized has his sins remitted, and receives sanctifying grace by his "baptism of blood."

Such necessary means, set up by God's ordinance, are said to be not absolutely, but *disjunctively*[7] necessary. That is, the means must be employed either *actually* or in *desire* (*in re* or *in voto*). Notice, however, that the external means as actually employed and the substitute for it—the internal desire of making use of the external means—are not two distinct and different means. Rather, they are related to one another as the perfect and imperfect, the full and partial use of one and the same means.[8]

4. Finally, the desire of using some means requisite for salvation signifies the sincere will to make use of the means instituted by God. This act of the will may be *explicit*, as in the case of a martyred catechumen who longed to receive baptism of water but was prevented by his own death; or *implicit*, that is, necessarily interwoven and included in some more extensive act of the will.* So, for example, a pagan who loved God with his whole heart and was innocently ignorant of the necessity of Christian baptism, would implicitly desire baptism by the following act: "I want to use *all* the means that God has prescribed for salvation," or, "I want to do everything that God wants me to do to get to heaven."

From the preceding discussion of terminology it should be clear that anything which is required for salvation by necessity of means is likewise required by precept, either by a positive or, at least, a connatural precept: for whoever obliges a man to reach a goal, by that very fact obliges him to use the means necessary to the goal.

160 PROPOSITION. *By Christ's institution the Roman Catholic Church is necessary for salvation for every man by necessity of means.*

Analysis of Proposition:

This proposition asserts that the Church is necessary for salvation not only by precept, but also *by necessity of means*. Secondly, it asserts that the "necessity of means" spoken of arises not from the very nature of the case, but by the *positive institution* of God. Thirdly, the "necessity of means" spoken of should be understood not absolutely, but *disjunctively;* i.e., the means must be employed either *actually* or at least *in desire*. Finally, the desire of using the means does not have to be *explicit;* it may also be *implicit*.

Theological label for the proposition. That the Church is necessary for salvation by divine precept is a dogma of *divine and Catholic faith;* that the Church is necessary by *necessity of means* is *theologically certain*.[9] The distinctions between necessity of precept and necessity of means are not explicitly stated in the official documents of the Church.[10]

161 *Proof:*

1. *From the Church's Magisterium:* (a) The *professions of faith* used by the Church clearly testify to the necessity of the Church for salvation as a dogma of faith. So the profession of faith proposed to the Waldensians by Innocent III: "We believe in our heart and profess with our lips one Church, not a church of heretics, but the holy, Roman, Catholic, apostolic Church. We

---

* It need hardly be added that such an act of the will must be under the influx of God's grace, since no purely natural act bears any proportion to man's supernatural destiny: the beatific vision.

believe that outside this Church no one is saved" (DB 423; TCT 150).

(*b*) *Ecumenical councils* proclaim clearly the same dogma. The *Fourth Council of the Lateran* (1215) declares: "Indeed, there is but one universal Church of the faithful outside of which no one at all is saved and in which the priest himself, Jesus Christ is the victim" . . . (DB 430; TCT 659). The *Council of Florence** (1438-1445) is even more explicit:

> The holy Roman Church believes, professes, and preaches that "no one remaining outside the Catholic Church, not just pagans, but also Jews or heretics or schismatics, can become partakers of eternal life; but they will go to the 'everlasting fire which was prepared for the devil and his angels' (Matt. 25:41), unless before the end of life they are joined to the Church. For union with the body of the Church is of such importance that the sacraments of the Church are helpful to salvation only for those remaining in it; and fasts, almsgiving, other works of piety, and the exercise of Christian warfare bear eternal rewards for them alone. And no one can be saved, no matter how much alms he has given, even if he sheds his blood for the name of Christ, unless he remains in the bosom and the unity of the Catholic Church."—DB 714; TCT 165.

(*c*) From *papal pronouncements:* Pius IX (1846–78) recapitulates the traditional Catholic teaching on the necessity of the Church in the following lucid statement which precludes any distortion of the Church's doctrine either by minimizing it, or exaggerating it:

> It must, of course, be held as a matter of faith that outside the apostolic, Roman Church no one can be saved, that the Church is the only ark of salvation, and that whoever does not enter it will perish in the flood. On the other hand, it must likewise be held as certain that those who are affected by ignorance of the true religion, if it is invincible ignorance, are not subject to any guilt in this matter before the eyes of the Lord. Now, then, who could presume in himself an ability to set the boundaries of such ignorance, taking into consideration the natural differences of peoples, lands, native talents, and so many other

---

* For a proper interpretation of this statement, see Scholion *below:* "Outside the Church no salvation."

factors? Only when we have been released from the bonds of this body and see God just as he is (*see I John 3:2*) shall we really understand how close and beautiful a bond joins divine mercy with divine justice. But as long as we dwell on earth, encumbered with this soul-dulling, mortal body, let us tenaciously cling to the Catholic doctrine that there is one God, one faith, one baptism (*see Eph. 4:5*). To proceed with further investigation is wrong.—DB 1647; TCT 174.

Similarly Pius XII in his encyclical *Mystici Corporis* emphasizes the necessity of the Church for salvation in his warm, urgent appeal to non-Catholics to return to the Church of Christ:

From a heart overflowing with love We ask each and everyone of them to be quick and ready to follow the interior movements of grace, and to look to *withdrawing from that state in which they cannot be sure of their salvation*. For even though unsuspectingly they are related to the Mystical Body of the Redeemer in desire and resolution, they still remain deprived of so many precious gifts and helps from Heaven, which one can only enjoy in the Catholic Church. May they then enter into Catholic Unity, and united with us in the organic oneness of the Body of Jesus Christ may they hasten to the one Head in the society of glorious love. With persevering prayer to the Spirit of love and truth We wait for them with open arms to return not to a stranger's house, but to their own, their Father's house.—121; italics ours.

The words of Pius IX cannot possibly be understood as meaning merely necessity of precept; he clearly brings this out by the comparison with Noah's ark, which last was surely a necessary *means* for escaping the flood. The pope's teaching implies a real necessity of means, but not absolute necessity, since he admits an exception in the case of those who labor under unconquerable ignorance. And the same exception shows that the passage must necessarily be understood as referring to actual membership in the visible Church. Similarly the words of Pius XII clearly signify necessity of means and refer to actual membership in the Church. If non-Catholics are begged to withdraw from that state in which they cannot be sure of their salvation it is because the Church is a necessary means to salvation, and remaining outside it, they are "deprived of so many precious gifts and helps from Heaven which can be enjoyed only in the Catholic Church." Still, the necessity of means alluded to should be interpreted not absolutely, but disjunctively (it is necessary to be joined to the Church *in fact* or at least *in desire*), since the pope admits such non-Catholics may be unwittingly joined to the Church by some more generic act of the will even though they verbally deny any such affiliation: "For even though *unsuspectingly* they are related to the Mystical Body of the Redeemer *in desire and resolution*. . . . "

2. *Patristic testimony:* From the very earliest days of the Church, sacred tradition shows a clear-cut view of the Church as a religious society outside of which no one can be saved. This truth is enunciated in a threefold way: (*a*) in the axiom: "Outside the Church there is no salvation"; (*b*) in the metaphor of the ark of Noah outside which no one is saved; (*c*) in the figure of the Church as a mother without whom no one can receive life. Here are a few citations of many others which could be adduced:

161a

Ignatius Martyr: "Do not be deceived, my brethren: if anyone runs after a schismatic, he will not inherit the Kingdom of God" (*Epistula ad Philadelphenses* 3. 3).

Irenaeus: "Those who are outside the Church, are outside the truth. . . . Those who cause schisms are fools who do not have the love of God" (*Adversus haereses* iv. 33. 7).

Cyprian: "You cannot have God for your Father if you have not the Church for your mother. If there was escape for anyone who was outside the ark of Noe, there is escape too for one who is found to be outside the Church" (*De unitate ecclesiae* 6; ACW trans.).

Lactantius: "The Catholic Church alone possesses the true religion. Here is the fountain of truth, here the household of faith, here the temple of God, into which if one does not enter, or if he departs from it, he is excluded from the hope of eternal life and salvation" (*Divinae institutiones* iv. 30. 11).

Augustine, commenting on Cyprian's words cited above, observes:

> Let us love the Lord our God, let us love His Church; He as a Father, she as a Mother; He as our Lord, she as His bride, for we are the children of that bride. But this marriage is accompanied by immense love. No one can offend the one and please the other. Let no one say, "Yes, I go idol-worshipping and con-

sult fortunetellers, but I do not quit the Church of God. I am a Catholic." Holding on to the Mother, you have insulted the Father. Neither let someone else say, "Heaven forbid that I should consult fortunetellers, or go in for sacrilegious divinations, or adore demons; but I admit that I am partly a Donatist." What good does it do you not to offend the Father, if you insult the Mother? What good is it if you confess the Lord, you honor God, you even preach God, acknowledge His Son and confess Him to sit at the right hand of the Father when you blaspheme His Church?

You ought to be able to learn these truths even from the example of human marriage. If you had a famous employer for whom you worked daily, whose portals you crossed, and before whom you—I do not say saluted, but prostrated—and to whom you showed constantly the deepest reverence, and you were to prattle just *one* misdeed of his wife; would you dare enter his home again? Cling therefore, dearly beloved, cling completely to both God, your Father, and to your Mother, the Church.—*Enarrationes in psalmos* 88. 2. 14.

Still, even though the fathers of the Church insist on the necessity of the Church as a means to salvation, it is also clear from their writings that the necessity spoken of is to be taken not absolutely, but disjunctively. On the one hand, all the fathers vehemently teach that the Church alone leads to salvation; nonetheless they admit that not all those who are actually outside the Church's membership are necessarily damned. Let St. Augustine act as a witness for both points. Speaking of the necessity of the Church for salvation, he says, "No one arrives at salvation and life eternal unless he has Christ for his Head. But no one can have Christ for his Head, unless he be in Christ's body which is the Church" ([?] *De unitate ecclesiae* 19. 49).

Still, Augustine does not exclude the possibility of salvation for those who are not actually members of the Church for, (*a*) speaking of *catechumens* who die in charity before they have received baptism, he says: "For then is fulfilled invisibly [the effect of baptism] when it is not contempt of religion, but the necessity of death that prevented its actual administration" (*De baptismo* iv. 22. 9). (*b*) Speaking of *heretics* who are innocently in error, he says:

Those who defend their own doctrine, without stubborn bitterness, no matter how perverse or false that doctrine may be, and particularly if they have not given rise to that doctrine because of any outrageous presumption, but have simply received it from parents who were seduced and fell into error, and provided they are in search of truth with prudent inquiry, and are prepared to relinquish their errors should they discover the truth, should in no wise be rated as [formal] heretics.—*Epistula* 43 (162). 1.

(*c*) Finally, Augustine constantly teaches that in addition to the public road which leads to salvation, there are also hidden and extraordinary paths: "Since Divine Providence does not simply take care of individual men in private fashion as it were, but takes care of the entire human race—you might say—in public fashion, what He does for individuals, the God who does it and they for whom it is done alone know; but what He does for the entire human race, He willed to make known by history and revelation" (*De vera religione* 25. 47).*

3. *Theological argument.* That the Church is necessary for salvation by necessity of means in the sense previously described can be argued theologically in this way:

Christ conferred on His Church alone all the means which lead to salvation. For Christ decreed and ordained that it was through the ministry of His Church alone that all men should receive that *faith* without which *it is impossible to please God;* and the *sacraments* "through which all real holiness either begins, or having been begun is increased, or having been lost, is restored;"[11] and, finally, the *instruction* which is necessary to attain holiness in this life.

But if union with the Church is the only way to share in all the means designed for salvation, this union itself is necessary by necessity of means. But then arises the question: Is this necessity absolute or not? At this point we presuppose what we shall prove in another place, and what God's own justice evidently requires anyhow: namely, that men who are in invincible ignorance of the true Church of Christ, but are seeking God with their whole heart,

---

* This metaphor of the "public road" (the Church) and the "private paths" should not be pushed in its figurative expression as though it meant these "private paths" are other "churches" inferior to the Catholic Church but sufficient for salvation. If that were Augustine's meaning he would not have had to refer us to the inscrutable mysteries of Divine Providence. His problem would have been solved.

will not incur eternal damnation. But if these two facts are simultaneously true: that the Church is necessary by necessity *of means* for salvation, and yet, some men purely by accident can obtain salvation without actually becoming members of the Church, the consequence is that the Church is a means necessary for salvation not absolutely, but disjunctively: one must be joined to the Church if not in fact, at least in desire.

That the Church is necessary for salvation by necessity of precept needs no laboring; it is clear from the words of Christ Himself: *"Preach the gospel to all creation; he that believes and is baptized will be saved; he that does not believe will be condemned"* (Mark 16:15–16). And, *"But should the people not make you welcome and not listen to your preaching, leave that house or town, and shake the dust off your feet. I tell you the plain truth: on Judgment Day it will go less hard with Sodom and Gomorrha than with that town"* (Matt. 10:14–15). And *"I am telling you the plain truth: unless a man is born of water and the Spirit, he cannot enter the kingdom of God"* (John 3:5; conjoin with I Cor. 12:13).

162 Corollary

Some union with the Church, at least in desire, is absolutely necessary for all men for salvation.

Although this point has recurred constantly in the demonstration of the Church's necessity, it has done so incidentally. Here it will receive explicit discussion. "Union in desire" means simply the sincere desire or will of actually entering the Church. This desire may be either explicit or implicit. An implicit desire of entering the Church is included in the determination to do *all* that God has commanded. The corollary states that a spiritual union or relationship with the Church (as opposed to actual membership), by at least the implicit desire of joining its ranks, is absolutely necessary for those who without fault of their own are actually wandering around outside the Church. There is only one exception to this principle, namely, for nonbaptized children who die by martyrdom. But this is an altogether singular privilege which will be discussed when we take up the sacrament of baptism.

The truth of the corollary flows from two facts which are demonstrated in other tracts of theology. The *first* fact is that absolutely no one is saved unless he dies in the state of sanctifying grace. The *second* fact is that no one (with the exception mentioned above) who is actually outside the Church receives the gift of sanctifying grace unless he has elicited such acts as necessarily include the desire of entering the Church.

Scholion 1. "Outside the Church there is no salvation."

From the matter previously discussed, it should be relatively easy both to explain and to defend that slogan—often misunderstood and bitterly complained against by non-Catholics—which the fathers of the Church and the Church itself take as an axiom: "outside the Roman Catholic Church there is no salvation." The axiom should be strictly understood as referring to actual union with the visible Church; but its full and correct meaning is: anyone who *by his own fault* lives and dies outside the Church will definitely be damned. That the axiom is understood by the Church only with that qualification is obvious from its clear teaching that no one will go to hell without serious guilt on his part.

We all know that those who are afflicted with invincible ignorance with regard to our holy religion, if they carefully keep the precepts of the natural law that have been written by God in the hearts of all men, if they are prepared to obey God, and if they lead a virtuous and dutiful life, can attain eternal life, by the power of divine light and grace. For God, who reads comprehensively in every detail the minds and souls, the thoughts and habits of all men, will not permit, in accordance with his infinite goodness and mercy, anyone who is not guilty of voluntary fault to suffer eternal punishment.—Piux IX, *Quanto conficiamur mœrore* (1863); DB 1677; TCT 178.*

* The condemnation of proposition 17 in the *Syllabus of Errors* (Dec. 8, 1864): "There is good reason at least to hope for the eternal salvation of all those who are in no way in the true Church of Christ" (DB 1717; TCT 187) —might seem, on casual reading, to contradict the teaching given above. But an inspection of the context of that condemnation (see DB 1647 and 1677; TCT 174 and 178) clearly shows there is no contradiction. Proposition 17 was condemned because and precisely insofar as it favors religious indifferentism. For enunciated in such universal and unqualified fashion it implies that any religion at all leads equally to salvation. See Heiner, *Der Syllabus*, p. 96; C. Romein, *Extra ecclesiam nulla salus, secundum doctrinam s. Augustini* (1908, *Forschungen*, VIII, 4); P. Lippert, "Die alleinseligmachende Kirche," *Stimmen*, 84 (1913), 1.

Finally, since no man can presume to set the boundaries of invincible ignorance (Pius IX, see DB 1647; TCT 174 cited above), no man can declare peremptorily that this or that individual, who apparently died outside the Church, is saved or damned. And no one can state confidently whether

Why, then, do we not usually add explicitly the words: "by his own fault," and thus avoid unnecessary confusion? For two reasons. *First*, because the axiom is a penal sentence, and the notion of penalty by its very nature presupposes guilt. *Secondly*, because the axiom helps to inculcate the truth that by the ordinary decrees of God's providence only the Church can lead one to salvation and consequently that anyone who is outside the Church, no matter how he got there, is there where salvation is *per se* unobtainable. *Finally*, Christ Himself did not speak in any less brusque fashion, for He did not use any expressed qualification when He stated: "*He who does not believe will be condemned*" (Mark 16:16; see Matt. 10:14-15).

So much for the exact meaning of the axiom we have been discussing. Now if one seeks not the historical usage and meaning of the axiom, but the Catholic truth about the necessity of the Church for salvation, there is nothing to prevent one's explaining the axiom in this manner: no one is saved who *in nowise whatsoever* belongs to the Catholic Church, i.e., who is not related to the visible Church by even an implicit desire.

164 *Scholion 2. Tolerance.*

Because the Catholic Church, in view of the doctrine contained in this article, is constantly accused of being intolerant, we should note a few points about tolerance in the sphere of religion.

Etymologically the word *tolerate* means not to repress, or to bear patiently with something which we know is evil. Whether bearing with an evil is something virtuous or vicious depends on the circumstances of the case and the motive of the person practicing tolerance. But apart from its etymological meaning, the term tolerance has often been used in modern times to signify a broad-minded, benevolent view of all religions, however erratic they may be, and a kindly attitude to all their members.

Apart from these preliminary notions, it has been customary in theological manuals to distinguish three types of tolerance: *dogmatic*, *political*, and *individual*.

---

the number saved, of those who factually die without being members of the Church, is large or small. Notice this one point: from the fact that salvation without actual membership is achieved only by way of exception (*per accidens*), it does not directly follow that salvation is obtained in this manner only *rarely*.

a. Dogmatic tolerance* is that type by which a man professes that the various Christian religions—and, in fact, all the religions—are equally good or equally bad. This conception which masquerades under the pleasant name of tolerance is nothing other than *religious indifferentism* and is proscribed and condemned by the Catholic Church. Really, it is a fatuous viewpoint as one non-Catholic theologian has acutely observed: [12]

> What "religious" tolerance means is often misunderstood both by professedly Christian people and, equally important, by disbelievers and the indifferent. Tolerance does not consist of an eager assertion that religion and unreligion are all of a piece or that one religion is as good as another: that snake worship in the backwoods of Kentucky is as noble as what goes on at the Riverside Church under Dr. Fosdick; that voodoo incantations are as intelligent as that which is taught at the Catholic University in Washington or at Andover Newton Theological School; that there is no difference, really, between casting one's babies into the fire before Moloch, on the one hand, and the Sacrifice of the Mass or the Friends Meeting on the other; that every form of Christianity is equally reverent, perceptive, and moving; that you pay your money and nonchalantly take your choice and it makes no difference whatever.
>
> To say such things is not to be tolerant but to talk nonsense. Tolerance means, rather, a willingness to let any man have cult, creed, and code that are different from one's own until one can persuade the man that one's own are better. . . .

b. Political tolerance means that the civil authority in a Catholic country may grant public liberty of worship and equal political rights to the adherents of false religions as well as to Catholics. Such tolerance, in circumstances such as are found in many countries today, is not only licit but it can even be necessary. This point will be discussed at length in the chapter: "Church and State."

c. Individual tolerance means that acting as individual men

---

* Some recent theologians feel that the commonly used phrase "dogmatic tolerance" is an unhappy choice of terminology because it is literary coinage belonging strictly to the philosophy of religious indifferentism. "One is then in the position of borrowing the language of relativist tolerance, outside of which the expression makes no sense" (Albert Hartmann, S.J., *Toleranz und Christlicher Glaube* [1955] p. 65; see RSR [1955], p. 629). Briefly, one cannot speak accurately of truth as such being "intolerant." Truth as such simply asserts itself for what it is: universal and exclusive of error.

we should sincerely fulfill our duties of justice, fairness, and charity towards our non-Catholic brothers. This type of tolerance should really be described as fraternal charity; it is not only licit, but strictly obligatory.

Generally speaking, the Catholic Church is animated by a loving zeal to spread the true faith everywhere and, once it has been planted, to preserve it in its integrity. But the Church never commands or approves that in spreading or conserving the faith its children should indulge in dishonest or imprudent tactics. It condemns and strenuously combats errors, but those who are in error are followed with maternal love in accord with that saying of St. Augustine: "Hate only sin; love sinners" (*Sermo* 49[232]. 7).

Experience itself usually testifies that Catholic men in their normal daily life do not usually hate or consider their non-Catholic fellow citizens to be of little value, or worthless. Contrariwise, it is not an unusual thing to find that men who are forever talking and writing about tolerance, and proclaiming it as the epitome of virtue, are frequently infected with religious indifference or animated by an implacable hatred towards the Catholic Church. One has only to glance through the history of nineteenth-century Continental "Liberalism" to see that the noble name of liberalism was often used as a mask for an antireligious crusade.

Notes

1. Zapalena, *op. cit.*, II, 309.
2. *Humani generis,* 27 (NCWC translation); for "false eirenism" see 11–12 and 43.
3. See the letter of the Holy Office (August 8, 1949), to Archbishop Cushing of Boston. The Latin text, *Haec suprema* is given in AER, 128 (1952); English translation in TCT 266–80.
4. *In Soft Garments,* chap. 13, "The Unconscious Catholic," p. 110–19. A number of statements in this essay are loosely formulated. So, for example, in describing the plight of those who in invincible ignorance have joined heretical sects, Knox concludes: "That means there are quantities and quantities of people who, as far as we can determine, are already members of the Mystical Body of Christ without knowing it" (p. 114). Such people may be *related* to the Mystical Body; they are definitely not *members* of it.

Still, one should not carp on the subject. Msgr. Knox wrote this essay many years prior to *Mystici Corporis* and was attempting a popular exposition of a knotty problem to undergraduates, not a theological disquisition. If one were obliged to write popular apologetics in the style of a theology textbook, few people would write them; no one would read them.

THE MEMBERS OF THE CHURCH

5. As Karl Adam observes:

[The Roman Catholic Church] alone is the Body of Christ and without her there is no salvation. Objectively and practically considered she is the ordinary way of salvation, the single and exclusive channel by which the truth and grace of God enter our world of space and time. But those who know her not receive these gifts from her; yes, even those who misjudge and fight against her, provided they are in good faith, and are simply and loyally seeking the truth without self-righteous obstinacy. Though it be not the Catholic Church itself which hands them the bread of truth and grace, yet it is Catholic bread that they eat.—*The Spirit of Catholicism* (New York, 1954), p. 185.

See Cardinal Billot's development of this same point, *De ecclesia Christi* (5th ed.; 1927), p. 121.

6. This opinion is cited and rebutted in Zapalena, *op. cit.*, II, 325-6.

7. See Salaverri, *op. cit.*, I, bk. III, no. 1091.

8. Lercher, *op. cit.*, I, 247-8.

9. See *ibid., loc. cit.;* Parente, *Theologia fundamentalis, op. cit.*, p. 142; Salaverri, *op. cit.*, no. 1095, p. 864. Zapalena, for his part, suggests that the doctrine of the Church's necessity by a necessity of means is not only theologically certain, but implicitly defined: *op. cit.*, II, 311.

10. Lercher, *op. cit.*, no. 432; Salaverri, *op. cit.*, no. 1095.

11. DB 843a.

12. Dr. Bell, canon of the Episcopalian cathedral of SS. Peter and Paul, Chicago, as cited in J. Cavanaugh, *Evidence for Our Faith* (Notre Dame, Ind., 1952), p. 316.

CHAPTER III

The Roman Pontiff

Article I

PRELIMINARY POINTS

I. *The Connection of Papal Primacy with the See of Rome*

   Corollary: The imperishability of the Roman See.

II. *The Origin of Jurisdiction in Individual Roman Pontiffs*

CHAPTER III

The Roman Pontiff

The first section of this book demonstrated that the Roman pontiff, the successor of St. Peter, by Christ's own decree possesses a primacy of jurisdiction over the entire Church. The *nature of this primacy* must now be examined in detail, and also the prerogative of *papal infallibility* which is included in that primacy. But prior to those lengthy questions, two preliminary points connected therewith need a brief discussion:
1. The *connection* of the primacy with the See of Rome.
2. The *origin* of jurisdiction in the individual Roman pontiffs.

Article I

PRELIMINARY POINTS

I. The Connection of the Primacy with the See of Rome[1]   **165**

It was stated above that the primacy over the universal Church is factually bound up with the episcopal see of the city of Rome (see no. 61). It was also stated that the proximate cause of this connection was *the fact of Peter:* (i.e., the historical fact that St. Peter went to Rome, assumed the episcopal chair of that Church, and remained its bishop until his death (see no. 62). Two speculative questions arise at this point: First, was St. Peter's choice the sole and total cause of the connection between the primacy and the see of Rome? Second, could this connection at some time be severed, or is it indissoluble? We shall begin with the second question.

1. *Could the primacy be severed from the See of Rome* so that, for example, it might be transferred to another see like Lyons or New York, or even continue to exist without being bound up with any particular see whatsoever? In dealing with this question note the following points:

a. This is not a question of *residence*. The Roman pontiff does not cease to be the bishop of Rome merely by the fact of living elsewhere, as for example occurred under the various pontiffs who lived for 70 years at Avignon.

b. The possibility of such a severance cannot be denied on the *sole* score of the *fact of Peter* considered in itself. For when Peter left Antioch to come to Rome, he transferred the primacy from one see to the other; and whatever Peter the first pontiff could do in his own person, Peter can also do as living in his successors, unless from *some other source* there is a reason which makes such a transfer impossible.

Now first of all it is *certain* that no secular power, and no ecclesiastical power inferior to the sovereign pontiff can effect such a separation of the primacy from the see of Rome. For that is what was meant by the condemnation of proposition no. 35 contained in the *Syllabus:* "There is nothing to prevent the supreme pontificate from being transferred from the Roman bishop and the city of Rome to another bishop and another city by the general decision of some *council,* or by the decision of all the *people*" (DB 1735).

Secondly, the *most probable* opinion holds that not even the pope himself, nor an ecumenical council together with the pope, could effect such a separation, but that the connection of the primacy with the see of Rome is absolutely indissoluble. This matter has never been defined, but the tone of the language employed by both popes and councils in reference to it strongly implies this indissolubility; furthermore, it is far and away the more common teaching of theologians. Finally, it is the staunch conviction of the faithful, to whom the idea of the Church of Christ becoming at same future date, say the Lyonnaise-Catholic Church, appears unthinkable.

2. *Is the connection between the primacy and the see of Rome the result of ecclesiastical or divine law?* In addition to that handful of theologians who in the past held that the primacy was "separable" from the Roman see, some theologians who stoutly defend its inseparability nonetheless maintain that the connection between the two is only by *ecclesiastical* law. Such theologians maintain that a separation of the primacy from the see of Rome, in all situations that one might conjure up, would be extremely harmful to the Church; and that actually God by His assistance

would prevent any pope or council from ever making such a change as would cause serious harm to the Church.

But the *more common** opinion holds that the connection between the primacy and the see of Rome does not stem merely from the bare will of Peter and the fact of Peter insofar as he was acting simply as the first pope; rather it holds that in some way or other this setup is by *divine decree*. It holds that either Christ or the Holy Spirit positively indicated that the primacy should be perpetually conjoined with the see of Rome (by divine law *antecedent* to the fact of Peter); or that it was divinely decreed that whichever see Peter should factually select would thenceforth have to be kept as a perpetual condition for succession in the primacy (by divine law *consequent* to the fact of Peter). However one explains the matter, the opinion which holds that the connection stems from divine law, seems both to account more satisfactorily for the factual indissolubility and perhaps to be a bit more plausible from the viewpoint of the tone of the language employed by both councils and popes. Strictly, however, no coercive argument can be drawn in favor of any of these three Catholic opinions from the language of the Church, since the Vatican Council deliberately refused to settle the question.[2] In this whole difficult question, as Salaverri wisely observes, two extremes should be avoided:

1. one should not too readily grant to the *see of Rome* privileges by divine law which might perchance overly restrict the very power granted by divine law to the *supreme pontiff* as the formal successor of St. Peter in the primacy;
2. one should not unthinkingly concede that the supreme pontiff has the power to separate the primacy from the see of Rome, since the ancient, constant, and unanimous tradition of the Church seems to proclaim their inseparability.—Salaverri, *loc. cit.*, p. 635.

---

* A third opinion, mediating between these two holds that a Roman pontiff succeeds Peter to the primacy by divine law, but to the Roman chair by ecclesiastical law and, consequently, that occupying the episcopal chair of Rome is only a *condition* for succession by divine right to the primacy. From the fact of Peter, these theologians infer that the primacy and the Roman episcopacy *have become absolutely inseparable.*—Salaverri, *loc. cit.*, p. 634. This opinion is classified by Zapalena as more common among recent authors (*loc. cit.*, note no. 35). For a fuller discussion of this whole matter, see Salaverri, *loc. cit.*, nos. 439–458.

Corollary. The imperishability of the Roman See

The above teaching on the complete inseparability of the primacy from the see of Rome involves the *imperishability* of that episcopal see and consequently of the *Roman Church*. Be sure, however, not to confuse the city of Rome taken in a purely physical sense with the Roman Church itself, i.e., the faithful of that region united with their bishop. The imperishability of the Roman Church, then, means simply this one thing: God will see to it that there will never be completely lacking in or from * that region a group of the faithful united to their bishop.

167 II. The Origin of Jurisdiction in Individual Roman Pontiffs

The point at issue is: *from whom* do the individual Roman pontiffs, the successors of St. Peter, receive their power of jurisdiction? We say "power of jurisdiction," because their power of orders, like that of other bishops, is conferred upon them by sacred ordination. In answering this question it is necessary to distinguish between the choice of a person for the papal office and the bestowal of power upon that person.

The *choice of a person* is made by the Church. Since Christ willed the primacy to endure forever, and yet He Himself does not personally handpick and indicate by name which man is to be pope, it follows that He left this task to be performed by the Church. Similarly He left to the Church's discretion the particular manner in which the selection of the candidate was to be made.

The *bestowal of power*, however, is not made by the electors, nor in any way by the Church. The bestowal of power is made by God alone. Earlier in this book we exposed and rejected the error of those who taught that the fulness of sacred power was originally and radically conferred on either the Church as a whole, or on the college of bishops (see no. 44); it was conferred on Peter alone. It follows, then, that when any individual pope dies no one in the Church possesses that power of the primacy and, consequently, no one can bestow that power upon the person legitimately chosen

---

* We add the alternative preposition *from* because it does not seem inconceivable in this nuclear age that hydrogen bombs might some day so lay waste to Rome and its surrounding territory that it would be impossible for the faithful of the Roman Church to dwell *in* that region. Even in such an hypothesis, if the bishop of Rome and a remnant of his flock were living in exile in London or New York, the Roman Church would still be in existence despite the obliteration of its familiar physical landmarks.

to be the new pope. Finally, it is quite connatural that the man who is constituted Christ's vicar should receive his power directly from Christ Himself.

Do not, however, misconstrue the matter in such fashion as to imagine that in each individual election of a pope there must occur a new bestowal of power. For that ancient bestowal of power by which Peter originally received the primacy that was destined to endure through the ages, always has its effect, always, as it were, comes to life again as soon as anyone is legitimately chosen to succeed Peter. That is why the Vatican Council teaches that to the Roman pontiff: *"in the person of St. Peter* was given *by Our Lord Jesus Christ* the full power of feeding, ruling, and governing the whole Church" (DB 1826; TCT 206; italics ours).

Notes

1. On this matter see the following authors: De Groot, *op. cit.*, q. 14, art. 5; Franzelin, *op. cit.*, thesis 12; Granderath, *Constitutiones dogmaticae Conciliae Vaticanae explicatae*, p. 137; Palmieri, *De Romano pontifice* (2nd ed.), p. 409; *Der Apostolische Stuhl und Rom* (1895). For more recent treatments, see: Lercher, *op. cit.*, I, 210–2; Salaverri, *op. cit.*, vol. I, bk. III, p. 633–5; Zapalena, *op. cit.*, I, 385–7.

2. See Salaverri, *loc. cit.*, nos. 443–4.

Article II

THE NATURE OF THE ROMAN PONTIFF'S PRIMACY

I. *The Catholic Dogma on the Nature and Power of the Primacy*

II. *The Power of the Supreme Pontiff*
    Assertion 1. The power enjoyed by the supreme pontiff is a real jurisdiction.

III. *The Jurisdiction of the Supreme Pontiff*
    Assertion 2. His jurisdiction is universal
    Assertion 3. His jurisdiction is ordinary
    Assertion 4. His jurisdiction is direct and episcopal
    Assertion 5. His jurisdiction is supreme
    Assertion 6. His jurisdiction is absolutely complete in itself

IV. *Conclusions*
    Objections

Article II

THE NATURE OF THE ROMAN PONTIFF'S PRIMACY

I. The Catholic Dogma on the Nature and Power of the Primacy

A generic notion of the primacy was given above when its existence was proved (see nos. 44–50). There it was defined briefly as: "the full and supreme power of teaching and ruling the universal Church." The exact nature of that primacy and the extent of its power must now be described more in detail. Our opponents in this matter are those who, while admitting along with us some sort of primacy established by divine law, pervert the notion of that primacy and diminish its rights and power. All such people may be classified under the generic label of *Gallicans* (see no. 43).

The *Catholic dogma* on the nature and power of the primacy was defined by the Vatican Council in these words:

> If anyone says that the Roman Pontiff has only the office of inspection or direction, but not the full and supreme power of jurisdiction over the whole Church, not only in matters that pertain to faith and morals, but also in matters that pertain to the discipline and government of the Church throughout the whole world; or if anyone says that he has only a more important part and not the complete fullness of this supreme power; or if anyone says that this power is not ordinary and immediate either over each and every church or over each and every shepherd and faithful member: let him be anathema.–DB 1831; TCT 211.

We shall *explain* this doctrine of the Vatican Council through a series of distinct assertions. *Dogmatic* proof of the doctrine is the council's own proclamation; *apologetic* proof of this can easily be found by referring to the arguments already given at length in proving the existence of the primacy of St. Peter (see nos. 44–56), and in proving the continuation of that primacy in the Roman pontiffs (see nos. 61–68). There is no need to repeat those arguments here.

II. The Power of the Supreme Pontiff

169 *Assertion 1. The power enjoyed by the supreme pontiff is a real jurisdiction.*

It is a real binding authority which demands as its correlative effect a duty, not simply of reverence, but of obedience in the strict sense of the term. The primacy, then, is worlds apart from any mere function of a presiding officer over his associates or confreres. Such an officer is merely an equal among equals and has primacy over the others only insofar as he directs the order to be followed in debating, voting, etc. Neither is the primacy of the pope simply an office of *direction,* for the notion of direction connotes counsel and persuasion rather than the exercise of genuine authority.

III. The Jurisdiction of the Supreme Pontiff

Assertion 2. The jurisdiction of the supreme pontiff is universal.

It is universal both in regard to *place* and to the *business* involved. It is universal in regard to place because it extends to all the churches spread throughout the entire world; in regard to the business involved, because it extends not only to matters of faith and morals (the ecclesiastical magisterium) but also to the discipline and government (rule–*imperium*) of the entire Church. Finally, it is universal in regard to *persons,* because no Christian is exempt from it.

Assertion 3. The jurisdiction of the supreme pontiff is ordinary.

In other words, the pope always possesses this jurisdiction in virtue of his office and can exercise it at any time. This assertion rules out the opinion of those who thought that the pope could act in dioceses outside of Rome *only in very special circumstances,* say for example, when great disturbances occurred in a given diocese, or when lesser prelates had not yet been appointed to their office and so forth.

170 *Assertion 4. The jurisdiction of the supreme pontiff is direct and episcopal.*

Thus, the pope can act not only upon the bishops and through them indirectly upon the faithful committed to their care, but he can exercise his own authority directly upon the individual flocks and individual members of those flocks without the mediation of their bishop. The pope himself is a true bishop, i.e., shepherd, teacher, ruler, and the proper bishop of all the faithful. Consequently, the power of the pope—the *use* of that power in daily affairs is quite another matter—extends just as much to the faithful of the whole world as it does to the faithful of the diocese of Rome.

As a result, the primacy of the supreme pontiff is not merely a primacy of *inspection*. A person who enjoys prime authority merely by right of inspection, does not himself by his own power directly rule a society; he simply watches over it. He watches to see that laws laid down for ruling that society are correctly observed and so forth. If, for example, a committee from the United Nations were granted the right to inspect atomic installations in various countries and to report its findings to the United Nations, it would not thereby possess any right to rule the countries where it carried out its work of inspection. Finally, it should be clear from this assertion, that the primacy is altogether different from the office of an archbishop or patriarch: they do not possess direct and episcopal power over the flocks of their suffragan bishops.

Because the Roman pontiff enjoys direct pastoral authority over the entire Church, he is sometimes called: *the bishop of the Catholic Church.*[1] And because not only lay people, or simple priests, but even the bishops themselves are subject to his power, the pope can also be called: *the bishop of bishops.*

Assertion 5. *The jurisdiction of the sovereign pontiff is supreme.*

There cannot be found in any other person or persons, taken singly or collectively, a power that is greater or even equal to his. This assertion states, then, that the power of the supreme pontiff is greater than:

    a. the power of any individual bishop or patriarch;

    b. the power of the whole college of bishops taken collectively (without the pope).

Assertion 6. *The jurisdiction of the supreme pontiff is absolutely complete in itself (per se plena).*

The supreme pontiff possesses in himself alone the plenitude of supreme power, and not merely the *major* portion of that power. For if the plenitude of sacred power were to reside in the college of bishops (including the pope) in such fashion that the pope had more power than the rest of the bishops, even considered collectively, he would still possess only the *largest* share of that power; but he would not strictly possess the total power without any restriction. In that hypothesis, the power of the Roman pontiff could still be called "supreme," but it would not be *absolutely complete in itself*. It is true that in the aforesaid hypothesis no individual bishop, and no collection of bishops (exclusive of the pope) would have power equal to the pope; but the power of the pontiff would not be absolutely complete in itself. As a matter of fact, however, the supreme pontiff, alone and without the consent of the bishops or of the Church, can do anything that pertains to the jurisdictional powers of the Church. That is why this fourth article of the *Declaration of the Gallican Clergy* was condemned: "In matters of faith the supreme pontiff has the principle share and his decrees pertain to all and each of the Churches, but his judgment is not irreformable unless it receives the consent of the Church" (DB 1325).

171 ## IV. Necessary Conclusions

From the doctrine outlined above it should be clear that the jurisdiction of the supreme pontiff has no other limits than those laid down by divine law, or which the nature and goal of the Church—a spiritual kingdom—imply. The pope consequently can:

1. Dispatch ambassadors to all parts of the Church, reserve certain cases to himself, summon or transfer any ecclesiastical case whatsoever to his own tribunal, and receive appeals and recourse in any case whatsoever and from any and all tribunals.

2. The pope is not bound by customs or by ecclesiastical laws laid down in any way whatsoever. Thus the third article of the *Declaration of the Gallican Clergy* was rightly condemned: "The use of the apostolic power must be restrained by the canons, for they have been founded by the Spirit of God and consecrated by the reverence of the entire world. . . . " (DB 1325).

3. The pope is superior to any general council (of all the bishops *without* the pope) and is not inferior even to an ecumenical council (all the bishops *together with* the pope). That is why the second article of the *Declaration of the Gallican Clergy* was condemned (see DB 1323). With good reason, then, did the Vatican Council state:

> We declare that the judgment of the Apostolic See, whose authority is unsurpassed, is not subject to review by anyone; nor is anyone allowed to pass judgment on its decision. There-

fore, those who say that it is permitted to appeal to an ecumenical council from the decisions of the Roman Pontiff (as to an authority superior to the Roman Pontiff) are far from the straight path of truth.—DB 1830; TCT 210.

Finally, from the doctrine outlined above, one should not leap to the absurd conclusion that all things are licit to the pope; or that he may turn things topsy-turvy in the Church at mere whim. Possession of power is one thing; a rightful use of power quite another. The supreme pontiff has received his power for the sake of building up the Church, not tearing it down. In exercising his supreme power he is by divine law strictly bound by the laws of justice, equity, and prudence. These laws require that unless necessity or great utility urge the contrary, the pope should, for example, respect the legitimate customs obtaining in various places, observe prescribed ecclesiastical laws, etc. These laws, even though they do not possess a binding power for the pope, do nonetheless normally have for him a directive power. They also demand that in normal circumstances the pope should leave the full running of dioceses to their individual bishops in accord with the advice given by St. Bernard to Pope Eugene III:

> What could be more unworthy of you than if, while possessing the whole, you should not be content with the whole unless you also busied yourself feverishly with even the small portions and minutiae of the entire business committed to your care, as though they were not really yours and you were still struggling, heaven alone knows how, to make them really yours. . . . You are wrong if you think that your supreme apostolic power, set up by God Himself, is also the *only* power set up by Him.—*De consideratione*, III, c. 4, n. 15–17.

It is possible, of course, as in all affairs governed by men, for abuses to creep in and for aberrations to occur; but the Divine Bridegroom of the Church, who has promised that the Holy Spirit will be with the Church forever, will always see to it that the Church herself is not exposed to catastrophe by the weakness or imprudence of individual men. One final point remains to be mentioned: the Roman pontiff is subject to no one on earth and consequently cannot be called to judgment by anyone. He is obliged to render an account for his decisions to no one but Him alone whose visible vicar he is, Jesus Christ.

Objections against the Primacy of the Roman Pontiff

Objection 1. This tremendous authority of the Roman pontiff took its origin in large measure from the decretals of Pseudo-Isidore.

Answer. The Pseudo-Isidorian fraud (middle of the ninth century) amounts to little more than this: the ascribing of false *dates* to certain official Church pronouncements. Briefly, the commands and utterances of popes and councils of a later era were attributed to pontiffs of an earlier era. This fact alone should make clear that the Isidorian collection neither created, nor increased the rights of the primacy.

As a matter of record, the collection attributes nothing new to the supreme pontiff except this one point: *no* council of bishops may be held without the consent of the supreme pontiff. But this arrangement was not ratified, nor has it ever yet been ratified.[2] The collection did contribute something to a stricter observance of the discipline then in vogue, particularly in this that it drove home more forcibly the point that a bishop might never be deposed by a definitive judgment without the consent of the pope. Finally, it is quite a remarkable thing that the popes throughout two whole centuries (i.e., until St. Leo IX, 1049–54) never invoked these false decretals to bolster their supreme authority even though they were well acquainted with them.[3]

173 *Objection 2. The Council of Florence* taught that the Roman pontiff has indeed full power, but only within the limits laid down by the councils and canons:

> we define . . . that to him in [the person of] St. Peter was handed over by our Lord Jesus Christ the full power of feeding, ruling, and governing the universal Church (*kath hon tropon kai en tois praktikois tōn oikoumenikōn, synodōn, kai en tois hieros kanosi dialambanetai*).

The Greek should be translated: "according to that measure which is contained in both the decisions of the councils and in the canons." Consequently, the meaning of that last section is *restrictive.*

Answer. The whole objection rests upon a false interpretation of that last section. In the Florentine archives there is still preserved one of the five originals of this decree, written both in Greek and Latin, and signed by both the Latin and the Greek fathers. In that original document here is how that last section reads in Latin: "Quemadmodum *etiam* in gestis oecumenicorum conciliorum et in sacris canonibus continetur"[4] (". . . as *likewise* is stated in the decrees of the ecumenical councils and in the sacred canons"). The meaning, therefore, is not restrictive but *confirmatory*. It gives approbation to what has been said. Furthermore, this reading cannot be repudiated on any pretext whatsoever, for it is not simply a version but a text equally original and equally authentic with the Greek text. Finally, the Greek text itself can hardly sustain the interpretation made of it by our opponents. Even if the words *kath hon tropon,* viewed grammatically, do admit of a restrictive meaning, such a meaning is completely excluded by the context. How on earth could these two points ever be reconciled: Christ Himself conferred on the supreme pontiff absolute fulness of power, yet nonetheless this power is limited by the councils and the canons?

Objection 3. The Council of Constance taught that every man "of no matter what position or dignity, including even the papal dignity," owes obedience to a general council.[5]

Answer. (*a*) That decree was not ratified by Pope Martin V and consequently has no binding force. (*b*) These decrees of the fifth session were not issued by the whole council but only by one of its three sections.[6] (*c*) At least a large number of the very members of the Council of Constance which issued the decree seem to have had in mind only the case of a *doubtful* pope.* And in such a case most canonists even now use as an axiom: "A doubtful pope is no pope."[7] We must admit, however, that Gerson and some other theologians attributed a universal meaning to the decree cited.

Objection 4. If the pope enjoys direct jurisdiction even over the faithful outside the Roman see, then there would be two imme-

---

* This decree asserts that a doubtful pope is held to obey the authority of a council in order to bring about the "extirpation of the said schism," i.e., the Western Schism. From the council's own admission, "an elected pope cannot be so bound." I. Turrecremata, who was present at the council, writes: "That definition or declaration was not issued in a universal or unqualified fashion, but for a singular occasion" (*De ecclesia*, II, 100). See Zapalena, *op. cit.,* I, 381.

diate pastors governing the same flock, namely the pope and the bishop of this or that diocese. But this is so awkward as to be untenable: for it could lead to only one thing—confusion.

Answer. It would lead to confusion if governing the same flock there were two *coequal* and *independent* pastors, but not if the one is supreme and the other is subordinated to him. This should be obvious from the normal setup of an army in which the supreme commander had direct authority not only over his subordinate officers but also over all the soldiers and over each individual soldier. Good sense dictates simply this one thing: a supreme commander ought not to take over the normal functions of his subordinate officers either too frequently, or without a good reason.

176 *Objection 5.** If the supreme pontiff were the bishop of the Catholic Church, St. Gregory the Great would not have rejected the title, "Universal Bishop," as a "title smacking of blasphemy." (*Epistulae* v. 18, 20).

Answer. St. Gregory rejected this new and unusual title of "ecumenical bishop," or "universal bishop":[8] (*a*) so that by giving a lesson in humility he might restrain the pride of "Fasting John," the bishop of Constantinople, who had arrogated that title to himself. Notwithstanding his rejection of the title, the same Gregory asserts: that to St. Peter was committed the care of the entire Church (*Epistulae* v. 20); and that he, Gregory, was bound "by the commissioned duty of sollicitously caring for all the Churches."[9] (*b*) Furthermore, Gregory was considering the title under a pejorative connotation—which it could have—as meaning that the dignity of other bishops was excluded completely by that title. That is why he called it a "title smacking of blasphemy": "Let that blasphemous title be far from Christian hearts by which the honor of all priests would be wiped out through the madness of one man attributing it to himself" (*Epistulae* v. 20).

The same reasoning underlies Gregory's rejection of the title in other passages cited:

> For as your venerable holiness knows, this title of universality was offered by the sacred synod of Chalcedon to the bishop of the Apostolic See, which I by God's ordinance take care of. But no one of my predecessors ever consented to use this ill-sound-

---

* For a few additional objections to the doctrine of the primacy and their solutions, see: Zapalena, *op. cit.*, I, 376–84; and Salaverri, *op. cit.*, I, 644–5.

ing title for the reason that if one patriarch is called universal, the title of patriarch is taken away from the rest of the patriarchs.—*Ibid.*, v. 43.

And again: "It is a very regrettable thing, and one not to be put up with patiently that the aforementioned brother and my fellow bishop [Fasting John] should try to get himself called the only bishop" (*Epistulae* v. 21).

It should be noted, however, that this sinister connotation does not belong to the title necessarily.

Notes

1. See, for example, the subscription of the Council of Trent.
2. See CIC, 283 taken in conjunction with 281.
3. On this point, see Palmieri, *op. cit.*, thesis 20; C. Bottemanne, "Over den invloed der valsche Decretalen op de pauselijke macht," *De Katholiek*, 77–78 (1880); De Smedt, "Les fausses Décrétales," *Etudes Réligieuses*, 2 (1870), 77.
4. The word *etiam* ("likewise") is fully written out. Consequently the reading which is sometimes found, "Quemadmodum et . . . et . . . ," is a corruption of the original text. Its origin can easily be explained on the grounds that scribes customarily made use of abbreviations. See *Coll. Lac.*, VII, 1480; C. Bottemanne, "De vervalsching van den tekst der Kerkvergadering van Florence," *De Katholiek*, 57 (1870), 188.
5. Council of Constance, Sessions IV and V; see Hefele, *op. cit.*, VII, 1, 103.
6. See Zapalena, *op. cit.*, I, 381.
7. See, however, the position of Franzelin, *op. cit.*, p. 230 ff.
8. On the meaning of this title and its usage, see S. Vailhé, "Le titre de patriarche oeconomique avant S. Grégoire le Grand," *Echos d'Orient* (1908), p. 65.
9. *Epistulae* vii. 19.; see H. Grisar, "Der römische Primat nach der Lehre und Regierungspraxis Gregors des Groszen," ZkTh (1879), p. 655.

Article III

THE INFALLIBILITY OF THE POPE

I. *The Catholic Dogma*

II. *Explanation of the Dogma:*
  1. The meaning of papal infallibility
  2. The efficient cause of papal infallibility
  3. The person endowed with the prerogative of infallibility
  4. The scope of papal infallibility
  5. The conditions required for exercising papal infallibility

  PROPOSITION: When the pope speaks *ex cathedra,* he is infallible.
   Proof: 1. from Christ's own words
   2. from tradition
   Objections: from history.

Epilogue: The Pope's Temporal Sovereignty

Article III

THE INFALLIBILITY OF THE POPE

The infallibility of the Church's magisterium, viewed as a whole, has already been demonstrated (see nos. 79–99). Granted that fact, the primacy of the pope, since it comprises both teaching and ruling authority, must also include the prerogative of infallibility. If the Church's magisterium cannot err, and if the pope by himself possesses the full power of that magisterium, it follows inevitably that the pope in exercising that magisterium is preserved from error. In other words, he is infallible. Still, the matter is so serious it must be discussed *ex professo*.

I. The Catholic Dogma 177

The Catholic dogma is expressed in the following words of the Vatican Council:

> And so, faithfully holding on to that tradition recognized from the very beginning of the Christian religion . . . with the approval of the sacred council, we teach and define as a dogma revealed by God: that the Roman pontiff when speaking *ex cathedra*, that is, when exercising his office of supreme shepherd and teacher of all Christians, defines, in virtue of his supreme apostolic authority, that some doctrine on faith or morals must be held by the universal Church, he possesses, thanks to the divine assistance promised to him in the person of St. Peter, that infallibility with which the Divine Redeemer willed His Church to be endowed in defining doctrines on faith or morals; and consequently that definitions by the same pontiff are by their very nature, and not because of the consent of the Church, irreformable.—DB 1839.

II. Explanation of the Dogma 178

1. **The meaning of papal infallibility.** The notion of infallibility was explained earlier in this book (see nos. 77 and 79). Many non-Catholics, however, still have distorted notions about

this matter. It may be helpful, therefore, to clear aside some misconceptions by stating the following points: (*a*) The pope was declared infallible in his *teaching* activity, not in his other activities. It would, then, be pure wantonness to confuse the notion of infallibility with impeccability.[1] How infallibility may have an indirect bearing on the Church's ruling power was explained above (see nos. 91 and 93). (*b*) The prerogative of infallibility does not make the pope's will the ultimate standard of truth or goodness. (*c*) Infallibility is not omniscience. (*d*) Finally, infallibility does not imply inspiration. An infallible decree does not possess the same sort of dignity as Sacred Scripture.

179   2. The efficient cause of papal infallibility is God's assistance. That assistance was promised to the Roman pontiff in the person of St. Peter. Keep in mind, however, that the popes in preparing an infallible decree do not neglect normal means of inquiry, research, discussion, or deliberation:

> The Roman Pontiffs on their part, according as the condition of the times and circumstances dictated, sometimes calling together ecumenical councils or sounding out the mind of the Church throughout the world, sometimes through regional councils, or sometimes by using other helps which divine Providence supplied, have, with the help of God, defined as to be held such matters as they had found consonant with the Holy Scripture and with the apostolic tradition.—DB 1836; TCT 216.

3. **The person endowed with the prerogative of infallibility is the currently-reigning Roman pontiff.** That is why the Gallican theory could not possibly be squared with the Vatican Council definition. The Gallicans make a distinction between the see and its occupant. Thus the individual popes could err, but God would prevent "error from taking deep root" in the Roman see or Roman Church. In other words, God would see to it that an error committed by one pope would be swiftly repaired either by the same pope or at least by his successor. Obviously this opinion is not reconcilable with the statement of the council that *"the Roman pontiff,"* is infallible when speaking *ex cathedra;* nor with the necessary conclusion of the same council: "and consequently definitions made by the same pontiff are *of themselves*, and not because of the consent of the Church, irreformable."

THE ROMAN PONTIFF

The Gallicans wrongly appeal to Leo the Great's epigram, "Sees are one thing, those who sit upon them another" (*Epistula* 106. 6). By that saying, Leo simply meant that the rights of a see do not depend upon the *holiness* of its occupant, "For even though those who occupy sees may differ at times in their merits, still the rights of the sees remain" (*Epistula* 119. 3).

Notice, however, that only the pope himself *personally* enjoys infallibility; not other people to whom he may delegate some share in his teaching authority. For example, even though the Roman congregations are organs of the papacy, they are not the pope himself. The reason for the restriction is this: the pope cannot cause the divine assistance, promised to himself personally, to come to the aid of other people. It should be clear, then, what is meant by saying that infallibility is a *personal prerogative*. It is *personal* insofar as it belongs to each individual pope and cannot be delegated to other people; it is *not* personal in the sense that it belongs to the pope as a private person, that is, in virtue of his personal qualifications.

4. The scope of papal infallibility is exactly the same as for the Church as a whole: "He possesses that infallibility with which the Divine Redeemer willed His Church to be endowed in defining doctrines on faith or morals." The fathers of the Vatican Council did not mean to delineate the precise boundaries of papal infallibility by the words: "doctrine on faith or morals to be held by the entire Church," for it was their intention to take up this point later. Hence they indicated the scope of his infallibility only in a general way by the formula normally used by theologians. It was by deliberate design, however, that they employed the phrase: "must be held" (*tenendam*) rather than the phrase: "must be believed" (*credendam*). They used the former phrase so that they might not appear to be restricting the prerogative of infallibility exclusively to those truths which have been *revealed*.[2]

5. The conditions for papal infallibility are summed up in the words: "when he speaks ex cathedra." A throne (*cathedra*—chair—judicial bench) is normally a symbol of authority and particularly of doctrinal authority.[3] The consecrated formulae: "to speak ex cathedra," or "an ex cathedra definition" were in use in theological schools long before the Vatican Council. They designated the *full* exercise of the papal magisterium. The Vatican Council, however, added this precise explanation: "that is: when exercising his office of supreme shepherd and teacher of all Christians, he defines, in virtue of his supreme apostolic authority, that some doctrine on faith or morals must be held by the universal Church."

Keeping in mind, then, what has already been explained in discussing the object of infallibility (see nos. 85–96), "to speak ex cathedra" signifies two things: (*a*) the pope is *actually* making use of his *papal* office—of supreme shepherd and teacher of all Christians; (*b*) the pope is using his papal authority at its *maximum power*. Both these facts must be made known clearly and indisputably. It makes no difference, however, whether they be made known by the words the pope uses, or by the circumstances of the case. Briefly, no set formula, and no particular type of solemnity is required for an ex cathedra statement.*

In reference to point *a*:—A man holding public office does not always act in his *official* capacity. Again, if the same person holds several offices simultaneously, he does not have to be constantly exercising his highest function. We must keep these points in mind when discussing the pope's infallibility, for he fulfills several positions simultaneously. He is not only the pope of the whole Catholic Church, he is also the local bishop of the diocese of Rome, metropolitan of its surrounding sees, and temporal sovereign of the Vatican state. Consequently, if the pope speaks merely as a private individual, or as a private theologian, or as a temporal sovereign, or precisely as ordinary of the diocese of Rome, or precisely as metropolitan of the province of Rome, he should not be looked on as acting infallibly. He may, for example, as a private individual air his private views—political, economic, or spiritual. As a private theologian he might write a book on some aspects of the spiritual life. As temporal sovereign of the Vatican state, he might issue decrees on taxes, or economic reform, or might set up a law grant-

---

* For example, it is not inconceivable that some pope in the future might use the medium of television to broadcast a solemn definition to the world. It is the pope's office that guarantees him the divine assistance, and the pope's decision to make a definitive declaration that calls that assistance to his aid, not any magical formula of words. Some literal-minded people wish that St. Peter had laid down some one introductory phrase, or clause for all popes to follow in making infallible statements. They forget that phrases which in apostolic times might be very clear to apostolic contemporaries might be very obscure to us; and that phrases which would be very clear to us might be very obscure to future generations. The Church is always contemporary; its magisterium is a *living* magisterium and it knows how to make its message known in any age.

ing religious liberty to non-Catholic worship in return for territory restored to himself and so on. Speaking precisely as ordinary of the diocese of Rome he might give a series of instructions or a retreat to the people of some definite parish in the city.[4]

What is required for an infallible declaration, therefore, is that the pope be acting precisely as pope; that is, as the supreme shepherd and teacher of all Christians so that his decision looks to the universal Church and is given for the sake of the universal Church. It is not necessary, however, for the document containing an infallible decision to be *addressed* directly to the universal Church. A decision intended for the whole Church can be immediately addressed, for example, to the bishops of a particular region in which a condemned error is flourishing.

With reference to point *b:*—A man who acts in an official capacity does not always make use of his full power, of the whole weight of the authority which he possesses by his very position. A president may, for example, disagree with a bill of Congress, and express his disapproval and yet not take the step of vetoing the bill. Thus the pope, even acting as pope, can teach the universal Church without making use of his supreme authority at its maximum power. Now the Vatican Council defined merely this point: the pope is infallible if he uses his doctrinal authority at its maximum power, by handing down a binding and definitive decision: such a decision, for example, by which he quite clearly intends to bind all Catholics to an absolutely firm and irrevocable assent.

Consequently even if the pope, and acting as pope, praises some doctrine, or recommends it to Christians, or even orders that it alone should be taught in theological schools, this act should not necessarily be considered an infallible decree since he may not intend to hand down a definitive decision. The same holds true if by his approval he orders some decree of a sacred congregation to be promulgated; for example, a decree of the Holy Office, in which the congregation itself condemns some doctrine. It is one thing to be willing to allow a decision of a congregation to be published—a decision which is by its very nature revocable—but quite another matter for the pope himself to make the final decision.

For the same reason, namely a lack of intention to hand down a final decision, not all the doctrinal decisions which the pope proposes in encyclical letters should be considered definitions. In a

CHRIST'S CHURCH

word, there must always be present and clearly present the intention of the pope to hand down a decision which is final and definitive.

181 Thus far we have been discussing *Catholic teaching*. It may be useful to add a few points about purely *theological opinions*—opinions with regard to the pope when he is not speaking ex cathedra. All theologians admit that the pope can make a mistake in matters of faith and morals when so speaking: either by proposing a false opinion in a matter not yet defined, or by innocently differing from some doctrine already defined. Theologians disagree, however, over the question of whether the pope can become a *formal heretic* by stubbornly clinging to an error in a matter already defined. The more probable and respectful opinion, followed by Suárez, Bellarmine and many others, holds that just as God has not till this day ever permitted such a thing to happen, so too he never will permit a pope to become a formal and public heretic. Still, some competent theologians do concede that the pope when not speaking ex cathedra could fall into formal heresy. They add that should such a case of public papal heresy occur, the pope, either by the very deed itself or at least by a subsequent decision of an ecumenical council, would by divine law[5] forfeit his jurisdiction. Obviously a man could not continue to be the head of the Church if he ceased to be even a member of the Church.

182 PROPOSITION: *When the pope speaks ex cathedra, he is infallible.*

This is *of faith*, from the Vatican Council. The proposition can be proved both by Christ's own words and by the witness of tradition. Tradition makes unmistakeably clear the position the infallible Church has always held in this matter.

Proof:

1. *From Christ's own words:*

" . . . *And I, in turn, say to you: You are Peter, and upon this rock I will build my Church, and the gates of Hell shall not prevail against it. I will give you the keys of the kingdom of heaven, and whatever you bind on earth shall be bound in* *heaven, and whatever you loose on earth shall be loosed in heaven."*—Matt. 16:18–19.*

Peter—and his successors—was established as the rock, or unshakeable foundation, which would make the Church perpetually indestructible. Now nothing pertains so much to the stability of the Church as immunity from error in matters of doctrine. Peter, then, was to be the means by which the Church would always uphold the faith in its purity and integrity. But if Peter is to be made equal to that task, two things are necessary: first, he must always have the power to bind all Christians absolutely to believe this doctrine and to reject that; second, in taking such action Peter must himself be necessarily immune from error.

If Peter could not bind all Christians in an absolute fashion, he would not be a foundation. On the other hand, if in binding all Christians he himself were liable to error, he would not be an unshakeable foundation, but a very shaky one. That Christ clearly intended to lay an unshakeable foundation is evident from the metaphor of the rock, and especially from the conclusion He drew: *"and the gates of Hell shall not prevail against it."*

Peter—and his successors—received the keys of the kingdom of heaven with such full power to bind and to loose that whatever Peter bound would also be bound by God. Usually the keys of the kingdom are listed as two: the key of knowledge (teaching power—magisterium) and the key of power (ruling power—jurisdiction). Consequently Peter can also bind absolutely by a doctrinal decision, and this decision by the very fact of its utterance is ratified by God. Now if this is the way matters stand, one is forced to conclude: either that a pope cannot err when making a definitive decision, or else that God Himself could at some time ratify a false doctrine.

Again:

After they had breakfasted, Jesus said to Simon Peter: "Simon, son of John, do you love me more than these others do?" "Yes, my Master," he replied; "you know that I really love you." "Then," Jesus said to him, "feed my lambs." He asked him a second time: "Simon, son of John, do you love me?" "Yes, Mas-

---

* A full *exegetical* discussion of this text is given in the appendix at the end of this volume.

> ter," he replied, "you know that I really love you." "Then," he said to him, "be a shepherd to my sheep." For the third time he put the question to him: "Simon, son of John, do you really love me?" It grieved Peter that he had asked him the third time: "Do you really love me?" and he replied: "Master, you know everything; you know that I really love you!" "Then," Jesus said to him, "feed my sheep."—John 21:15–17.

Peter—and his successors—clearly received the task and the full power to feed the entire flock of Christ. Before anything else, then, he is bound to nourish the entire flock, both bishops and the ordinary faithful, on healthy doctrine and to keep them away from poisonous pasture. This task itself necessarily implies infallibility on the part of the pope, in the sense already explained. Suppose a pope were to make a mistake in defining Christian doctrine. What would happen? Either the entire Church would accept the pope's decision—and that would be the end of the infallibility and indestructibility of the Church; or, the Church would rebel against the pope's decision and would correct his doctrine—and that would be the end of the arrangement set up by Christ Himself, for the flock would be feeding the shepherd!

Again:

> "Simon, Simon, mark my words: Satan has demanded the surrender of you all in order to sift you like wheat; but I have prayed for you personally, that your faith might not fail. Later on, therefore, when once thou hast turned again, it is for you to strengthen your brethren" (su pote epitrepsas stērison tous adelphous sou).—Luke 22:31–32.

Now we must show that this text implies infallibility in the sense already explained; and, furthermore, that it implies infallibility not only for Peter himself but also for his successors.

a. That Christ's words here guarantee Peter real indefectibility in faith, or *infallibility*, seems quite clear. First of all, Christ's unqualified prayer that Peter's faith might not fail, could not possibly go unanswered. Second, by the force of this prayer and the assistance begged for in it, Peter was to be made equal to the task of strengthening or stabilizing his brothers in the faith. If Peter were to be made equal to this task, the very minimum required was that he be necessarily free from error at least at such times as he would be actually instructing his brothers in the faith with the maximum of his authority.

b. That this text refers to Peter in his *official* capacity, and consequently to Peter living in his successors is clear: first, from the very nature of the office entrusted to him. Strengthening in the faith is no less necessary for later generations: in fact it is even more necessary for them than for the apostles and the first Christians. Second, that this text refers to Peter in his official capacity is clear likewise from the real parallelism between this passage and those of Matt. 16 and John 21. If the office of acting as a foundation for the Church and of being shepherd to the Church is something perpetual, how could the office of confirming in the faith be not always perpetual since it is already contained in those other two functions? But if this office is perpetual, so must the aid Christ prayed for be perpetual.[6]

2. *From tradition.* Even though the fathers of the Church do not discuss the pope's infallibility in absolutely explicit and unmistakeable terms, his infallibility was nonetheless acknowledged from the very earliest days. It was acknowledged both in theory and in practice. This fact is clear from: (*a*) the statements of the fathers; (*b*) the practice of the popes; (*c*) the statements of ecumenical councils.

a. The statements of the fathers.

St. Irenaeus (c. 140–c. 202) not only admits that the Roman Church possesses "a more powerful authority" (*potiorem principalitatem*) but he explains the reason for this authority. It stems from the fact that the Roman Church is the *standard of faith* for the rest of the churches. Irenaeus teaches that to have a sure knowledge of the Christian truth all one has to do is consult the faith of the Roman Church, because the faithful throughout the world are obliged to agree with this Church in matters of belief (see no. 64). Now if the faith of the Roman Church is the standard and norm for all the other churches, this very fact presupposes the infallibility of the Roman Church, or what amounts to the same thing both objectively and also in the mind of Irenaeus, the infallibility of the bishop of Rome.

St. Cyprian (c. 200–258) praises: "the Romans whose faith was extolled in the very preaching of the apostle [Rom. 1:9] men to whom perversion of faith could have no access" (see no. 65).

184

St. Ephiphanius (c. 315–403) states: "The faith receives its stability in every way from him who received the keys of the kingdom and who looses things on earth and binds them in heaven. For from him may be found out [the answer] to even the deepest problems of the faith" (*Ancoratus* 9).

St. Jerome (c. 342–419) when a great dispute was raging in the East over the question of whether one should acknowledge one or three "hypostases" in the Trinity, sought the answer from Pope Damasus, "Therefore, I thought I ought to consult the chair of Peter and that faith recommended by the mouth of the Apostle. For by you people alone is preserved incorrupt the tradition of the fathers" (*Epistula* 15. 1).

St. Augustine (354–430) says of the Pelagian controversy, "For this reason two deputations were sent to the Apostolic See, and that see has sent back the answers. The case is finished" (*Sermo* 131. 10).

In another place, Augustine writes, "All doubts about this matter were completely removed by the letters of Pope Innocent of blessed memory" (*Contra duas Epistulas Pelagianorum* ii. 3. 5).

St. Peter Chrysologus wrote to Eutyches, "In all ways we implore you, honorable brother, to heed obediently the directions written by the blessed pope of the city of Rome; because St. Peter who lives in and presides over this his own see offers to all who seek it the truth of the faith" (Among the *Epistulae* of St. Leo 25).

St. Leo the Great (390?–461): "The firmness of that faith, which was recommended in the prince of the apostles, is something perpetual" (*Sermo* 3[1]. 2).

John, bishop of Jerusalem (572–92), after citing Matthew 16:18–19 concludes, "Now in the heads of that holy, first, and venerable see his [Peter's] successors are sound in the faith and according to our Lord Himself, infallible."[7]

185   *b. The practice of the popes:*

At the beginning of the *third* century, Pope Callistus by a peremptory decree rejected Montanism.*

---

* Montanism was a heresy of an *ascetical* nature, placing more emphasis on a rigorous mode of life than on doctrine. It dates from about 170 A. D. Its founder, Montanus, thought he had been inspired by the Holy Spirit to start a more rigid Christianity, prohibiting second marriages, advocating prolonged fasts, fierce physical mortifications, etc. Its most famous convert was Tertullian who succumbed to its austere appeal and died as a heretic outside the Church. See Parente, *Dictionary of Dogmatic Theology*, p. 195–6.

At the beginning of the *fifth* century, Innocent I, by confirming the decrees of the councils of Carthage and Mileve in the year 416 definitely condemned the errors of Pelagius and Celestius. That the entire Church accepted his decision as binding irrevocably is clear, for example, from the testimony of St. Augustine mentioned above.

Pope Celestine I (422–432) condemned Nestorius. A brief time later his legates went to the *Council of Ephesus* (431) to see that the decisions he had previously laid down should be executed (see no. 67). The fathers of the council humbly accepted the pope's decision: "Constrained by the sacred canons and the letter of our holy father and co-minister, Celestine, the bishop of the church at Rome . . . we have necessarily reached this painful decision against him [Nestorius]."[8]

The fathers of the *Council of Chalcedon* (451) received in the same way the Tome of St. Leo I to Flavian, bishop of Constantinople, in which he condemned the doctrines of Eutyches (see no. 67). The fact that Leo intended his decision to be accepted as definitive is clear from his letter to the Council of Chalcedon: "It is not permissible to defend what is not allowed to be believed, since in accord with the authority of the gospels, the words of the prophets, and the doctrine of the apostles, what is the true and holy doctrine about the mystery of the Incarnation of our Lord Jesus Christ was stated fully and clearly in the letter which we sent to Bishop Flavian" (*Epistula* 93. 2).

In the *seventh* century Pope Agatho condemned Monotheletism even before the *Third Council of Constantinople* (680–681) did. At the same time in a letter to Constantine Pogonatus, he greatly extolled the apostolic see, "Which has never turned aside from the road of truth to any sort of error . . . and has never become depraved and surrendered to heretical novelties, but in the true faith known from the very beginning remains unpolluted to the very end" (*Epistula ad Augustos Imperatores*). The fathers of the council applauded* the decision of Pope Agatho: "The paper and ink were seen and Peter spoke through Agatho."[9]

---

* Philip Hughes describes the incident briefly and vividly:
To this council the pope—Agatho—sent a letter setting out the traditional Catholic teaching on the dogmatic point at issue, viz. whether in Our Lord there were one or two wills, as St. Leo had sent the like kind of letter to Chalcedon. As at Chalcedon so now the 174 eastern bishops present received the pope's teaching with acclamations, crying out: 'It is Peter who speaks through Agatho.' The doctrine defined, the council turned to con-

In the *fourteenth* century Clement VI (1342-52) required the Armenian church to believe "that only the Roman pontiff can, when doubts arise about Catholic faith, by a guaranteed decision impose that faith which must be adhered to without qualification; and that whatever he, by the authority of the keys handed over to him by Christ, decides is true is the true and Catholic doctrine; and that what he decides is false or heretical must be judged to be so" (DB 570q).

186   c. *The Testimony of ecumenical councils:*

Three ecumenical councils "in which the East and the West united in a union of faith and charity" (DB 1833), even if they did not declare the pope's infallibility in explicit terms, did declare it in equivalent terms.

The fathers of the *Fourth Council of Constantinople* (870) subscribed to the following solemn profession of faith: °

> The first condition of salvation is to keep the norm of the true faith and in no way deviate from the established doctrine of the Fathers. For it is impossible that the words of our Lord Jesus Christ who said, "Thou art Peter, and upon this rock I will build my Church" (*Matt. 16:18*) should not be verified. And their truth has been proven by the course of history, for in the Apostolic See the Catholic religion has always been kept unsullied. . . .
>
> Following, as we have said before, the Apostolic See in all things and proclaiming all its decisions, we endorse and approve all the letters which Pope St. Leo wrote concerning the Christian religion. And so I hope I may deserve to be associated with you in the one communion which the Apostolic See proclaims, in which the whole, true, and perfect security of the Christian religion resides.—DB 171 f.; TCT 147 f.

In the *Second Council of Lyons* (1274) the Greeks who returned to the unity of Church made the following profession:

---

demn the authors of the heresy, and with them it condemned Pope Honorius, not indeed as an author of the heresy but 'because in his reply to Sergius he followed in all things that wicked man's opinion, and confirmed his impious teaching.'—*A Popular History of the Catholic Church* (New York, 1947), pp. 46–7.

° This profession of faith stems back to Pope St. Hormisdas who, in dealing with the Acacian Schism, included it in a letter to the bishops of Spain in the year 517. For the *authenticity* of the text see BLE (1904), p. 152 and (1905), p. 333.

THE ROMAN PONTIFF

The holy Roman Church has supreme and full primacy and jurisdiction over the whole Catholic Church. This it truly and humbly recognizes as received from the Lord himself in the person of St. Peter, the Prince or head of the Apostles, whose successor in the fullness of power is the Roman Pontiff. And just as the holy Roman Church is bound more than all the others to defend the truth of faith, so, if there arise any questions concerning the faith, they must be decided by its judgment.—DB 1834; TCT 214.

In the *Council of Florence* (1439) the Greeks as well as the Latins defined that:

The Roman pontiff is the true vicar of Christ, the head of the whole Church, the father and teacher of all Christians; and that to him, in the person of St. Peter, was given by our Lord Jesus Christ the full power of feeding, ruling, and governing the whole Church.—DB 1835; TCT 215.

If the Roman pontiff is the teacher of all Christians, so much so that he possess the *full* power of feeding—and hence of teaching—the universal Church, which cannot fall into error, it follows inescapably that he is himself infallible.

There you have the mind of the Church. Fourteen hundred years of unswerving tradition. Unfortunately, the frightful Western Schism at the end of the fourteenth century caused near chaos in Christendom. With three rivals claiming to be the legitimate pope, people were bewildered during a period of some forty years.[10] This schism was the occasion also of causing confusion in the minds of some western theologians. Not only did it obscure for them the doctrine of papal supremacy in governing the Church, it also cast its shadow over the related doctrine of the pope's infallibility. Actually, it was particularly at the time of the Council of Constance (1414–1418) that the pope's infallibility began to be seriously questioned and attacked.* Gallicanism and Josephinism vehemently supported the opinion denying papal infallibility.

---

* "This council which met at Constance (November, 1414) is the strangest in all Church history from its composition, its procedure, and the nature of what was effected through it. The full effect of the chaos of forty years was now seen. All the wildest theories about the source of ecclesiastical authority seemed likely to be realized when there descended on the town (in addition to the 185 bishops) 300 doctors in theology and law, 18,000 other ecclesiastics, and a vast multitude of lay potentates, of princes, and of representatives of

But how startingly this negative opinion departed from Catholic mentality and tradition, Gerson himself (d. 1419) admitted at the very beginning of the controvery: "Before the Council of Constance that traditional teaching [of the pope's infallibility] was so completely accepted by most Catholics that if any one had tried to teach an opposite opinion he would have been either censured or condemned for heretical depravity."[11]

And Tournely admitted the same thing at the beginning of the eighteenth century when he stated:

> One should not disguise the fact that it is difficult in the face of the vast amount of evidence which Bellarmine and others have assembled, not to recognize the unquestionable and infallible authority of the Apostolic See or of the Roman Church: but it is even more difficult to reconcile that testimony with the *Declaration of the Gallican Clergy* with which we are not allowed to disagree.[12]

Ruard Tapper of Enkhuizen (d. 1559) has excellently summed up the whole history of the dogma of papal infallibility in these remarks:

> But whether this head [of the Church—the pope] can make an error when he makes a decision concerning the faith and morals of the faithful . . . began to be controverted and disputed pro and con about 150 years ago. . . . For from the time of the councils of Constance and Basle some doctors teach that only

---

towns and corporations, to the number of more than a hundred thousand. . . . This same council that had brought the schism to an end had sown the seeds of much future dissension. Whatever the niceties of Canon Law that had safeguarded the legitimacy of its liquidation of a complex problem, the fact remained that the Council of Constance had judged two claimants to the papacy and condemned them, and that it had also elected a new pope. And it had also declared, in explicit terms, that General Councils were superior to popes, and it had provided that every five years this General Council should reassemble and the pope, in some measure, give to it an account of his stewardship. As far as the wishes of the Council of Constance went, a revolution had been achieved, and the Church for the future was to be governed in a parliamentary way, and not by the absolute, divinely given authority of its head, the Vicar of Christ. The forty years that followed the Council were to see the successive popes—Martin V, Eugene IV, and Nicholas V—wholly taken up with the effort to destroy this new theory and to control the councils which it bred and inspired. The full fruits of the mischief were only reaped in the long-drawn-out dissensions of the Council of Basle (1431–1449)" (Hughes, *Popular History*, *op. cit.*, p. 141–3).

an ecumenical council enjoys the privilege of infallibility. . . . But the older writers unanimously argue from the Scriptures that this privilege of infallible decision belongs to Peter and to the Roman pontiff and his see, since he is the supreme vicar of Christ on earth in Peter's place and, as such, has alone received the keys of binding and loosing everything.[13]

As a final point, note that the Roman pontiffs did not refrain from handing down definitive decisions in matters of faith even during the period of the controversies;[14] and all the churches, even those among whom the new opinion had more or less made headway, in practice accepted these decisions as being of themselves irrevocable and infallible.

Objections: 188

Many facts from the Church's history are adduced as objections to the infallibility of the pope. Here, only the main ones will be considered. In dealing with these facts, we are interested in one point only: whether the pope ever made a mistake when speaking ex cathedra.

1. Against *St. Peter* himself two objections are raised. First, he denied Christ on the night of His passion; secondly, he forced Gentile converts to adopt Jewish religious practices (see Gal. 2:11–14).

At the time of the passion Peter was not yet the supreme shepherd and teacher of the Church. Obviously, then, he could not act in that capacity at that time. As a private individual he sinned seriously, but he did not lose the faith.

The second objection is closer to the point, for Peter was then head of the Church. It is, however, a rather superficial argument against infallibility. When Peter deliberately separated himself from the Gentile way of life—so not to shock Judaic-Christians—he did act imprudently. He did cause some harm to the progress of the faith. (That is why St. Paul scolded him for it: he knew how much Peter's example meant.) Whether Peter was acting in good conscience or not is not here our concern. One fact is abundantly clear: Peter by no means handed down any doctrinal decision on the matter. That is why Tertullian could write, "It was indeed a fault of *conduct*, but not of teaching" (*De praescriptione* 23).

2. *Pope Liberius* (352–366) is alleged to have betrayed St. 189

Athanasius and the whole Catholic faith by signing the formula of Sirmia which was either Arian or semi-Arian in doctrine.

a. For the sake of argument let us grant that Liberius did actually sign this heretical document (some historians dispute the point). The mere signing of the document could not possibly be considered an ex cathedra decision. Even anti-Catholic critics admit that the pope, after two years of exile and captivity, only finally signed to release himself from persecution. Such circumstances,* far from showing that the pope intended to hand down a decision binding the universal Church, exclude any such intention.

b. Even in the supposition that Liberius did sign his name to one of the formulae at Sirmia, the one he signed would have been the third formula (in the year 358). This formula was not in itself heretical. Even though the formula, by omitting the term *homoousios* made sacrosanct by the Council of Nicaea, contained a *less accurate* formulation of the Catholic faith and was consequently more acceptable to the semi-Arians; strictly speaking it was not erroneous.

c. Finally, a number of historians think there can be some real doubt whether Liberius actually signed or not.[15]

3. Pope *Vigilius* (537–555) is accused of first condemning "The Three Chapters,"[16] then of forbidding their condemnation, and finally of once more condemning them.

Vigilius did not change in the slightest his decision about the doctrinal matter in question. He always and clearly rejected the Nestorianism with which "The Three Chapters" were infected (see no. 89). But the pope was under extremely difficult circumstances (as Justinian's prisoner), and, surrounded by deceit and political intrigue, hesitated to make a *prudential judgment.* He did hesitate about the wisdom of condemning, *at that time,* those writings of Theodore of Mopsuestia, Theodoret of Cyrrhus, and Ibas, bishop of Edessa, which were called the *Tria Capitula* (the authors themselves were already in their graves). The writings did deserve

---

* Basil of Ancyra the leader of a group which, though Catholic, disliked the term *homoöusion,* because of its misuse in a third century controversy, gained the emperor's favor. He then endeavored to unite all the Catholics on the basis of a non-Nicene (but not anti-Nicene) formula. In the Catholic sense in which this was offered, and with an explanation making clear what he was doing, Liberius, still a captive, signed this. The forgeries of Arian pamphleteers are probably the original cause of the confusion around which the discussion centers.—Hughes, *Popular History, op. cit.,* p. 53.

censure, but since their authors, after explicitly rejecty Nestorianism, had been welcomed back by the fathers of the Council of Chalcedon, condemnation of the writings would have been a stumbling block to many people, particularly the Westerners. These people would have taken the condemnation as a slap at the authority of the Council of Chalcedon.* Consequently, even if the pope acted a bit imprudently in this matter, he definitely made no error in matters of faith. For a fuller treatment of this extremely complicated matter, consult the historian cited in no. 89 above.

4. It is alleged of Pope *Honorius I* (625–38) that: (*a*) in two letters to Sergius, bishop of Constantinople, he taught Monotheletism † and, did so, indeed, so clearly that (*b*) he was afterwards for this very reason condemned as a heretic by the sixth ecumenical council (Third Constantinople) in the year 680.

a. The letters of Honorius do not contain any ex cathedra statement. The pope made no doctrinal decision; he approved the request of Sergius that *silence* should be observed in the question of "a single or double operation" in Christ, "Exhorting you that avoiding the use of the newfangled term of a single or double operation . . . " (Kirch 1064); and again, "It is not necessary for

---

* The Roman objection to issuing the condemnation was that since Theodoret and Ibas had been solemnly reinstated at Chalcedon any attack on them must have a prima facie appearance of a move away from Chalcedon. And indeed this was the first and immediate reading in the west of the very qualified condemnation issued by the pope in 548. There were passionate scenes everywhere, but in Africa especially, where the pope was excommunicated.

The pope's position was all the more delicate—and his acts open to misinterpretation—from the fact that he was at this time Justinian's prisoner, having been kidnapped in 545 and shipped to the capital when his first hesitancy about complying with the imperial will had shown itself.

Between the condemnation of 548, which the pope withdrew, and the meeting of the council—May 553—there were a succession of crises, and the council met with the pope refusing to take any part in it. There were thus separate condemnations. One, by the pope, of the writings of Theodore of Mopsuestia, the other, by the council, of the Three Chapters—or rather an acceptance by the council of Justinian's condemnation of them.

It remained to win the pope's assent, and after six months more of bullying, of isolation and imprisonment, Vigilius, an old man past eighty years of age, yielded. He was then allowed to leave for Rome, whence he had been absent nearly ten years.—Hughes, *Popular History, op. cit.*, pp. 43–4.

† Monotheletism (from *monos* "single" and *thelo* "I will") is the last of the great Christological heresies and an offshoot of Monophysitism. It maintained that Christ had only one will—a divine will—and consequently denied to Christ's human nature that which is connatural to it—a human will. See Parente, *Dictionary, op. cit.*, p. 194–5.

us to give a definitive decision on this matter of one or two operations" (Kirch 1068).

But to urge silence on a matter is just the reverse of a peremptory definition!

The letters of Honorius do not contain any doctrinal error. Even though the pope does refrain from using the term of a double will or double operation, he does teach in equivalent terms the existence of two wills and a twofold operation by asserting that Christ possesses two complete, unconfused natures, which operate and are sources of operation, and one operator.

The phrase: "We confess that there is *one will* of our Lord Jesus Christ" (Kirch 1073) in nowise prevents this conclusion. In the context in which the clause occurs, the meaning is simply this: in Christ's human nature there is perfect harmony between His rational will and His sensitive appetite (for the latter is perfectly subject to the former), hence there is in Christ's *humanity* but one will, one that is to say, not physically but morally.[17] Pope John IV (640–42) ratified this orthodox meaning in his *Apologia pro Honorio* coauthored, it is interesting to note, by the same John Sympon who had cosigned the letters of Honorius himself.

It must be admitted, however, that the clause "we confess one will," even though it did not have a Monotheletic meaning in Honorius' mind and does not have such a meaning objectively—provided the context be considered carefully, not casually—could be easily twisted to give it a perverted sense.[18]

b. Before anything else, this much is absolutely sure: Honorius was not condemned as guilty of preaching heresy in his official capacity (ex cathedra). Something more, he was not even condemned as being privately a heretic. Strictly speaking, he was condemned for being a *helper* of heresy. Whatever might have been the intention of the fathers of the sixth ecumenical council, this much is certain: the decree of the council would be of no value except insofar as it was ratified by the Apostolic See. Now Leo II, who had succeeded Agatho as pope before the end of the council, in his ratification of the fathers' decree either explained the decree in such fashion or so mitigated it that the upshot was that Honorius was to be stigmatized not as a heretic, but as a helper of heresy.

Here are Leo's words to Constantine Pogonatus ratifying the council's decree: "We anathematize the inventors of the new error, that is, Theodosius, Cyrus, Sergius, Pyrrhus, Paul, Peter . . . and also Honorius who *did not enlighten* this apostolic see with the doctrine of apostolic tradition, *but allowed* its immaculate faith to be soiled by profane betrayal" (Kirch 1085).[19] A short time later, Leo wrote to the bishops of Spain explaining the matter. Honorius was condemned along with the others: "because instead of extinguishing the incipient flame of heretical doctrine, as befits the holder of apostolic authority, he rather fanned it *by his negligence.*"

Was, then, Honorius actually a helper of heresy? Prescinding from the question of serious subjective guilt, from which many authors excuse the pope, this much must be said: Honorius was a bit gullible in relying so readily on Sergius' advice and he acted unwisely in persuading people not to preach about the twofold operation which he himself, nonetheless, personally admitted. He acted still more unwisely by adding that odd-sounding clause about "one will in Christ." Because of these imprudences he did (unwittingly) help to fan the rising blaze of the Monotheletic heresy. Instead, he should have combatted the heresy energetically with a clear and distinct explanation of apostolic doctrine as befitted his apostolic office. Finally, it seems probable that the only reason the Apostolic See acquiesced in this grave censure of Honorius was to prevent even further damage by making some concessions to the Greeks who were quite incensed about the condemnation of some of their leaders.[20]

All this explanation is offered on the hypothesis that both the letters of Honorius and the acts of the sixth council are completely authentic. Quite a few scholars—whose opinion has not won wide acceptance, however—have tried to show that a number of interpolations have been inserted in either the letters of Honorius or the acts of the council.

5. Pope Zacharias (741–752) is said to have erred by condemning St. Virgilius for teaching the existence of the antipodes.

We still do not know much about this case of Virgilius. Nothing about the case has been handed down to posterity except this reply of the pope to St. Boniface:

> as for that perverse and evil doctrine in which he has spoken against God and against his own soul—if he has actually taught that there is another world and other men under the earth or another sun and moon—after convening a council throw this

man out of the Church and deprive him of the priestly honor. But we ourselves in writing to the aforesaid duke [Otilo, duke of Bavaria, and defender of Virgilius] have sent summoning letters to the aforesaid Virgilius: that he should come before us for careful questioning and if he should be found in error, he shall be condemned in accord with the canonical sanctions.[21]

a. It was the commonly accepted opinion of earlier ages that to make a journey to the other side of the earth was absolutely impossible. Consequently anyone who would subscribe to such an impossibility and at the same time accept the existence of the antipodes would be implicitly asserting that some men on this earth are not descended from Adam. This assertion, since it negates the universality of original sin, is contrary to the Catholic faith.* It should be clear, then, that the pope called that doctrine "perverse and evil" not in the sense that there should actually *exist* antipodes, but in the sense that there should exist antipodes not descended from Adam.

b. This censure of the pope does not bear the earmarks of an ex cathedra decision. The replies of the pope to some bishop who asks for advice on a particular matter are not usually ex cathedra decisions. Again, perversity of doctrine is rather implied than declared *ex professo*: the pope considered that further investigation was necessary. It is hardly probable that Pope Zacharias wished to make *subtle* inquiries as to whether Virgilius admitted the existence of the antipodes; what he wanted to know was precisely in what way Virgilius accounted for them.

Finally, even though we do not know precisely how he did so, it seems clear Virgilius gave the pope a satisfactory answer, for he soon received the cathedral of Salzburg and his name was added by Gregory IX to the catalogue of the saints.[22]

6. Finally, we have the widely publicized case of *Galileo* whose teaching on the motion of the earth and the immobility of the sun was condemned as "false and completely opposed to Divine Scripture."

a. It should be candidly admitted, we think, that the sacred congregation did condemn Galileo's teaching by what was actually a *doctrinal* decree. The opinion of some theologians that the decree

---

* Catholic doctrine holds that all men on this earth, naturally descended from Adam, contract original sin. It has nothing to say about the possibility or condition of men on other planets.

of March 5, 1616 was a purely *disciplinary* decree, merely forbidding the reading of books containing Galileo's theory and nothing more than that, is, in our opinion, difficult to square with the facts of the case. Likewise it should be frankly admitted that the Congregations of the Inquisition and of the Index committed a *faux pas* in this matter. Even though that mistake is easily understandable in the circumstances of the time, it cannot be completely excused.*

b. It is beyond question that in the whole case of Galileo no ex cathedra decision was ever handed down. The pope was aware of the decree of the congregation, and approved it *as a decree of the congregation*, even though (as was customary at the time) no explicit mention of papal approbation is found in the decree itself. But the pope himself in his capacity as pope did not hand down any decision. Neither did he make the congregation's decision his own in any special way. In the Galileo case, therefore, we have a decision which is by its very nature *revocable* and nothing more. As a matter of fact, both the more sensible theologians of the time and a fair number of the scientists of the day understood the matter in exactly that light.†

Likewise, the decree of July 22, 1633 which ordered Galileo to abjure his errors and, furthermore, did so under pain of certain penalties—even though it was sent to all the bishops by order of Urban VI—possesses no other authority than the authority of the Sacred Congregation of the Inquisition. This is quite clear from

---

* Monsignor Journet feels that the authors of the decrees of 1616 and 1633 committed a fault against prudence due to a failure of nerve. They failed to act quickly enough and resolutely enough in detaching the scriptural question from the scientific one:

Where precisely were the authors of these fallible decrees at fault? They lacked the courage to detach the question of Scripture at once from the dispute over the geocentric issue. That, it seems, would have been the prudent thing to do. "Cardinal Baronius," wrote Galileo to the Grand Duchess of Tuscany, "used to say that God did not wish to teach us how the heavens go, but how we are to go to heaven." One wishes that all the theologians of that day had spoken like Cardinal Baronius! Then they would not have involved the fallible magisterium of the Congregations in a prudential and doctrinal error.—*Church of the Word, op. cit.*, I, 356–7.

† See, for example, the statements by the theologian, St. Robert Bellarmine, and the astronomer, Laplace, cited in Journet, *loc. cit.* A recent work, detailing all the intrigues surrounding the Galileo incident, is now available to English readers: George De Santillana, *The Crime of Galileo* (Chicago, 1955). Unfortunately, the multitudinous Latin and Italian footnotes are, for the most part, untranslated.

the ending of a decree of this type: "And so, we, the undersigned cardinals, pronounce . . . "; there then follows a list of their names without any mention made of the pope.

Since in this whole question, he who occupied the chair (*sedebat in cathedra*) never handed down a decision, there is simply no ex cathedra decision in the Galileo case.* Consequently it is futile to adduce it as an objection to papal infallibility.

* Since the other objections against Catholicism in general that arise at the mention of the word "Galileo" (v.g., that a scientific mind is irreconcilable with acceptance of religious teaching by authority) have no precise bearing on the question of papal infallibility, they cannot be gone into at this point. They come into focus under the more generic question of the relationship obtaining between faith and reason and will be discussed in the next volume of this series, *Sources of Revelation* and *Divine Faith*. It is impossible to discuss such a question intelligently until one understands precisely the various types of assent required by the ecclesiastical magisterium and in precisely what matters. These points are all discussed *ex professo* in the next volume.

The actual proceedings of the case of Galileo have been edited by A. Navarro, *Il processo di Galilei* (1902) and A. Favarro, *Galileo e L'Inquizione. Documenti del Processo* (1907).

Among the best treatments of the Galileo case are the following: H. Grisar, *Galilei-Studien* (1882); Funk, *Manual of Church History*, vol. II; Linsmeijer, "Riccioli's Stellung im Galileistreit," *Natur and Offenbarung* (1901); A. Müller, *Der Galilei-prozesz 1632 nach Ursprung, Verlauf und Folgen;* R. Maiocchi, *Galileo e la sua condamna* (1919); J. Stein, "Galilei en zijn tijd," *Studiën*, 85 (1916), 392.

Notes

1. Because the word "infallibility" when rendered into other languages might possibly leave the door open to misinterpretations of this sort, the fathers of the Vatican Council took the fourth chapter which had been tentatively titled "On the Infallibility of the Roman Pontiff" and re-entitled it, "On the Infallible Magisterium of the Roman Pontiff." See *Coll. Lac.*, VII, 406.

2. See Granderath, *op. cit.*, p. 190 ff. The importance of this distinction will be seen in the controversy over "ecclesiastical faith"; see volume III of this series, nos. 246–50.

3. See, for example, Matt. 23:2: "*The Scribes and the Pharisees occupy the chair* [cathedram] *of Moses.*"

4. So, John XXII in sermons preached at Avignon stated three times that the souls of the saints do not enjoy the intuitive vision of the Divine Essence prior to the General Judgment. See Hefele, *op. cit.*, VI, 299. The matter had not yet been defined.

5. Pertinent to this point are the words of Innocent III: "He [the Roman pontiff] can be judged by men, or rather can be shown to be already judged, if for example he should wither away into heresy; because he who does not believe is already judged" (*Sermo* 4); see *Decreta Gratiani*, III, d. 40, c. 6.

6. We have changed the Kleist-Lilly translation in this instance:

Some scholars maintain that this text refers exclusively to the time of our Lord's Passion and consequently cannot be used in favor of Peter's successors. They base their stand on a double argument:

(1) By supposing that Luke 22:31 is a parallel passage with Matthew 26:31 and Mark 14:17, they conclude that the *sifting* Luke was talking about must refer to the scandal which all the apostles were to undergo on the night of the Passion.

But this hypothesis is not terribly convincing since all the apostles and Peter in particular actually succumbed to scandal on that night; whereas the sifting spoken of in Luke seems to indicate that the brethren will come through it unscathed: Peter first of all, and then, because of Peter, the other apostles. As a matter of fact later events confirmed the distinction between the two types of danger: for there is no shred of probability for maintaining that Peter "strengthened" the rest of the apostles on the night of the Passion. He failed even more than the others.

(2) Opponents of our interpretation state: there is a *restrictive* sense to the passage implied from the fact that Peter is ordered to confirm his brethren *after* his own conversion from the fall of the denial: "and do thou, *when once thou hast turned again*" (*aliquando conversus—su pote epitrepsas*).

But: *a.* It is not certain that the word, "turned" (*conversus*) should be understood in this sense, since Christ had not yet predicted Peter's denial. Consequently, many scholars render the word (*conversus*) this way: "but you *in your turn* (*vicissim*) confirm," or, "You *turn yourself to* your brethren and confirm them."

b. Even if the word *conversus* may be understood of a conversion from a fall, it does not follow at all that the task of strengthening the brethren should be fulfilled *immediately* after the conversion, and at that time *exclusively*. Furthermore, the particle (*pote*) seems to indicate a time-period that is more remote (see Palmieri, *De Romano pontifice*, 2nd ed., p. 353). At all events, even if the explanation proffered by our opponents might seem to have some probability to it, *considering Sacred Scripture alone*, the *interpretation of tradition* is of such a kind that "for men who follow the Church's interpretation of Scripture, there can and should be no doubt at all about the true meaning of the passage" (*Relat. Ep. Brixin.* in *Coll. Lac.*, VII, 282).

Now if the text in question, at least from the viewpoint of tradition simply must be understood of Peter as the foundation and supreme pastor of the Church, obviously the quibblings of Jos. Langen fall apart; for he contended that the indefectibility promised Peter does not prevent him from innocently falling into error in matters of faith, but only prevents him from losing the virtue of faith by sinful apostasy from Christ. It would certainly not be much help if the one who holds the office of strengthening his brethren in the faith could not become a "formal heretic," but could in some circumstances go astray from the truth (see Palmieri, *loc. cit.*).

A recent, excellent article on this subject by a Scripture scholar is to be found in Edmund F. Sutcliffe, "Et Tu Aliquando Conversus" CBQ, 15 (July 1953), 305–310. This study corroborates the interpretation given here; it adds to the theological reasoning here employed, some cogent exegetical and philological arguments.

7. *Epistula ad Abatem albanorum catholicum;* see H. Hurter, "Ein Zeugnis aus dem 6. Jahrhunderte für die Unfehlbarkeit des Papstes," ZkTh (1910), p. 219.

8. See Hefele, *op. cit.,* II, 188.

9. *Conc. Constantinop.* III, act. 18; cited in Labbe, VI, 1053.

10. Philip Hughes describes their confusion neatly in the following words: All the cardinals—with one exception—recognized Clement VII as pope [i.e., in a second election attempting to disqualify the legitimately elected Urban VI]. What was Christendom to do? How was it to decide between the conflicting accounts of the rivals? And how was it to judge on which occasion this same body of cardinals had really, by its unanimous vote, elected a pope, in April or September? Christendom speedily divided, along lines more or less political, according as its sympathies were French or anti-French. And both camps were equally representative of the Church, holy people, since canonized, being found among the supporters of the Avignon pope as well as among those of his Roman antagonist. Was the Church divided? On one point only, the point of fact, was Urban truly pope or was Clement? On all points of doctrine, on the point of papal powers and the obedience due to the pope, all were in agreement. There was nowhere any rebellion against an admittedly lawful pope. The division was not a schism in any real sense of the word. But it was a very real division, and it lasted for just short of forty years.—*Popular History, op. cit.,* p. 139.

11. *De potestate ecclesiae,* constit. 12; in *Opera omnia* (Paris, 1606), I, 135.

12. *De ecclesia Christi,* q. 5, a. 3 (Paris, 1727), II, 134.

13. *Orat. theol.,* 3, no. 7. Then the illustrious theologian mentions his personal opinion, stating that the privilege of papal infallibility, "is, in our judgment, certain because of the teaching of the fathers and the councils" (no. 8).

14. This is obvious, for example, from the condemnations of Baius (DB 1001 ff.); Jansenius (DB 1092 ff.); Quesnel (DB 1351 ff.); and Synod of Pistoia (DB 1501 ff.), and so forth.

15. See Hefele, *op. cit.,* I, 681 ff.; Hergenröther-Kirsch, *Kirchengeschichte,* I, 374; BLE (1905), p. 223; (1907), p. 279; A. Feder, "Neue Literatur zur Liberiusfrage," ThR (1910); F. di Capua, *Il ritmo prosaico nelle lettere dei Pape,* I (1937), p. 236–47.

16. See below p. 336, note.

17. Others give a different explanation, namely that Honorius was referring to a kind of moral unity between the divine and human wills in Christ; see Hefele-Leclercq, *Histoire des conciles,* III, 376 ff.

18. See Hefele, *op. cit.,* III, nos. 296–8; Hergenröther-Kirsch, *op. cit.,* I, 625.

19. In Greek: *Tē bebēlō prodosia mianthēnai tēn aspilon parexōrēsen.* Thus, certain versions err by translating the text as, "he tried to stain," rather than, "he allowed to be stained."

20. See Hefele, *op. cit.,* III, no. 324.

21. Jaffé, *Monumenta moguntina,* p. 91.

22. See Hefele, *op. cit.*, III, 557; Barthélemy, *Erreurs et mensonges historiques* (1873), I, 269–86; *Kirchenlexikon*, XII, col. 1002; Gilbert in *Revue des questiones scientifiques* (1882); Krabbo in *Mitteilungen des Institut für Oesterreichisch Geschichtsforschung*, 24 (1902), 1.

Epilogue: The Pope's Temporal Sovereignty *

194 After the middle of the nineteenth century the Italian states burned with a desire for political unity. When they were finally coalesced into "One Italy with Rome as its Capital" even the *ecclesiastical state,* which the popes had ruled over as kings for long centuries, was first of all vastly diminished in territory and then, in the year 1870, completely subjugated by military might. The following year the new government through its "law of grants" decided to bestow upon the pope a personal privilege of sovereignty and inviolability, free commerce with foreign nations, and an annual pension. But since all these things depended exclusively on the good pleasure of the Italian government, the pope could not accept the arrangement.

First, Pius IX and then the succeeding popes protested strongly against the injury done to the Holy See and the resultant shameful and intolerable conditions forced upon the pope.[1] They did not recognize the Italian government with Rome as its capital until Feb. 11, 1929 when "the Roman Question" was definitively settled by a solemn concordat. By this concordat the Holy See recognized: "the kingdom of Italy under the dynasty of the house of Savoy together with Rome, the capital of the Italian nation"; and at the same time Italy recognized: "Vatican City as a state under the supreme sovereignty of the supreme pontiff."[2]

195 To understand why the popes insisted so strongly and so unwaveringly: (*1*) that they should not be deprived of their temporal sovereignty; (*2*) that the plunder committed should be repaired, at least to the degree that the head of the universal church might cease to find himself in that deplorable condition to which he had been reduced in the year 1870, we mention the following points:

The protests of the popes always reiterated the same point: it

---

* For a lively, unbiased, historical presentation of this whole matter by a non-Catholic, see: *Pio Nono,* by E. E. Y. Hales (New York, 1954): "The Prisoner in the Vatican," pp. 313–331. The whole book, indeed, is commendable for its balanced, scholarly assessment of the struggles between the papacy and nineteenth century liberalism.

is of immense concern to the entire Christian world that the pope in ruling the Church should not only *be* free, but should be *clearly seen* to be free and subject to no earthly government:

> the individual faithful all over the world and various nations would never cease suspecting, or at least fearing, that the pope might bend his actions to meet the whims of the prince or government on whose bounty he lived. As a result, various peoples might not hesitate to refuse to obey his decisions on this pretext.[3]

But the pope will always be the citizen of some government, unless he has a territory of his own. Consequently some sort of temporal sovereignty is a necessity for the pope.

The pope's need of temporal sovereignty, then, is viewed in relation to the exercise of his spiritual power. Obviously this necessity of temporal sovereignty is not an *absolute* necessity. Since the Church in the early centuries lacked all temporal sovereignty, it is clear that she could, strictly speaking, exist without it. In other words, the popes could exercise the duties and rights of their primacy in some fashion without that temporal sovereignty. The necessity for temporal sovereignty, therefore, is a *moral* necessity. It amounts to this: the pope's spiritual power cannot be exercised in suitable fashion and with unhampered fruitfulness without such temporal sovereignty.

Since from very ancient times, viz., the collapse of the Roman Empire: "it came about by the very striking plan of Divine Providence that the Roman pontiff should be possessed of civil sovereignty,"[4] the popes did not feel free to simply abandon at whim this guarantee of their liberty which they had justly acquired and possessed peacefully throughout so many centuries. That explains why the popes who succeeded Pius IX took an oath to strive to the best of their power to restore the temporal sovereignty.

196 In this constant demand the popes quite reasonably prescinded from the question of whether perhaps some other guarantee might be found to safeguard and make plain to the world the complete liberty of the Roman pontiff. Since up to this time "neither Divine Providence has pointed out, nor have human suggestions hit upon anything similar which might suitably compensate for the protection brought about [by one's own sovereignty],"[5] the popes rightly

(314)

demanded the restitution of that one safeguard which throughout so many centuries had suitably guaranteed their liberty—a safeguard which was destroyed by obvious injustice and military might.

In demanding restitution for the territory that had been stolen from them, the popes refrained from laying down the exact amount of restitution to be made. Since the freedom of the head of the Church does not necessarily depend upon the size of the papal territory, and since it is up to the popes alone to decide how much territory would suffice for their purpose, Pius XI deserves great praise for his wise generosity. He was content with the tiny state of Vatican City and decided to leave all the rest of the papal territory to Italy so that the Roman Question might be finally and definitively brought to an end.

Notes

1. See DB 1775–6 and the statements of Pius IX cited in 1776a; Leo XIII, encyclical *Inscrutabili* (April 21, 1878) in *Allocutiones Leo XIII* (Desclée ed.), I, 10; Pius X, allocution of Nov. 9, 1903 in *Civ. Catt.* S. 18, vol. 12, p. 386; Benedict XV, encyclical, *Ad beatissimi* (Nov. 1, 1914) in AAS (1914), p. 511. Pius XI, encyclical, *Ubi arcano* (Dec. 23, 1922) in AAS (1922), p. 699.
2. See AAS (1929), p. 221.
3. Pius IX, allocution, *Quibus quantisque* (April 20, 1849).
4. Pius IX, apostolic letter, *Cum catholica* (March 26, 1860).
5. Pius XI, encyclical, *Ubi arcano*, *loc. cit.*, p. 699.

CHAPTER IV

The Bishops

Article I

THE BISHOPS CONSIDERED SINGLY

I. *Preliminary Remarks*

II. *Jurisdiction of Ordinaries:*

    Assertion 1: Bishops possess ordinary jurisdiction over their own dioceses by divine right.

    Assertion 2: The jurisdiction of bishops over their own dioceses is complete in its own kind, but is not a supreme and independent jurisdiction.

    Assertion 3: With the exception of the Roman pontiff, no bishop possesses authority over other bishops by divine right.

    Assertion 4: Bishops, to be able to exercise jurisdiction over their flocks, must be adopted by the authority of the pope.

    Assertion 5: Bishops receive jurisdiction over their flocks directly from the Roman pontiff.

    Assertion 6: No one else in the Church besides the bishops possesses jurisdiction by divine law.

CHAPTER IV

The Bishops

Christ so arranged the government of His Church that He joined to Peter, the supreme shepherd, other shepherds to help him rule the flock. Those other shepherds were the rest of the apostles. As the pope fills the post originally occupied by St. Peter, so the bishops fill the post of the apostles. The pope's powers have already been discussed; it now remains to discuss the power of the bishops. First, we shall discuss the bishops viewed individually; then, viewed collectively.

Article I

THE BISHOPS CONSIDERED SINGLY

I. Preliminary Remarks

Since the power of orders* possessed by the bishops will be explained in the treatise, *Christ's Sacraments,* here our discussion focuses exclusively on their power of jurisdiction. Hence, the term "bishops" does not here refer to those who enjoy the fulness of the priesthood, yet do not rule over individual dioceses (titular bishops). We are discussing here only bishops in the fullest sense of the word: those who are usually called the "ordinary bishops" of various places, or, simply, "ordinaries."

---

* The power of *orders* is immediately directed to the sanctification of souls through the offering of the sacrifice of the Mass and the administration of the sacraments. The power of *jurisdiction,* on the other hand, is immediately directed to ruling the faithful with reference to the attainment of life eternal, and is actuated through the authoritative teaching of revealed truths (*sacred magisterium*), and through the promulgation of laws (*legislative power*), together with the authoritative decision of legal actions involving its subjects (*judicial power*), and the application of penal sanctions against transgressors of the law (*coactive* or *coercive power*). These last three powers are functions of the same sacred jurisdictional authority with which the Church is endowed as a perfect society.—Parente, *Dictionary, op. cit.,* p. 124.

II. The Jurisdiction of Ordinaries

197 *Assertion 1: Bishops possess ordinary jurisdiction over their own dioceses by divine right.*

This assertion is *theologically certain.*

Ordinary jurisdiction in the canonical sense is that jurisdiction which is annexed to an *office;* delegated jurisdiction is that which is bestowed on a *person* by another. The first assertion, then, is that the bishops rule over their flocks, not in the name of another man such as the pope, as mere vicars of that person, but in their own name. By the very nature of the office once bestowed upon them, they themselves, through themselves, are the true shepherds of their flock.[1]

The bishops are said to possess this ordinary power by *divine right* because their office was established not by the Church but by God. For God Himself—Christ or the Holy Spirit—laid it down that in normal circumstances particular churches should be ruled by their own individual bishops. In this sense it is said: "The Holy Spirit has placed the bishops to rule the Church of God." Consequently not even the pope himself can cancel that office, by decreeing, for example, that *vicars apostolic* * should universally † preside over particular churches, or that *groups* of bishops should take over that office.

The jurisdiction of individual bishops is limited to their own dioceses. The fact that their jurisdiction is thus restricted today, and always has been thus restricted is quite obvious from the ancient custom of adding to the name of the bishop the name of the see which he occupies: bishop of Antioch, bishop of Alexandria, etc. One citation will suffice to bring this point out clearly. Already in his day St. Augustine could write:

---

* A *vicar apostolic* is a prelate commissioned by the Holy See to administer a diocese whose see is vacant or whose ordinary is incapacitated; or to administer ecclesiastical affairs in regions where an ordinary hierarchy has not yet been established. For their rights and duties see CIC, 293–311.

† Note the term *universally*, i.e., as a general rule. There is nothing to prevent having portions of the Church, either recently established or temporarily in a state of distress, in which ecclesiastical matters have not yet been set up on a regular basis, from being run temporarily by vicars apostolic or prefects apostolic. It is one thing to change the constitution of the Church; it is another thing entirely to provide for extraordinary circumstances in an extraordinary way.

It is ridiculous to say this as though I had any proper government over any church but the church of Hippo . . . for we only act in other cities in ecclesiastical matters insofar as the bishops of those cities, our brothers and co-priests, either allow or commission us to do so.—*Epistula* 34. 5.

198 *Assertion 2: The jurisdiction of bishops over their own dioceses is complete in its own kind, but it is not a supreme and independent jurisdiction.*

The power of the bishops is said to be *complete in its own kind* because it covers both the internal and external forum, and because it extends to all parts of the diocese. Consequently, their jurisdiction includes both teaching and ruling power (legislative, judicial, and coercive); otherwise the bishops would not really be shepherds, that is, teachers and rulers of their flocks: "as far as each one's own diocese is concerned, they [the bishops] each and all as true Shepherds feed the flocks entrusted to them and rule them in the name of Christ" (MCC 52). Still, by the very fact that the jurisdiction of a bishop over his own flock is always subordinate to the power of the supreme pontiff, it cannot be *supreme and independent:* "Yet in exercising this office they are not altogether independent, but are duly subordinate to the authority of the Roman Pontiff; and although their jurisdiction is inherent in their office, yet they receive it directly from the same Supreme Pontiff" (*ibid.*).

Two conclusions flow from this fact:

a. The *teaching power* of the individual bishop is not infallible. Obviously a bishop's doctrinal decision, by the very fact of stemming from a subordinate pastor, can be retracted and corrected by the supreme pastor. It would, then, be contradictory to say that some decision is by its very nature simultaneously reformable and irreformable, or, fallible and infallible. Because of this subordination it follows that a bishop's magisterium (besides being limited to a definite locality) does not extend to a decision in controverted matters; rather, it extends to the handing down, safeguarding, and defense of those matters which are already established either by an explicit definition, or by the universal consent of the Church.

Be careful, however, not to conclude from the restrictions laid down that when a bishop is teaching in his official capacity he carries practically no more weight than any other learned man.

The opinion of any private doctor can be rejected by anyone without injuring the duty of religious obedience. Indeed, common prudence itself usually dictates that one should carefully weigh his arguments. But the case is entirely different when a bishop is officially exercising his magisterium in his own diocese. For the bishop in virtue of his very office, that is, not because of his renown for learning, and not because of the power of the arguments he may adduce, but because of the very public authority he possesses in the Church, should out of religious obedience be heeded by his subjects in such fashion that they feel obliged to accept his teaching as the true doctrine of Christ, unless there be special reasons to prove the contrary. This is what theologians mean by saying that the bishop possesses for his own diocese a *magisterium* which is not indeed infallible, but which is *authentic,* i.e., authoritative.[2]

b. The *ruling power*—jurisdiction taken in a very strict sense—of bishops over their own flocks can be restricted to a greater or lesser degree by the pope so that certain kinds of cases or persons may be withdrawn from their power. Obviously the jurisdiction of a bishop can be more or less broad without thereby ceasing to be genuinely pastoral. Since its extent has not been determined in individual cases by divine law, it can be limited by the pope. Furthermore, the fact that the jurisdiction of individual bishops extends to only one diocese, indicates that it is by its very nature subject to some limitation: for those matters which pertain to the common good of the Church Universal cannot be left to the decision of individual bishops.

199 *Assertion 3: With the exception of the Roman pontiff, no bishop possesses authority over other bishops by divine right.*

The body of bishops continues the college of the apostles. Now among the apostles no one was placed in authority over the rest of them by Christ, except St. Peter. The conclusion is obvious. Consequently, all the degrees of hierarchical rank factually existing between the papacy and the episcopacy—patriarchial, primatial, and archiepiscopal—are ecclesiastical in origin. From this it follows that: (*a*) the office of patriarch, primate, etc., considered precisely as an office, consists in a kind of participation in the papal office; (*b*) the supra-episcopal authority possessed by patriarchs, etc., over bishops within their orbit is bestowed upon them by the pope. This fact is symbolized by the cloak (*pallium*) which

THE BISHOPS

"taken from the body of St. Peter," is sent to them as a sign of their sharing in a supra-episcopal jurisdiction.³

Assertion 4: Bishops, to be able to exercise jurisdiction over their flocks, must be adopted by the authority of the pope. 200

The way in which individual bishops are established must now be discussed. Even though the episcopal office is something established by God, it is quite obvious that individual rulers of individual dioceses are directly established not by God, but by men. At this juncture we are not inquiring from whom the bishops proximately receive their jurisdiction (see below no. 202), but what is required for them *actually to function* as pastors of their diocese and *to exercise* their jurisdiction there. To be able to do this, we state, they must be adopted by the authority of the supreme pontiff. *Adoption* (*assumptio*) is a short form standing for "adoption or assumption into the corporate body of the pastors of the Church." It designates the factor by which the formal admittance of a selected or elected candidate is brought to its final conclusion. We use the phrase, "by the authority of the pope," to indicate that a direct, personal intervention by the pope is not necessarily required. So long as the adoption be done by someone to whom the pope has entrusted the task (regardless of the precise way in which the pope commissions him to do so), or in accord with regulations already established or approved by the pope. In saying that papal adoption is *necessary*, we do not mean it is merely necessary because of ecclesiastical law currently in force; we mean it is necessary by the divine law itself. Even though this necessity has never been explicitly defined, it follows absolutely from Catholic principles.

It is a fact that a bishop cannot act as a pastor of the Church unless he be a member of that body which is a continuation of the apostolic college. Now the Roman pontiff, as Christ's vicar, presides over that college with full and supreme authority. It would be ridiculous, therefore, to think that someone could be constituted a member of that body in such fashion as not to need to be acknowledged or adopted in any way by the very head of that body, i.e., the Roman pontiff. Again, the Roman pontiff is the supreme shepherd of the entire Church to which the bishops may be compared as subordinate shepherds for each individual part of the Church. Clearly it would be nonsensical to think someone could take charge of part of the sheepfold without the agreement of the one who rules the universal sheepfold with complete authority.

201   The *objection* is raised: in ancient times the popes did not intervene in any way at all in the selection of bishops. That they did not always intervene directly and by explicit consent, is *granted;* that they did not intervene at all, not even mediately and by legal consent, we *deny*. In the absence of historical testimony, it is admittedly impossible to prove this statement directly.

Still, keeping in mind Catholic principles, it is fair enough to reconstruct the process somewhat as follows.[4] The apostles and their principal aides, in accord with Peter's consent and will, both selected the first bishops, and decreed that thereafter when sees became vacant the vacancy should be taken care of in some satisfactory way, and in a way which at the very least would not be without the intervention of the neighboring bishops. As often, therefore, in accord with this process, established with Peter's approval, a new bishop was constituted in the early Church, Peter's authority ratified that selection implicitly. Later on, when ecclesiastical affairs were arranged more precisely by positive law, the patriarchs in the Eastern churches and the metropolitans in the Western churches used to establish the bishops; but they did so only in virtue of the authority of the Apostolic See by which they themselves had been established, even though in a variety of ways. Finally, in later centuries the matter of establishing bishops was set up in different fashion; indeed in such a way that in the Latin church especially, the direct intervention of the Roman pontiff was required. For details in this matter, consult the canonists.

202   *Assertion 5: Bishops receive jurisdiction over their flocks directly from the Roman pontiff.*

This is *certain*.

In the previous assertion it was pointed out that the establishment of individual bishops always involves some intervention by the pope. The bishops, we saw, cannot actually exercise their jurisdiction over their flocks without the consent, explicit or implicit, of the pope. Another question now remains to be answered: what is the precise connection between papal confirmation in office and episcopal jurisdiction? Is papal intervention simply a *condition* for the reception of episcopal jurisdiction, or is it a *cause?*

Briefly, do the bishops receive jurisdiction directly from God, or only indirectly through the mediation of the Roman pontiff?

Prior to *Mystici Corporis,* two opinions were held by Catholics:

1. Some theologians taught that God directly confers episcopal jurisdiction in each individual instance, either by the very consecration of the bishop, or in some other way. Consequently those authors were of the opinion that the pope either merely assigned the bishop his flock, or limited the bishop's divinely conferred jurisdiction to a definite church, or by his consent fulfilled some condition without which Christ would not confer jurisdiction on the individual bishop, etc. But no matter how they explained the matter, they all admitted that jurisdiction was bestowed from heaven always in dependence upon and with subordination to the supreme pontiff, so that the pope could always restrict, extend, or even completely prohibit the exercise of that jurisdiction. This opinion, once hotly defended in the Council of Trent, was described by Benedict XIV as: "backed by valid arguments."[5]

2. The other, and always the majority opinion, maintained that bishops received their jurisdiction not directly, but indirectly from God. They receive it, in other words, through the supreme pontiff who, in establishing them as bishops, at the same time by explicit will, or at least by legal will, confers jurisdiction upon them. This second opinion, in the judgment of the same Benedict XIV, "seems: (*a*) more in harmony with reason; and (*b*) more in harmony with authority."[6]

In reference to (a): It harmonizes better with the monarchical structure of the Church that all jurisdiction should be communicated to subordinate pastors by the supreme pastor, the vicar of Christ. Again, since there is no doubt at all that the *power* of the supreme pontiff suffices to confer jurisdiction on bishops, the direct intervention of God is adduced without any real need for it. Furthermore, this second opinion gives a far easier explanation of why it is that the pope can diminish, increase, restrict, or even completely take away the jurisdiction of a bishop. Finally, it is a fact[7] that:

> A bishop appointed to a diocese, but not yet consecrated, possesses jurisdiction; contrariwise, a bishop already consecrated, but not yet established over a diocese, lacks jurisdiction. Two consequences follow immediately from that fact: first, that

episcopal jurisdiction is not conferred by consecration; secondly, that it is conferred through the mediation of papal confirmation [i.e., adoption].—Zapalena, *loc. cit.*

In reference to (b): St. Optatus of Mileve says, "St. Peter alone received the keys of the kingdom of heaven to confer them on others" (*De schismate Donatistarum* 7. 3). In these words, Optatus seems to have been considering, not the apostles * themselves, but their successors, the bishops.

Innocent I states that especially in questions of the faith, all bishops should consult St. Peter: "the originator of both his [the bishop's] name and honor" (*Epistula* 30).

St. Leo I says of St. Peter, "If [Christ] willed the rest of the rulers to have anything in common with him [Peter], He never gave except through him whatever it was He did not deny to the others" (*Sermo* 4. 2).

Pius VI praises the Roman pontiff "from whom the bishops themselves receive their own authority, just as he himself has received his supreme authority from God" (DB 1500).

Finally, in his epoch-making encyclical, *Mystici Corporis*, Pius XII states explicitly and without any qualification that the bishops receive their jurisdiction directly from the pope:

> as far as each one's own diocese is concerned, they [the bishops] each and all as true Shepherds feed the flocks entrusted to them and rule them in the name of Christ. Yet in exercising this office they are not altogether independent, but are duly subordinate to the authority of the Roman Pontiff; and although their jurisdiction is inherent in their office, yet they receive it *directly* from the same Supreme Pontiff.—MCC 52; italics ours.

Following this explicit, even though brief, declaration by Pius XII the first opinion is, we feel, no longer tenable. We would agree with Cardinal Ottaviani's statement that the second opinion "should now . . . be rated as absolutely certain because of the words of the supreme pontiff, Pius XII."[8]

---

* The apostles themselves, according to the more common opinion, received both their jurisdiction and their mission from Christ Himself directly (Zapalena, *loc. cit.*, p. 105).

Assertion 6: No one else in the Church besides the bishops possesses jurisdiction by divine law.

This assertion must be held contrary to the position of some Gallicans and Jansenists who taught that even the office of "parish pastors" was instituted by Christ in his seventy-two disciples.[9] That idea is utterly nonsensical. Even though the priesthood (and likewise the diaconate) is of divine institution, the position of parish pastor was introduced by the Church, and introduced no earlier than the fifth century. Consequently, the jurisdiction of parish pastors in the internal forum, even though it is ordinary, comes to them only by ecclesiastical law.

Notes

1. See DB 1828; TCT 208; and MCC 52.
2. What is said here about the obligation to heed the teaching of an individual bishop in his own diocese can be applied in some fashion to parish pastors and other authorized preachers of God's word; namely, *insofar* as they are in unison with the local bishop and acting at his behest.
3. See *Pontificale Romanum*, p. 1, *De pallio*.
4. For a fuller and stricter theological demonstration of this question, see Zapalena, *op. cit.*, II, 94–115.
5. *De Synodo diœcesana*, I, 4, 2.
6. *Ibid.*
7. For a brief, cogent proof of this point, see Zapalena, *loc. cit.*, p. 107–8.
8. *Institutiones juris publici ecclesiastici* (Rome, 1947), I, 413; see Zapalena, *loc. cit.*, p. 112.
9. To this category belong propositions 9 and 10 of the Synod of Pistoia condemned by Pius VI; see DB 1509–10.

Article II

THE BISHOPS CONSIDERED COLLECTIVELY

I. *Preliminary Remarks:*

    PROPOSITION: The college of bishops, whether gathered in an ecumenical council, or dispersed throughout the world but morally united to the supreme pontiff, in its teaching on matters of faith and morals, is infallible.

    Proof: contained in the previous proof for the infallibility of the Church's *magisterium*.

    Scholion: Ecumenical Councils:
        1. Conditions
        2. Usefulness
        3. A list of ecumenical councils

Article II

THE BISHOPS CONSIDERED COLLECTIVELY

I. Preliminary Remarks   204

Viewing the bishops "collectively" does not mean considering them simply as a mathematical total of many persons individually placed in charge of individual dioceses. If that were the case, there would be nothing special to add to what has already been stated in the previous article. Rather, it means considering the bishops insofar as all of them along with the Roman pontiff form a *corporate entity,* or *a single body* of pastors placed in charge of the entire Church. Since they do not form a single body except insofar as they are united to the supreme pontiff and are subject to him, it should be clear that formulae like: "college of bishops," "body of bishops," "the Catholic episcopate," etc.—always include the pope, the head and crown of the rest.

Note, too, that in asserting that all the bishops (insofar as jointly with the Roman pontiff they form one body) are in charge of the universal Church, we do not imply that the bishops possess two kinds of jurisdiction: one which is particular and received directly from the pope; the other which is universal and received directly from Christ Himself in their episcopal consecration.[1] Not at all. We maintain that the bishops do not possess any other jurisdiction than that which they receive from the Roman pontiff. All the same, when the bishops scattered throughout the world—but in harmony with their head—are governing their individual flocks, they are by that very fact simultaneously concurring with the Roman pontiff in governing the entire flock of Christ. Similarly, when a large group of bishops, assembled in a council, is adopted by the pope into a unity of a single agent, all of them as a group concur in ruling the universal Church, even though they do so only in virtue of the power transmitted to them by the Roman pontiff.

205 PROPOSITION. *The college of bishops, whether gathered in an ecumenical council, or dispersed throughout the world but morally united to the supreme pontiff, in its teaching on matters of faith and morals, is infallible.*

This proposition is *of faith.*

In the analysis of this proposition, keep in mind the principles laid down above (see nos. 77–99) about the object, nature, and conditions of infallibility.

The *first* part of this proposition states that the college of bishops is endowed with the charism of infallibility when it is assembled together somewhere in an ecumenical council. What is required to constitute an ecumenical council will be explained in detail below (no. 207). Here we emphasize simply one point: there cannot be an ecumenical council without the consent and cooperation of the supreme pontiff (CIC 222).

The *second* part of the proposition states that the college of bishops is also endowed with infallibility when dispersed throughout the world, but morally united with the Roman pontiff. In other words, when the individual bishops, residing in their home dioceses, unanimously propose the same doctrine as the pope and impose that doctrine in unqualified fashion, they are infallible.

The doctrinal agreement of the bishops dispersed throughout the world can be discerned in a variety of ways: for example, from the catechisms they allow to be published for the instruction of the faithful; from the pastoral instructions the bishops issue to oppose some erroneous doctrine which is beginning to spread; from the decrees of local councils held in various parts of the world; from the fact that a given doctrine is normally preached throughout the entire Catholic world in sermons to the people, or is found regularly in prayerbooks possessing episcopal approbation, and so forth.

It hardly needs stating that the unanimity of the bishops does *not* have to be mathematically universal, as though the dissent of one or two bishops would cripple the teaching power of the rest of the episcopal college. What suffices is a *morally* universal unanimity[2] which in most instances will not be difficult to determine, even though it is impossible to fix mathematically the minimum requirements for such unanimity. On the other hand, no matter how unanimous the agreement of bishops might conceivably be, such unanimity would never suffice for infallibility if the Roman pontiff were to be in opposition to it. We deliberately use the phrase, "might conceivably be," because the more probable opinion of theologians maintains that factually it could never happen that a majority of the bishops would depart from the doctrine of the pope.

Even though the proposition as laid down above has never been explicitly defined, it is *a dogma of faith* in both its parts. For ecumenical councils have really been proclaiming their own infallibility every time they exercised it; and they have exercised it every time they have handed down a definitive decree condemning heresies. As for the second part of the proposition, the infallibility of the episcopal college dispersed throughout the world was implicitly asserted by the Vatican Council when it stated: "By divine and Catholic faith must be believed all those matters which are contained in the written or handed-down word of God and which are proposed by the Church to be believed as divinely revealed, whether she does so by a solemn judgment or *by her ordinary and universal magisterium*" (DB 1792).

Proof: **206**

Proof of the proposition is contained in all the arguments given previously (no. 79 ff.) to prove the infallibility of the Church's magisterium; for the magisterium of the Church, viewed concretely, is the body of the bishops united to their head.

The following three brief theological arguments will pinpoint the reasons why the Catholic episcopate, when united to the pope, is endowed with infallibility in teaching matters on faith and morals. Although these arguments speak formally of an "ecumenical council," they are equally applicable to the college of bishops dispersed throughout the world.[3]

1. It has been proven: (*a*) Christ instituted an infallible magisterium in the apostolic college; (*b*) this magisterium was to be perpetual or continued in the legitimate successors of the apostles; (*c*) the apostolic college is continued by the episcopal college; (*d*) but an ecumenical council is the episcopal college together with its head. Consequently we have present in an ecumenical council the infallible magisterium instituted by Christ.

2. If the teaching Church in an ecumenical council could fall into error, the universal Church would also err in *believing*. But the universal Church cannot err in believing, otherwise (contrary

to the promise of Christ), "the gates of hell would prevail against her."

3. If an ecumenical council were to err, so too would the pope speaking ex cathedra. But the pope when speaking ex cathedra cannot err, as was previously demonstrated. The conclusion is clear.

First of all, then, the Roman Catholic episcopate exercises infallibility when assembled in conciliar fashion, for a definition by an ecumenical council is the clearest and most solemn way in which the magisterium instituted by Christ can exercise its prerogative. That is why St. Athanasius stated in reference to a decree of the Council of Nicaea: "The word of the Lord expressed through the ecumenical Council of Nicaea will remain forever" (*Epistula ad Afros* 2); and St. Gregory the Great stated: "For just as I accept and venerate the four books of the Holy Gospel, so, too, do I accept and venerate the four councils. And I likewise equally venerate a fifth council [i.e., should there be a fifth council]" (*Epistulae* i. 25).

Second, the Roman Catholic episcopate exercises its infallibility when dispersed throughout the world. For Christ's promise of divine assistance to the magisterium of the Church was given in unqualified fashion. Consequently there are no grounds whatsoever to support the restriction of Christ's promise exclusively to the extraordinary case of an ecumenical council. Indeed, in saying: "*And mark: I am with you at all times,*" Christ declared in very plain terms that His help would primarily pertain to that daily and ordinary exercise of teaching power carried on by the episcopacy dispersed throughout the world.*

207 *Scholion. On Ecumenical Councils.*

A *council* may be defined as an authorized assembly of the Church's rulers to judge and legislate in matters of doctrine and

---

* What Pius XII affirmed of the papal ordinary magisterium as exercised through encyclical letters is equally applicable to the ordinary magisterium of the bishops dispersed throughout the world but in agreement with the Roman pontiff: " . . . these matters are taught with the *ordinary* teaching authority, of which it is true to say: '*He who hears you, hears Me*' " (*Humani generis*, NCWC trans., 20).

Finally, in all reverence, one might say Christ's promise to assist His Church perpetually would not be very helpful if it were restricted to the extraordinary case of ecumenical councils. There have been only 20 ecumenical councils in the 2,000 year period since the founding of the Church. Are we to suppose that Christ left His Church to fumble with purely human aids during the several hundred year intervals between ecumenical councils?

ecclesiastical discipline. Councils are divided into two major categories: *particular* and *general* (*ecumenical*). A *particular* ° council is one in which bishops from a single province, or from several provinces, gather together; an *ecumenical* council is one in which the entire episcopal college is represented.[4]

1. *Requirements for an Ecumenical Council*. Two things are necessary by divine law † to have such a council: (*a*) that all bishops who are ordinaries of dioceses throughout the world be summoned and that a sufficient number from different parts of the world actually attend so that, morally speaking, they are judged to represent the entire episcopal college.[5] Given such a representation, those bishops who are actually absent from the council are judged to yield their own right and to agree tacitly to all decrees which may be handed down.

Titular bishops need not, apparently, be summoned to an ecumenical council. They can, of course, be invited and if present possess a deliberative vote. On them and other invited clerics ‡ the pope, out of the fulness of his own power of jurisdiction, confers a quasi-episcopal jurisdiction for the occasion.

(*b*) That the authority of the pope be joined to the council and

---

° This category is subdivided into *provincial* and *plenary* councils: . . . a council is described as *provincial* when there are present at it the bishops of a single province, under the presidency of its Archbishop or Metropolitan; *plenary* (at one time called *national*) when composed of the bishops of one kingdom or nation; *general* or *ecumenical* . . . when representing the Universal Church, with the Roman Pontiff presiding, either personally or through his representative.—Aelred Graham, O.S.B., "The Church on Earth," in *The Teachings of the Catholic Church*, II, 724.

† We say by *divine* law because this matter is inextricably interwoven with the constitution of the Church as established by Christ. By divine law Peter and his successors, the popes, received the *primacy*; and by divine law only the bishops are the successors of the apostles, co-ruling with Peter the universal Church. Finally, do not misconstrue the phrase "by divine law" as if it meant: God Himself or Christ has decreed that ecumenical councils should be convoked at regular intervals. It means simply, *if* the Church decides to hold an ecumenical council, certain conditions for such a council are requisite by divine law (Zapalena, p. 177). *Ecclesiastical* law governing matters pertaining to ecumenical councils is found in CIC 222–229.

‡ Those summoned to an Oecumenical Council, and having a deliberative vote, are the Cardinals of the Holy Roman Church, whether or not they be bishops; Patriarchs, Primates, Archbishops, and Prelates *Nullius;* the Abbot Primate, the Abbot Superiors of Monastic Congregations, and the Chief Superiors of exempt religious orders of clerics. Titular bishops also have a deliberative vote when called to a Council. The expert theologians and canonists who always attend are there in an advisory capacity, not as judges and witnesses in matters of faith.—Aelred Graham, *loc. cit.*, p. 725; see CIC 223.

invest it. No matter how numerous the gathering of bishops, it does not constitute the body of the pastors of the Church unless Peter be joined to it. Consequently, even if all the bishops are assembled in one place, they do not possess supreme authority over the Church, nor infallible teaching power except insofar as they are united with the Roman pontiff and together with him form one moral person.

If we scrutinize more closely the relationship which, because of the primacy and hence by divine law, obtains between the pope and an ecumenical council, the following points stand out:

(1) The pope alone has the right to *convoke* an ecumenical council.[6] To understand this point correctly, it is necessary to distinguish carefully between convocation viewed simply as a *material* action, and viewed as an *authoritative* action.

Material convocation of an ecumenical council is simply the physical act which causes the assemblage of bishops in one geographical location; convocation viewed as an authoritative act is what makes the gathering take on the nature of an ecumenical council. Material convocation of a council is not legitimate unless it be done either by the pope or with the consent—tacit or expressed—of the pope. Briefly, then, regardless of the particular fashion in which a council may be supposed to be physically convoked, the council itself is always legitimate, provided it does not lack papal convocation in the second sense of the term. This papal approbation is *ipso facto* possessed when the pope, either personally or through his ambassadors, joins himself to the gathering. In so doing he adopts the gathered bishops into unity with himself so that together with himself they constitute one moral person teaching and judging. It should be clear, therefore, that papal convocation is of the essence of an ecumenical council only insofar as the term is taken to designate that action of the pope which establishes the council in its specific character.

Convocation of councils in the light of history: turning from a purely doctrinal exposition of this matter to the facts of history, it is certain that the first eight councils were materially convoked by the emperors* in whose hands in those days lay practically all

---

* Zapalena's exposition of this point is both succinct and convincing:
A rather serious historical objection arises here; the first eight Eastern councils were convoked by the Christian emperors. So the First Council of Nicaea was convoked by Constantine I; the First Council of Constan-

the preparations for and the expenses of the councils. Nor can it be proven that the emperors always sought the consent of the Roman pontiffs in this business. Nevertheless, with the exception of the First and Second Councils of Constantinople (which will be discussed separately below), the pope's formal convocation, in the sense described above, was never missing.[7]

(2) The pope alone has the right to *preside* over an ecumenical council, not merely in the sense of giving some sort of direction to it, such as we mean by presiding over parliaments, but presiding with real and complete jurisdiction; for the relationship obtaining between the pope and the bishops gathered together cannot be any different than his relationship to them when they are dispersed throughout the world. Consequently, the pope alone has the right to determine the matters to be discussed, the methods of procedure to be followed, and so on. Likewise he has the right to transfer, suspend, or dissolve a council. The pope can do all these things either personally, or by one or several legates.—As for the fact that we sometimes read that an emperor "presided" over some

---

tinople by Theodosius I; the Council of Ephesus by Theodosius II . . . nonetheless these councils were from the very beginning acknowledged as truly ecumenical.

Two theories have been proposed to meet this difficulty. The first opinion holds that the Christian emperors convoked these councils by *ministerial* power, in other words, really as agents of the pope. The second opinion holds that the Christian emperors were really acting on their own authority but that their assembling of the councils was a purely material convocation. The councils received legitimate authorization through subsequent papal approbation. And the fact that papal approbation was never lacking at these Eastern councils is proven beyond cavil by the mere fact that the supreme pontiff sent his delegates to those councils.

This second theory is, in our opinion, far more probable and far more in conformity with historical evidence. There are extant six imperial letters of convocation; two for the Council of Ephesus—two for the Council of Chalcedon—one for the little Council of Ephesus—one for the First Council of Nicaea. To anyone reading these letters it appears quite clear that the emperors were acting not as ministers of the pope, but in their own name and authority. In this business one has constantly to keep in mind on one hand the factor of caesaropapism, and on the other, a political-religious zeal that was coupled with theological ignorance. Finally, one must distinguish between the native *right* to convoke a council and the actual *use* or exercise of that right. The pope indeed enjoys the native right of convoking ecumenical councils for the universal good of the Church, but he is not bound to exercise that right. Nor is there any difficulty in the fact of the pope's allowing a Christian emperor to take the initiative in this whole business seeing that the pope would hardly have been able to carry out such an enterprise successfully all on his own.—*Loc. cit.*, p. 176-7.

ancient councils, the meaning is not that the emperor was the genuine head of the council, but simply that he was given the honor of acting as host to and protecting the council.

210 (3) The decrees of an ecumenical council must be *ratified* by the pope. They must be ratified in the sense that no decree, no matter how drawn up, could have coercive value unless it be quite clear that the Roman pontiff has consented to it. From this fact, it should be clear that ratification can take place in various ways. If the pope is personally present it suffices for him to add his vote to the votes of the other bishops. If the pope is absent but has proposed a predetermined opinion to be followed by the fathers of the council, their adherence to it does away with any *necessity* for subsequent ratification. If the pope while absent sends his legates without any definite instruction, then his subsequent ratification is required. This subsequent ratification may be either explicit or tacit and consists in this, that the pope allows the decrees formulated with the consent of his legates to be promulgated: for a commander who does not revoke the acts of his legates by that very fact approves and ratifies them.[8] In ancient times the emperors likewise approved the decrees of councils by giving them the power of law in the *civil* forum.

If the decrees of some council, convened without the cooperation of the supreme pontiff, are later on solemnly approved by the Apostolic See, or are received by the universal Church, they obtain the force of the decrees of an ecumenical council. It is for this reason that the First Council of Constantinople (381) and the Second Council of Constantinople (553), which strictly speaking were only *plenary* councils of the Eastern Church, are usually classified as ecumenical councils; for the amplification of the Nicene Creed made by the First Council of Constantinople to condemn the heresy of Macedonianism, etc.; and similarly the anathematization made by the Second Council of Constantinople, in which "The Three Chapters"* were condemned, were gradually approved

---

* The expression, "The Three Chapters," was first applied to certain portions of the writings of Theodore of Mopsuestia, Ibas of Edessa, and Theodoret of Cyrrhus, dealing with Christology. Later on the expression was applied, not to the writings, but to the authors themselves: Theodore, Ibas, and Theodoret. A recent scholarly account of the authors and their Christology is given by H. M. Diepen, O.S.B., *Les trois chapitres au concile de Chalcédoine: une étude de la christologie de l'Anatolie ancienne* (Oosterhout, 1953). A brief analysis of this book is given by Thomas Clarke, S.J., in TS, 16 (1955), 140-3.

by the universal Church.⁹ Consequently, even though these two councils were not ecumenical in their *assemblage,* they were later on made ecumenical in *authority,* but only with reference to the matters mentioned; for the disciplinary decrees of the council of the year 381 were not received by the universal Church.

2. *The Usefulness of Ecumenical Councils.* Ecumenical councils **211** are not strictly necessary, since there may be a coercive condemnation of errror or a definitive declaration of Catholic truth without such councils. Still, they are extremely useful, because, (*a*) in an ecumenical council, where there are gathered together the lights of the entire Church, there are abundant means for investigating the tradition and mind of the Church and for laying down the disciplinary laws best suited to meet the necessities of the times; (*b*) the splendor of authority, native to the decrees of an ecumenical council, does a great deal to incline men to obey more easily; (*c*) decrees of reform, laid down in an ecumenical council are more smoothly and efficaciously put into practice: for it is quite connatural that the bishops should with greater zeal urge the fulfillment of those very decrees in whose formulation they themselves had a hand.

3. *List of Ecumenical Councils.* Here it may be useful to **212** append a list of the twenty ecumenical councils and the major points decided at them.

(1) The *First Council of Nicaea* was held in the year 325 under Pope St. Sylvester and Constantine the Great. This council condemned the heresy of Arius who denied that the Word was *consubstantial* with the Father.

(2) The *First Council of Constantinople* was held in the year 381 under Pope St. Damasus and Theodosius the Elder. This council condemned the heresy of Macedonius who denied the divinity of the Holy Spirit. Later on, this council attained ecumenical stature through the approval of the Church.

(3) The *Council of Ephesus* was held in the year 431 under St. Celestine, the Pope, and Theodosius the Younger. This council condemned Nestorius who claimed there were two persons in Christ, and denied that the Blessed Virgin could be called the *Mother of God.*

(4) The *Council of Chalcedon* was held in the year 451 under Pope St. Leo I and Marcianus. This council condemned Eutyches who claimed there was only one nature in Christ (*Monophysitism*).

(5) The *Second Council of Constantinople* was held in the year 553 under Pope Vigilius and Justinian. Later on this council attained ecumenical stature through the approval of the Church.

(6) The *Third Council of Constantinople* was held in the year 680 under Pope Agatho and Constantine Pogonatus. This council condemned the Monothelites who acknowledged only one will and one kind of activity in Christ.

(7) The *Second Council of Nicaea* was held in the year 787 under Pope Adrian I and Constantine VI, against the Iconoclasts.

(8) The *Fourth Council of Constantinople* was held in the year 869 under Pope Adrian II and Basil I. This council deposed Photius.

(9) The *First Lateran Council* was held in the year 1123 under Pope Callistus II. This council solemnly ratified the Callistine Agreement (Concordat of Worms) of the preceding year which put an end to the quarrel over the investiture of bishops.

(10) The *Second Lateran Council* was held in the year 1139 under Pope Innocent II, to put an end to the schism that started during the reign of Anacletus II.

(11) The *Third Lateran Council* was held in the year 1179 under Pope Alexander III. This council established numerous disciplinary laws.

(12) The *Fourth Lateran Council* was held in the year 1215 under Pope Innocent III. This council condemned the Albigensian heresy and established disciplinary laws, among which was the law of yearly confession and Easter Communion.

(13) The *First Council of Lyons* was held in the year 1245 under Pope Innocent IV. This council deposed Frederick II.

(14) The *Second Council of Lyons* was held in the year 1274 under Pope Gregory X. In this council the Greeks in union with the Latins defined the procession of the Holy Spirit from both Father and Son.

(15) The *Council of Vienne* was held in the year 1311 under Pope Clement V. This council condemned various errors and suppressed the Order of Templars.

(16) The *Council of Constance* held in the years 1414–1418 was *partially* ecumenical; that is to say, those sessions which were conducted under the presidency of Pope Martin V, and previous decrees insofar as they were ratified by the same pope.

(17) The *Basel-Florence Council* was held during the years 1431–1442 under Pope Eugene IV. The council begun at Basel

was in the year 1438 transferred to the city of Ferrara; and was transferred in the year 1439 from Ferrara to Florence. The things decided at Basel for the most part do *not* possess ecumenical value, since they were *not ratified*[10] by Eugene IV. At Florence the Greeks were once again united with the Latins.

(*18*) The *Fifth Lateran Council* was held during the years 1512–1517 under Popes Julius II and Leo X. This council dealt mainly with disciplinary matters.

(*19*) The *Council of Trent* was held during the years 1545–1563 under Popes Paul III, Julius III, and Pius IV. It defined many points on *grace* and the *sacraments* and *condemned* the various errors of the Protestants.

(*20*) The *Vatican Council* was held in the years 1869–1870 under Pope Pius IX. This council formulated two dogmatic constitutions, namely, *On Catholic Faith*, and *On the Church of Christ* and then was suspended because of the violence of the times.

Notes

1. This was the opinion taught by Bolgeni at the beginning of the nineteenth century, and some canonists followed him. They added, however, that bishops could make use of that universal jurisdiction received directly from Christ only in a council.—This opinion is no longer tenable after the statement of Pius XII that the jurisdiction of bishops is received directly from the pope: "Yet in exercising this office they [the bishops] are not altogether independent, but are duly subordinate to the authority of the Roman Pontiff; and *although their jurisdiction is inherent in their office, yet they receive it directly from the same Supreme Pontiff*" (MCC 52).

2. Zapalena denies that a moral unanimity is an *essential* requirement for episcopal infallibility when the bishops are gathered in ecumenical councils; all that is required is a simple *conciliar majority*.

If it be asked whether *moral unanimity* be an essential requirement, the more common answer is in the negative. First of all because its necessity cannot be demonstrated; secondly, because there is no sure criterion for determining precisely [such moral unanimity], as should be clear from the controversies about this point in the very Vatican Council; finally, because, once such a necessity is admitted, there arises the danger of disputes. Therefore, a *conciliar majority*, such as is customary in all human gatherings, suffices. Perhaps you will ask: what if the majority section should disagree with the pope? The first reply to that is: is such a case possible under the guidance of Divine Providence? up to this time it has certainly never occurred. Even granting such a possibility, I think one should reply as follows: the minority side in unison with a pope *defining* would have to prevail; and one further question only could be asked: whether in such a case one was really discussing *conciliar* infallibility, or rather papal? But this question (since it is purely hypothetical) is of little practical importance.—*Op. cit.*, II, 180–1.

Actually the learned author's disagreement with the position outlined in this text, seems more a quarrel over terminology than the ideas involved: since it is admitted to begin with that: (*a*) no majority could prevail over the pope; (*b*) it is impossible to determine mathematically what constitutes moral unanimity; (*c*) historically no instance has ever occurred in which even a majority of the episcopate was in opposition to the pope; (*d*) that such a case seems impossible, granted the constant guidance of the Church by the Holy Spirit.

However, the same author (Zapalena), in our opinion, overemphasizes the difficulties of determining the moral unanimity of the teaching of the episcopate scattered throughout the world; and thus perhaps practically—not theoretically—underrates the value of that episcopal ordinary magisterium. See *ibid.*, p. 185 ff.

3. These arguments are taken directly from Zapalena, *loc. cit.*, p. 182. The same author applies them also to the episcopate dispersed throughout the world (*ibid.*, pp. 188–89).

4. The terms *council* and *synod* are roughly synonymous and are used interchangeably, except that a synod held by a single bishop with his local clergy, since it is not a gathering of bishops, is not usually called a council.

5. For an historical digest of the numbers of bishops present at various councils, see Zapalena, *loc. cit.*, pp. 178–79.

6. See CIC 222.

7. See Hefele, *op. cit.*, I, 5–14; Funk, *Abhandl.*, I, 39 ff.; Kneller, "Papst und Konzil im ersten Jahrtausend," ZkTh (1903), 1 and 391; *idem*, "Zur Berufung der Konzilien," ZkTh (1906), 1 and 408.

8. If one approaches the matter from history alone, it does not seem to be proven that the decrees of the first councils were always dignified with an explicit, subsequent ratification by the supreme pontiff. See Hefele, *loc. cit.*, pp. 46–50; Funk, *loc. cit.*, p. 87 ff.

9. Though many assert the contrary, it does not seem to be established that Pope Damasus ratified the First Council of Constantinople: see Funk, *loc. cit.*, p. 99; Hergenröther-Kirsch, *op. cit.*, I, 319. And, strictly speaking, Pope Vigilius did not ratify the Second Council of Constantinople, although, by condemning "The Three Chapters" by his own decree, he did as a matter of fact consent to the council's decisions.

10. See Hefele, *loc. cit.*, p. 60 ff.

CHAPTER V

Church and State

Article I. Teaching of the Church
Article II. Theological Value of Leo XIII's Teaching

CHAPTER V

Church and State

I. Preliminary Remarks

The relationship of Church and State is a delicate, practical, and complex problem. Delicate because it touches two of man's deepest allegiances: patriotism and religion. It is a practical problem: it is not restricted to the quiet, scholarly sphere of theological or philosophical speculation, but enters the noisy market place of politics and government. It is a complex problem: its adequate solution involves three or four distinct sciences—theology, canon law, political science, and history. No one of these sciences can afford to neglect the others in scrutinizing this problem.* Finally, it is an explosive problem because it involves living people who feel strongly on the matter and often start from diametrically opposed principles. Devotion to truth does not give us the right to trample ruthlessly underfoot other people's feelings; yet charity toward one's neighbor does not justify any tampering with truth. A delicate problem indeed.

To avoid confusion and unnecessary haggling, it should be stated plainly what will be treated here and what will not be treated.

The first point to be noticed is that we are here primarily concerned with stating the *theological principles* involved. Matters primarily historical, political, or canonical will be mentioned only insofar as they are necessarily intertwined with a proper theological presentation.[1]

---

* Although each of these sciences has something to contribute to an adequate understanding and solution of this problem, the theologian will bear in mind that theology, in addition to being a science, is a wisdom. Functioning precisely as a science, it could contribute only its own special slant of the matter; but functioning as a wisdom, it can shed light on the other sciences. It has a higher vantage point and can discern when another science is trespassing its proper limits. For an interesting, recent article on the functioning of theology as a wisdom, see William O'Connor, "The Grandeur and Misery of Theology," CTSA (1955), pp. 285–94.

Second, we are concerned with principles governing the relationship between the State and the *Roman Catholic Church;* not the relationship between the State and non-Catholic Churches. Catholic doctrine does not discuss the latter point.[2]

Third, we are not exclusively nor primarily concerned with the Church-State problem in the United States of America. This problem existed for 1400 years before America was discovered and will probably continue for centuries after the American civilization has disappeared like others before it. Our concern is to delineate the unchanging principles which are pertinent to any era and which admit of analogical *application*[3] to the most diverse situations. We shall nonetheless devote some space to the American situation for the sake of our American readers. Our aim in this section will be twofold: (1) to allay the honest but mistaken fears of many non-Catholic Americans—fears engendered largely by a caricature of the Church's doctrine as presented in the writings of bigots; (2) to show there is no incompatibility between Catholic principles and the cherished traditions of this land, and no inconsistency between Catholic thought and practice, provided Catholic principles be understood in all their delicate balance. This matter will appear in two *scholia* respectively entitled: *The position of non-Catholics in a Catholic state,* and, *Where the "ideal" is unobtainable.*

Division of treatment. Since this is a theological discussion, we shall first consider the Church's magisterium to see her positive teaching on this problem. Second, we shall give an evaluation of the binding force of that teaching.

Special Bibliography for Church and State

Books and Documents

BENDER, L. *Jus publicum ecclesiasticum.* Holland, 1948.
BILLOT, L. *De ecclesia Christi,* vol. 2. Rome, 1929.
BONGHI, A. *Stato e Chiesa.* Milan, 1942.
CAPPELLO, F. *Summa juris publici ecclesiastici.* Turin, 1932.
CORONATA, M. *Jus publicum ecclesiasticum.* Turin-Rome, 1934.
EDITORS OF "COMMONWEAL." *Catholicism in America.* New York, 1954.

CHURCH AND STATE

EHLER, S., AND MORRALL, J. *Church and State Through the Centuries.* Westminster, Md., 1954.

GARRIGOU-LAGRANGE, R. *De revelatione,* vol. 2, 4th ed., pp. 411–25. Rome, 1945.

GILSON, E. *The Church Speaks to the Modern World.* New York, 1954.

GURIAN, W., AND FITZSIMONS, M. *The Catholic Church in World Affairs.* Notre Dame, Ind., 1954.

HALES, E. E. Y. *Pio Nono.* London, 1954.

HARTMANN, A. *Toleranz und Christlicher Glaube.* Frankfurt-am-Main, 1955.

HERBERG, W. *Protestant-Catholic-Jew.* New York, 1955.

JUNG, N. *Le droit publique de l'Eglise,* pp. 109–37. Paris, 1948.

LECLERCQ, J. *Histoire de la tolérance au siècle de la Reforme.* Paris, 1955.

LEO XIII. Encyclicals: *On Human Liberty,* (*Libertas praestantissimum,* June 20, 1888); *On Freemasonry,* (*Humanum genus,* April 20, 1884); *On Civil Government,* (*Diuturnum,* June 29, 1881); *On the Christian Constitution of States,* (*Immortale Dei,* Nov. 1, 1885); *On Christian Citizenship,* (*Sapientiae Christianae,* January 10, 1890); *On Christian Democracy,* (*Graves de communi,* January 18, 1901).

LERCHER, L. *Institutiones theologiae dogmaticae,* vol. 1, 5th rev. ed., by F. Schlagenhaufen, pp. 244–45, and 251. Innsbruck, 1951.

MARCHESI, F. *Summula juris publici ecclesiastici.* Naples, 1948.

MARITAIN, J. *Man and the State.* Chicago, 1953.

OTTAVIANI, A. *Institutiones juris publici ecclesiastici,* 3rd ed., vol. 2. 1948.

PARENTE, P. *Theologia fundamentalis,* 3rd rev. ed., pp., 185–90. Turin, 1950.

PIUS IX. Encyclical: *Quanta cura,* (Dec. 8, 1864).

PIUS X. Encyclical: *Vehementer Nos,* (Sept. 8, 1906).

PIUS XI. Encyclicals: *The Kingship of Christ,* (*Quas primas,* Dec. 11, 1925); *The Church in Germany,* (*Mit brennender Sorge,* March 14, 1937).

PIUS XII. Encyclical: *On the Function of the State in the Modern World,* (*Summi pontificatus,* October 20, 1939); Christmas Message, Dec. 24, 1944; allocution to the Sacred College: *Catholics and World Reconstruction,* (*Ancora Una Volta,* June

1, 1946); *Address to Catholic Lawyers of Italy*, (*Ci Riesci*, Dec. 6, 1953); *Address to Historians*, (Sept. 7, 1955).

RUNCIMAN, S. *The Medieval Manichee*. Cambridge, 1955.

SALAVERRI, I. *Sacrae theologiae summa*, vol. I, 2nd ed., pp. 805–817. Madrid, 1952.

Articles and Essays

CANNAVAN, F. P. "Subordination of the State to the Church according to Suarez," TS, 12 (1951), 354 ff.

Christian Herald. 69 (August, 1946), p. 51.

CONNELL, F. J. "Freedom of Worship," Paulist Press, 1944. "Christ the King of Civil Rulers," AER, 119 (October, 1948), 244 ff. "Theory of the Lay State," AER, 125 (July, 1951), 7 ff. "Reply to Father Murray," AER, 126 (January, 1952), 49 ff.

FENTON, J. C. *"Time* and Pope Leo," AER, 114 (May, 1946), 369 ff. "The Catholic Church and Freedom of Religion," AER, 115 (October, 1946), 286 ff. "The Status of a Controversy," AER, 124 (June, 1951), 451 ff. "Principles Underlying Traditional Church-State Doctrine," AER, 126 (June, 1952), 452 ff. "The Teachings of the *Ci Riesci*," AER, 130 (February, 1954), 114 ff. "Toleration and the Church-State Controversy," AER, 130 (May, 1954), 330 ff.

HASSEVELDT, R. "The Church and Civil Society," in *The Church: a Divine Mystery*, Transl. by Wm. Storey, 1955, 183 ff.

MARTIN, T. O. "The Independence of the Church," AER, 122 (January, 1950), 37 ff. "The State: Its Elements," AER, 125 (Sept., 1951), 177 ff.

McMAHON, F. E. "Orestes Brownson on Church and State," TS, 15 (1954), 175 ff.

MESSINEO, A. "Democrazia e libertà religiosa," *Civiltà Cattolica*, CII, vol. 2 (1951), 126 ff.

MURRAY, J. C. "Freedom of Religion," TS, 6 (March, 1945), 85 ff. "Freedom of Religion: I. The Ethical Problem," TS, 6 (June, 1945), 229 ff. "Separation of Church and State," *America*, 76 (December 7, 1946), 261–63. "Religious Liberty—Concern of All," *America*, 78 (Feb. 7, 1948), 513–16. "St. Robert Bellarmine on the Indirect Power," TS, 9 (December, 1948), 491 ff. "Governmental Repression of Heresy," CTSA (March, 1949), 26 ff. "The Problem of the Religion of the State," AER, 124 (May, 1951), 327 ff. "The Problem of State Religion,"

TS, 12 (June, 1951), 155 ff. (reply to G. W. Shea). "For the Freedom and Transcendance of the Church," AER, 126 (January, 1952), 28 ff. (reply to F. J. Connell). "Leo XIII on Church and State: the General Structure of the Controversy," TS, 14 (March, 1953), 1 ff. "Leo XIII: Separation of Church and State," TS, 14 (June, 1953), 145 ff. "Leo XIII: Two Concepts of Government," TS, 14 (December, 1953). 551 ff. "On the Structure of the Church-State Problem," in *The Catholic Church in World Affairs*, Indiana, 1954, 11 ff. "Problem of Pluralism in America," *Thought*, 29 (Summer, 1954), 165 ff.

OTTAVIANI, ALFREDO CARDINAL. "Church and State: Some Present Problems in the Light of the Teaching of Pope Pius XII," AER, 128 (May, 1953), 321 ff.

ROMMEN, H. "The Church and Human Rights," in *The Catholic Church in World Affairs* (1954), 115 ff.

RYAN, A. H. "The Church and Civil Government," *Studies*, 41 (1952), 151.

SERER, R. "The Church in Spanish Public Life Since 1936," in *The Catholic Church in World Affairs* (1954), 305 ff.

SHEA, G. W. "Catholic Doctrine and 'the Religion of the State'," AER, 123 (September, 1950), 161 ff. "Catholic Orientations on Church and State," AER, 125 (December, 1951), 405 ff.

SIMON, Y. "The Doctrinal Issue between the Church and Democracy," in *The Catholic Church in World Affairs* (1954), 87 ff.

Time. 48 (July 29, 1946), p. 56.

WEIGEL, G. "The Church and the Democratic State," *Theology Digest* (Autumn, 1953), 169–175 (digest of longer article in *Thought*, 27, [Summer, 1952], pp. 165–84).

YANITELLI, V. "A Church-State Controversy," *Thought*, 26 (Autumn, 1951), 443 ff. "A Church-State Anthology," *Thought*, 27 (Spring, 1952), 6 ff. (excerpts from J. C. Murray).

Article I

TEACHING OF THE CHURCH

I. *Positive Teaching of the Church as Found in the Ordinary Magisterium*
   Leo XIII's Teaching

II. *Theological Principles Based on Leo's Teaching*

III. *Principle 1:*
   God is the author of all true authority, civil and religious alike.

IV. *Principle 2:*
   Church and State are really distinct societies. Each is a complete society and independent in its own sphere.

V. *Principle 3:*
   Church and State should not be hermetically sealed off from one another. They should cooperate peacefully for their own mutual benefit.
   Scholion: The "Indirect Power" of the Church

VI. *Principle 4:*
   The Church transcends the State because of the nobility of its nature and its goal.

VII. *Principle 5:*
   A really Catholic state is per se obliged to make public profession of Catholicism.

   Meaning of the Principle
   Scholion 1: The position of non-Catholics in a Catholic state
   Scholion 2: Where the "ideal" relationship is not obtainable

Article I

TEACHING OF THE CHURCH

I. Positive Teaching of the Church as Found in the Ordinary Magisterium

213

The Vatican Council intended to discuss the problem of Church and State, but it was interrupted before it had the time to consider the matter. The Church's teaching is therefore to be found in the ordinary papal magisterium. The classic places are primarily, though not exclusively, the encyclicals of Leo XIII. Pius XI and Pius XII have precised still further some points of Leo's teaching, while reiterating it in substance.

Leo XIII's Teaching

Before summarizing the points taught by Leo, it is important to notice that Leo is concerned primarily with stating what is the *ideal* relationship that should obtain between the Catholic Church and a Catholic State.° The pope is concerned with the

---

° The English term, "state," is to say the least, ambiguous. It can signify anything from an amorphous mass of people in a given geographical location to the top echelon of government. Contrariwise the Latin language has four or five different words to designate the various notions included within the meaning of "State." According to Etienne Gilson: "from the point of view of the English usage, the word State is correctly employed in most passages of the encyclicals. The word signifies both the 'body politic' and that which Jacques Maritain describes as 'that part of the body politic especially concerned with the maintenance of the law, the promotion of the common welfare and public order and the administration of public affairs.'" See Gilson, *The Church Speaks to the Modern World* (New York, 1954), p. 28. Gilson is careful to render the exact nuance of the various Latin terms, *"res publica," "civitas," "civilis potestas,"* etc. For Maritain's careful delineation of the differences between "nation," "state," "body politic," etc., see *Man and the State* (Chicago, 1951) pp. 1–12. Although some political philosophers might dispute his usage of this or that term to cover the same conceptual content, one cannot gainsay the need of distinctions in this matter of political vocabulary, nor Maritain's neatness in precising and justifying his terminology.

As for the term, "a Catholic state," one need not fall into the trap of reducing it to a purely statistical concept. It is not purely a matter of head-counting: 90% makes a Catholic state; less than 90% a "pluralistic" state.

relationship between the Church and states with a pluralistic religious background only secondarily and incidentally. Still, in dealing with the latter question, the pope—in a few memorable paragraphs which we shall quote later on—does clearly show how Catholic governments may grant full religious liberty to its non-Catholic citizens without being inconsistent with Catholic principles.

With this background we may state that Leo XIII's *Immortale Dei (The Christian Constitution of States)* is a kind of Magna Charta laying down a blueprint for an ideal Catholic society organized according to Catholic principles. In it is found his clearest and fullest teaching on the relationships between Church and State in such a society.[4]

The main teachings of the encyclical may be summarized in the following points: *

1. God is the author of all true authority, civil and religious alike (3).

2. God's authority backs up any legitimate form of government (4).

Analogously, one would not be tempted to deny there is an England merely because a large group of Irish were to immigrate to Manchester; nor that there is a reality called America merely because several hundred thousand Americans were once fellow-travelers of the Communist party. Without haggling about the matter, one would simply describe a Catholic state as a country where the people as a whole—allowing for individual or large group dissidents—subscribe to the Catholic philosophy of life, have historically joined the Catholic Church and accept it as Christ's kingdom on earth and accept all the revealed truths taught by it. It is somewhat in this way that we accept the concept of the American state as a group of people committed to an American way of life, who historically have accepted the Constitution and traditions of this land, without bothering to count heads to see which ones may in their hearts be anarchists, or may be embittered by certain articles of the Constitution. Everybody, Catholic and non-Catholic alike, seems to take such a healthy, broad view of the matter and, without further quibbling, immediately classifies as "Catholic countries," Italy, Ireland, Poland, Portugal, etc. Pius XII in addressing Italians (see *Ci Riesci*) takes it for granted Italy may be classified as a Catholic state, without worrying over the fact that there are large groups of Italians who are at present Communists. For a more technical justification of this usage of traditional terminology, see George W. Shea, "Orientations on Church and State," AER, 125 (1951), 405–416. — A final caution: to say that a state or a country is a "Catholic state" does not mean that it is necessarily admirable in all its ways. Just as individuals can be Catholics but bad men (because they fail to live up to Catholic principles) so "Catholic states" may, from time to time in their history, behave disgracefully by betraying the Catholic principles they are supposed to follow.

* The numbers given at the end of each proposition are the paragraph numbers used in Gilson's edition of the encyclical.

3. The Church has no preference for any one kind of government. It is opposed only to governments that would trample underfoot either the rights of God or the rights of man (4 and 36).

4. In their own sphere civil governments should behave as agents of God's authority and in their concern for public welfare should imitate God's fatherly care and justice (5).

5. Civil society, since it derives its powers from God, is, in the objective order of things, bound to make public profession of the religion established by God (7, 25, 26, 34, 35).

6. Church and State are two distinct, complete, and independent societies (13).

7. The goal of the Church is the eternal supernatural happiness of mankind; it alone possesses authority over matters purely spiritual (14).

8. The goal of civil society is man's earthly welfare; it alone has authority over matters purely secular (14).

9. Church and State should cooperate with one another for the benefit of their common citizens (14).

10. The idea that civil authority has its ultimate origin in the multitude of the citizens and not in God is a philosophical error and leads to evil consequences for civil society (25 and 31).

11. Freedom is necessary to the Church for the fulfillment of its mission (34).

12. In matters of mixed jurisdiction, Church and State may work out some harmonious arrangement through a concordat (35).

13. Catholics should be public spirited and do their best, by all honorable means, to help restore modern society to Christian ideals (44-46).

14. No fixed method can be prescribed for helping to Christianize modern society: methods will vary according to time, place, circumstances (46).

15. The doctrine set forth in this encyclical is Catholic teaching on the ideal setup for a society organized according to Christian principles (16, 35, 36, 40, 50).

II. Theological Principles Based on Leo's Teaching

The pontiff's teaching as contained in those points may be summarized in the following five theological principles:

1. God is the author of all true authority, civil and religious alike.

2. Church and State are really distinct societies. Each is a complete society and independent in its own sphere.

3. Church and State should not be hermetically sealed off from one another. They should cooperate peacefully for their own mutual benefit.

4. The Church transcends the State because of the nobility of its nature and its goal.

5. A really* Catholic State is per se obliged to make public profession of Catholicism.

214 III. Principle 1

God is the author of all true authority, civil and religious alike.

This principle is a truth both of natural reason and revelation. Reason points out that no man is an island: he needs the companionship of his fellow men if he is to live a fully human life. No man can be simultaneously farmer, doctor, lawyer, engineer, physicist, bricklayer, tailor, undertaker, and priest. Consequently it is an instinct of man's nature that moves him to live in society: domestic, civil, or religious. Since it is impossible for a multitude of men to live together harmoniously unless there be order among them and some legitimate ruling authority to safeguard the individual rights of each and the common good of all, ruling authority, like society itself, has its ultimate basis in nature. Since God is the ultimate creator of all things and all things continuously depend upon Him, so too every genuine, natural society has God as its ultimate author. Consequently all genuine authority over societies is ultimately the result of God's design, intended by Him and delegated to men through various, legitimate modes of organizing different societies. Leo puts the matter aptly this way:

> Man's natural instinct moves him to live in civil society, for he cannot, if dwelling apart, provide himself with the necessary requirements of life, nor procure the means of developing his mental and moral faculties. Hence it is divinely ordained that he should lead his life—be it family, or civil—with his fellow men, amongst whom alone his several wants can be adequately

---

* The adjective "really" is added because it is possible for a state which was once Catholic to become pluralistic or even non-Catholic say, for example, by the apostasy of half its citizens from the faith. (See Bender, *Jus publicum ecclesiasticum, op. cit.,* p. 199, where he envisages and discusses such a possibility.)

supplied. But, as no society can hold together unless some one be over all, directing all to strive earnestly for the common good, every body politic must have a ruling authority, and this authority, no less than society itself, has its source in nature, and has, consequently, God for its author.—*Immortale Dei* (hereafter ID) Gilson ed., No. 3.

This same truth which is attainable by natural reason has also been proclaimed by God's revelation. St. Paul reminds the Roman Christians in forceful terms that they must respect and obey civil authority, for its ultimate author is God:

Let everyone submit himself to the ruling authorities, for there exists no authority not ordained by God. And that which exists has been constituted by God. Therefore he who opposes such authority resists the ordinance of God, and they that resist bring condemnation on themselves. . . . Accordingly we must needs submit, not only out of fear of punishment, but also for conscience sake.—Rom. 13:1–6.

This principle is so sound that one might wonder why Leo XIII should stress it at such length. The reason is that in the rampant liberalism of the nineteenth century, various queer political theories about the origin of civil power were in vogue. One theory—no less aberrational for the fact that it was extremely popular—was the so-called "cab-driver theory" of government.[5]

According to this theory the rulers are purely and simply the *instrument* of the multitude. No real civil authority, capable of obliging in conscience, exists, and, consequently, no corresponding duty of obedience.

Let the last effects of the traditional myths concerning the dignity of the ruling person be dissipated: men in government are reduced to the capacity of agents, managers, secretaries, instruments that are traversed by power but have no power of their own. They take orders, yet, in spite of appearances, are not entitled to give any order. . . . They are leaders by order of the led. *Their leadership involves no authority.* Even though the governing person is allowed to utter sentences grammatically undistinguishable from commands, the government, like hired and paid servants, takes the orders of the governed and leads them where they want to go.—Yves R. Simon, *art. cit.*, p. 91.

In extreme form this theory takes a mystical turn and the "will of the people" becomes glorified as an impersonal, infallible force which automatically regulates all things for the common good.

In sum, the origin and ultimate source of civil authority is not God but the people. The obvious mistake here is to confuse a pipeline with a reservoir, a telephone line with a dynamo. Because civil authority is channeled through the votes of the people, that does not mean it originates with the people. This is precisely the gist of Leo XIII's protest against a false conception of civil authority in vogue in his day:

> The sovereignty of the people, however, and this without any reference to God, is held to reside in the multitude; which is doubtless a doctrine exceedingly well calculated to flatter and to inflame many passions, but which lacks all reasonable proof, and all power of insuring public safety and preserving order. Indeed, from the prevalence of this teaching, things have come to such a pass that many hold as an axiom of civil jurisprudence that seditions may be rightfully fostered. For the opinion prevails that rulers are nothing more than delegates chosen to carry out the will of the people; whence it necessarily follows that all things are as changeable as the will of the people, so that the risk of public disturbance is ever hanging over our heads.— ID 31.

215 IV. Principle 2

Church and State are really distinct societies. Each is a complete society and independent in its own sphere.

a. They are really *distinct* societies. Even though the same men may be both members of the Church and citizens of a definite country, that does not mean that Church and State somehow become amalgamated into one hybrid society. Men can belong to both a chess club and a golf club, but that does not make chess golf, nor golf chess. The simplest proof for this part of the proposition is that societies are most easily distinguished by the different goals for which each has been instituted. The goal of the Church is the supernatural[6] and eternal happiness of mankind; the goal of civil society is the temporal welfare and, in fact, directly (per se), the external welfare of its citizens.

b. Both Church and State are *complete* societies. A complete, or perfect* society is one whose goal is supreme in its own sphere and which possesses, theoretically at least, all the means needed to achieve that goal. Any society lacking either of these two requisites is necessarily an incomplete, imperfect society, destined by its very nature to be part of some larger organization. The family, for example, even though endowed with certain inalienable rights, is an incomplete, imperfect society. It needs the resources of civil society to help it achieve its own ends.

Hardly anyone but an anarchist would deny that the State is a complete or perfect society. The same is not true, however, of the Church. Vast numbers of non-Catholics either fail to see or vehemently deny that the Roman Catholic Church is a complete or perfect society. They view it merely as one of the many private and subordinate societies contained within the framework of the State. Despite their protests, we must maintain the truth of the matter: the Church is a complete or perfect society and fulfills all the requisites for such. As a matter of fact, the goal of the Church is not only supreme in its own sphere, it is unqualifiedly supreme. Consequently, the Church possesses in itself full and supreme power to teach, govern, and sanctify. These are the normal means proportioned to its goal. Strictly speaking too, the Church can by its own right demand[7] of its subjects such temporal goods as it needs to pursue its goal; actually however, it prefers to have them fulfill such obligations voluntarily. Notice the phrase, *by its own right.* Just as the Church received its universal power neither from the State itself, nor even through the mediation of the State, so too, it possesses the right just mentioned directly from Christ and independently of the State. As Leo XIII put it:

> The only-begotten Son of God established on earth a society which is called the Church, and to it He handed over the exalted and divine office which He had received from His Father, to be continued through the ages to come.—ID 8.
>
> [The Church] is a society chartered as of divine right, perfect in its nature and *in its title, to possess in itself and by itself,* through the will and loving kindness of its Founder, *all needful provision for its* maintenance and action.—ID 10; italics ours.

---

* The term "perfect society," in this usage, carries no connotation of moral beauty, or spotlessness. It means simply (*perficere-perfectus*) something finished, or complete. Perfect, then, refers, not to moral perfection, nor economic perfection, but to *structural* perfection.

c. Both Church and State are *independent in their own spheres*. This follows from what has already been laid down: a complete or perfect society, since it is self-sufficient both from the viewpoint of its goal and the means to the goal, is, by that very fact, in its own sphere, independent of any other society. The *State*, consequently, is independent within its own proper boundaries, i.e., in all *purely civil** matters. For example, to lay down laws governing taxes, to enact penal codes, to make nuclear experiments, to safeguard public health, to enter into treaties with other nations, to erect or do away with tariff barriers, to safeguard the defense of the nation—these and hundreds of similar items belong by their very nature to civil society. Over such affairs the Church has no power.

> Whatever is done in temporal matters with reference to the temporal goal is outside the goal of the Church. Now the general norm is that societies have no power over matters which lie outside their own proper goal.—Tarquini, *Juris ecclesiastici publici institutiones*, 16th ed., p. 49.

But the *Church* is no less independent in its own sphere. Consequently, it can by an inalienable right teach its doctrine throughout the entire world, exercise its jurisdiction and priestly powers everywhere, and so forth, without needing any authorization or permission from civil society. The State has no power over *purely religious* matters. That is why the apostles never went searching for civil rulers to beg their permission to preach the gospel, or to found churches, or to carry out acts of worship. As a matter of fact, when necessary, the apostles openly rejected the intervention of the secular powers, by appealing to their own authority—an authority granted by God. See Acts 4:18–20; 5:29, 40–42. The Church has always vindicated its independence by its words, deeds, and very blood.

The independence of each society in its proper sphere is brought out clearly by Leo XIII in these words:

---

* Notice the modifier purely: *purely* civil matters, *purely* religious matters. Some matters (usually described by theologians and canonists as *mixed* affairs) like matrimony and education are neither exclusively civil nor exclusively religious. They have both a sacred and a civil aspect to them: the sacred aspect belongs to the province of the Church; the civil aspect to the province of the State. For a full discussion of this matter, consult the canonists. L. Bender's presentation of this matter is quite original, provocative, and penetrating. See *op. cit.*, chap. 6, pp. 201–16.

CHURCH AND STATE

The Almighty, therefore, has given the charge of the human race to two powers, the ecclesiastical and the civil, the one being set over divine, the other over human, things. Each in its kind is supreme, each has fixed limits within which it is contained, limits which are defined by the nature and special object of the province of each, so that there is, we may say, an orbit traced out within which the action of each is brought into play by its own native right.—ID 13.

Some object that the Church cannot be considered a complete and independent society because it does not possess its own territory. This is a naïve objection. The entire earth is the Church's territory in spiritual affairs:

Jesus then came closer to them and spoke to them the following words: "Absolute authority in heaven and on earth has been conferred upon me. Go, therefore, and initiate all nations in discipleship: baptize them in the name of the Father and of the Son and of the Holy Spirit, and teach them to observe all the commandments I have given you. And mark: I am with you all times as long as the world will last."—Matt., 28: 18–20.

There is nothing contradictory in the idea of the same territory and the same men being simultaneously subject to two powers, each of which is independent in its own sphere; the reason is that each society has its own proper field of activity: the one is in charge of spiritual affairs, the other in charge of civil affairs. Conflicts can, of course, arise and historically have arisen. Such conflicts come about accidentally: i.e., not from the simple fact of there being two societies, but from the fact that individuals, lay or ecclesiastic, may overstep their proper boundaries, and trespass on the other's territory. Legitimate means of resolving such quarrels peaceably are always at hand. Leo XIII foresaw this objection and answered it with his usual wisdom. Such disputes can always be resolved either by reviewing the respective spheres of the two societies in relation to the matter in question, or by explicit contractual agreement, "concordats," between Church and State drawing up strict lines of demarcation in areas where disputes are liable to originate:

Whatever, therefore, in things human is of a sacred character, whatever belongs either of its own nature or by reason of the end to which it is referred, to the salvation of souls, or to the worship of God, is subject to the power and judgment of the Church. Whatever is to be ranged under the civil and political order is rightly subject to Civil authority. Jesus Christ has Himself given command that what is Caesar's is to be rendered to Caesar, and that what belongs to God is to be rendered to God. —ID 14.

There are, nevertheless, occasions when another method of concord is available for the sake of peace and liberty: We mean when the rulers of the State and the Roman Pontiff come to an understanding touching some special matter. At such times the Church gives signal proof of her motherly love by showing the greatest possible kindliness and indulgence.—ID 15.

216 V. Principle 3

Church and State should not be hermetically sealed off from one another. They should cooperate peacefully for their mutual benefit.

This principle must be maintained against those who proclaim as a self-evident dogma that there *must* be "a wall of separation" between Church and State. Such self-described "liberals" even though they theoretically grant the Church's liberty, at least assert the following: by the very nature of the case (per se) the best relationship and the one devoutly to be wished for under all circumstances is that the Church should pay no attention to the State, and the State should ignore the Church. Please note the words: "by the very nature of the case" the best and to be wished for "under all circumstances." It is one thing to accept a complete separation (in the sense of non-cooperation) of Church and State in a given situation, and to welcome that state of affairs as the only sensible one in the given circumstances. It is a horse of an entirely different color to regard such a state of affairs as *per se ideal*.

Here we are merely discussing principles. We are not asking what can, may, or should be welcomed in this or that set of circumstances ("hypothesis"). We are simply asking what should be laid down as a positive principle ("thesis"), prescinding from any given historical context, for an ideal relationship between Church and State in a *Catholic* country. In other words, what relationship is per se ideal—even though in a given historical context some other relationship might be quite good—and consequently what should every Catholic man honestly and earnestly like to see wherever and to whatever extent a given set of circumstances warrants it? For the liberalistic doctrine, in the sense above described and in no other sense, was condemned in the *Syllabus of Errors:* "The Church *must* be separated from the State, and the State from the Church" (DB 1755). Leo XIII repeatedly condemned this nineteenth-century liberal doctrine as *pernicious.* See the encyclicals, *Arcanum* (Feb. 10, 1880); *Immortale Dei* (Nov., 1885); *Libertas* (June 20, 1888); *Longinqua* (Jan. 6, 1895).

And pernicious it was. The type of liberalism Leo XIII was protesting is obvious from the detailed list of complaints he raises. Nineteenth-century liberalism used "separation of Church and State" as a war cry. By it, the nineteenth-century liberal meant not separation of the two societies, but *subjugation* of the Church to the State; denial of its rights even in its own proper sphere:

> They claim jurisdiction over the marriages of Catholics, even over the bond as well as the unity and the indissolubility of matrimony. They lay hands on the goods of the clergy, contending that the Church cannot possess property. Lastly, they treat the Church with such arrogance that, rejecting entirely her title to the nature and rights of a perfect society, they hold that she differs in no respect from other societies in the State, and for this reason possesses no right nor any legal power of action, save that which she holds by the concession and favors of the government. If in any State the Church retains her own agreement publicly entered into by the two powers, men forthwith begin to cry out that matters affecting the Church must be separated from those of the State. . . . Accordingly, it has become the practice and determination under this condition of public policy (now so much admired by many) either to forbid the action of the Church altogether, or to keep her in check and bondage to the State. Public enactments are in great measure framed with this design. The drawing up of laws, the administration of State affairs, the godless education of youth, the spoliation and suppression of religious orders, the overthrow of the temporal power of the Roman Pontiff, all alike aim to this one end—to paralyze the action of Christian institutions, to cramp to the utmost the freedom of the Catholic Church, and to curtail her every single prerogative.—ID 27–29.*

---

* The pontiff's condemnation is not a condemnation of genuine liberalism (see *ibid.*, nos. 38–39 and also the encyclical, *Libertas*); it is simply a condemnation of an anti-religious philosophy masquerading under a noble name.

How sane and reasonable it is that Church and State in a Catholic country should cooperate harmoniously will be clear from the following points:

a. The Church and State have the same subjects. Unless they work out in friendly agreement such matters as are of mutual concern (mixed affairs) quarrels will easily arise. Such quarrels do harm both to the Church and to civil society. The bewildered citizen caught in the middle of such a conflict will either turn away from his religious duties; or he will cease to exhibit the respect and obedience he owes to civil authority. Harmonious cooperation, therefore, is something to be sought for on both sides.

b. Even though the goals of the State and Church are distinct and pertain to different spheres, God did not institute these goals in such fashion that there is no relationship interconnecting them, or in such fashion that the State and Church have not the slightest need of one another. Leo affirms that the All-wise God does not act in such a fashion (see ID 13–14). The sincere practice of religion and pursuit of holiness contribute a great deal, even though indirectly, to temporal happiness. Vice versa, tranquility in society and an equitable distribution of material goods is a great help, even though indirectly, to the sanctification of souls and eternal salvation (see ID 20). If, then, each society can be benefited greatly in the pursuit of its own goal by the indirect help of the other, reason itself suggests that they should not ignore one another but should cooperate peacefully. Such cooperation should be especially welcomed by the State because the Church can continue to exist and function without any aid from the State (provided it be not persecuted by the State), whereas civil society has so great a need of religion that without religion all things would be topsy-turvy and civil society itself would crumble.

c. Finally, just as individual citizens are obliged to worship God, so, too, society as a whole is bound to worship Him.* In fact it is bound to worship Him through the religion He Himself instituted, the only true religion, Catholicism. Now if civil society, precisely as a society, is obliged to profess the Catholic religion †

---

* See the first volume of this series, *The True Religion,* no. 7, p. 17.

† Please observe that this third argument for peaceful cooperation between Church and State (drawn from the obligation of society *qua* society to worship God) refers to a *Catholic* State. Obviously no one—neither pope nor theologian—expects a Mohammedan country or Israel to make public profession of Catholicism: Catholicism is the one, true religion, but they are

it cannot, without violating its obligation (to God), behave with utter indifference towards that Church in which the true religion is incorporated.

Scholion: The "Indirect power" of the Church. **217**

Even though Church and State have their own direct spheres in which each exercises its power directly over the affairs committed to it, it would be a trifle naïve to think that they do not indirectly affect one another. Human life itself is not so neatly compartmentalized that one can say: "here is the political sphere, here is the religious sphere, here is the medical sphere, here is the educational sphere." One can reason abstractly in such fashion but in concrete, real life, the unity of the living subjects who enter into politics, medicine, education, or religion prevents such happy mental vivisection.*

If the Church has laws on fast and abstinence, it indirectly affects the economic market: less meat is sold on Friday. If the Church prescribes rest from servile work on Sunday, it again indirectly affects economic life: for large numbers of people will not be working in farms or factories one day in the week. Similarly if the State drafts men into the army it indirectly affects the life of the Church: male attendance at Mass in parishes declines and the number of curates in a parish is cut down as numbers of them become chaplains. Again, if the State has fire laws restricting the number of people in a given space, small churches may have to keep half their congregation standing on the front steps. State laws against bingo lessen returns for charity, etc.

Apart from these almost fortuitous effects on one another, which are too trivial for serious discussion, Church and State *necessarily* have an indirect effect on one another in areas that are of *mutual concern*. These are dubbed by theologians and canonists, *mixed affairs*. The same concrete things or actions may have simultaneously *several* aspects to them. Under one aspect they may be spiritual and pertain directly to the province of the Church; under

---

not aware of the fact. The *objective* obligation of all men *freely* to embrace Catholicism is for them, *subjectively*, nonexistent.

* Thus we find statesmen having to draw up laws safeguarding society from the too-easy selling of dangerous drugs; we find doctors lobbying politically to prevent socialized medicine; educators entering politics to guarantee teachers adequate salaries, and clergymen delivering sermons against political ideas or social practices that threaten to undermine public morality.

another aspect they are secular and pertain to the province of the State. The most obvious and best-known example in this area is a marriage between baptized persons, (Bender *op. cit.*, "Potestas Indirecta," p. 119). Such a marriage is simultaneously a sacrament and a contract. One and the same act of consent produces both supernatural effects (sanctifying grace) and natural effects (the obligation of living together, supporting and educating children, rights of inheritance, etc.; *ibid.*). The same concrete reality, consequently, falls directly under the scope of both Church and State: the Church has direct power over the supernatural aspect of marriage (all that pertains to marriage as a sacrament: its correct form, its indissolubility, etc.): the State has direct power over the natural aspect of marriage (the contractual effects such as obligation to support, laws of inheritance, etc.).

This is not the only instance in which the same concrete reality may be directly subject to the power of the Church under one aspect, and directly subject to the power of the State under other aspects. For example, matters economic and political seem to belong exclusively to the State, yet they frequently have moral aspects to them. In passing judgment on that moral aspect of an economic or political affair, the Church will not be stepping out of its proper sphere; the moral aspect falls under the Church's direct power. Communism, for example, is not simply a political phenomenon; it is also an atheistic philosophy of life. As such, the Church has a perfect right to condemn it and to forbid its members to join it. If they obey in a particular Catholic country, the Communist party will cease to exist there. While perfectly within its rights in condemning the moral aspect of Communism—its purpose is to lead men to eternal life and one of the chief means is pointing out what leads to that goal and what leads away from it—it indirectly affects the life of the Communist party. Similarly, in the economic sphere, such concrete realities as labor unions pose problems that are not exclusively the concern of the economist or politician. Some questions are moral: has a man a right to a living wage? Has a union the right to strike? What are the conditions for a just strike? etc. In these and similar questions one aspect of a concrete reality falls directly under the power of the Church; and another or several aspects fall directly under the power of the State.

That the Church has *some* power over temporal matters, has the right to intervene in them, and pass judgment on them, no theologian would deny. The opposite proposition has been explicitly condemned: "The Church has not the power of using force, *nor has she any temporal* power, direct or indirect" (apostolic letter, *Ad apostolicae,* Aug. 22, 1851). When theologians maintain the Church's power over temporal matters they are stating this one point only: the Church can pass judgment on temporal matters when and insofar as those affairs have a definite connection with spiritual welfare, that is, insofar as such control is necessary if the Church is to be able to provide for its own special goal, the salvation of souls.

How describe this power of the Church to intervene in temporal matters? Even though, as was stated above, all theologians admit the right of the Church to intervene in temporal affairs insofar as they have a connection with its spiritual goal, their theological *terminology* in describing the same phenomenon has not been the same in all ages, nor equally precise. As Bender wisely states:

> We know that what holds true of other sciences also holds true of the teaching and science of theologians: they are not and have not always been perfect. Even in explaining a truth known to them from matters which are contained in the doctrine of faith and traditional practice, men usually make progress gradually.—*Op. cit.,* p. 118.

He then goes on to apply this general norm to the matter we are here discussing. He points out that St. Robert Bellarmine, in describing the intervention of the Church in temporal affairs, described it under the formula: the *indirect power of the Church.* Even though he states St. Robert was teaching the exact same doctrine we have described above, Bender feels that more precise terminology should be used because nonprofessional theologians might misunderstand the phrase, much as many people misunderstand the phrase *extra ecclesiam nulla salus.* While not rejecting Bellarmine's terminology—it is traditional and clear enough to theologians—he would prefer more exact terminology. A number of other modern theologians feel the same way.

> In the seventeenth century the famous theologian, St. Robert Bellarmine, in explaining and justifying how the Church could use her power to intervene in many temporal and natural mat-

ters, proposed his teaching of the *indirect power of the Church.*
. . .

It seems to us that Bellarmine by his theory did a great deal to explain and justify the extensions of ecclesiastical power to many secular affairs. But the use of the phrase which became customary—"indirect power," does not appear praiseworthy in all respects. If the reality designated by this phrase is not lucidly explained, confusions can arise quite easily. For if someone reads that the Church has a direct power over spiritual matters and an indirect power over temporal matters he is easily led to think that the Church possesses a *double* power, one direct and one indirect. In our judgment, this is an error. We hold the same doctrine as Bellarmine about the power of the Church, its object and its extension, because in all these matters we are all bound to hold the doctrine contained in the Church's tradition. Still it seems to us that the same doctrine should be proposed in another way. —*Loc. cit.*, p. 118.

The distinguished author then goes on to describe at some length the matter we have previously synopsized: namely, the reason the Church's spiritual power can reach even into temporal matters is that one and the same concrete reality may have several aspects to it. The Church directly touches the spiritual aspect of the matter and indirectly affects the State only insofar as the one same concrete reality belongs to the State under another aspect. The same holds true in reverse. What is to be done should a conflict arise between Church and State concerning the same concrete reality that belongs to both of them under separate aspects, brings up the fourth principle for discussion.

218 **VI. Principle 4**

The Church transcends the State because of the nobility of its nature and its goal. In a Catholic State, therefore, the Church's rights take precedence.

Whenever God establishes anything He establishes it in orderly fashion. Consequently if God wills that there should exist two perfect societies which simultaneously strive to provide for the complete welfare of the same citizens, there must exist some orderly relationship between those societies: some norm by which possible conflicts in the field of mixed affairs can be resolved. Since neither of these societies is subject to the other (each is supreme

CHURCH AND STATE

and independent in its own sphere), obviously neither can simply order the other society about. The norm for resolving conflicting rights is to be found, not in the sphere of power but of *dignity*. If one society is nobler both in its nature and its goal than the other, then reason itself suggests that the nobler society should prevail. This does not mean that the other society becomes subject to or subordinate to the nobler society; it simply means that it freely yields or postpones its rights in a given situation for the sake of the common welfare. That the Church eminently surpasses the State in dignity because of the transcendent dignity of its goal and its nature (as the Mystical Body of Christ) hardly needs statement. God, then, as Bender puts it, did not have to promulgate explicit directions giving the Church precedence over the State: that fact is *implicit* in the very goals He set for each:

> God, the single Supreme Authority which is above both these perfect societies He instituted, has not *explicitly* laid down a norm for dealing with this case [conflicts in "mixed affairs"]. There was no need to do so. For the very establishment of the Church and the State, such as they are with their own proper nature and goals, *implicitly* states the norm. The only reasonable solution, and consequently willed by God and to be observed by us, is that which applies this norm: if two societies, not subordinate to one another, under diverse aspects have control over the same matter and in a given concrete case the regulations of both powers cannot be observed, one power should take precedence and the other should yield. If one power is obviously far nobler and much more worthy than the other, that is the power which should prevail. . . .
> It follows that if opposition should arise between an act of ecclesiastical authority and an act of civil authority, it is the Church's right that her ordinance should be sustained and should prevail; and civil authority has the juridical obligation, founded in divine law, to abide by those matters which the Church commands, putting aside its own ordinance—*Ibid.*, p. 124.

Many theologians describe this precedence of the rights of the Church by the formula: "the indirect subordination of the State to the Church," or, "the State is indirectly subject to the Church." While the teaching they give is the same as just outlined, the formulae used are, in our opinion, less accurate in expressing the reality. They could easily be misinterpreted to sound as though the State were not an *independent* society. How can a society be simultaneously "subject" or "subordinate" and yet "independent"? The adjective *indirect* clarifies matters somewhat but not completely. We feel with Bender that:

> It would be doctrinally more accurate to speak not of the *subjection,* however indirect it may be, but of the *precedence* of the other society. We normally use the word [precedence] in cases of this kind. For example when two men who are in no sense subject to one another approach the same house. If space allows they both proceed together and there is no need for a norm of action. But if they have to pass through a doorway so narrow that they cannot simultaneously pass through it, some sort of norm of action becomes imperative. If someone says it is more fitting for Titus to enter first, he does not thereby mean that the other man is "subject" to Titus, or "subordinate" to him, not even indirectly. He simply acknowledges that the two persons are not equal in dignity, and from this very inequality he deduces that it is right for Titus to precede the other.—*Ibid.,* pp. 125–6.

Two *consequences* follow immediately from this principle: (*a*) The State may not, just at its own fancy and with absolute disregard for the Church, lay down laws on *mixed affairs. Mixed affairs,*[8] as previously mentioned, are matters which are, though under different aspects, simultaneously spiritual and civil. For example, matters connected with marriage, public institutions for children, education and the like, are mixed affairs. In such matters the State should either abide by the Church's laws, or else the State should enter into some concordat[9] with the Church, ironing out precisely the jurisdiction of each society. The Church, as history itself bears out, will always respect the needs and rights of the State in such affairs. It realizes better than anyone else there is no authority but from God, and the injunction of its Head, "*Render to Caesar what is Caesar's.*"

(*b*) The Church should not become enmeshed in politics; nor in the administrative affairs of any government. But if, in mixed matters, civil rulers should inflict damage on religion, or injure man's natural rights by unjust laws, the Church can declare that such a law does not bind in conscience, or even that citizens must not obey such laws. It can, finally, when the rulers are Catholic—as is the case in the hypothesis we are discussing—warn, rebuke, and even level spiritual punishments like excommunication, on such tyrannical rulers.*

Objections: Some statesmen feel that this teaching on the primacy of the rights of the Church, in a conflict about mixed affairs, poses a real danger to the State, since the Church could trespass beyond its lawful limits. How groundless this fear is should be clear from this one fact alone: physical force is always on the State's side, while the Church has only moral force on its. That is why even in the Middle Ages the quarrels which arose between the secular power and the spiritual power were almost always caused by the usurpation of the rights of the Church by the State and not vice versa. Even Auguste Comte (the founder of Positivism and no lover of the Church) admitted this fact candidly:

219

> When one examines today, with a truely philosophic impartiality, the ensemble of those great struggles which occurred so frequently between the two powers during the Middle Ages, one quickly recognizes that they were almost always essentially defensive on the part of the spiritual power, which even when it had recourse to its own powerful weapons, often did no more than to wrestle nobly for the reasonable maintenance of a just independence, which the real accomplishment of her mission demanded of her, but without being able, in most cases, to do so successfully.—*Cours de Philosophie Positive,* 2nd ed., V, 234.

The objection is raised: *no one should act as a judge in his own case.* But if it comes to a case of deciding, in mixed affairs, whether

---

* This last mentioned point, of spiritual sanctions, seemed horrifying to the nineteenth-century liberal. After the sobering experiences with the twentieth century totalitarian States, even non-Catholics have been better able to appreciate how healthy a thing it is to have some power which can at least place a moral check on the State when it verges on tyranny. See, for example, the non-Catholic writer, E. E. Y. Hales:
He died a hero to his followers; to the world, apparently, a failure. Few thoughtful men, in 1900, thought he had been right. It was necessary to find excuses for the Syllabus—better, even, to forget it. But we, today, who have met the children and the grandchildren of European Liberalism and the Revolution, who have seen Mazzini turn into Mussolini, Herder into Hitler, and the idealistic early socialists into the intransigent communists are able from a new vantage ground to consider once more whether Pio Nono, or the optimistic believers in an infallible progress, like his cultured friend Pasolini, will have, in the eyes of eternity, the better of the argument.—*Pio Nono* (New York, 1954), p. 331.

(367)

the supernatural aspect of the matter is more important than the natural, or civil aspect, the Church alone can make that decision, since the Church alone is the competent authority in the supernatural sphere. And in that case, it would be acting as judge in its own case.

Reply: The axiom that one should not act as judge in his own case is a sound, general axiom; but it does not possess absolute and universal validity. If it be impossible, from the nature of the case, to have another judge—if there be no higher authority available—one may act as judge in his own case. If, for example, the Supreme Court wanted to reverse one of its own prior decisions, given the light of new evidence, it would have to pass judgment on its own case because legally there is no higher court of appeal. The highest authority in any sphere, in other words, is necessarily the judge of all cases in that sphere, including its own. If the Church were not to pass judgment on, and lay down the extent of, its authority, this task—in the opinion of those who propose the objection—would pertain to civil authority; but in this alternative, the State would be acting as judge in its own case. For the matter we are discussing is precisely the marking off of lines of demarcation for the proper spheres of these two societies, Church and State. The meaning of the axiom, then, is not: acting as judge in one's own case is always and everywhere wrong. The real meaning is that to act as judge in one's own case is normally perilous and consequently, insofar as it is possible to do so, such procedure should be avoided and prohibited by law. In the case at hand—judging the extension of the power of the supernatural—it is impossible to have any other judge than that society to which God Himself has committed the care of supernatural reality, His Church. (Bender, *op. cit.*, p. 94).

Objection: A final objection is raised that even if the Church's position be theoretically sound, still it is practically dangerous. Men being men, even ecclesiastics can abuse rightful authority.

Reply: One must candidly admit there is danger. But the danger of abuse necessarily accompanies use. And the general axiom: *abusus non tollit usum* is valid here too. The only way to prevent the possibility of the abuse of authority, civil or ecclesiastical, would be to wipe out authority altogether. That, in turn, would only induce even greater danger to society—anarchy; we say nothing of such an abolition's being against God's institution of authority. No reasonable man would expect society to be able to exist without some authority. Bender's answer to this objection seems quite sensible:

> *Objection:* Is there not a danger of abuse, when the decision is left to persons who are live participants in the case? It seems we must reply there is some danger. But the danger of abuse is always and everwhere present whenever you have the use [of a good thing]. If some one wishes to suppress all danger of abuse of power and authority he would have to remove power and authority from men altogether. We would not say a man was making a wild judgment if he were of the opinion that nothing in the history of mankind has ever been the object of so much abuse and such terrible abuse as supreme civil authority. Yet no one ever proposes, or at least wisely proposes, that we should wipe out altogether such supreme authority. In this life we do not expect to be able to wipe out all danger of abuse, for that is something impossible. Our obligation is to order social life in such fashion that the danger of abuse is reduced to such a minimum as is possible without, however, thereby causing or introducing either greater dangers or definite evils. Even if the fact that ecclesiastical authority has the right of deciding the proper limits of its own power entails the possibility of some abuse of that competency, it would be wrong to conclude that the concession, in such matters, of this competency was not made according to God's plan and for the usefulness of the human race. Someone ought to have competence in such matters. In practice, that competence would have to be bestowed either on the supreme rulers of the Church, or on civil rulers. Hardly anyone would deny that the latter alternative would not only not lessen the danger of abuse, but enormously increase it.—*Ibid.,* pp. 97–98.

It is perfectly true that the principles explained above cannot, most of the time, receive their full application, because religious unity has been torn asunder in almost all formerly Catholic nations. Despite that fact, it is not right for the Church's members to keep silent—in fact they are not free to do so—about the rights of the Church which its adversaries ascribe to the State as the fountain source of all rights.

Obviously, we neither expect, nor can we reasonably demand that non-Catholics, whether Protestants, Jews, Agnostics, or Atheists, fully recognize the rights of the Church so long as they fail to recognize the Church for what she is: the Mystical Body of Christ and the Kingdom of God on earth. The facts that God has instituted a supernatural order and a supernatural society are known only from revelation and by faith. Indeed, the whole nub of the Church-State problem for non-Catholics lies not in the logical consequences the Church deduces from her premises but in those very *premises* themselves. *Hypothetically* they can see the logic of concluding that there should be harmonious cooperation between the State and the Roman Catholic Church *if:* (1) Jesus Christ is really the Son of God; (2) Jesus Christ did institute a real church destined for all mankind; (3) that church established by Christ is none other than the Roman Catholic Church. If non-Catholics deny any one of these three premises they necessarily and logically deny the Church's conclusions about the Church-State relationship. These premises are dealt with prior to the Church-State problem. Of course if a non-Catholic is totally unaware of these prior premises, it is impossible to carry on an intelligent discussion of the Church-State problem with him even in hypothetical terms.

Even though non-Catholics do not yet recognize or acknowledge them, our beloved Mother the Church still possesses those rights and prerogatives which she received, not from the rulers of this world, but from Jesus Christ the King of the Ages, for the salvation of both individuals and nations.

220 VII. Principle 5

A really Catholic State is per se obliged to profess Catholicism publicly.

Terminology. The term "state" as used here means primarily the "body politic" (the individual citizens viewed as a collective entity), and secondarily governmental rulers functioning precisely as representatives of the body politic. The term "Catholic State" has been described previously (see p. 349 note).

Meaning of the principle. The proposition states simply that the people of a Catholic State should openly proclaim their loyalty to Jesus Christ and His Church and should perform acts of public Catholic worship. This proposition is based on the prior proposition, already established (see *The True Religion,* no. 7), that man as a social being, or that society *qua* society has an obligation to pay public worship to God because God is its ultimate author.

CHURCH AND STATE

Since society continuously depends upon its Creator, it should acknowledge that dependence by appropriate acts of worship. This obligation stems directly from the natural law. In a Catholic country this obligation to offer public worship is simply made precise. Briefly, if man as a social being is obliged to worship God not merely privately but publicly as well, any society which *knows* that God has revealed the Catholic religion is obliged to honor God by Catholic worship. Speaking, as the context * clearly shows, of a Catholic State, (and of a Catholic State in its *ideal* relationship to the Church) Leo XIII puts the matter very plainly:

> As a consequence, the *State* [*civitas*—body politic], constituted as it is, is clearly bound to act up to the manifold and weighty duties linking it to God, *by the public profession of religion*. Nature and reason, which command every individual devoutly to worship God in holiness, because we belong to Him and must return to Him, since from Him we came, bind also the *civil community* by a like law. For, men living together in society are under the power of God no less than individuals are, and society, no less than individuals, owes gratitude to God who gave it being and maintains it and whose ever-bounteous goodness enriches it with countless blessings. Since, then, no one is allowed to be remiss in the service due to God, and since the chief duty of all men is to cling to religion in both its teaching and practice—not such religion as they may have a preference for, but the religion which God enjoins, and which certain and most clear marks show to be the only true religion—it is a public crime to act as though there were no God. So, too, *is it a sin for the State not to have care for religion*, as something beyond its scope, or as of no practical benefit; or out of many forms of religion to adopt that one which chimes in with the fancy; *for we are bound absolutely to worship God in that way which He has shown to be His will*. All who rule, therefore, should hold in honor the holy name of God, and one of their chief duties must be to favor religion, to protect it, to shield it under the credit and sanction of the laws, and neither to organize nor enact any measure that may compromise its safety.

---

* "It is not difficult to determine what *would* be the form and character of the State *were* it governed according to the principles of *Christian* philosophy." —ID 3. And again: "Such, then, as We have briefly pointed out, is the *Christian* organization of civil society; not rashly or fancifully shaped out, but educed from the highest and truest principles, confirmed by natural reason itself."—ID 16.

This is the bounden duty of *rulers* to the people over whom they rule.—ID 6; italics ours.

From the pope's words it is clear that this obligation of a Catholic State to offer public Catholic worship applies to both the body politic (the collective citizenry) and the top part of the body politic (or its rulers).

Some distinctions about the principle. *Three* closely connected but really distinct questions underlie the principle as enunciated above in generic terms. Failing to keep them distinct, we feel, causes needless confusion.* The first question asks: is a Catholic state *obliged* to profess Catholicism publicly? The second: is there any *special mode* in which this public profession must take place? In other words, to fulfill the obligation of professing Catholicism publicly it is necessary to have a *juridical* setup, a constitutional declaration, or an official concordat installing the Catholic religion as the official state-religion, and the Catholic Church as the official state-church? The third question concerns the *consequences* that flow from an affirmative answer to the first two questions. Briefly, if a Catholic State is obliged to profess Catholicism publicly, and if it must make such profession by juridically installing Catholicism

---

* We feel that some of the controversial writing engaged in by American Catholic theologians in recent years, touching the Church-State problem, was really occasioned by a failure to clarify the three distinct questions indicated above. In other words, we think a large part of their disagreement in this area was more verbal than real because they were not actually discussing the same problem. Failing to detach the three separate questions and to discuss them separately they never really joined issue. One side was engaged in defending the generic principle that "a Catholic state is *per se* obliged to profess Catholicism publicly" (in which they were perfectly correct); whereas the other side (while not denying that principle at all), was concerned with the subtler question of whether there was a strict obligation to have a juridical institution of Catholicism as a state-religion.

As for their real disagreement on lesser matters—particularly the usage and usefulness of various technical formulae like "error has no rights," "the indirect subordination of the State to the Church," "dogmatic intolerance," etc., the interested reader will find ample bibliography at the beginning of this section. Rather than attempt any premature, and peremptory judgment as to which side had the better of the argument in the *many* matters touched upon, we would rather pay tribute to both sides with this quotation from the Saskatchewan Hierarchy: "Among scholars, a discussion of the union or separation of Church and State has long been carried on. In recent years, *much light* has been shed on the various theories of Church-State relations in a series of articles in the *American Ecclesiastical Review* and *Theological Studies*" (*The Catholic Mind*, 54 [1956], p. 592).

as the state-religion, is the state further obliged to prohibit juridical recognition to other religions and to take some sort of repressive measures against proselytizing by non-Catholic sects?

Briefly, we think the answers to those three questions supplied by papal teaching are as follows:

1. Is a Catholic State per se *obliged* to make public profession of Catholicism?—Yes.

2. Is it absolutely necessary for such profession to take *juridical* form by instituting Catholicism as the state-religion (proclaimed as such in the State's constitution)? No, it is not absolutely necessary. But it is the Catholic *ideal*—something to be hoped for and welcomed, unless in given circumstances it would do more harm than good. Pius XII tells us:

> The Church does not hide the fact that in *principle* she considers such collaboration [i.e., between Church and State in a Catholic country] normal and that she regards the unity of the people in the true religion and the unanimity of action between herself and the state as *an ideal*.
> But she also knows that for some time events have been evolving in a rather different direction.—*Address to Historians* (Sept. 7, 1955), NCWC translation; italics ours.

3. Even if a Catholic State makes juridical profession of the true religion, legally establishes Catholicism as the official religion, *it may also give juridical recognition to other and false religions* for the sake of safeguarding rights of conscience and the common good. Catholic people should, however, make clear in such juridical conventions that they are not thereby subscribing to religious indifferentism.

4. *There is neither any per se obligation on the part of a Catholic State to suppress false religions, nor any right bestowed upon the state by God to do so.* Per accidens, for the sake of preventing the undermining of public morality, or of preventing frightful disorders in society, any State—Catholic or non-Catholic—might be forced to curtail the activities of a really vicious religion. If, for example, someone were to revive the ancient custom of sacrificing babies to Moloch, the State, as the guardian of public welfare would be obliged to prevent such a perverted religion from carrying its perverse ideas into action. A fuller discussion of points 3

and 4 will be found below in the *scholia* entitled: *The position of non-Catholics in a Catholic State* and *Where the "ideal" is not obtainable*. There it will be seen that there is nothing inherent in Catholic principles to curtail the full civic rights of any citizen, Catholic or non-Catholic.

221 *Scholion 1. The position of non-Catholics in a Catholic State.*

One point that troubles fair-minded* non-Catholics is the specter that even though the Catholic Church goes along with religious liberty in those countries where it has not a dominant majority, it would reverse its position were Catholics to become the majority. They fear that if America were to become 90% Catholic all remaining Protestants, Jews, Agnostics, or Atheists would be persecuted, or at a minimum, be treated as second-class citizens. They feel that this is a logical and inexorable consequence of the teaching that there is but one, true religion, and that a Catholic State is (per se) obliged to make public profession of that true religion.

This fear was largely engendered by the caricature of the Church's doctrine presented by nineteenth-century liberals. It may have been further nurtured by some overly-strict theologians who took the view that a Catholic State would always be bound to repress heretical sects.

The best way to allay that fear is to show that it is a caricature

---

* It seems difficult to include in this category individuals like Paul Blanshard, or Agnes Meyer, or an organization like the P.O.A.U. However sincere may be their personal motives, they seem to be suffering from a kind of group-hysteria we might label *ecclesiaphobia*. As John Courtney Murray points out ably, wittily, yet charitably, they have simply revived in less gross form the ancient, hysterical, anti-Catholic prejudices of the days of *The Menace* and *Ku Klux Klan*. ("Religious Liberty: the Concern of All," *America* [Feb. 7, 1948] pp. 513–16.) With such people it is difficult to carry on an intelligent discussion. As Maritain pertinently remarks, our efforts to make Catholic teaching in this area intelligible should be directed primarily to open-minded non-Catholics, not to those whose minds are temporarily obscured by bigotry or hysteria:

> I am alluding to serious-minded authors, not to Mr. Paul Blanshard. His handling of the question (*American Freedom and Catholic Power* [Beacon Press, 1949], ch. iii) is not worth discussing because it is simply unfair, like the rest of his book, whose criticisms, instead of clarifying matters, are constantly vitiated by biased and devious interpretation, and which confuses all issues in a slandering manner, up to ascribing to the Catholic Church "*a full-blown system of fetishism and sorcery.*"—*Op. cit.*, p. 184, n. 36.

of oversimplification, by simply adducing explicit papal teaching on the matter under discussion.* Leo XIII after pointing out the obligation of a Catholic State to acknowledge publicly the true religion, states plainly:

> Nor is there any reason why anyone should accuse the Church of being wanting in gentleness of action or largeness of view, or of being opposed to real and lawful liberty. The Church, indeed, deems it unlawful to place the various forms of divine worship on *the same footing* as the true religion, *but does not, on that account, condemn those rulers who, for the sake of securing some great good or of hindering some great evil, allow patiently custom or usage to be a kind of sanction for each kind of religion having its place in the State.* And, in fact, the Church is wont to take earnest heed that no one shall be forced to embrace the Catholic faith against his will, for, as St. Augustine wisely reminds us, "Man cannot believe otherwise than of his own will."—ID 36; italics ours.

Again, the same pope in his encyclical *On Human Liberty* (1888) in his discussion of liberty of conscience, after pointing out the absurdity of thinking there is some right † to worship God or ignore Him at one's whim, goes on to lay down the principle governing the patient permission of objective evils, including the objective evil of false religions. This principle is simply a faithful reflection of God's own method of government. Even though God abhors evil, He does permit some evils either to prevent still worse ones, or for the protection of some greater good:

> Yet, with the discernment of a true mother, the Church weighs the great burden of human weakness, and well knows the course down which the minds and actions of men of this our age are being borne. For this reason, while not conceding any *right* to anything save what is true and honest, she does not forbid public authority to tolerate what is at variance with truth and justice, for the sake of avoiding some greater evil, or of ob-

---

* It is not uncommon to find even the most fundamental tenets of Christianity caricatured by such oversimplification. Thus the Trinity is presented as "three gods," the Incarnation means Christ is a fantastic hybrid, "half god—half man," the Redemption means God used Christ as a "whipping boy," etc.

† We mean a *moral* right, not *civic*.

taining or preserving some greater good. God Himself in His providence, though infinitely good and powerful, permits evil to exist in the world, partly that greater good may not be impeded, and partly that greater evil may not ensue. In the government of States it is not forbidden to imitate the Ruler of the world; and, as the authority of man is powerless to prevent every evil, it has (as St. Augustine says) to overlook and leave unpunished many things which are punished, and rightly, by Divine Providence. But if, in such circumstances, *for the sake of the common good* (and this is the only legitimate reason), human law *may or even should* tolerate evil, it may not and should not approve or desire evil for its own sake; for evil of itself, being a privation of good, is opposed to the common welfare which every legislator is bound to desire and defend to the best of his ability. In this, human law must endeavor to imitate God, who, as St. Thomas teaches, in allowing evil to exist in the world "neither wills evil to be done, nor wills it not to be done, but wills only to *permit it* to be done; and this is good." This saying of the Angelic Doctor contains briefly the whole doctrine of the permission of evil.—*On Human Liberty*, Gilson ed., no. 33; italics ours.

Leo's teaching—that non-Catholic religions, even though objectively false, may have a legal status in a Catholic State and that their adherents should not suffer civic disabilities because of their honest convictions, has been reiterated, endorsed, and presented in even stronger terms by Pius XII several times. In his address to Italian Catholic lawyers, *Ci Riesci* (Dec. 6, 1953), he appeals to this principle of Christian tolerance of objective religious or moral evil for the sake of a greater good, even when a Catholic State possesses the power to repress such evils. He rebukes strongly the opinion that because "evil has no objective right to exist" there always corresponds a duty to repress it. To put it another way, the pope rebukes the bald, unqualified statement that "to tolerate religious or moral evils when one has the power to stop them is itself an immoral way of acting." He points out that in some circumstances toleration of evil is not only permissible but may be the better course to follow. In laying down these principles Pius XII appeals not only to the principle used by Leo, but cites in addition the words of Christ about not attempting to root out the cockle before the harvest time:

We have just adduced the authority of God. Could God, although it would be possible and easy for Him to repress error and moral deviation, in some cases choose the "non-impedire" without contradicting His infinite perfection? Could it be that in certain circumstances He *would not give men any mandate, would not impose any duty, and would not even communicate the right to repress what is erroneous and false? A look at things as they are gives an affirmative answer.* Reality shows that error and sin are in the world in great measure. God reprobates them, but He permits them to exist. Hence the affirmation: religious and moral error must always be impeded, when it is possible, because toleration of them is in itself immoral, is *not valid absolutely and unconditionally.*

Moreover, God has not given even to human authority such an absolute and universal command in matters of faith and morality. *Such a command is unknown to the common convictions of mankind, to Christian conscience, to the sources of Revelation and to the practice of the Church.* To omit here other scriptural texts which are adduced in support of this argument, Christ in the parable of the cockle gives the following advice: "let the cockle grow in the field of the world together with the good seed in view of the harvest" (see *Matt.* 13: 24–30). The duty of repressing moral and religious error *cannot* therefore be an *ultimate* norm of action. It must be subordinate to *higher and more general norms,* which in some circumstances *permit,* and even perhaps seem to indicate as *the better policy,* toleration of error in order to promote a greater good.

Thus the two principles are clarified to which recourse must be had in concrete cases for the answer to the serious question concerning the attitude which the jurist, the statesman and the sovereign Catholic state is to adopt in consideration of the community of nations in regard to a formula of religious and moral toleration as described above. *First:* that which does not correspond to truth or to the norm of morality *objectively* has no right to exist, to be spread or to be activated. *Secondly:* failure to impede this with civil laws and coercive measures *can nevertheless be justified in the interests of a higher and more general good.*—Translation from AER, 134 (1954), pp. 134–5; italics ours.*

---

* The language of this address is worded with extreme care, with many nuances. An ordinary reader, unused to papal preciseness, might conclude the pope was "hedging" on the question. "Why did he not just say 'yes' or 'no'?" an irritated layman might ask. The reason is that there are no simple answers to problems in themselves delicate and complex. Simple answers are for simple

Even more recently, in his *Address to Historians* (Sept. 7, 1955), Pius XII states emphatically that the Church always has respected and always will respect the conscience of non-Catholics, even while she disapproves of the erroneous principles to which they may in good faith subscribe. Their position is entirely different from that of apostate Catholics who wilfully reject the faith in which they have been educated. The Church regards such Catholics as committing sin by their apostasy. It does not blame non-Catholics who honestly disagree. *The Church respects their conscience while rejecting their principles:*

Let no one object that the Church herself scorns the personal convictions of those who do not think as she does. The Church has considered and still considers that the wilful abandonment of the true faith is a sin. When beginning about 1200, such a defection entailed penal proceedings on the part of the spiritual as well as the temporal power, it was only to avoid the destruction of the religious and ecclesiastical unity of the West.*

---

problems. The matter here in question involves a delicate balance of principles which cannot be simply squelched, but must be counterbalanced. The address was to legal minds, in legal phraseology, and would be appreciated by minds attuned to the refinements of legal terminology. For a careful analysis of this address, see J. C. Fenton's commentary in "The Teaching of *Ci Riesci,*" *ibid.,* pp. 114-23.

* There were no Protestants involved in the medieval inquisition because no Protestants yet existed. As the erudite non-Catholic historian, Runciman, aptly notes, "Writers who seek to find the heirs of the Cathars in the Protestants of the Reformation or even in the earlier Protestants that we call the Lollards and the Hussites, do Protestantism an injustice" (*The Medieval Manichee* [Cambridge, 1955], p. 178). All involved were Catholics. As such, they were subject to the Church's jurisdiction and subject to such spiritual penalties as she has a right to impose. The fact that these apostate Catholics also received punishments from the State (from fines to exile or execution) was due to the peculiar circumstances of the medieval Church-State setup, in which to be a Catholic was to be a citizen and vice versa. Consequently, heresy was regarded as a crime simultaneously against the Church and the State.

The modern mind recoils at the very mention of the word "inquisition." Without attempting to excuse many of the real horrors which accompanied it (extortion of evidence by torture, secret witnesses, etc.), we think it can be safely said that the general reading public has been given a far more bloodcurdling description of the whole business than calm historical evidence seems to warrant. The medieval Manichee (Albigensian) was no theoretical dissenter, politely and sincerely clinging to his personal convictions of conscience the way a twentieth-century university professor might; he seems to have been an active conspirator against society in the way that a twentieth-century Communist is. He put his peculiar ideas into action. Many of his ideas—like

To *non-Catholics* the Church applied the principle contained in the Code of Canon Law, "Let no one be forced against his will to embrace the Catholic faith" (*Ad amplexandam fidem catholicam nemo invitus cogatur,* canon 1351). *She believes that their convictions constitute a reason,* although not always the principle one, *for tolerance.* We have already dealt with the subject in our address of December 6, 1953 to the Catholic lawyers of Italy.—NCWC translation; italics ours.

---

his conviction of the basic depravity of marriage, or his right to assassinate fellow Manicheans to keep them from relapsing—were, to say the least, subversive of society. While making generous allowance for pious exaggeration, Runciman admits that these theories were certainly held by the medieval Manichee and, at least from time to time, carried out in practice (cf. *op. cit.,* p. 151, 158, 176–7).

But the inquisition is too knotty a problem to be disposed of in summary fashion. For an honest appraisal of the inquisition by Catholic historians see Vacandard, *The Inquisition,* and Maycock, *The Medieval Inquisition.* Also worth reading on this point are the brief essay by Heinrich Rommen, professor of political sicence at Georgetown University, "The Church and Human Rights" in *The Catholic Church in World Affairs* (Notre Dame, Ind., 1954), pp. 115–53, and Monsignor Journet's treatment of the inquisition in *The Church of the Word Incarnate,* I, 262–304.

None of the Catholic historians, philosophers, or theologians mentioned above attempt to whitewash the inquisition entirely; but they do seek to place it in its proper perspective against the medieval milieu and to make it intelligible, at least in those terms. Runciman, too, though non-Catholic, does not seem surprised that repressive measures were taken against the medieval Manichee; it was something one might naturally expect in the given circumstances:

> It is not remarkable that the spread of Dualism terrified not only right-thinking Churchmen but also many of the lay authorities. It was considered heresy, and correctly so considered. . . . There is no room for Christ in a truly Dualist religion.

> Thus all good Christians must necessarily fight against Dualism. And the State will usually support them. For the doctrine of Dualism leads inevitably to the doctrine that race-suicide is desirable: and that is a doctrine that no lay authority can regard with approval. Moreover there was another reason why Church and State alike detested the Dualist Tradition. To their minds it was associated with orgiastic obscenity. It is possible to discount the horrible hints of orthodox writers as mere propaganda, but the regularity of the charges makes some investigation necessary. . . . Indeed, the account of Dualist orgies cannot be all entirely fictitious. Dualism necessarily disapproves of the propagation of the species. It therefore disapproves of marriage far more than of casual sexual intercourse, for the latter represents merely one isolated sin, while the former is a state of sin. Similarly, sexual intercourse of an unnatural type, by removing any risk of procreating children, was preferable to normal intercourse between man and woman. Moreover till his initiation ceremony the Dualist Believer was merely a creation of the Devil's. To indulge his carnal appetites would make him no worse.—*Op. cit.,* 175–7.

That American Catholics, hierarchy and laity alike, subscribe to such papal teaching, and are genuinely interested in safeguarding all the rights and dignity of their non-Catholic fellow citizens is a fact easy enough to substantiate for anyone willing to do a bit of patient research. The famous reply of Cardinal Manning to Gladstone on the question of religious freedom would be heartily endorsed by any American Catholic and is only typical of like utterances by American bishops * issued at various times in this country's history:

> "If Catholics were in power tomorrow in England," Cardinal Manning wrote, "not a penal law would be proposed, not a shadow of constraint put upon the faith of any man. We would that all men fully believed the truth; but a forced faith is a hypocrisy hateful to God and man. . . . If the Catholics were tomorrow the 'Imperial race' in these kingdoms they would not use political power to molest the divided and hereditary religious state of the people. We would not shut one of their Churches, or Colleges, or Schools. They would have the same liberties we enjoy as a minority."—Henry E. Manning, *The Vatican Decrees in Their Bearing on Civil Allegiance* quoted in Maritain, *op. cit.*, p. 181.

Whether America will ever become 90 or 95 per cent Catholic we do not know. Perhaps hydrogen bombs will preclude any such possibility; perhaps two hundred years from now all American Catholics will either have apostatized from the Church, or will have been thrown to the lions like their ancestors, because of the hysteria of "true Romans" who fear the overthrow of the national gods. Perhaps America will become 100 per cent Catholic and then there will be no one left to tremble about the unknown dangers of Catholicism. Who knows? There are many possibilities, but we do not pretend to the mantle of prophecy. For all who wish to prophecy, we can only say: there have been false prophets.

* See, for example, the statement by the late Archbishop John T. McNicholas: "We deny absolutely and without any qualification that the Catholic Bishops of the United States are seeking a union of Church and State by any endeavors whatsoever, either proximate or remote. If tomorrow the Catholics constituted a majority in our country, they would not seek a union of Church and State."—"The Catholic Church in American Democracy," NCWC press release, January 26, 1948 as quoted in J. Cavanaugh, *Evidence for Our Faith* (Notre Dame, Ind., 1952), p. 296.

Finally, it might be useful, instead of trying to glimpse the purely hypothetical future, to study something of the present. One Catholic country, which in its constitution publicly affirms its devotion to Catholicism, no less vehemently affirms the rights of its non-Catholic citizens, and recognizes the legal status of various non-Catholic religions. We refer to the Republic of Ireland. A perusal of excerpts from its constitution will indicate that there is nothing inherent in Catholic principles to pose a threat to civic and religious freedom:

CONSTITUTION OF EIRE

1. In the Name of the Most Holy Trinity, from Whom is all authority and to Whom, as our final end, all actions both of men and States must be referred,

We, the people of Eire,
humbly acknowledging all our obligations to our Divine Lord Jesus Christ . . . and seeking to promote the common good, with due observance of Prudence, Justice and Charity, so that the dignity and freedom of the individual may be assured, true social order attained, the unity of our country restored and concord established with other nations, do hereby adopt, and give to ourselves this Constitution.

Personal Rights

Article 40. All citizens shall, as human persons, be held equal before the law.

The Family

Article 41. The state recognizes the Family as the natural primary and fundamental unit group of Society, and as a moral institution possessing inalienable and imprescriptible rights, antecedent and superior to all positive law.

Education

Article 42. 1. The State acknowledges that the primary and natural educator of the child is the Family and guarantees to respect the inalienable right and duty of parents to provide, according to their means, for the religious and moral, intellectual, physical and social education of their children.

2. Parents shall be free to provide this education in their homes or in private schools or in schools recognized or established by the State.

CHRIST'S CHURCH

3. The State shall not oblige parents in violation of their conscience and lawful preference to send their children to schools established by the State, or to any particular type of school designated by the State.

Religion

Article 44. 1. (i) The State acknowledges that the homage of public worship is due to Almighty God. It shall hold His Name in reverence and shall respect and honour religion.

(ii) The State recognizes the special position of the Holy Catholic Apostolic and Roman Church as the guardian of the Faith professed by the great majority of the citizens.

(iii) The State also recognizes the Church of Ireland, the Presbyterian Church in Ireland, the Methodist Church in Ireland, the Religious Society of Friends in Ireland, as well as the Jewish Congregations and the other religious denominations existing in Ireland at the date of the coming into operation of this Constitution.

2. (i) Freedom of conscience, and the free profession and practice of religion are, subject to public order and morality, guaranteed to every citizen.

(ii) The State guarantees not to endow any religion.

(iii) The State shall not impose any disabilities or make any discrimination on the ground of religious profession, belief or status.

(iv) Legislation providing State aid for schools shall not discriminate between schools under the management of different religious denominations, nor be such as to affect prejudicially the right of any child to attend a school receiving public money without attending religious instruction at that school.

(v) Every religious denomination shall have the right to manage its own affairs, own, acquire, and administer property, moveable and immoveable, and maintain institutions for religious or charitable purposes.

(vi) The property of any religious denomination or any educational institution shall not be diverted save for necessary works of public utility and on payment of compensation.— *Church and State Through the Centuries: A collection of historic documents with commentaries*, trans. and ed. by S. Z. Ehler and J. B. Morrall (Westminster, Md., 1954), 595–9.

222 *Scholion 2: Where the "ideal" relationship is not obtainable.*

Even though the establishment of *juridical* relations between

CHURCH AND STATE

Church and State is the Catholic *ideal*, the Catholic "thesis," it is no necessary corollary, it seems to us, that any other arrangement is necessarily *evil (per se malum)*. The dichotomy proposed: "either you have the ideal, or you have something per se evil" surely seems a false one. There are many gradations between ideal and evil: there is ideal (best), better, good, and only then, evil. The dichotomy is a false presentation of our position, or at least an overly rigid representation of it by some Catholic theologians. Because the Church affirms the superiority of virginity to marriage, it does not mean she despises the latter, but rather venerates it highly. Similarly, though the Church praises and wishes her members to seek the ideal Church-State relationship * by all honorable means, the while respecting the consciences of non-Catholics in their midst, she by no means despises or considers evil other relationships called for by particular circumstances. The Church has not just one principle to keep in mind—man's obligation as a social being to make social profession of his religion—there are other Catholic principles: that individual persons are obliged to follow their consciences, even erroneous consciences; that no man may be constrained to accept Catholicism; and finally, that the State has the obligation to provide for the common welfare of all, not simply its Catholic citizens. Where, then, the ideal is unrealizable without injury to other principles, the Church is content with something good, though less good. That is why the present Holy Father took special pains to point explicitly to America to show that the Church can prosper in the most diverse situations:

> The Church does not hide the fact that in *principle* she considers such collaboration [i.e., between Church and State in a Catholic nation] normal and that she regards the unity of the people in the true religion and the unanimity of action between herself and the state as *an ideal.*
> But she also knows that for some time events have been evolving in a rather different direction, that is to say towards the multiplicity of religious beliefs and conceptions of life within the same national community, where Catholics are more or less a strong minority. It may be interesting and surprising for the

---

* What could be more natural than that a deeply Catholic people should wish publicly and proudly to proclaim their love and loyalty to Jesus Christ and His Church? Every people, including the American, instinctively proclaims aloud its native loyalties and ideals.

historian to encounter *in the United States of America one example, among others, of the way in which the Church succeeds in flourishing in the most disparate situations.—Address to Historians,* NCWC trans.; italics ours.

As Pius XII points out in the same address, the Church, even though her goal reaches into eternity, has, like her Founder, entered into all the complexities of time. Without relinquishing principles, the Church adapts herself with a marvelous flexibility to all the multitudinous cultures she has passed through, without becoming simply an artifact of any particular era—ancient, medieval, or modern. Her goal in every age is primarily religious and moral, but because she is situated in historical circumstances and always has man as her object, the Church is interested in all that affects mankind in any period and strives to promote anything that promotes man's welfare:

> The Church knows that her mission, although by its nature and its goals it belongs to the religious and moral domain, situated in the beyond and eternity, nevertheless penetrates to the very heart of human history. Always and everywhere, by unceasingly adapting herself to the circumstances of time and place, she seeks to model persons, individuals and, as far as possible, all individuals according to the laws of Christ, thus attaining the moral basis for social life. The object of the Church is man, naturally good, imbued, ennobled and strengthened by the truth and grace of Christ.—*Ibid.*

This sympathy of the Church for man governs not only her relations to the individuals in any historical era, but also human societies. That is why she shows the same marvelous flexibility in being able to deal with vastly disparate types of State. Although her ideal is intimate collaboration with the State among a people religiously unified, she does not thereby hesitate to enter into concordats with societies where the religious background may be pluralistic. In some concordats the Church and State may express their common religious convictions; in others the Church may simply desire an honorable independence to do her own work; in yet others she may simply wish to help preserve social tranquility by marking out lines of demarcation between the State and herself, thus avoiding or lessening the possibility of future conflicts:

CHURCH AND STATE

In the history of relations between the Church and State, the Concordats, as you know, play an important part . . . in Concordats, let us say, the Church seeks the juridical security and independence necessary to her mission.
It is possible, let us add, for the Church and State to proclaim in a Concordat their common religious convictions. But it may also happen that the Concordat has for its goal, among others, the prevention of conflicts about questions of principle and avoidance from the beginning of possible occasions for conflict. When the Church puts her signature to a Concordat, the approval applies to all its contents.
But the deeper meaning may include shades of meaning about which the contracting parties both know. It may signify an expressed approval, but it may also provide for simple tolerance . . . according to the principles which serve as a norm for the coexistence of the Church and her faithful with the powers and men of different belief.—*Ibid.*

Briefly put, the Church does her best in any given society— Catholic, Protestant, or secular—to promote the welfare of the individual and the good of society as a whole. She respects and defends all lawful civil authority as having God for its ultimate author. She instructs the faithful—whether they be a minority, or a majority—to respect and obey civil authority. She tries to be "all things to all men that she may win all men for Christ." St. Augustine beautifully describes this unchanging attitude in all ages when he addresses the Catholic Church in these words:

Thou dost teach and train children with much tenderness; young men with much vigor, old men with much gentleness; as the age not of the body alone, but of the mind of each requires. Women thou dost subject to their husbands in chaste and faithful obedience, not for the gratifying of their lust, but for bringing forth children, and for having a share in the family concerns. Thou dost set husbands over their wives, not that they may play false to the weaker sex, but according to the requirements of sincere affection. Thou dost subject children to their parents in a kind of free service, and dost establish parents over their children with a benign rule . . . Thou joinest together, not in society only, but in a sort of brotherhood, citizen with citizen, nation with nation, and the whole race of men, by reminding them of their common parentage. Thou teachest kings to look to the interests of their people, and dost admonish the people to be submissive to their kings. With all care dost thou teach all to whom honor is due, and affection, and reverence, and fear, consolation, and admonition, and exhortation, and discipline, and reproach, and punishment. Thou showest that all these are not equally incumbent on all, but that charity is owing to all, and wrongdoing to none.—*De moribus* i. 30. 63; see ID 20.

For anyone who would calumniate the Church as being hostile to the State or inimical to society's welfare, St. Augustine's answer to the same calumny in his own day is worth pondering deeply:

Let those who say that the teaching of Christ is hurtful to the State produce such armies as the maxims of Jesus have enjoined soldiers to bring into being; such governors of provinces; such husbands and wives; such parents and children; such masters and servants; such kings; such judges, and such payers and collectors of tribute, as the Christian teaching instructs them to become, and then let them dare to say that such teaching is hurtful to the State. Nay, rather will they hesitate to own that this discipline, if duly acted up to, is the very mainstay of the commonwealth.—*Epistula* cxxxviii. 2. 15; see ID 20.

Leo XIII in modern times answered the same calumny this way:

Therefore, when it is said that the Church is hostile to modern political regimes and that she repudiates the discoveries of modern research, the charge is a ridiculous and groundless calumny. Wild opinions she does repudiate, wicked and seditious projects she does condemn, together with that attitude of mind which points to the beginning of a willful departure from God. But, as all truth must necessarily proceed from God, the Church recognizes in all truth that is reached by research a trace of the divine intelligence. And as all truth in the natural order is powerless to destroy belief in the teachings of revelation, but can do much to confirm it, and as every newly discovered truth may serve to further the knowledge or praise of God, it follows that whatsoever spreads the range of knowledge will always be willingly and even joyfully welcomed by the Church. She will always encourage and promote, as she does in other branches of knowledge, all study occupied with the investigation of nature. In these pursuits should the human intellect discover anything not known before, the Church makes no opposition. She never objects to search being made for things that minister to the refinements and comforts of life. So far, indeed, from opposing these she is now, as she ever has been, hostile alone to indolence and sloth, and earnestly wishes that the talents of men may bear more and more abundant fruit by cultivation and exercise.—ID 39.

Notes

1. For a treatment of this matter from the viewpoint of political philosophy see Jacques Maritain, *Man and The State;* for an excellent canonical presentation of the problem, see L. Bender, *Jus publicum ecclesiasticum* (1948); for some historical background on the nineteenth-century Church-State problem, see E. E. Y. Hales, *Pio Nono.*

2. Bender, *op. cit.*, p. 200.

3. On this point see Maritain, *op. cit.*, pp. 156–57.

4. "The encyclical *Immortale Dei,* dated November 1, 1885, can be considered the most perfect exposition and clarification of the problem of Church and State contained in the letters of Pope Leo XIII. It presupposes a conception of the State conformable to the principles of Christian philosophy, that is, to the principles of St. Thomas. The foundation for such doctrine is provided by the teachings of the gospel" (Gilson, *op. cit.*, p. 157).

5. This theory is historically connected with the French Revolution. Its name is found explicitly in the works of Paul-Louis Courier (1773–1825). Its richest, subtlest formulation is found in the philosophy of Rousseau. For a clear, brief analysis of this theory and its radical opposition to a Christian concept of democracy see Yves R. Simon, "The Doctrinal Issue Between the Church and Democracy" in *The Catholic Church in World Affairs*, pp. 87–114, edited by Gurian and Fitzsimons (Notre Dame, 1954).

6. Bender objects that it is not quite accurate to distinguish Church and State as "Religious vs Secular" society as do Ottaviani and other jurists. In another economy of things there might have been a purely natural religion and then the basis of division would be acceptable. As a matter of fact, however, God instituted a supernatural order, a supernatural religion, and a supernatural society, the Church. See his *Jus publicum ecclesiasticum*, pp. 26, and 43 where he writes: "The goal of the one is the supreme natural good; the goal of the other the supreme supernatural good. It follows that we now have two societies each of which has as its proper goal some complete good or a good which is an ultimate goal of human life. But each in its own sphere. Each is *in its own sphere* perfect from the viewpoint of its goal, since the goal is a perfect good of human life *in that order*." Briefly, by God's ordinance there exist two orders. The Church is in charge of one, civil society of the other. Each is supreme in its own sphere. The supernatural society is not

intended to swallow up the natural, nor vice versa; they are mutually complementary.

7. See I Cor. 9:4–14.

8. For the difficulty of defining "mixed affairs," see Bender, *op. cit.*, p. 201.

9. For a discussion of the nature and extent of concordats see Bender, *op. cit.*, pp. 217–232. The same author treats the rights of Church and State relative to matrimony and education not under the title of "Mixed Affairs," but in a special chapter titled: *Special Questions touching the cooperation of Church and State,* (pp. 201–216). His strictures against a Catholic State which would oblige all its citizens to go through a civil marriage ceremony are witheringly logical (*ibid*, pp. 206–209).

Article II

THEOLOGICAL VALUE OF LEO XIII'S TEACHING

I. *Preliminary Remarks*

II. *Leo XIII's Teaching is Catholic Doctrine:*
   1. The very nature of an encyclical
   2. An inspection of the *Immortale Dei* itself
   3. The unanimous agreement of theologians
   4. Subsequent papal endorsement

Article II

THEOLOGICAL VALUE OF LEO XIII'S TEACHING

223 **I. Preliminary Remarks**

A brief summary of the Church's teaching on the ideal relations that should exist between Church and State in a Catholic country has just been given. Most of that teaching has been synthesized by Leo XIII in his famous *Immortale Dei* and other related encyclicals. What is the theological value of Leo's teaching in this matter? Does his teaching represent simply his views as a private theologian? Is it merely authoritative teaching guaranteed as safe for a time, but restricted in its value to the peculiar problems which faced the Church in the midst of a rampant nineteenth-century anti-religious liberalism? Or is it something of universal application, expressing clearly the mind of the Church: a perennial norm for all theologians and the faithful in dealing with this ever delicate and complex problem of Church and State?

We raise this question explicitly because in the light of some recent controversial writings in America, non-theologians and particularly non-Catholics might mistakenly arrive—and not necessarily because of any of the theological participants in the debate*—at the notion that Leo's teaching was something merely pertinent to a peculiar historical context and hence able to be revamped in the light of every changing "historical constellation," to use Maritain's poetic phrase.[1]

II. Leo XIII's Teaching is Catholic Doctrine

An assay of the value of Leo's teaching on Church and State may be rapidly gained from a brief consideration of these points: 1. the very nature of an encyclical; 2. an inspection of the *Immortale Dei* itself; 3. the unanimous agreement of theologians; 4. the endorsement of Leo's teaching by subsequent popes.

---

* All the theologians involved emphatically declared their loyalty and submission to Leo's teaching; they simply disagreed as to what would be the proper understanding of this or that section of his writings.

1. **The very nature of an encyclical.** An encyclical is an important papal document designed to carry the pope's ordinary teaching to the entire Catholic world, even if it be addressed to some particular church. Consequently, an encyclical gives the clear mind of the Church on the matter under discussion. Its contents viewed as a whole will always require, at the minimum, an assent of internal religious obedience. At the most, some of its contents might require an assent of divine and Catholic faith: for example, it is not unusual for encyclicals to repeat points which have been already solemnly defined by the Church. To use an all-embracive label, then, the best way to classify the contents of an encyclical, viewed as a whole, would probably be: *Catholic teaching.* This is an elastic label used to cover a variety of assents. It means doctrine that is taught throughout the entire Catholic world, and hence not something in the mere realm of opinion. Lest anyone mistake the importance of encyclical letters, the present pope reminded theologians in his *Humani generis* (August 12, 1950) that encyclicals demand our consent. They are an expression of the ordinary teaching power of the Church to which it is correct to apply Christ's dictum: "He that hears you hears me."

2. **An inspection of the Immortale Dei itself** bears out the fact that Leo was not restricting his teaching merely to a special situation he was facing, nor simply expressing his own views as a private theologian. Over and over again in the encyclical he refers to the fact that he is exercising his apostolic office of teacher of the entire Church; secondly, that his teaching on Church and State is ultimately grounded in revelation and sound philosophy. A few citations will suffice to show this clearly. After stating that many have tried to work out plans for civil society based on doctrines other than those approved by the Catholic Church, he writes:

> But, though endeavors of various kinds have been ventured on, it is clear that no better mode has been devised for building up and ruling the State than that which is *the necessary growth of the teachings of the gospel.* We deem it, therefore, of the highest moment, and *a strict duty of Our apostolic office,* to contrast with *the lessons taught by Christ* the novel theories now advanced touching the State.—2; italics ours throughout.
>
> Such, then, as We have briefly pointed out, is the *Christian* organization of civil society; not rashly or fancifully shaped out,

(391)

but educed from the highest and truest principles, confirmed by natural reason itself.—16.

This, then, is *the teaching of the Catholic Church* concerning the constitution and government of the State.—36.

Since truth when brought to light is wont, of its own nature, to spread itself far and wide, and gradually take possession of the minds of men, *We, moved by the great and holy duty of Our apostolic mission to all nations,* speak, as We are bound to, with freedom.—40.

Finally, at the close of the encyclical Leo states unequivocally that his teaching is directed not simply to one country but to the entire Catholic world:

This, venerable brethren, is what We have thought it *Our duty to expound to all nations of the Catholic world touching the Christian constitution of states,* and the duties of individual citizens.—50.

225   **3. The unanimous agreement of theologians.** Finally all theologians and canonists from Leo's own day to the present refer to Leo's teaching as the classic source of the Church's teaching on relations between Church and State. It would be wearisome to list them all. Here are a few of the standard theologians: Billot, Tanquerey, Hervé, Pesch, Zapalena, Tromp, Garrigou-Lagrange, Parente and Salaverri. Here are a few of the standard canonists: Ottaviani, Cappello, Coronata, and Bender.[2]

4. Subsequent papal endorsement. Leo XIII in his own encyclical referred to the fact that he was only repeating and developing what previous popes before him had taught on the same fundamental principles. He cites explicitly Gregory XVI and Pius IX (ID 34). St. Pius X reiterated Leo's condemnation of the liberalistic doctrine of Church and State in his *Vehementer Nos,* addressed to France in 1906.[3] Pius XI repeated Leo's doctrine on the obligation of civil society to pay public worship to Christ the King in his encyclical *Quas primas.*[4]

If any doubt could remain that Leo's XIII has represented the clear mind of the Church in his teachings on Church and State, Pius XII has dissipated any such illusions in his recent *Address to the Historians* (Sept. 7, 1955). Noting that scholars have been recently attentive to the history of relations of Church and State, the present Holy Father affirms that Leo has put into a kind of formula the proper relations which ought to obtain between the two societies. After stating that Leo has given "an enlightening explanation" of those relations in his encyclicals *Diuturnum illud* (1881), *Immortale Dei* (1885), and *Sapientiae Christianae* (1890), Pius XII refers to the value of Leo's teaching on Church and State in these words:

> One can say that with the exception of a few centuries—for all the first 1,000 years as for the last 400—*the statement of Leo XIII reflects more or less explicitly the mind of the Church.* Even during the intervening period, moreover, there were representatives of the doctrine of the Church—perhaps even a majority who shared the same opinion.—Translation and italics ours. For original French see AAS, 47 (1955), 678.

In other words, Pius XII tells us plainly that Leo's teaching on Church and State represents in explicit terms what was the teaching of the Catholic Church over the centuries—some 1400 years—with perhaps a brief interlude in which the Church's teaching was temporarily obscured (the Medieval Era)—and that even during that era there were representatives of the true doctrine of the Church. Leo's teaching, therefore, cannot possibly be reduced to simply an *ad hoc* solution produced to meet the peculiar needs of the nineteenth century. It is *Catholic teaching (doctrina catholica).*

Notes

1. *Op. cit.,* p. 160.
2. The following theologians and canonists appeal to Leo XIII's authority as a source of their teaching on the proper relations between Church and State:

Theologians: L. Billot, *De ecclesia Christi* (3rd ed., 1929), II, *passim* and especially p. 82–93; R. Garrigou-Lagrange, *De revelatione* (4th ed., 1945), II, p. 411–9; J. M. Hervé, *Manuale theologiae dogmaticae* (5th rev. ed., 1951), p. 244–5; L. Lercher, *op. cit.,* p. 244–5; Parente, *Theologia fundamentalis, op. cit.,* 185–90; C. Pesch, *Compendium theologiae dogmaticae* (2nd ed., 1929), I, 160–3; I. Salaverri, *op. cit.,* (1952), I, 805–17; A. Tanquerey, *Synopsis theologiae dogmaticae* (26th ed., 1949), I, 686–701.

Canonists: L. Bender, *op. cit.,* p. 177–8; Cappello, *Summa iuris publici ecclesiastici* (4th ed., 1936), p. 128–41; M. Coronata, *Compendium iuris canonici* (1937), p. 25–48; A. Ottaviani, *Institutiones iuris publici ecclesiastici* (3rd ed., 1947), I, p. 157–72.

3. Bender, *op. cit.,* p. 178.
4. See Pius XI, *The Kingship of Christ (Quas primas),* translated by Gerald Treacy (New York, 1944), nos. 20 and 24.

APPENDIX

THE PRIMACY TEXT IN THE GOSPEL OF MATTHEW *

St. Peter's confession of his Master's divinity is found in Matthew 16:13–16; Mark 8:27–30; Luke 9:18–21. The promise of primacy which followed as the reward of this confession appears only in Matthew 16:17–20. St. Matthew's account of the incident is accordingly the key passage in this whole discussion.[1] In our treatment of it, we shall:

1. *Give an analysis of the passage*, so that an idea may be formed of its general contents.

2. *Examine more in detail some of the expressions used therein* (especially in verses 18–19), so that their real force may be the more clearly understood. This will be a supplement and justification of what will have been said under the previous step.

3. *Consider some of the various objections* raised against the Catholic interpretation of the passage.

1. Analysis of the passage 226

The Gospel account places the scene in the neighborhood of Caesarea Philippi, but gives no indication which would help us fix exactly the precise place of the event. Hence the view of some authors that it was near the source of one of the branches of the Jordan, close by the temple of Augustus built on a rock near a cavern suggestive of the entrance to Hades may be very interesting and stimulating from the oratorical viewpoint, but it has no support in the Gospel text.

Jesus Himself brings up the question regarding His identity (vv. 13b–14). In order to lead His apostles to an expression of their faith in Him, He questions them about the opinions current among the people about Him, and finally calls upon them directly

---

* This will be a strictly exegetical treatment, with little, if any, reference to the authority of Tradition or the Magisterium of the Church. For a really full appreciation of the passage, recourse to these latter is necessary, but it is quite impressive to see the force of the passage considered all by itself.

to declare *their* view of Him (v. 15). Peter answers (v. 16). No doubt he speaks in the name of all, but primarily and immediately it is his own faith that he expresses. It is not a question of his formulating something already present in the minds of the whole group, as the sequel shows. The others may have believed in Jesus' Messiahship before this; they may also have suspected that there was something more than human about their Master; but Jesus' reply to Peter implies that there was something new and far more definite in Peter's confession. Peter confesses not only the Messiahship of Jesus, but also *His divine Sonship*. The words "Son of the living God," peculiar to the first gospel, are not a meaningless addition, repeating and explaining the "Christ" of the preceding phrase. There is no proof for the claim that the two expressions, "Christ" (Messias) and "Son of God" are synonymous. Even critics like Loisy explain the words "the Son of the living God" as a confession of the divine nature of Jesus, and this explanation agrees perfectly with the tenor of the whole context.

Jesus, addressing Peter directly (v. 17), accepts his confession and insists on its exceptional significance. He congratulates His apostle, acknowledging that the latter's words were spoken under the influence of a divine revelation which enabled him to realize the mystery of Jesus, the relation existing between the Son of God and His heavenly Father. Peter had, then, just given expression to a mystery, inaccessible of itself to human understanding, knowable only in virtue of a special grace, a supernatural illumination.

Jesus thus fully endorses and represents as guaranteed by the authority of God Himself the confession made by Peter. But all this, wonderful as it is in itself, serves, in addition, as an introduction to our Lord's words to Peter in vv. 18 ff. In return for his singular confession, Peter is to receive a singular reward. He is to have in the Church of Christ an exceptional place of honor and of authority.[2]

227 Clearly alluding to the significance of the name He had previously given His apostle (John 1:42), Jesus discloses that the apostle is to be the rock on which, like the wise builder (Matt. 7:24–25), He intends to build His Church. Christ, therefore, contemplates something new. The Chosen People had been the "Church of the Lord" or the "Church of God." Christ means to replace this congregation by *His own Church*, a new building which is to rest securely on a new foundation (v. 18a, b). The strength of the edifice will be such that Hades itself will be powerless against it (18c).

APPENDIX

This verse therefore describes Peter's place in the Church: he is the foundation on which it stands immovable, beyond any danger of falling. By means of different metaphors, Jesus declares in the next verse the power (authority) which He will bestow on His apostle and thus defines more precisely the place of Peter in the Church. The latter is to have supreme power in the Kingdom of God upon earth. He is to act as the agent or representative of Christ, who of course remains the Master and Owner ("*I will build my Church*"). Biblical and Rabbinic usage (Isai. 22:22; Apoc. 1:18; 3:7; 9:1; 20:1) forbids us to see in the metaphor of the keys the idea that Peter is merely the porter who admits or keeps out. On the contrary, it demands the idea of one delegated by the owner to administer the affairs of his house in his name and in his place. Peter is thus to be the vicar of Christ on earth (19a).

The next two clauses may be considered as specifications of the power given by Christ to His representative. The words (*deo*) and (*luo*) as used by Jesus here evidently cannot be explained in the sense in which they are found so often in Greek magical formulae. The words occur very frequently in Rabbinic writings and must be understood along the general lines of Rabbinic usage. "To bind" and "to loose" are sometimes used by the Rabbis in the sense of "exclude," "excommunicate," and "admit," "release from excommunication." From this point of view, the expressions would denote the disciplinary power conferred on Peter. But in this same Rabbinic usage, "to bind" and "to loose" are also very frequently employed in the sense of "forbid" and "permit." Since this is so, then Peter has authority in the Kingdom of Heaven to decide what is wrong and what is right. And since the terms are used also of doctrinal decisions, they mean that Peter has the authority to teach. This all amounts to saying that the expressions are to be taken in their widest possible meaning, as even so very radical a critic as Oort admits:

228

> In this case [i.e., if the words are a translation from a Hebrew or Aramaic original], there is given to Peter here a twofold power: the management of discipline and the authority to decide what is true and good: the office of overseer and that of teacher. And so the Church has understood it.

A similar conclusion is reached by Strack and Billerbeck, conservative Protestants, in their commentary on this passage, a commen-

CHRIST'S CHURCH

tary based on Rabbinic usage: the words of our Lord include disciplinary and doctrinal authority.[3]

Peter is thus invested with full power to rule the Church of Christ in His place. And to enhance, if possible, the authority thus entrusted to Peter, Jesus assures the apostle that the exercise of this authority will be ratified by God. Peter's decisions will therefore be, as it were, those of God Himself. His word, whatever it may be—commanding, forbidding, or teaching—will have to be listened to as that of God Himself.

The section concludes (v. 20) with Jesus' charge to His apostles not to speak of His Messiahship. The following verses reveal Jesus' conception of the Messianic office. In His mind, the latter is something wholly unlike the Messianic office of popular imagination, so unlike it, indeed, that even the apostles themselves are as yet unable to understand properly. Indiscreet proclamation of His Messiahship would therefore result only in vain agitation. Hence the need for silence on this point. There would be no need to impose silence with respect to Jesus' divine Sonship. The disciples would hardly be tempted to bruit that about in a Jewish milieu just then.

229 We have explained the words of our Lord as a promise to St. Peter of a unique position in the Church. Many Protestants would accept this interpretation, provided Christ's words were taken as addressed to Peter exclusively, in the sense that our Lord meant His promise to be entirely personal and restricted to Peter and that He meant Peter's privileged position to belong to him exclusively and not to be passed on to others after him.

It is true that the words of the text do not mention a successor directly and explicitly. But that Peter was to have successors in office is clearly suggested by the whole passage, which would otherwise be pointless. The Church is to continue throughout the ages, built on Peter as its firm foundation. Now he cannot fulfill this function personally throughout the history of the Church; but what Peter cannot do personally he can do through his successors, who will be to the different generations of men making up the Church of Christ in each successive age what Peter was to be to the Church of Christ in his day. That means that the words of Christ are a promise (*a*) of the institution of an office by which the proper continuation of the Church to the end of time is to be secured, and (*b*) of the bestowal of that office on Peter first. These

(398)

APPENDIX

words are likewise a prophecy that the Church will continue to the end of time, a prophecy whose fulfillment demands that the Church have at all times one who will be Peter, the Rock to her.[4]

In favor of the above view of our text, we may appeal to all those critics who reject the genuineness (authenticity) of these verses. If, as they hold, the verses were added to the Gospel, the intention of the interpolator was obviously to support the claims of Rome to a position of unique authority over the other Churches, and not to champion the useless authority of an already dead Peter. Accordingly, the purpose of the author of the verses was evidently to attribute to Christ the promise of founding an office, not merely the bestowal of a purely personal privilege to Peter.

When, therefore, Catholics appeal to this text in favor of the primacy of the Holy See, they are not reading too much into it. They are drawing a perfectly legitimate and obvious conclusion from the words of Christ.

2. Explanation and justification of some points mentioned above 230

Verse 18a. In this verse there is a significant play on words which is fully clear only in Aramaic and can be preserved to some extent in Greek and Latin (and some other languages), but is lost in other languages (e.g., English, German). To realize the full meaning of the text we must bear in mind always that the sense is to be determined not by the meaning which the words may have in Greek—or in Syriac, but by their meaning in the Aramaic which our Lord used when He uttered them.

From different passages in the New Testament which have preserved it in its original (Aramaic) form, we know that the name *Petros* represents the word *Kepha'* (see John 1:42; I Cor. 1:12; 3:22; 9:5; 15:5, etc.). Now this word *Kepha'*, which does not seem to have been used before as a personal name, is found in various Aramaic dialects with the meaning of "rock." Thus in the Targum of the Old Testament written in the Jewish Palestinian dialect of Western Aramaic, the word appears as the translation of the Hebrew word for "rock" (Num. 20:8, 10, 11; Ps. 39[40]:3). The same word, translating the Hebrew word for "rock," is found also in the Syriac Bible, written in one of the dialects of Eastern Aramaic (Num. 20:8, 10, 11; Matt. 16:18; 27:51, for the Greek *petra*, "rock").

Accordingly, the original words spoken by our Lord to Peter

will have been: "Thou are *Kepha'*, and upon this *kepha'* I will build my Church," as they are in the Syriac versions (Cureton and Peshitto) of this passage. To preserve the play on words perfectly, the Greek translator should, strictly speaking, have rendered the same word, *kepha'*, by the same word, *petra*, in both instances, But he no doubt felt that such a literal translation would have resulted in a rather strange form of name for a man: *petra* is feminine. Now the masculine form *petros*, means "stone." Since the idea of "stone" is closely related to that of "rock," even though it is not identical with it, the translator felt that he was doing sufficient justice to the original by rendering the first *kepha'* by *petros*, as Peter's name, and the second one by *petra* (as Peter's function), with its usual meaning.

It is, then, altogether wrong to draw any kind of argument from the fact that the Greek text uses two different words, *petros* and *petra*. It is a complete waste of time to insist that these two words have different meanings, *petra* being properly "rock, mass of live rock," and *petros* being "a detached stone, a boulder," and that good Greek usage maintains a distinction between them. *The distinction does not exist in the Aramaic*,[5] but, as explained above, the translator had to make some distinction in the Greek. Moreover, such a distinction as that which explains *petros* as the name of the apostle and *petra* as his faith or something of the sort makes the words of our Lord pointless. The demonstrative pronoun in "this rock" remains without a natural explanation.

We may conclude, then, that our Lord is here addressing the apostle directly by the significant name of *Kepha'*—"Rock," which He had given him before this, and that He is here explaining the reason for having conferred it upon him: He intends to make him the rock upon which He means to build His Church.

231 *Verse* 18b. The figure under which Christ describes the strength of the Church has been understood in various ways by Catholic as well as by non-Catholic commentators. According to some, Hades (hell) is the abode of the dead, and the word is used in the sense it usually has in the Old Testament. The gates of hell thus signify the power of death, and the sense is that death will be powerless against the Church of Christ. Although everything in the world of men must fall prey to death, *"debemur morti nos nostraque"* (Horace *Ars poetica* 63), the Church shall live on immortal. Others take Hades as the name of the abode of the

APPENDIX

damned. It is the empire of Satan, and the power of wickedness referred to by this expression is that of the empire of evil waging relentless war against the Church. According to this interpretation, Christ is promising that His Church will always successfully resist and overcome the attacks of Satan. If the Greek verb translated by "prevail against" had to be taken as implying a hostile attack, it would settle the controversy in favor of the latter view. The verb, however, does not necessarily suggest a hostile attack and, therefore, does not decide the point. It is clear that both views are orthodox and are in agreement on the ultimate sense. But the second is perhaps the more natural in the present context.[6]

In this context, which clearly presupposes a semitic original, the expression "gates of Hades" represents the same expression in the Aramaic. Still it may be noted that the figure is not unknown in classical Greek, where it is a periphrasis for the netherworld.

Verse 19. The metaphors used here to describe the power given to Peter are distinctly semitic.

The figure of the keys (19a) as a symbol of authority is natural enough and is therefore to be found in literatures other than the semitic. Strange to say, however, it does not occur in Greek, classical or nonclassical, as far as can be determined. But it is found in Latin, where the expression *"claves alicui tradere"* means "to entrust the management of one's affairs to someone." Still it does not constitute an idiom in Latin as characteristic as it is in semitic languages. Outside the Bible, we find it in Rabbinic sources. Thus God is said to have reserved for Himself four keys which He has not given to any creature, and which denote His sovereign power over rain, food, death, and birth. It is used in the Koran as an image of the power of the Creator over His creation: Sura 39:63: "Allah is the creator of all things and He of all things is the guardian. His are the keys of the heaven and of the earth." This latter phrase occurs again in Sura 42:10. However, as the word translated "keys" may also mean "treasure rooms," some Arabic commentators understand the word in this latter sense, so that the passages would not really constitute parallels to our text. But Arabic has another expression which is indisputably parallel to that of the Gospel. To entrust the management or disposal of one's affairs to another is expressed in Arabic by "he delivered to him the keys of the affairs."

We may then say that the Gospel metaphor, understood in the

light of biblical and extra-biblical semitic usage, represents Peter as invested with full power over the kingdom of heaven, established as its administrator with power to manage its affairs—in accordance, of course, with the will of the One whom he represents.

The figure of binding and loosing in 19b, c has been sufficiently explained above. It will suffice to note here that it is exceedingly common in Hebrew and Aramaic among the Rabbis, especially in the sense of "forbidding" and "allowing." The expression "to loose," in the sense of "to allow," has passed into Arabic, which also has the expression, "the master of the binding and of the loosing," to denote one who has the right to decide or solve, and whose decision is to be accepted. If our Lord's words in this part of the verse were to be understood in this special sense which they have so often among the Rabbis, we might say that Peter is set up by Christ as the supreme doctor or teacher in the Church. But in view of the wider meaning which the expression may have in Rabbinic usage, and in view of the whole context, it is better to take these words in as general a sense as possible, i.e., as denoting supreme authority to pass any sentence—doctrinal, disciplinary, etc.—that may be required by Peter's position as vicar of Christ, with the assurance that his decision will be ratified by God.[7]

233 3. Authenticity of the promise to Peter

Modern criticism may be said in general to accept as well founded the Catholic interpretation of Christ's promise to Peter. It might almost be said that the more radical the attitude of the critic, the more Catholic his *interpretation* is. But these critics agree in denying in different ways the *authenticity* of vv. 17 and 19; either the whole passage is an interpolation, or the original words of Christ have been changed by additions which give them their present Catholic sense.

In favor of the authenticity of these verses are the Catholics and conservative Protestants. But the latter disagree with the former in the interpretation of the passage. Obviously they cannot admit that Christ gave Peter and his successors primacy over the Church. Consequently, as seen above, in their endeavor to strip the text of its distinctive Catholicism, they offer explanations which are more or less strained and unnatural. In favor of their interpretation they also appeal to the authority of several of the fathers who appear not to have understood the text in its full Catholic sense. It was pointed out above, among other things, that these fathers, when treating the phrase in a strictly exegetical manner, did give the usual Catholic interpretation. But in homilies and moral exhortations they gave it different meanings and applications in accordance with the moral lesson they were trying to put across. Further discussion of this question would take us too far afield and is better left to patrologists and historians.[8] For our present purpose, we have now only to prove the value of the text by considering the problem of its authenticity that has been raised by radical criticism.

Some objections are based on rather broad tendentious views of the whole Christian message. The text is to be rejected because it does not square with the rest of Christ's teaching. Thus, according to the eschatological theory, Jesus did not intend to found a society or Church which would continue after Him. He preached the kingdom of God which He was to inaugurate within a short time when He would reappear as the Messias in glory. Hence there was no need to make provision for the future, since He was expecting the consummation of all things in the very near future. Jesus therefore preached the kingdom of heaven. But instead of this kingdom, there came the Church. Since the Parousia did not take place and the world continued to move on, the followers of Jesus, in order to survive, were forced to accommodate themselves to circumstances and to organize themselves into a society under an authority which gradually came to be considered as founded by Christ Himself. It follows necessarily from such a conception of the teaching of Christ that anything implying an enduring organization was wholly foreign to the mind of Jesus and is therefore to be rejected, since it merely grew out of the conditions of the later Christian community. Clearly, then, the present text with its reference to a Church which is to last forever and is organized under a supreme head, Peter and his successors as representatives of Christ—such a text, so strikingly "ecclesiastical," cannot be part of the teaching of Jesus, but corresponds to a later situation and is therefore an interpolation.

It is naturally impossible at this point to discuss fully the view on which this rejection of our text is based. It involves a study of the nature of the kingdom as preached by Christ and of His claims concerning His own Person. A few words of reply to this revolutionary system must suffice here. There are some words of our

Lord's which, taken all by themselves, might suggest the idea of an immediate Second Coming or the like (e.g., Matt. 10:23). But alongside of such passages, which are admittedly difficult, there are many others which are certainly authentic and which cannot be construed in the eschatological sense. Thus, in Matthew 13, several of the Kingdom Parables suggest anything but a kingdom to be established in a miraculously divine manner and within a short time, not, at least, in the eschatological sense. Likewise the parts of the instructions in Matthew 10 which regard the future do not imply a view of the kingdom like that supposed by the Eschatologists. So also the choice of the Twelve and the care given to their training by our Lord imply at least the intention of preparing for the future. Our Lord's teaching concerning Himself should be taken into account, too. Unless we are ready to admit that He was completely mistaken about His Person and His mission, we cannot consistently force the eschatological system upon Him. And if we grant that His horizon was not limited to the immediate future by the thought of the impending kingdom and Second Coming, then we cannot deny the possibility of His thinking of the future development of His work and of providing for it.[9]

235 Some objections are of a more specific character. It is claimed, for instance, that the text is not authentic for reasons derived from the context. Thus from the point of view of the Two Source Theory, the promise betrays itself as an addition since it is wanting in the Gospel of Mark, the main narrative source of the first Gospel. And it was not in Q or the *Logia*, since St. Luke, who also used Q, does not record these two verses.* To this difficulty we may reply that even from the standpoint of the Two Source Theory of the origin of *Matthew*, the conclusion of the critics is unwarranted. For, however the absence of these verses from *Mark* and *Luke* may be explained, the fact remains that they have a very

---

* The so-called "Two Source Theory" is an hypothesis devised in an attempt to solve the well-known Synoptic Problem, i.e., the problem of the literary interrelationships of the three synoptic gospels. According to this theory, the sources of Matthew's Gospel are Mark and an hypothetical collection of our Lord's sayings (*Logia*). For want of a better name, this collection is called simply Q, the first letter of the German word *Quelle* (source). Catholic scholars reject this hypothesis in its crude form as being quite arbitrary, lacking in solid evidence, and contrary to the sure data of historical tradition. See B. C. Butler, *The Originality of St. Matthew*, (Cambridge, 1951). While Abbot Butler's positive solution leaves something to be desired, his critique of the Two Source Theory is devastating and highly interesting. See also G. Ricciotti, *The Life of Christ* (Milwaukee, 1949), 126 ff.

APPENDIX

pronounced semitic flavor. In addition to the expressions discussed above, there are, in verse 17, the words "Simon bar Jona" (Simon, son of Jona), and "flesh and blood." Of these semitisms, one at least, the play on words in verse 18, is explicable only in Aramaic, and points clearly to an Aramaic original for our text. The linguistic character of the passage, therefore, establishes its Aramaic origin and, consequently, the early date of the tradition to which it belongs. Hence from the point of view of language alone we might hold, even on the Two Source hypothesis, that Matthew added these verses on the authority of an ancient Aramaic source which we should have no right to set aside lightly. Abstracting from the Two Source Theory and accepting the tradition of the Aramaic origin of the first Gospel, we may maintain that the striking Aramaic character of this text proves that it must have belonged to the Aramaic Gospel itself.

In favor of this conclusion, we may add that the promise in verses 17–19 forms the natural sequel to Peter's confession in the preceding verses rather than betrays itself as an adventitious addition. Jesus had not questioned His disciples in order to find out for Himself, for His own personal information, what people in general or His disciples thought of Him. His intention was to obtain a profession of faith from them. When this profession, which He has Himself elicited, is forthcoming, we should expect Him to make some comment on the answer He has obtained. This comment we have in the words given in verses 17–19, which thus form an appropriate conclusion.

Consequently, whether we consider the peculiarities of the language of these verses or their relation with the preceding context, there is no solid reason for rejecting their early date and authenticity. It may be noted in addition that the later the date when the verses were supposed to have been introduced into the text (during the second century, according to some), the more difficult it becomes to explain their origin satisfactorily. We should hardly expect a forger at such a late date to try to create the impression of authenticity by giving his production its strong Aramaic flavor.[10] Nor could we explain readily how such an addition would have passed into *all* the MSS and into *all* the ancient versions. *The text is found everywhere in the form in which it is known to us.* There are some variants, but they are no more serious than they are in other parts of the Gospel.

As a final reason confirming the authenticity of these verses, we may appeal to the unquestionable fact attested by the New Testament in various places that Simon, the brother of Andrew, received from Jesus the name of Peter (*Kepha'*). Such a strange and significant name, which finds no explanation in the character or temperament of its bearer, must have been explained on some occasion. This is just what Matthew reports to have taken place on the occasion of Peter's confession.

The conclusion from this review of the arguments against the authenticity of verses 17-19 is that there is no evidence compelling us either to reject or even to question their authenticity, but rather that a number of reasons speak distinctly and loudly in favor of that authenticity. And so it is not surprising to see some critics, unable to reject or condemn the text as a whole, rejecting only some words as interpolated.[11] Or, if they keep the text as it stands, they try to force upon it an altogether different interpretation. Their frantic and often embarrassed efforts to be rid of or to adulterate the passage offer eloquent testimony to the importance they attach to it.

Notes

1. The literature on this text is, of course, enormous, and we shall not even attempt to give here a formal bibliography. We want to acknowledge our debt of gratitude to Dr. Edward P. Arbez, S.S. of the Catholic University of America for his kind permission to reproduce here, with some slight changes, his unpublished notes on the matter at hand. Our thanks, too, to Dr. John P. Weisengoff, who edited Dr. Arbez' notes for classroom use.

2. Abbé Hasseveldt has drawn attention to the significant fact that "throughout the whole of history there has always been a correlation between the Revelation of the Mystery of God and the Revelation of the Mystery of the Church" (*The Church: A Divine Mystery*, p. 97-98). Thus God revealed Himself to Abraham and chose him as the progenitor of the Chosen People, the Church of the Old Testament; He revealed Himself yet more intimately to Moses, chose him as the leader of that People and established a covenant with him as their representative; He revealed Himself uniquely in Christ, and anointed Him in Mary's womb as Head of the Mystical Body. But the analogy does not stop there. He revealed the divinity of His Son to Peter, and chose the latter, through His Son, as the Rock on which the Church, the Mystical Body, was to be established.

3. *Kommentar zum neuen Testament aus Talmud und Midrasch* (1922-1928).

4. In 1952, a prominent Protestant theologian, Oscar Cullmann, published at Zurich a work which received wide notoriety, even in the secular press.

APPENDIX

It was entitled *Petrus, Jünger, Apostel, Märtyrer*. In the same year it was translated into English by Floyd V. Filson: *Peter, Disciple, Apostle, Martyr*, (Philadelphia, The Westminster Press). Reviews and critiques followed in short order, one of them assuming book proportions, Msgr. Charles Journet's *The Primacy of Peter*, translated by John Chapin (Westminster, Md., 1954). Other splendid and readily available reviews are to be found in TS, 15 (1954), 129; AER, 130 (1954), 209 ff. An excellent full-length article devoted to a discussion of Prof. Cullmann's work is that of Kevin Smyth, S.J., "The Primacy of Peter," *Studies*, 43 (1954), 271 ff. We shall limit ourselves to a brief summary of this abundant material.

Cullmann admits that "the solution of the Reformers, that the rock is only the faith of Peter, does not satisfy. . . . The parallelism, 'You are rock, and upon this rock I will build' shows that the second rock refers to nothing different from the former one. The Roman Catholic exegesis must be regarded as correct" (p. 207). But here he parts company with Catholics, for he sees in the promise not the institution of an enduring office, but only a personal favor to Peter. A foundation can be laid only once, and Peter's function is therefore unique and limited to the initial stages of the Church. Since the function of founding the Church in the manner of a workman who lays the foundations is common to all the apostles, Peter's power does not differ essentially from that of the other apostles. What Prof. Cullman fails to see at this point is that Peter did not *lay* the foundation; he *was* the foundation rock. He states further that there is no distinction between the apostolic privileges common to all the apostles and the transapostolic privilege belonging to Peter, which would make them unequal. (On this question, see *above*, nos. 53, 57). In Cullmann's view, Peter is superior to the others because he was the first to see the risen Christ. His purely accidental superiority is due to his "chronological preeminence." Because of this latter he becomes the leader of the Church at Jerusalem, and thus Christ's promise to him finds its fulfillment. But he is quickly supplanted by James. Opposed to the small group of Churches with James at the head is the group headed by Paul. "Thus there occurred even in Primitive Christianity a decisive Church split" as the result of differences "which concerned a *central point*, that is, the conception of grace" (p. 218). Peter then becomes subordinate to James, whom he "fears" (Gal. 2:12), and must accept a rebuke from Paul (*ibid.*, 2:11). When he finally arrives in Rome, he has long since ceased to possess the power of the keys and to be head of the universal Church. He dies a martyr at Rome without having anything to leave his successors. See Journet (*op. cit.*, 130 ff.) who reacts to all the above as follows:

> Let us meditate on these . . . propositions which give us a sufficient idea of the theses of Prof. Cullmann. Let us meditate especially on the fact that he begins by asserting the authenticity of the Gospel text, but then, in order to avoid giving it the Catholic interpretation of *Tu es Petrus*, consigns the apostolic Church itself, which has scarcely emerged from the hands of Christ and is still enlightened by the graces of Pentecost, to a "decisive church split." Let anyone compare his laborious historical reconstruction with the profound coherence of the Catholic interpretation and the conclusion inevitably seems to be that he has failed in his attempt. It is difficult not to think once again of the saying of Chesterton: "In place

of supernatural history which is likely, they give us natural stories which are unlikely" (p. 133).

Still, Dr. Cullmann recognizes that the foundation-rock must somehow persist in its function, not merely virtually but actively. And it does—through the apostolic writings:

> Here in these writings we today, in the midst of the twentieth century, meet the person of the apostles, the person of the first of the apostles, Peter; In this way they continue to support, he continues to support, the structure of the Church (p. 221).

As Fr. Smyth remarks (*art. cit.*, p. 284), there might be something in Dr. Cullmann's explanation of how the primacy persists, if the primacy had consisted of teaching, and had not included the exercise of the supreme authority, of giving decisions that bound in heaven and on earth. Or again, there might be something in it if Peter had "inspired" the whole New Testament and still effectively guided the reader to the true sense. But not even Catholic reverence for St. Peter will allow us to affirm, "Peter has spoken through Paul, through Luke, through John." It is simply not true that the Christian who reads the Bible is obeying Peter. And surely to make the Petrine text mean "Read the New Testament" is to substitute for the person of Peter his faith, in other words, to return to the Protestant position which Dr. Cullmann rejects as untenable.

5. This is a fact which must never be lost sight of even for a moment in any discussion of the text: our Lord did not address Peter in Latin or Greek or even in Syriac, but in Aramaic. (See Edward F. Siegman, "The Yonan Codex of the New Testament," CBQ, 18 [Apr., 1956] 151 ff.) In what will be a very widely distributed book, if past experience is any criterion, the Jehovah's Witnesses have given the world a sadly misleading, pseudo-scientific translation of the New Testament entitled *The Christian Greek Scriptures*. A lengthy note is devoted to an explanation of Matthew 16:18, which they translate: "You are Peter, and on this rock-mass I will build up my congregation." In the note they point out that the two words in Greek (*petros*, Peter—*petra*, rock-mass) do not both apply to Peter. Instead of belaboring this oft repeated argument in the usual way, they give it an aura of deep scholarship by appealing to the Syriac version of the New Testament. The approach would have been more fundamental—and more sincerely scientific—if they had appealed to the dialects of Aramaic which Jesus might have used, instead of going to a secondary source like the Syriac, which is itself a translation from the Greek. In Syriac, as in Greek, the word for rock is feminine, and they make capital of this fact. However, this is not true in Aramaic, and there is consequently absolutely no basis for distinguishing one *kepha'* from the other. In the *original*, the play on words is perfect and unambiguous. Here is Burney's reconstruction of the words as they fell from the lips of Christ:

$$w^e \text{ 'amarna lak} \quad de \text{ 'att hu kepha'} \text{ (masc.)}$$
$$w^e \text{ 'al haden kepha'} \text{ (masc.)} \quad \text{'ebne' liknishti.}$$

See Burney, *The Poetry of Our Lord* (1925), 117; J. Mattingly, S.S., "Jehovah's Witnesses Translate the New Testament," CBQ, 13 (1951), 442–443.

6. See M. Meinertz, *Theologie des Neuen Testamentes*, I, 75; I. Salaverri, *op. cit.*, p. 681.

APPENDIX

7. See M. Meinertz, *loc. cit.*
8. See *above,* nos. 55 and 65, and esp. notes 61-64.
9. See *above,* nos. 19 ff.; Van Noort, *The True Religion* (Westminster, Md., 1955), 285 ff.; John A. McEvoy, "Realized Eschatology and the Kingdom Parables," CBQ, 9 (1947), 329 ff.
10. Especially if, as would be logical in the hypothesis, the forger were a member of the Roman Church. See Meinertz, *op. cit.*, 76.
11. Some mention should be made here of the rather desperate attempt of Harnack, in his 1918 essay on *Peter as the Rock of the Church,* to disprove the authenticity of the crucial verse 18. He appeals to the fact that St. Ephraem, in his commentary on Tatian's *Diatessaron,* does not quote 18b, but only 18a and c, and that in 18c, instead of "shall not prevail against it," he has "shall not prevail against thee." But although St. Ephraem quotes an incomplete text and has a change of pronouns, it does not follow that his source, the *Diatessaron,* had this shorter text and in this form. For the rest of St. Ephraem's explanation, wherein he describes the building of the Church, proves that he was acquainted with 18b also. To say with Harnack that this knowledge of 18b was derived from the "Separated Gospels" and not from the *Diatessaron* is a poor explanation. According to the conclusions of recent critics who have thoroughly examined this point, all the evidence shows that St. Ephraem used only the *Diatessaron.* Hence if it is admitted that his comment on the verse reveals his knowledge of 18b (even though he does not quote it), it follows that he read 18b in his Gospel text, i.e., in the *Diatessaron.* Therefore, the absence of 18b from the words of the text quoted by St. Ephraem proves merely that he did not feel bound to quote the text in full. And if he felt that way, we cannot hold that he must necessarily have reproduced with scrupulous care the part which he actually did use. Since he dealt freely with his text by omitting part of it, we may conclude that he dealt freely with the part which he actually did use. Thus, though he says "shall not prevail against *thee,*" there is no real proof that the *Diatessaron* had the second person pronoun instead of the third. Rather, since he omitted 18b with its mention of the rock and of the Church, he had to change the pronoun "it" to "thee" in order to make sense. This change, required by the turn he gave the sentence, may have suggested itself to him all the more readily since, like other commentators of antiquity, he understood that the gates of hell would not prevail against the rock on which the Church is built instead of against the Church itself, and he identified the rock with Peter.

Hence nothing can be concluded against the traditional text of verse 18 from St. Ephraem's commentary. There is no serious evidence that the *Diatessaron* had an older form which lacked 18b, and thus there is no external evidence permitting us to regard this clause as a later insertion into the verse. And even if Harnack had proven beyond a shadow of a doubt that St. Ephraem—and the *Diatessaron*—did not read 18b, what would he have proven? Simply the fact that *one* father and *one* version of the Gospel omitted part of verse 18. What possible conclusion would this solitary instance permit us to draw regarding the authenticity of the text in the face of its otherwise universally attested integrity?

Scriptural Index

Genesis
1:28   123
17:5   87
22:18   145
32:28   87

Exodus
19:6   35

Numbers
13:17   87

II Kings
7:12–16   28

I Paralipomenon
17:11–14   28

Psalms
2:1–4   148
2:8   145
44:12   233
71:5–7   28
71:7   137
71:17   145
88:38   27

Canticle of Canticles
6:13   184

Isaias
2:2–3   17, n. 29
9:6–7   28
54:2–5   147
54:17   148
62:12   138

Ezechiel
37:28   138

Daniel
2:34   44–45
2:44   28

Micheas
4:1–2   148

Zacharias
12:3   148

Malachias
1:10–11   148

Matthew
1:21   21, 87
4:12–17   11
4:17   15, n. 12, 16, n. 16
4:23   15, n. 12
5:13   136
5:14   17, n. 26, 158
5:14–16   137
5:16   164
7:16–17   137
7:24–25   25
7:24–27   87
10   404
10:1 ff.   51, n. 6
10:2–3   87
10:5–7   15, n. 12
10:7   16, n. 16
10:14–15   264, 266
10:23   148
12:6–8   16, n. 21
13:24–30   26, 139, 253, 377
13:31–32   148
13:31, 34   16, n. 16
13:33   136
13:38–40   26
13:40   26
13:44   14
13:47   17, n. 26
13:47–50   26, 253
13:48–50   139
16   66–68, 73, 297

Matthew
16:13–19   86
16:13–20   395 ff.
16:16   90
16:18   16, n. 16, 17, n. 26, 25, 300
16:18–19   8, 65, 155, 295
17:27   64
18   67
18:15–17   248
18:17   17, n. 26, 245
18:18   9, 34, 66
24   17, n. 26
24:3   26
24:9   148, 196
24:14   148
24:27   17, n. 28
25:1–12   139, 253
25:14–30   198
25:35–45   220
25:41   259
28:16–20   16, n. 18
28:17–20   21, 155
28:18–19   34
28:18–20   26, 127, 155, 357
28:19   145
28:19–20   9, 16, n. 13, 122
28:20   38, 105, 122, 137

Mark
1:15   17, n. 26
1:36   88, n. 18
3:16   63
3:16–19   87
6:7 ff.   51, n. 6
14:17   311, n. 6
16:7   64

(411)

Mark

16:15–16	16, n. 13, 34, 122, 264
16:15–17	127
16:15–18	139
16:16	21, 106, 266
16:20	34

Luke

1:32–33	26
5:1–10	64
6:14	51, n. 6
6:14–16	87
9:1 ff.	51, n. 6
10:19	21
12:14	22
17:21	14
18:8	149
19:10	21
22:19	22, n. 14, 34
22:24–26	35
22:27	35
22:31	87, 311, n. 6
22:31–32	88, n. 19, 296
24:34	64
24:46–48	145

John

1:16	221
1:42	63
1:44	87
3:5	8, 264
5:39	124
6:48, 57–58	217
6:52–54	22, n. 14
6:54–59	136
10:10	21
10:11–16	63
10:16	8, 16, n. 16, 17, n. 26, 148
10:27–28	249
11:52	16, n. 16, 158
13:6	64
13:13	51, n. 11
14:12	139
14:16	122
14:16–17, 26	105
14:17	119

John

15:1, 4–6	217
15:18–20	196
16:13	105, 119, 155
17:20–21	162
17:21–23	129
18:36	22
20:21	16, n. 18, 21, 34
20:21–23	9
20:23	21, 34, 249
21:15	87, 91
21:15–17	9, 16, n. 18, 17, n. 26, 63, 155, 296, 297

Acts

1:3	37
1:5, 8	105
1:8	145
1:13	87
1:15 ff.	65
1:15–26	51, n. 7
1:17	34
1:25	34
2:14	88, n. 18
2:14 ff.	65
2:37–42	9
2:41	238
2:41–42	9
2:42	16, n. 20
2:46	16, n. 20
3:6	65
3:11	16, n. 20
4:18–20	356
4:34–35	9
4:36	51, n. 7
5:3–8	65
5:11	16, n. 19
5:12–13	16, n. 20
5:29	88, n. 18
5:29, 40–42	356
5:42	34
6:1–6	36
6:2–6	9
8:5, 38	36
8:14	70
8:17	34

Acts

8:37	9
9:1–18	51, n. 7
9:4–5	220
9:12	9
9:27	51, n. 7
9:31–32	16, n. 17, 65
10	65
10:33 ff.	9
10:42	34
11:22	51, n. 7
12:17	54, n. 26
13	51, n. 7
13:1–3	51, n. 15
13:2–4	51, n. 7
14:4	51, n. 7
14:22	10, 36
15	16, n. 17, 51, n. 7
15:2, 6, 23	36
15:5 ff.	10
15:6 ff.	65
15:13	54, n. 26
15:28	51, n. 9
16:4	16, n. 17, 36, 51, n. 9
20:24	51, n. 8
20:28	10, 16, n. 17, 17, n. 27, 45
21:18	54, n. 26
22:6–16	51, n. 7
26:12–18	51, n. 7

Romans

1:8	148
1:9	297
10:10	127
12:5	232
12:6	163
13:1–6	353
16:17	9

I Corinthians

1:10	127
3:11	66
3:22	15, n. 12, 35
4:1	34
4:21	51, n. 10
5	138
5:3 ff.	10

SCRIPTURAL INDEX

I Corinthians
5:3–5	35
5:12	238
6:15	232
9:16	51, n. 8
10:17	9, 16, n. 17
11:2	51, n. 9
11:18 ff.	138
11:19	148
11:23–30	16, n. 14
11:26	26
11:34	10
12:4–11	139, 163
12:8–11	51, n. 13
12:12	220
12:12 ff.	17, n. 27
12:12–14, 27	218
12:13	9, 16, n. 17, 238, 264
12:27	220
14:28–30	36
15:5	64
15:10	90

II Corinthians
5:18–20	34
10:3–8	51, n. 10
10:8	10
12:20–21	138
13:2, 10	51, n. 10
13:10	10

Galatians
1:8	9, 127
1:13	16, n. 19
1:18–19	51, n. 7
1:19	54, n. 26
2:7–9	70
2:9	51, n. 7, 87
2:11	70, 407, n. 4
2:11–14	303
2:12	54, n. 26, 407, n. 4

Galatians
2:20	220
3:28	32
4:19	220
5:2–4	17, n. 23

Ephesians
1:10	219
1:22–23	217
2:20	10, 66
4:4, 25	232
4:5	9, 127, 260
4:11 ff.	15, n. 12, 17, n. 27
4:11–13	136, 233
4:11–16	16, n. 17
4:15–16	218
5:22	233
5:23, 25–27	224
5:23, 29	137, 226, 232
5:25–27	10, 136, 249
5:25–28	28
5:26–27	136

Colossians
1:6, 23	148
1:18–20	217
1:19	220
1:24	218, 220
2:9	232

II Thessalonians
2:3	148, 149
2:15	51, n. 8
3:14	51, n. 9

I Timothy
1:19–20	51, n. 8
2:4	227
3:14–15	106
3:15	17, n. 27, 119

I Timothy
4:6–7	52
5:22	38

II Timothy
1:6	34
2:17–18	51, n. 8
2:23–25	52
4:2–3	52
4:5–6	38

Titus
2:14–15	136
3:10–11	127
3:10–12	9

Hebrews
3:6	10, 249
4:12	28
9:11 ff.	16, n. 21
10:14	21
12:28	26

James
2:24–26	194

I Peter
2:4–5	10
2:5, 9	35
5:2–4	17, n. 27

I John
3:2	260
3:8	28

II John
9–11	9

Apocalypse
1–3	43
1:6	35
21:9	233

Index of Proper Names

Adam, xix, 97, n. 11, 269, n. 5
Agatho, 299, 306
Aldama, 124, n. 21
Algermissen, xi, xix, 171, nn. 1 and 2, 172, 173, 174, 175, 177, 179, 183, 191, 207, n. 2, 208, nn. 5 and 9, 210, n. 17
Ambrose, St., 69, 84
Aphraates, St., 65
Arbez, 406, n. 1
Arius, 113
Arnauld, 72
Athanasius, St., 27, 79, 96, 107, 304, 332
Attwater, xi, xix, 171, n. 2, 175, 176, 177, 183
Augustine, St., 16, n. 22, 17, n. 29, 23, n. 2, 66, 68, 81, 85, 90, nn. 40 and 43, 107, 127, 129, 145, 148, n. 13, 185, 190, 198, 210, n. 16, 219, 226, 227, 232, 233, 239, 248, 249, 251, 253, n. 21, 256, 261, 262, 263, 268, 298, 299, 320, 375, 376, 385, 386

Bainvel, xix
Baius, 312, n. 14
Bardy, 93, n. 59
Baronius, 309
Barthélemy, 313, n. 22
Bartmann, 16, n. 12
Basil of Ancyra, 304
Basil, St., 45
Batiffol, xix, 16, n. 15, 86, n. 2, 89, n. 38, 93, n. 56
Bauer, F., 210, n. 20
Bauer, J., 87, n. 14
Baur, 208, nn. 11 and 12
Bavinck, 15, n. 3
Bell, 269, n. 12
Bell, G., xix
Bellarmine, St. Robert, xix, xxviii, n.
 10, 89, n. 35, 148, n. 12, 227, 252, n. 5, 294, 309, 346, 363, 364
Bender, 56, n. 37, 344, 352, 356, 362, 363, 365, 366, 368, 369, 387, nn. 2 and 6, 388, nn. 8 and 9, 392, 393, nn. 2 and 3
Benedict XIV, 123, n. 17, 325
Benedict XV, 315, n. 1
Benson, xix, 28, n. 2, 140, n. 1, 228, 230, 231, 233
Bernard, St., 283
Bévenot, 94
Billot, xix, 89, n. 36, 166, n. 4, 269, n. 5, 344, 392, 393, n. 2
Billuart, 252
Blanshard, 374, n. 1
Bluett, xi, xix, 230, 231
Bolgeni, 339, n. 1
Bonghi, 56, n. 37, 344
Boniface VIII, xix, 47
Boniface, St., 307
Bonsirven, 230, 232
Bottemanne, 287, n. 3
Bougaud, 211, n. 31
Bouyer, 191
Bremond, 211, n. 29
Brownson, 346
Bülow, von, 209, n. 13
Burney, 408, n. 5
Butler, A., 201
Butler, B., 404
Buzy, 87, n. 13

Caerularius, 169, 171, 173, 188, 189
Cajetan, 89, n. 34
Calcagno, xix
Callistus I, St., 78, 298
Calvin, 27, 160, 166, n. 4, 178, 179, 192, 194, 247
Cannavan, 346
Cano, 148, n. 12

Cappello, 56, n. 37, 344, 392, 393, n. 2
Cavagnis, 56, n. 37, 89, n. 35
Cavanaugh, xix, 269, n. 12, 380
Celestine I, St., 81, 299
Celestius, 299
Cerfaux, xix, xxi, 16, n. 12, 230, 232
Chapin, 52, n. 19, 407, n. 4
Chapman, 91, n. 48
Chesterton, 196, 407, n. 4
Chotkowski, 210, n. 22
Choupin, xxi, 56, n. 34
Clark, 336
Clarkson, xi
Clarus of Mascula, 42
Clement of Alexandria, 41
Clement of Rome, St., 38, 44, 52, nn. 18 and 20, 76
Clement VI, 300
Comte, 367
Connell, 346, 347
Cordovani, 16, n. 12
Coronata, 56, n. 37, 344, 392, 393, n. 2
Courier, 387, n. 5
Cranston, 193, 203
Crehan, xxi, 89, n. 30, 92, nn. 50 and 54
Cristiana, 91, n. 46
Cullmann, 52, n. 19, 406, n. 4
Cyprian, St., 10, 17, n. 28, 42, 45, 65, 78–79, 84, 94, 95, 129, 143, n. 1, 219, 233, 261, 297
Cyril of Alexandria, St., 173
Cyril of Jerusalem, St., 66, 143 and n. 1

Damasus I, St., 340, n. 9
Daniélou, xxii, 15, n. 1
Davis, 51, n. 12
Dawson, 93, n. 56, 211, n. 31
De Brouwer, xix
De Dominis, 59
De Groot, 96, 114, 210, n. 20, 211, n. 25, 277, n. 1
De La Brière, 211, n. 31
De San, xix
De Santillana, 309
De Smedt, 54, n. 27, 253, n. 12, 287, n. 3
De Visscher, xxii, 15, n. 1
D'Herbigny, xix
Di Capua, 312, n. 15
Dieckmann, xix, 50, n. 1, 54, n. 25, 86–87, n. 8
Diepen, 123, n. 13, 336
Dionysius of Alexandria, St., 79
Dionysius, Pope St., 79
Dioscurus, 173
Doronzo, xi
Dorsch, xx
Downes, xii
Duchesne, 96
Dulles, xxii, 15, n. 1

Edwards, xi
Ehler, 345, 382
Ehrhard, 93, n. 56, 211, n. 30
Eleutherius, 41
Ephraem, St., 65, 409, n. 11
Epiphanius, St., 85, 298
Eusebius, 41, 54, n. 22, 78, 79, 92, n. 52, 93, n. 58, 132, n. 5
Eutyches, 172, 299, 337

Favara, 256
Favarro, 310, n. 5
Feeney, 256
Feder, 312, n. 15
Fenton, xxii, xxvii, nn. 3, 4, and 5, 17, nn. 24, 25, and 26, 51, n. 12, 53, n. 21, 54, n. 24, 56, nn. 39 and 41, 86, n. 5, 89, n. 36, 90, n. 44, 93, n. 55, 94, 95, 96, 97, 122, n. 2, 124, n. 23, 131, n. 1, 230, 231, 232, 233, 252, n. 9, 346, 378, n. 1
Feuillet, 231
Filson, 52, n. 19, 407, n. 4
Finegan, 90, n. 46
Firmilian, 42, 79
Fitzmyer, xxii, 88, n. 20, 132, n. 2
Fitzsimons, xx
Flavian, 299
Forget, 93, n. 56
Fosdick, 267

INDEX OF PROPER NAMES

Fraghi, 252
Franzelin, xx, 54, n. 23, 108, 119, 252, n. 9, 277, n. 1, 287, n. 7
Funk, 92, n. 54, 310, 340, nn. 7, 8, and 9

Garofalo, xi
Garrigou-Lagrange, 163, 345, 392, 393, n. 2
Gerson, 285, 302
Gilbert, 313, n. 22
Gilson, 345, 349, 350, 353, 376, 387, n. 4
Gladstone, 130
Goossens, xxi, 231, 232
Grabmann, xx
Graham, A., xxii, 325, 333
Graham, B., 178
Granderath, 277, n. 1, 310, n. 2
Gregory of Nyssa, St., 227
Gregory the Great, St., 43, 56, n. 34, 286, 332
Gregory IX, 308
Gregory XVI, 392
Grisar, 287, n. 9, 310, n. 5
Grosheide, 15, n. 2
Gruden, xx, 230
Grundner, xi
Gurian, xx, 345

Hales, xi, 313, 345, 367, n. 1
Hammerstein, 209, n. 14, 210, n. 23
Harapin, 96
Hardon, 181
Harnack, 15, n. 4, 90, n. 45, 91, n. 51, 148, n. 3, 211, n. 28, 409, n. 11
Hartmann, 267, 345
Hasseveldt, xx, xxvii, n. 5, 17, n. 29, 230, 346, 406, n. 2
Hefele, 93, n. 57, 96, 123, n. 13, 166, n. 3, 287, n. 5, 310, n. 4, 312, nn. 8, 15, 18, and 20, 313, n. 22, 340, nn. 7, 8, and 10
Hefele-Leclercq, 312, n. 17
Hegesippus, 41, 78
Heiner, 265
Heinrich, 124, n. 26
Herberg, xx, 345

Hergenröther-Kirsch, 312, n. 15, 340, n. 9
Hervé, 392, 393, n. 2
Hilary, St., 239
Holzhey, 87, n. 10
Horace, 400
Hormisdas, Pope St., 300
Honorius I, 300, 305, 306, 307, 312, n. 17
Huarte, xxii, 18, n. 31
Huby, 88, n. 26
Hughes, xii, xx, 53, nn. 20 and 21, 54, nn. 24 and 32, 90, n. 46, 93, n. 57, 95, 123, n. 13, 299, 302, 304, 305, 312, n. 10
Hürter, 312, n. 7
Huss, 247
Hutchinson, xii, 192

Ibas, 113, 305, 336
Ignatius of Antioch, St., 17, n. 28, 26, 41, 44, 77, 106, 129, 148, n. 1, 218, 261
Innocent I, 299, 326
Innocent III, 258, 310, n. 6
Innocent X, 72
Irenaeus, St., 17, n. 28, 41, 51, n. 14, 77, 78, 91, n. 50, 107, 127, 129, 219, 261, 297

Jaffé, 312, n. 21
Jansen, 112, 113, 312, n. 14
Jerome, St., 27, 43, 45, 46, 66, 80, 85, 107, 239, 248, 298
John of Jerusalem, 298
John Chrysostom, St., 66, 81, 129
John IV, 306, 307
John XXII, 310, n. 4
Journet, xii, xx, xxviii, nn. 5 and 10, 17, n. 24, 18, n. 31, 28, n. 2, 50, n. 4, 51, n. 5, 52, n. 19, 53, n. 20, 54, n. 33, 56, nn. 35 and 41, 86, n. 3, 88, n. 27, 89, nn. 34 and 36, 91, nn. 46 and 49, 96, 97, 131, n. 1, 140, n. 1, 198, 231, 309, 379, n. 1, 407, n. 4
Jugie, 88, n. 25
Julius I, 79–80
Jung, 345

(417)

Jurieu, 128
Justin, St., 10, 127

Kelly, xi
Kirch, 306, 307
Kilber, 252
Kirsch, 211, n. 30
Kissane, 17, n. 29
Kleist, xi, 18, n. 30
Kleist-Lilly, 311, n. 6
Knabenbauer, 14, 87, n. 14
Kneller, 90, n. 46, 94, 97, 340, n. 7
Knox, 182, 196, 253, n. 16, 256, 268, n. 4
Koesters, xx
Krabbo, 313, n. 22
Krose, 211, n. 31

Labbe, 96, 312, n. 9
Lactantius, 166, n. 1, 261
Lagrange, 99, n. 22
Langen, 311, n. 6
Laplace, 309
Lawlor, 252
Lebreton, xx
Lecler, 345
Leclercq, xx, xxvii, n. 5, 230, 231
Leo the Great, St., 291, 298, 299, 300, 326
Leo II, 306
Leo IX, 284
Leo XIII, xii, 22, 126, 131, 132, 224, 315, n. 1, 345–347, 349–357, 359–360, 371, 375–376, 386, 387, 389–390, 392–393, 393, n. 2
Lercher, xx, 243, 246, 252, 253, 269, n. 8, 277, n. 1, 345, 393, n. 2
Liberius, Pope, 303, 304
Lietzmann, 90, n. 45
Lilly, xi
Linsmeyer, 310, n. 5
Lippert, 265
Lubac, de, xix, 144, n. 2
Luce, 196
Luther, 177, 178, 179, 192, 210, n. 19
Lyonnet, 91, n. 46

Maas, xx

McCann, xix
McEvoy, 409, n. 9
McMahon, 346
Maiocchi, 310, n. 5
Maistre, de, 207, n. 1, 211, n. 26
Maldonatus, 145, n. 5
Manning, 380
Marchesi, 345
Marini, 88, n. 25
Maritain, 15, n. 9, 196, 211, n. 23, 345, 349, 374, n. 1, 387, nn. 1 and 3
Martin V, 247
Martin, T., 346
Mattingly, 408, n. 5
Maycock, 379
Mazella, 252
Médebielle, 231
Meindertz, 148, n. 3
Meinertz, 230, 232, 408, n. 6, 409, nn. 7 and 10
Mersch, v, xi, xx, 230, 231, 233
Mertens, 50, n. 1, 53, n. 21, 87, n. 8
Messineo, 346
Meyer, 374, n. 1
Michelitsch, 252
Michiels, 54, n. 29, 54, n. 32, 87, n. 8
Montcheuil, de, xix
Moran, 89, nn. 33 and 37
Morrall, 345, 382
Müller, 310, n. 5
Murphy, F., 96
Murphy, J., xx, 230
Murray, 166, n. 4
Murray, J. C., 346, 374, n. 1
Myers, xxii

Natalis Alexander, 69
Navarro, 310, n. 5
Neill, xxi
Nestorius, 113, 171, 299, 337
Newman, 196
Noort, van, v, 51, n. 5, 409, n. 9

O'Brien, 211, n. 27, 253, n. 14
O'Callaghan, 91, n. 46
O'Connor, 343
Optatus, St., 66, 84, 326
Origen, 17, n. 28, 41, 65

INDEX OF PROPER NAMES

Ottaviani, 56, n. 37, 345, 347, 387, n. 6, 392, 393, n. 2
Ottiger, xx

Pacha, 209, n. 13
Palmer, 130
Palmieri, xx, 89, n. 30, 90, n. 43, 277, n. 1, 287, n. 3, 311, n. 6
Papebroch, 96
Parente, xi, 171, n. 3, 230, 232, 233, 251, 252, nn. 2, 4, and 6, 253, n. 20, 269, n. 9, 298, 305, 319, 345, 392, 393, n. 2
Paris, xx
Paulus, 123, n. 20, 124, n. 22
Pelagius, 299
Pesch, xxviii, n. 10, 17, n. 23, 117, 252, n. 5, 392, 393, n. 2
Peter Chrysologus, St., 66, 74, 298
Peters, 209, n. 13
Photius, 160, 166, n. 3, 171, 188
Piolanti, xi
Pirot, 87, n. 13
Pirot-Clamer, 231
Pius VI, 27, 326, 327, n. 9
Pius IX, xx, 242, 259, 260, 265, 313, 314, 315, nn. 1, 3, and 4, 345, 367, n. 1, 392
Pius X, St., 315, n. 1, 345, 392
Pius XI, 172, 315, nn. 1 and 5, 345, 349, 392, 393, n. 4
Pius XII, xi, xii, xx, 51, n. 12, 216, 219, 221, 222, 224, 225, 227, 229, 230, 231, 236, 238, 241, 244, 245, 248, 255, 260, 326, 332, 339, n. 1, 345, 347, 349, 350, 373, 376, 378, 384, 385, 391, 392, 393
Polycarp, St., 41, 78
Pourrat, 211, n. 29
Poulpiquet, 144, n. 4
Prat, 230, 232
Pseudo-Isidore, 284
Pusey, 130

Quasten, xxi, 92, n. 54, 93, n. 56
Quesnel, 247, 312, n. 14

Räzy, 211, n. 27

Ranft, xxi, xxvii, n. 1
Rea, 51, n. 12
Reisinger, 15, n. 8
Ricciotti, xi, xxi, 16, n. 22, 404
Richer, 59
Roiron, 88, n. 22
Romein, 265
Rommen, 347, 379, n. 1
Rost, 211, n. 31
Rouse, xxi
Runciman, 346, 378, n. 1, 379
Ryan, 347

Sabellius, 79
St. John, xxii
Sainton, 208, n. 13
Salaverri, xxi, 16, n. 12, 50, n. 1, 54, n. 33, 131, n. 1, 132, n. 19, 139, n. 1, 230, 232, 246, 249, 252, nn. 5 and 9, 253, n. 20, 269, n. 7, 275, 277, n. 1, 286, 346, 392, 393, n. 2, 408, n. 6
Saviano, 56, n. 37
Scavenus, 209, n. 13
Scheid, 123, n. 19
Schlagenhaufen, 252, nn. 3 and 5
Schneemann, 93, n. 56
Schnürer, 211, n. 31
Schultes, xxi
Schweitzer, 183
Sell, 211, n. 32
Serer, 347
Sergius, 300, 305, 307
Sertillanges, xxi, 230
Shea, 347, 350
Siegman, 408, n. 5
Simon, xxi, 347, 353, 387, n. 5
Siricius, 80
Sloet, 87, n. 8
Smyth, 407, n. 4, 408, n. 4
Socrates, 80
Soloviev, xi, xxi, 85
Spedalieri, xxi, 123, n. 19
Spinka, 191
Staerk, 211, n. 24
Stanley, xxii, 16, n. 18
Stein, 310, n. 5
Stephen, Pope St., 79, 95

Stern, 196
Stolz, 252, n. 9
Storey, xxvii, n. 5, 230
Strack-Billerbeck, 397
Straub, xxi, 252
Suárez, 89, n. 35, 240, 241, 252, n. 9, 294
Sutcliffe, 311, n. 6
Sympon, 306

Tanquerey, 208, nn. 4 and 13, 392, 393, n. 2
Tapper, 302
Tarquini, 356
Tatian, 409, n. 11
Tavard, xxi, 180, 207, n. 2, 208, n. 6
Taylor, 208, n. 13
Tertullian, 41, 42, 65, 66, 74, 78, 94, 95, 107, 143, n. 1, 189, 219, 239, 298, 303
Theodore of Mopsuestia, 113, 304, 305, 336
Theodoret, 113, 305, 336
Thomas Aquinas, St., 89, n. 31, 139, n. 1, 143, 192, 232, 376, 387, n. 4
Tournely, 302
Toynbee, 91, n. 46
Treacy, 393, n. 4
Tromp, xxi, 231, 392
Turrecremata, 285
Tyszkiewicz, xxi, 231

Urban VI, 309

Vacandard, 379, n. 1
Vailhé, 287, n. 8
Venantius Fortunatus, 72
Victor, Pope St., 78
Vigilius, 113, 304, 340, n. 9
Virgilius, St., 307, 308
Vollert, xi
Voltaire, 211, n. 25

Walz, 17, n. 24
Weigel, xxi, 15, n. 1, 347
Weisengoff, 406, n. 1
Welch, xi
West, 209, n. 13
Wilmers, xxi, 54, n. 32, 132, n. 17
Wright, xxii
Wycliffe, 247

Yanitelli, 347

Zacharias, Pope St., 307, 308
Zapalena, xxi, 16, n. 18, 50, n. 1, 53, n. 20, 87, n. 8, 92, n. 50, 93, n. 56, 95, 97, 230, 231, 232, 233, 242, 252, nn. 7 and 10, 253, n. 20, 269, n. 1, 267, n. 6, 275, 277, n. 1, 285, 286, 287, n. 6, 326, 327, nn. 4 and 7, 333, 334, 339, n. 2, 340, nn. 3 and 5, 392
Zeiller, xx
Zizzamia, xi, xxi, 17, n. 22
Zolli, 196

General Index

A

Abercius of Hieropolis, 78
"Adoption of a bishop," 323–24
Agatho, Pope, praises apostolic see for its infallibility, 299
Ancient Eastern Christian sects, brief sketch of, 171–77
Anglicanism, 31, 179–80
Anglicans, viewpoint of some on unity of Church, 130
Aphraates, St., on primacy of Peter, 65
Apostles: jurisdiction of, 71–72; purely personal privileges of, 39–40; twofold function of, 39; were they all equal?, 71–72
Apostolic College, its authority established by Christ, 32–35; objections to this doctrine, 35–36
Apostolicity: as a mark of the Church, see Mark of Apostolicity; notion of, 151; of a particular bishop, 152–3; of Church, 151 ff.; of doctrine, 151; of government, 151; of membership, 151
Archbishop, rank of, instituted by Church, 322
Augustine, St.: on bad Catholics vs. Church's holiness, 198; on infallibility of Church, 107, 298; on necessity of Church for salvation, 261–62; on primacy of Peter, 66; on salvation of non-Catholics, 262–63; repudiates charge that Church is harmful to State, 386; why name "Catholic" belongs to Roman Church alone, 185

B

Bad Catholics vs. Church's holiness, 198
Baptism, the cause of incorporation in Church, 237–8; b. of water does not suffice for membership, 240; invalid b. does not suffice for membership, 240
Barnabas, St., was he an apostle?, 51, n. 7
Basil, St., on divine origin of episcopacy, 45
Benedict XIV, on origin of episcopal jurisdiction, 325
Bernard, St., warns Eugene III that pope is not the sole authority in the Church, 283
Bishops and presbyters, see Presbyters and bishops
"Bishop of bishops," as title of pope, 281
"Bishop of the Catholic Church," 281; title of "universal bishop" rejected by St. Gregory the Great, 286
Bishops: does their jurisdiction come directly from God?, 324; do not possess a twofold kind of jurisdiction, 329; have ordinary jurisdiction by divine right, 320; must be ratified by pope to exercise jurisdiction, 323; historical objections against this doctrine, 324; successors of apostles, 40 ff.; their jurisdiction is complete, but subordinate, 321
Bolgeni, claimed bishops have two types of jurisdiction, 339, n. 1
Breviary, Roman, could it contain office of one not actually a saint?, 118
Buddhists, number of in world, 187

C

Calvin, as described by a modern Protestant, 192; on the marks of the Church of Christ, 160
Calvinism: its original tenets, 178–9; rejection of Calvin's doctrine of

predestination by present-day Calvinist churches, 179
Canonization: differs from beatification, 117; falls under scope of Church's infallibility, 117–18; notion of, 117
Catechumens are not members of the Church, 240–41
Catholic Church: statistics on, structure of, 181, 185, 186; verifies marks of Christ's Church, see Marks of Christ's Church; why non-Catholics fail to recognize it as Christ's Church, 206–7
Catholicity, "absolute," some day will be achieved, 144–46; c. "by right," 144; c. "in fact," 144; mark of c., see: Marks of Christ's Church; "moral" c., found in Church in every age, 146–47; c. notion of, 143
Catholics: not intolerant, 267–68; bad Catholics vs. Church's holiness, 198
Charismatics and co-workers of apostles, 36
Christ, head of the Church, see Mystical Body of Christ
Clement of Rome, St., exercised the papal primacy, 76; testifies that apostles provided for hierarchical succession, 38–39
Clement VI, defends infallibility of Roman pontiff, 300
Church: bride of Christ, 219, 233, n. 20; broad use of term, xxv; definition of, xxvi; is the religion of Christ in concrete form, 22; its distinction from synagogue in primitive Christianity, 11; its origin according to early and modern Protestants, 5–6; the Mystical Body of Christ, 215–234
Church and State: *Address to Historians* and, 373, 378–79, 392–93; American Catholics and papal teaching on, 380; authority of both is from God, 352–54; Blanshard's unfair handling of Catholic position on, 374; Church's respect for non-Catholic consciences shown in her teaching on, 378–79; *Ci Riesci* on, 376–77; conflicts between in "mixed affairs," 364–69; Constitution of Eire on, 381–82; delicacy of problem of, 343; as distinct and independent societies, 354–58; Leo XIII's teaching on, 349–51; medieval conflicts between as viewed by Auguste Comte, 367; medieval inquisition and its bearing on problem, 378 and 378–379; notion of "Catholic State" in discussion of, 349–350; note on American theological controversy over, 372, 379; obligation of Catholic State to profess Catholicism, 370–380; Pius XII on certain aspects of problem, 373, 378–79, 392–93; "position of non-Catholics in a Catholic state," 374–382; value of Leo XIII's teaching on, 389–93; "where the ideal relationship between is unobtainable," 382–87; why non-Catholics cannot be expected to agree with Church's teaching on, 369–70
Churches: Orthodox, brief sketch of, 173–77; doctrinal unity of, 182; not zealous for converts, 183; Protestant, statistics on membership, 135, 187
College of bishops, as successor to College of apostles, 40 ff.
Comte, Auguste, on cause of medieval conflicts between Church and State, 367
Council of Chalcedon, acknowledged infallibility of Roman pontiff, 299; and his primacy, 81–82; twenty-eighth canon of as objection to primacy, 82–83
Council of Constance, did it subordinate popes to an ecumenical council?, 285
Council of Constantinople, III, condemned Pope Honorius, 305–307
Council of Constantinople, IV, professed belief in infallibility of pope, 300

Council of Ephesus, acknowledged infallibility of pope, 299; and his primacy, 81

Council of Florence, did not teach pope's powers are limited by sacred canons, 284; recognized infallibility of pope, 301

Council of Lyons, II, acknowledged infallibility of pope, 300–301

Cyprian, St., on primacy of Roman pontiff, 65, 78; on infallibility of Roman Church, 297

Cyril of Jerusalem, St., on the name "catholic," 143, n.

D

Deacons, 36

Decretals, *see* False Decretals

Discipline of Church, *see* General discipline of Church

E

Ecumenical council: list of, 337–39; notion of, 332; pope alone has right to convoke, 334; ratification of, 336; requirements for, 333 ff.; what history discloses about emperors and convocation of, 334–335

Ecumenical movement: how viewed by Rome, 180

"Elders," lay helpers of apostles, 36

Episcopate, monarchical, its apostolic origin, 43; its ultimate origin from Christ, 44; notion of, 43

"*Et tu aliquando conversus,*" 296 and 311, n. 6

Ex cathedra pronouncement: conditions for, 291–94; notion of, 291

Excommunicates, are they members of the Church?, 244

Extra ecclesiam nulla salus, "outside the Church no salvation," *see also,* Necessity of Church for salvation

F

"Fact of Peter" (that Peter resided in Rome as its bishop), connection of with inseparability of primacy from Roman See, 273–75; proof of 75 and 90, n. 45

Facts, dogmatic: notion of, 112; object of infallibility, 112–13

False Decretals of Pseudo-Isidore, did not increase powers of papacy, 284

Fundamentalists, views on doctrinal unity, 128

G

Galileo, case of, 308–309

Gallican Clergy, Declaration of, 282

"Gates of Hell," meaning of, 87, n. 10

General discipline of Church, notion of, 114; object of infallibility, 115–116

Gerson, admits papal infallibility acknowledged everywhere prior to Council of Constance, 302

Gifts, of Christ to Church, 223

Goal of the Church, 20

Gregory the Great, St., rejected title of "universal bishop," 286

H

Harnack, claims Matthew 16:13 ff. a later addition to Gospel, 86, n. 8; impressed by testimonies of Clement of Rome and Ignatius Martyr on the primacy, 92, n. 51; on Peter's residence in Rome, 90, n. 45; praises institution of sacraments, 211, n. 28

Heretics, public, are not members of Church, 241; dispute over "occult" heretics, 242–3

Hierarchical society, notion of, 31

Hindus, statistics on, 187

Holiness: as mark of Christ's Church, *see* Marks of Christ's Church; of charisms, 139; of means, 135–36; of members, 136–37; various facets of Church's, 135

Honorius, did he err when speaking ex cathedra?, 305; in what sense was he condemned by Council of Constantinople, III?, 306–307

I

Ignatius Martyr, St.: on the episcopacy, 41; on primacy of Roman Church, 77; on viciousness of schism, 129

Indestructibility of Church, 25 ff.; errors on, 27; of Roman Church and See, 276

Infallibility,
———nature of: differs from revelation and inspiration, 120; does not exclude human study and effort, 120–121, 290; notion of, 102; refers only to definitions, 104
———object of: and approbation of religious orders, 116; and canonization, 117; and dogmatic facts, 112; and theological conclusions, 111; and general discipline of Church, 114
———persons endowed with: college of bishops, 330; Roman pontiff, 290–291
———proof of its existence, 104 ff.

Innocent III, on question of pope falling into heresy, 310, n. 5; possibility of pope becoming formal heretic, 294

Irenaeus, St., on bishops as successors of apostles, 41; on infallibility, 297; on primacy of Roman Church, 77–78; on unity of faith, 127; on viciousness of schism, 129

J

Jansenists: modern, deny the primacy, 59; their viewpoint on Church's infallibility, 103

Jansenius, and his book, "Augustinus," 112

Jerome, St.: does he teach that priests were originally equal to bishops?, 45; on infallibility, 107, 298; on primacy of Roman pontiff, 66

John of Jerusalem, on infallibility of pope, 298

John XXII, his erroneous view on beatific vision, 310, n. 4

Jews, statistics on, 187

Jurieu, his system on "fundamental articles" of belief, 128

Jurisdiction: differs from power of orders, 48; notion of, 48
———of bishops: from whom received, 324–325
———of Roman pontiff: from whom received, 276; its qualities, 280; use of, subject to norms of prudence, 283

"Just, The," not the only members of the Church, 247

K

"Kingdom of God," meaning of, 15, n. 12

L

"Lambs and sheep of Christ," meaning of, 63. *See also* Jurisdiction, Primacy

Leo XIII: on Church as simultaneously a spiritual and visible society, 22; on proper relationship between Church and State, 349 ff.; on unity of the Church, 126. *See also* Church and State

Lex orandi est lex credendi, 116

Liberius, did he err when speaking ex cathedra?, 303–304

Liturgies, diversity of, does not destroy Church's unity, 129–130

Luke 22:31–32, explained and defended in its traditional interpretation, 296 and 311, n. 6

Luther, sensed keenly lack of apostolicity in Reformation churches, 210, n. 19; brief description of by a modern Protestant, 192

Lutheranism, original tenets of, 178

M

Magisterium, of Church, established by Christ, 32 ff.; of bishops, extent and value, 321–22

Maistre, de, states enemies of Church know where to strike, 211, n. 26

Maldonatus, on not misunderstanding meaning of "one flock and one shepherd," 148, n. 5. *See also* Catholicity

Marks of Christ's Church: abstract discussion of, 158–167; application to various Christian Churches, 181–207;

———considered abstractly: notion of, 159; laid down by Catholics, 161–65; laid down by non-Catholics, 160–61; whether one mark alone suffices to identify Christ's Church, 165

———considered individually: of "apostolicity," meaning of, 164; of "catholicity," meaning of, 164; of "holiness," meaning of, 162–3; of "unity," meaning of, 162

———if discernible why not recognized by sincere non-Catholics, 206–207

———applied to Christian Churches: "Apostolicity" is found in Roman Catholic Church, 190 ff.; is not found in Orthodox or Protestant Churches, 188 ff.
"Catholicity," is found in Roman Catholic Church, 184 ff.; is not found in Orthodox or Protestant Churches, 181 ff.
"Holiness" is found in Roman Catholic Church, 195 ff.; is not found in Orthodox or Protestant Churches, 191 ff.
"Unity" is found in Roman Catholic Church, 184 ff.; is not found in Orthodox or Protestant Churches, 181 ff.

Marmontel, praises practice of confession, 211, n. 25

Martyrology, Roman, can have names of nonsaints appear therein, 123, n. 20

Means, necessity of, *see* "Necessity of means vs. necessity of precept"

Members of the Church: conditions for membership, 236–39; who are members, 237 ff.; who are not members, 239–245

Membership in Church, corollary: babies baptized by heretical sects are members of Roman Catholic Church, 245; objections to Church's doctrine on, from patristic writings, 250–252

Michael Caerularius, broke away from college of apostolic pastors, 188–89

Mission, extraordinary: whether "extraordinary mission" to reform Church, is possible, 154

"Mixed affairs," discussion of, 364–369; conflict over, 364–69; notion of, 356

Mohammedans, statistics on, 187

Mystical Body of Christ: apparent neglect of doctrine till recent times, 216; Church as continuation of Christ in the world, 227–29; coextension of concepts "Mystical Body" and "Church," 229–30; diagram of likenesses and differences between mystical body and moral or physical bodies, 223; explanation of the analogy of, 220–223; Holy Spirit as soul of, 224–225

———proof of doctrine: from words of Christ, 217; from fathers of Church, 218–19; from magisterium of Church, 219–220; from St. Paul, 217–18

———term and its significance, 222–23; theological label for doctrine of, 216

———where analogy between "soul" and Holy Spirit breaks down, 225

N

Necessity of Church for salvation: caricatures of this doctrine, 255; exact meaning of axiom, "outside the Church no salvation" in relation to, 265–266; proof of doctrine on, 261–264; theological terminology used in discussion of, 256–57; "tolerance" and its relation to the doctrine on, 266–268; salvation of non-Catholics and, 262–63 and 265–66

"Necessity of means vs. necessity of precept": meaning of terms, 256–258

Non-Catholics: cannot be expected to agree with Church's doctrine on Church and State, 369–370; position of, in Catholic State, 374–382; possibility of salvation for, 262–63 and 265–66; why so many sincere, fail to recognize Christ's own Church, 206–207

O

Orders, *see* Power of orders
Orthodox Church: does it have real unity of belief, 182–83; its long-time spiritual paralysis, 191; signs of new life in, 191

P

Pallium, what it signifies, 322–23
Parish pastor, office of, not of divine origin, 327
Patriarch, rank of, ecclesiastical in origin, 322
Paul, St., is an apostle, 51, n. 7; is not equal to Peter, 72; withstood Peter to his face, 70–71
Paulus, Dr. N., holds it possible for office of nonsaint to appear in Breviary, 124, n. 22
Peter, St.: after Ascension of Christ exercises primacy, 65; did not err when speaking ex cathedra, 303; dwelt in Rome as its bishop, 75 ff.; given task of feeding lambs and sheep, 62–63; his relationship to rest of apostles, 71; ordered to strengthen his brethren, 64, 296 ff.; receives keys of the kingdom, 62; receives new name, 63; resisted to his face by St. Paul, 70; specially honored, 64; the rock of the Church, 61, 65 and Appendix

Peter's residence in Rome: admitted by non-Catholic scholars, 90, n. 45; corroborated by recent archaeological findings, 90–91, n. 46

Pius IX, on necessity of belonging to the Church, 259–260, 265; on the temporal sovereignty of pope, 194–95, and 313–315

Pius XI, his solution of the "Roman Question," 313, 315

Pius XII: on Church and State, 349, 350, 373, 376–79, 383–85, 392–93; on jurisdiction of bishops, 326; on membership of Church, 236, 239, 241, 245; on Mystical Body, 219–20, 221, 223–24, 227, 233, n. 23; on necessity of Church for salvation, 255, 260; on presence of sinners in Church, 248–49

Pope, *see* Roman pontiff
Power of orders: differs from power of jurisdiction, 48–49; notion of, 48; often described as power of "the ministry," 49

Predestined, the, are not all members of the Church; nor are they its only members, 247

Presbyters and bishops, comparison of, 40, 52, n. 20, 54, n. 28

Priesthood of laity, 35
Priestly powers, conferred on apostles by Christ, 32

Primacy of Peter, conferred on Peter, 62–63; continued in bishop of Rome, 74; destined to last through ages, 72–74; is it separable from Roman See?, 273; its power and nature, 279 ff.; notion of, 60; was promised to Peter, 61; what kind of law annexes it to See of Rome?, 274–75

"Princes of the Apostles," meaning of, 72

Properties of the Church, 102
Protestantism: and its missionary ef-

forts, 183, 208–209, n. 13; origin of the name, 177; three original branches of, 177; *see also* Church, Marks of Christ's Church

Protestants: and Bible-reading, 195; and claim of "superiority" of Protestant nations, 203 ff.

——differences between original and modern, 161, 177–178, 179, 195

——many lead exemplary lives, 191; statistics on number of, 180–181, 187

——and ecumenical movements, how viewed by Rome, 180

Pseudo-Isidore, false decretals of, 284

Puseyites, their view of Church's infallibility, 103

R

Reformation, did not bring about improvement in morals, 192, 210, n. 23

Reformers, were not exceptionally holy, 192

Religion of Christ, not separable from church in which it is embodied, 22

Religions of world, statistics on, 180–81, 186, 187

Religious orders, as indirect object of infallibility, 116–117; notion of, 116; statistics on, 199–200

Roman Church: connection of primacy with Roman See, 273; indestructibility of, 276

Roman congregations are not infallible, 291; example of, in Galileo case, 308–309

Roman pontiff, his civil sovereignty, 313; is infallible, 289 ff.; power and nature of his primacy, 279 ff.; source of his jurisdiction, 276; relationship of, to an ecumenical council, 233–36; what would happen if he fell into heresy, 294; when infallible, 291 ff.; why he invokes authority of both Peter and Paul, 83

Roman See, its imperishability, 276

Rule of faith, meaning of, 121; which one are all bound to follow?, 122

Russian Orthodox Church: its enslavement to political government, 191; statistics on and structure of, 174–175

S

Sanctity, *see* Holiness

Saints and beatified: huge numbers of produced by Church, 201; impossibility of calculating number of, 201

Schism, Western, *see* Western Schism

Schismatics, notion of, 239–240; not members of Church, 243, 245–46; still belong to Church by law and obligation, 246

Separation of Church and State, *see* Church and State

Sinners, presence of, in Church no argument against its holiness, 138–139 and 198

Society: kinds of, 31; Church is a hierarchical, 31; Church is a monarchical, 59; Church is not an aristocratic, 59; Church is not a society of equals, 31

"Soul and body of Church," does not mean two churches, 225–26

"Soul of Church," Holy Spirit as, 224–225; where analogy breaks down, 225

State and its relations with the Church, *see* Church and State

Statistics: on religious membership, 180–181, 187; on morality, can be used only with extreme caution, 166, n. 6

Successor, meaning of, 40

Syllabus of Errors, proposition 17 of, properly explained, 265

Synagogue, its distinction from primitive Christian Church, 11–12;

whether it possessed an infallible magisterium, 108

T

Tapper, his judgment on papal infallibility, 302

Temporal prosperity: no criterion of value of a religion, 203 ff.; is Protestantism more conducive to, than Catholicism?, 204–205

"Three Chapters," the, and papal infallibility, 113, 304

Theological conclusion, as an object of infallibility, 111

Tolerance, Canon Bell on nonsensical notions of, 267; notion and kinds of, 266–68; term "dogmatic" t. disliked by some modern theologians, 267

Tournely, admits tradition heavily favors doctrine of papal infallibility, 302

U

Unity of Church, various facets of, 126–131

V

"Vicar of Christ on earth," notion, 60

Vigilius, did he err when speaking ex cathedra?, 304

Virgilius, his doctrine on existence of the Antipodes, 307–308

Visibility of Church, 12 ff.

Voltaire praises practice of confession, 211, n. 25

W

Western Schism, how is it compatible with unity of Church?, 131

Z

Zacharias, did he err when speaking ex cathedra?, 307–308